The Ministers Manual for 1973

By the same editor

Holy Holy Land
The Treasure Chest
Words of Life
Our American Heritage
1010 Sermon Illustrations from the Bible
Worship Resources for the Christian Year
Stories on Stone: A Book of American Epitaphs
The Funeral Encyclopedia
A Treasury of Story-Sermons for Children
Treasury of Sermon Illustrations
Selected Poems of John Oxenham
Poems of Edwin Markham
Notable Sermons from Protestant Pulpits
Treasury of Poems for Worship and Devotion
88 Evangelistic Sermons
Speaker's Resources from Contemporary Literature
Christmas in Our Hearts (with Charles L. Allen)
Candle, Star, and Christmas Tree (with Charles L. Allen)
When Christmas Came to Bethlehem (with Charles L. Allen)
The Charles L. Allen Treasury
Lenten-Easter Sourcebook
365 Table Graces for the Christian Home
Speaker's Illustrations for Special Days
Table of the Lord
The Eternal Light
Twentieth Century Bible Commentary (co-editor)
Prayers for Public Worship (co-editor)

FORTY-EIGHTH ANNUAL ISSUE

The MINISTERS MANUAL

(*Doran's*)

1973 EDITION

Edited by
CHARLES L. WALLIS

HARPER & ROW, PUBLISHERS
New York, Evanston, San Francisco, London

Editors of THE MINISTERS MANUAL

G. B. F. HALLOCK, D.D., 1926–1958
M. K. W. HEICHER, PH.D., 1943–1968
CHARLES L. WALLIS, B.D., 1969–

THE MINISTERS MANUAL FOR 1973
Copyright © 1972 by Charles L. Wallis. Printed in the United States of America. All rights reserved. For information address Harper & Row, Publishers, Inc., 10 East 53rd Street, New York, N.Y. 10022.

FIRST EDITION

STANDARD BOOK NUMBER: 06-069017-8
LIBRARY OF CONGRESS CATALOG CARD NUMBER: 25-21658

PREFACE

Through the words of more than 700 contributors, the forty-eighth annual publication of *The Ministers Manual* provides homiletic and worship materials and resources for pulpit and parish ministries and proclaims the redemptive life, death, and resurrection of the Lord Jesus.

Included in this volume is the Christian witness of writers of twenty centuries, representatives of the Christian fellowship from many lands, preachers laboring in obscure and well-known parishes, younger writers, women in the Church, and laymen. All of the major affiliations of the Body of Christ have been drawn together according to our common testimony.

Section VII includes illustrative, discussion, and resource items on the theme of youth and the Church.

Section XI features a description of the purposes and scope of KEY 73, a continent-wide evangelistic effort. The section includes an abbreviated calendar for KEY 73 and suggestions for involvement by the local church. Materials in this section have been read and verified for accuracy and definition by the KEY 73 leadership, who emphasize the cooperative nature of the endeavor and the need for adaptation according to local need and the programs of the participating denominations. An index of KEY 73 emphases identifies sermons in this volume by the six phases of the year-long witness to Christ.

The editor welcomes comments, suggestions, and contributions from readers for subsequent volumes. Reader suggestions are incorporated into each annual issue of *The Ministers Manual.*

Rev. Charles L. Wallis
Keuka College
Keuka Park, N.Y. 14478

CONTENTS

SECTION I. CALENDARS AND OTHER CLERGY AIDS	1
SECTION II. VITAL THEMES FOR VITAL PREACHING	10
SECTION III. RESOURCES FOR LENTEN AND EASTER SERVICES	26
SECTION IV. RESOURCES FOR COMMUNION SERVICES	33
SECTION V. RESOURCES FOR FUNERAL SERVICES	37
SECTION VI. RESOURCES FOR SMALL GROUPS	43
SECTION VII. RESOURCES FOR PREACHING ON THE CHURCH AND YOUTH	49
SECTION VIII. EVANGELISM AND WORLD MISSIONS	55
SECTION IX. CHILDREN'S STORIES AND SERMONS	63
SECTION X. SERMON OUTLINES AND WORSHIP AIDS FOR THE CHRISTIAN YEAR	83
SECTION XI. FOCUS ON KEY 73	253
SECTION XII. A LITTLE TREASURY OF ILLUSTRATIONS	256
INDEX OF CONTRIBUTORS	265
SERMON TITLE INDEX	270
INDEX OF SPECIAL DAYS AND OCCASIONS	274
INDEX OF KEY 73 EMPHASES	274
POETRY INDEX	275
SCRIPTURAL INDEX	276
TOPICAL INDEX	278

SECTION I. Calendars and Other Clergy Aids

Civil Year Calendars

1973

JANUARY	FEBRUARY	MARCH	APRIL

S M T W T F S
  1 2 3 4 5 6
 7 8 9 10 11 12 13
14 15 16 17 18 19 20
21 22 23 24 25 26 27
28 29 30 31
	S M T W T F S
	           1 2 3
	 4 5 6 7 8 9 10
	11 12 13 14 15 16 17
	18 19 20 21 22 23 24
	25 26 27 28
		S M T W T F S
		           1 2 3
		 4 5 6 7 8 9 10
		11 12 13 14 15 16 17
		18 19 20 21 22 23 24
		25 26 27 28 29 30 31
			S M T W T F S
			 1 2 3 4 5 6 7
			 8 9 10 11 12 13 14
			15 16 17 18 19 20 21
			22 23 24 25 26 27 28
			29 30

MAY	JUNE	JULY	AUGUST

S M T W T F S
     1 2 3 4 5
 6 7 8 9 10 11 12
13 14 15 16 17 18 19
20 21 22 23 24 25 26
27 28 29 30 31
	S M T W T F S
	              1 2
	 3 4 5 6 7 8 9
	10 11 12 13 14 15 16
	17 18 19 20 21 22 23
	24 25 26 27 28 29 30
		S M T W T F S
		 1 2 3 4 5 6 7
		 8 9 10 11 12 13 14
		15 16 17 18 19 20 21
		22 23 24 25 26 27 28
		29 30 31
			S M T W T F S
			           1 2 3 4
			 5 6 7 8 9 10 11
			12 13 14 15 16 17 18
			19 20 21 22 23 24 25
			26 27 28 29 30 31

SEPTEMBER	OCTOBER	NOVEMBER	DECEMBER

S M T W T F S
                    1
 2 3 4 5 6 7 8
 9 10 11 12 13 14 15
16 17 18 19 20 21 22
23 24 25 26 27 28 29
30
	S M T W T F S
	    1 2 3 4 5 6
	 7 8 9 10 11 12 13
	14 15 16 17 18 19 20
	21 22 23 24 25 26 27
	28 29 30 31
		S M T W T F S
		              1 2 3
		 4 5 6 7 8 9 10
		11 12 13 14 15 16 17
		18 19 20 21 22 23 24
		25 26 27 28 29 30
			S M T W T F S
			                    1
			 2 3 4 5 6 7 8
			 9 10 11 12 13 14 15
			16 17 18 19 20 21 22
			23 24 25 26 27 28 29
			30 31

1974

JANUARY	FEBRUARY	MARCH	APRIL

S M T W T F S
       1 2 3 4 5
 6 7 8 9 10 11 12
13 14 15 16 17 18 19
20 21 22 23 24 25 26
27 28 29 30 31
	S M T W T F S
	                 1 2
	 3 4 5 6 7 8 9
	10 11 12 13 14 15 16
	17 18 19 20 21 22 23
	24 25 26 27 28
		S M T W T F S
		                 1 2
		 3 4 5 6 7 8 9
		10 11 12 13 14 15 16
		17 18 19 20 21 22 23
		24 25 26 27 28 29 30
		31
			S M T W T F S
			    1 2 3 4 5 6
			 7 8 9 10 11 12 13
			14 15 16 17 18 19 20
			21 22 23 24 25 26 27
			28 29 30

MAY	JUNE	JULY	AUGUST

S M T W T F S
           1 2 3 4
 5 6 7 8 9 10 11
12 13 14 15 16 17 18
19 20 21 22 23 24 25
26 27 28 29 30 31
	S M T W T F S
	                    1
	 2 3 4 5 6 7 8
	 9 10 11 12 13 14 15
	16 17 18 19 20 21 22
	23 24 25 26 27 28 29
	30
		S M T W T F S
		    1 2 3 4 5 6
		 7 8 9 10 11 12 13
		14 15 16 17 18 19 20
		21 22 23 24 25 26 27
		28 29 30 31
			S M T W T F S
			              1 2 3
			 4 5 6 7 8 9 10
			11 12 13 14 15 16 17
			18 19 20 21 22 23 24
			25 26 27 28 29 30 31

SEPTEMBER	OCTOBER	NOVEMBER	DECEMBER

S M T W T F S
 1 2 3 4 5 6 7
 8 9 10 11 12 13 14
15 16 17 18 19 20 21
22 23 24 25 26 27 28
29 30
	S M T W T F S
	        1 2 3 4 5
	 6 7 8 9 10 11 12
	13 14 15 16 17 18 19
	20 21 22 23 24 25 26
	27 28 29 30 31
		S M T W T F S
		                 1 2
		 3 4 5 6 7 8 9
		10 11 12 13 14 15 16
		17 18 19 20 21 22 23
		24 25 26 27 28 29 30
			S M T W T F S
			 1 2 3 4 5 6 7
			 8 9 10 11 12 13 14
			15 16 17 18 19 20 21
			22 23 24 25 26 27 28
			29 30 31

Christian Year Calendar for 1973

JANUARY

- 1 New Year's Day
- 6 Epiphany
- 14 Missionary Day
- 18-25 Week of Prayer

FEBRUARY

- 11 Race Relations Sunday
- 18-25 Brotherhood Week

MARCH

- 2 World Day of Prayer
- 4 The Transfiguration
- 7 Ash Wednesday
- 11 First Sunday in Lent
- 18 Second Sunday in Lent
- 25 Third Sunday in Lent
  The Annunciation

APRIL

- 1 Fourth Sunday in Lent
- 8 Passion Sunday
- 15-21 Holy Week
- 15 Palm Sunday
- 19 Maundy Thursday
- 20 Good Friday
- 22 Easter
- 29 Easter (Orthodox)
  National Christian College Day

MAY

- 4 May Fellowship Day
- 6-13 National Family Week
- 13 Festival of the Christian Home
  Mother's Day
- 27 Rural Life Sunday
- 31 Ascension Day

JUNE

- 10 Pentecost (Whitsunday)
  Children's Sunday
- 17 Trinity Sunday
  Father's Day
- 24 Nature Sunday

JULY

- 1 Independence Sunday
- 4 Independence Day

AUGUST

- 6 The Transfiguration (alternate)
- 26 Festival of Christ the King

SEPTEMBER

- 2 Labor Sunday
- 3 Labor Day

OCTOBER

- 7 World Communion Sunday
- 14 Laymen's Sunday
- 21 World Order Sunday
- 28 Reformation Sunday
  Youth Sunday
- 31 Reformation Day

NOVEMBER

- 1 All Saints' Day
- 2 All Souls' Day
  World Community Day
- 4 World Temperance Day
- 11 Stewardship Day
- 18 Thanksgiving Sunday
  Universal Bible Sunday
- 22 Thanksgiving Day

DECEMBER

- 2 First Sunday in Advent
- 9 Second Sunday in Advent
- 16 Third Sunday in Advent
- 23 Christmas Sunday
- 25 Christmas
- 31 Watch Night

Four-Year Church Calendar

	1973	1974	1975	1976
Ash Wednesday	March 7	February 27	February 12	March 3
Palm Sunday	April 15	April 7	March 23	April 11
Good Friday	April 20	April 12	March 28	April 16
Easter	April 22	April 14	March 30	April 18
Ascension Day	May 31	May 23	May 8	May 27
Pentecost	June 10	June 2	May 18	June 6
Trinity Sunday	June 17	June 9	May 25	June 13
Thanksgiving	November 22	November 28	November 27	November 25
Advent Sunday	December 2	December 1	November 30	November 28

Forty-Year Easter Calendar

1971	April 11	1981	April 19	1991	March 31	2001	April 14
1972	April 2	1982	April 11	1992	April 19	2002	March 31
1973	April 22	1983	April 3	1993	April 11	2003	April 20
1974	April 14	1984	April 22	1994	April 3	2004	April 11
1975	March 30	1985	April 7	1995	April 16	2005	March 27
1976	April 18	1986	March 30	1996	April 7	2006	April 16
1977	April 10	1987	April 19	1997	March 30	2007	April 8
1978	March 26	1988	April 3	1998	April 12	2008	March 23
1979	April 15	1989	March 26	1999	April 4	2009	April 12
1980	April 6	1990	April 15	2000	April 23	2010	April 4

Four-Year Jewish Calendar

	1973	1974	1975	1976
Purim	March 18	March 8	February 25	March 16
Passover	April 17	April 7	March 27	April 15
Shabuoth (Revelation of the Law)	June 6	May 27	May 16	June 4
Rosh Hashanah (New Year)	September 27	September 17	September 6	September 25
Yom Kippur (Day of Atonement)	October 6	September 26	September 15	October 4
Sukkoth (Thanksgiving)	October 11	October 1	September 20	October 9
Simhath Torah (Rejoicing in the Law)	October 19	October 9	September 28	October 17
Hanukkah	December 20	December 9	November 29	December 17

Holidays begin at sunset on the evening before the date given.

Traditional Wedding Anniversary Identifications

1	Paper	7	Wool	13	Lace	35	Coral
2	Cotton	8	Bronze	14	Ivory	40	Ruby
3	Leather	9	Pottery	15	Crystal	45	Sapphire
4	Linen	10	Tin	20	China	50	Gold
5	Wood	11	Steel	25	Silver	55	Emerald
6	Iron	12	Silk	30	Pearl	60	Diamond

Colors Appropriate for Days and Seasons

Black: Good Friday

Crimson: Passion Sunday, Palm Sunday

Green: Nature Sunday, Labor Sunday, Thanksgiving Sunday

Purple: Lent, Advent

Red: Pentecost

White: Maundy Thursday, Easter, Ascension Sunday, Trinity Sunday, All Saints' Day, Christmas

Historical, Cultural, and Religious Anniversaries in 1973

5 years (1968). *January 30:* Tet offensive in Vietnam. *April 4:* Dr. Martin Luther King, Jr., slain in Memphis. *June 1:* Death of Helen Keller (b. 1880). *June 5:* Senator Robert F. Kennedy shot in Los Angeles. *December 24–25:* Apollo 8 Astronauts Borman, Lovell, and Anders made ten orbits around the moon.

10 years (1963): *May 15–16:* Major Gordon Cooper orbits earth 22 times. *June 12:* Civil rights leader Medgar W. Evers murdered in Mississippi. *June 17:* Supreme Court ruled that required recitation of the Lord's Prayer or Bible verses in public schools is unconstitutional. *June 21:* Cardinal Montini became Pope Paul VI. *August 5:* U.S., U.K., and U.S.S.R. sign partial nuclear test-ban treaty *August 28:* "Freedom March" on Washington, D.C.

15 years (1958). *January 31:* First U.S. satellite, Explorer I, established orbit. *February 1:* United Arab Republic (Egypt and Syria) founded. *October 4:* B.O.A.C. launched jet passenger service across Atlantic.

20 years (1953). *January 20:* Eisenhower inaugurated as President. *March 5:* Death of Stalin (b. 1879). *March 26:* Dr. Jonas Salk announced polio vaccine. *April 10:* Dag Hammarskjöld elected Secretary-General of the U.N. *May 29:* Edmund Hillary and Tenzing Norkay conquered Mt. Everest. *July 27:* Korean armistice signed. *August 20:* U.S.S.R. announced their first H-Bomb explosion.

25 years (1948). *January 4:* Burmese independence achieved. *January 30:* Gandhi assassinated. *April 7:* World Health Organization established. *April 30:* Charter of the Organization of American States signed. *May 14:* Israel independence proclaimed. *August 23:* World Council of Churches constituted at Amsterdam.

30 years (1943). *February 1–2:* German Sixth Army surrendered at Stalingrad in World War II. *September 8:* Italy surrendered.

40 years (1933). *January 30:* Hitler named Chancellor of Germany. *December 5:* Repeal of 18th (prohibition) Amendment of the Constitution.

50 years (1923). *November 12:* Hitler imprisoned after failure of Munich beer hall putsch and writes *Mein Kampf* while in jail.

70 years (1903). *December 17:* First successful airplane flight by the Wright brothers.

100 years (1873). Ibsen wrote *Emperor and Galilean.* *February 25:* Birth of Enrico Caruso (d. 1921). *October 20:* In New York City P. T. Barnum opened the "Greatest Show on Earth."

110 years (1863). *January 1:* Lincoln signed the Emancipation Proclamation. *July 1–3:* Battle of Gettysburg. *October 3:* Thanksgiving Day proclaimed a national holiday.

150 years (1823). *December 2:* Monroe Doctrine declared.

200 years (1773). *December 16:* Boston Tea Party.

250 years (1723). *February 25:* Death of Sir Christopher Wren (b. 1632), architect of St. Paul's Cathedral.

300 years (1673). Marquette and Joliet explored the Mississippi.

350 years (1623). Publication of First Folio Edition of Shakespeare's plays.

500 years (1473). Sistine Chapel built.

700 years (1273). Thomas Aquinas completed *Summa Theologica.*

Anniversaries of Hymns and Hymn Writers in 1973

20 years (1935). Death of Thomas Curtis Clark (b. 1877), American poet, author of "Where restless crowds are thronging," etc.; Karl P. Harrington (b. 1861), American educator, composer of hymn-tune CHRISTMAS SONG ("There's a Song in the Air"); Henry Hallam Tweedy (b. 1868), author of

"Eternal God, whose power upholds," "O gracious Father of mankind," and "O spirit of the living God."
25 years (1948). Death of Bates G. Burt (b. 1878), American Episcopalian, composer of hymn-tune SHADDICK ("City of God, how broad and far" and "Prayer is the soul's sincere desire"); David Evans (b. 1874), Welsh organist and editor, composer of hymntunes CHARTERHOUSE ("O Son of man, our hero strong and tender"), NYLAND ("In heavenly love abiding"), etc.
30 years (1943). Death of Allen Eastman Cross (b. 1864), author of "More light shall break from out thy word," etc.
40 years (1933). Death of Charles A. Tindley (b. 1851), American Negro Methodist clergyman, author of "We shall overcome," author-composer of "When the storms of life are raging"; Henry van Dyke (b. 1852), American clergyman, diplomat, and educator, author of "Joyful, joyful, we adore thee," "They who tread the path of labor," etc.
50 years (1923). Death of Mary Ann Thomson (b. 1834), London-born American librarian, author of forty hymns including "O Zion, haste."
60 years (1913). Writing of "The old rugged cross" by George Bennard; "We would see Jesus" by J. Edgar Park. Death of Ethelbert W. Bullinger (b. 1837), Anglican clergyman, composer of hymn-tune BULLINGER ("God, who touchest earth with beauty"); William C. Doane (b. 1832), American Episcopal bishop, author of "Ancient of days"; Mary A. Lathbury (b. 1841), "Laureate of Chautauqua," author of "Break thou the bread of life" and "Day is dying in the west."
70 years (1903). Writing of "Creation's Lord, we give thee thanks" by William DeWitt Hyde; "God of the strong, God of the weak" by Richard Watson Gilder; "Where cross the crowded ways of life" by Frank Mason North. Composing of hymn-tune RECESSIONAL ("God of our fathers, known of old") by John H. Gower. Death of Herbert Stanley Oakeley (b. 1830), British educator and organist, composer of hymn-tune ABENDS ("Sun of my soul"), etc.; Joseph Parry (b. 1841), Welsh musician, composer of 400 hymntunes including ABERYSWYTH ("Jesus, Lover of my soul"); Godfrey Thring (b. 1823), Anglican clergyman, author of "Crown him with many crowns"; Samuel A. Ward (b. 1847), American musician, composer of hymn-tune MATERNA ("O beautiful for spacious skies" and "O mother dear, Jerusalem").
75 years (1898). Death of William Chatterton Dix (b. 1837), Glasgow business man and scholar, author of "As with gladness men of old," etc.; H. Roy Percy Smith (b. 1825), Anglican clergyman, composer of hymn-tune MARYTON ("O Master, let me walk with thee").
80 years (1893). Writing of "Christian, rise, and act thy creed" by F. A. Rollo Russell; "O beautiful for spacious skies" by Katharine Lee Bates [see Samuel A. Ward above]. Composing of hymn-tune JUST AS I AM ("Just as I am, thine own to be") by Joseph Barnby. Death of Phillips Brooks (b. 1835), American Episcopal clergyman, author of "O little town of Bethlehem"; John Ellerton (b. 1826), Anglican clergyman, author of 68 hymns including "Behold us, Lord, a little space," "God the omnipotent," and "Savior, again to thy dear name we raise"; George Job Elvey (b. 1816), British musician, composer of hymntunes DIADEMATA ("Crown him with many crowns") and ST. GEORGE'S WINDSOR ("Come, ye thankful people, come"); Lucy Larcom (b. 1826), American writer, author of "Draw thou my soul, O Christ"; John Addington Symons (b. 1840), British scholar, author of "These things shall be"; William H. Walter (b. 1825), American organist, composer of hymn-tune FESTAL SONG ("Rise up, O men of God").
90 years (1883). Writing of "O perfect Love, all human thought transcending" by Dorothy F. Gurney. Birth of G. A. Studdert-Kennedy (d. 1929), Anglican clergyman, author of "Awake,

awake to love and work," etc.; Howard A. Walter (d. 1918), American YMCA leader, author of "I would be true."

100 years (1873). Writing of "All things are thine" by John Greenleaf Whittier; "Where is your God? they say" by James Martineau. Composing of hymn-tune NOX PRAECESSIT ("Lamp of our feet") by J. Baptiste Calkin. Birth of George Bennard (d. 1958), America evangelist, author-composer of "The old rugged cross" [see *1913* above]; John Hughes (d. 1932), Welsh Baptist, composer of hymn-tune CWM RHONDDA ("God of grace and God of glory" and "Guide me, O thou great Jehovah"). Death of George Hews (b. 1806), American musician, composer of hymn-tune HOLLEY ("Lord, speak to me").

125 years (1848). Death of John Quincy Adams (b. 1767), sixth U.S. President, author of "Send forth, O God, thy light and truth"; Sarah Flower Adams (b. 1805), British poet, author of "Nearer, my God, to thee"; Joseph Mohr (b. 1792), Austrian priest, author of "Silent night, holy night."

150 years (1823). Composing of hymn-tune MISSIONARY HYMN ("From Greenland's icy mountains") by Lowell Mason. Writing of "O Spirit of the living God" by James Montgomery. Birth of John B. Dykes (d. 1876), Anglican clergyman, composer of 300 hymn-tunes including KEBLE ("Strong Son of God, immortal love"), MELITA ("O Master of the waking world"), and ST. AGNES ("Jesus, the very thought of thee"); William Walsham How (d. 1897), Anglican bishop, author of "O Jesus, thou art standing" and "O Word of God incarnate"; William H. Monk (d. 1889), British organist, composer of hymn-tune DIX ("As with gladness men of old" and "For the beauty of the earth"); Henry Twells (d. 1900), Anglican clergyman and educator, author of "At even, ere the sun was set."

200 years (1773). Birth of Harriet Auber (d. 1862), British poet, author of "Our blest Redeemer, ere he breathed."

Quotable Quotations

The following quotations may be useful for church bulletin boards, printed Sunday worship programs, and church newsletters and other parish publications.

JANUARY

1. Some people miss heaven by just eighteen inches—the distance between the head and the heart.

2. The smile of God is victory. John Greenleaf Whittier.

3. The future begins today. Daphne du Maurier.

4. To snatch the passing moment and examine it for signs of eternity is the noblest of occupations. Louis J. Halle.

5. Sow the living part of yourselves in the furrows of life. Miguel de Unamuno y Jugo.

6. The question is not how I can attain my salvation but how I can stop being concerned about it. Alexander Miller.

7. Any crisis may be the hour when God gives birth to new dimensions in our lives. C. Neil Strait.

8. Prayer does not change God's mind but works principally to help us adjust to God's will in all things. Theodore Hesburgh.

9. You may give without loving, but you cannot love without giving.

FEBRUARY

10. The best cure for shaking knees is to kneel on them. Frederick Donald Coogan.

11. Unless our hearts are 25,000 miles in circumference, they are too small. Robert G. Lee.

12. Life is what is happening to you while you are making other plans. Robert Blazer.

13. Being a Christian means involvement in the world of want and

CLERGY AIDS

hunger, of technology and racial tension. Leonard Hodgson.

14. Most of the troubles of the world flow from the fact that few men are able to sit alone on a chair in an empty room for three or four hours. Blaise Pascal.

15. Monotony is the awful penalty of the careful. Ralph Pulitzer.

16. We throw our arms with a gesture of religion to the universe; we close them around a person. Robert Frost.

17. A Christian pays for his words with his life. Hendrikus Berkhof.

MARCH

18. A Christian is not one who withdraws but one who infiltrates. Bill Glass.

19. The man who neglects his prayers is guilty of overconfidence in his own self-sufficiency. Ray F. Magnuson.

20. There is no detour to holiness. Jesus came to the resurrection through the Cross, not around it. Leighton Ford.

21. The universe is true for all of us and different for each of us. Marcel Proust.

22. The Christian Gospel is a matter of decision. Paul Tillich.

23. I will never let a man build a wall around himself, but I will find some little crack to break through. Peter Ainslie.

24. We know more about teaching rats, and we are more effective with psychotics and neurotics than with freshmen. John Weir.

25. Ask all the questions you want about religion, but ask the questions of faith, not the questions of skepticism. Earl L. Douglass.

26. He who neglects the present moment throws away all he has. Johann Schiller.

27. Human things must be known to be loved, but divine things must be loved to be known. Blaise Pascal.

APRIL

28. Spring is God thinking in gold, laughing in blue, and speaking in green. Frank Johnson.

29. Sympathy is your pain in my heart.

30. Decisive battles are those fought in the scarred soul of a man. Gaston Foote.

31. The creation of the whole world is miracle, and only in light of that miracle does every form of light and life find its fullest meaning. Nels F. S. Ferré.

32. Our Lord has written the promise of the resurrection, not in books alone, but in every leaf in springtime. Martin Luther.

33. It may take a crucified church to bring a crucified Christ before the eyes of the world. William E. Orchard.

34. We are Easter men and "Alleluia" is our song. St. Augustine.

35. All streets are dead-end streets except the one to the empty tomb. Lon Woodrum.

36. Every time a Christian cheats on his income tax he perverts and obscures the Gospel. John Sanderson.

MAY

37. I love to lose myself in other men's minds. Charles Lamb.

38. The Church should be the society of the forgiven and the forgiving. Daniel A. Poling.

39. There can be no good, real genuine good, unless there exists the possibility to choose evil. Herbert Gezork.

40. The Almighty is working on a great scale and will not be hustled by our peevish impetuosity. W. Graham Scroggie.

41. It is easier to build and maintain a whole city than it is to build and maintain a single human relationship. John Killinger.

42. We are not a post-war generation but a pre-peace generation. Corrie Ten Boom.

43. Simply because a man falls in love with his wife does not mean that he is a good husband.

44. Let us have more of the Church in the world and we will have less of the world in the Church. Nels F. S. Ferré.

45. If you don't have any problems, you should get down on your knees and pray, "What's the matter, Lord, don't you trust me with a problem?" Norman Vincent Peale.

JUNE

46. The greatest pleasure in life is doing what people say you cannot do. *The Link.*

47. It is always easier to do something than to be someone. Kermit Long.

48. Prayer is not a lazy substitute for work. Roy M. Pearson.

49. Reach down and change the gears within us that we may go forward with thee. Peter Marshall.

50. One thing we can do for our children's future is to give them fine memories of today. John Paul Stafford.

51. He who ceases to make a response ceases to hear the word. Martin Buber.

52. Man cannot be filled with the spirit of blackness or whiteness and be filled with the spirit of Christ. Willie White.

53. More men fail for the lack of an aim than for any other reason. Winston Churchill.

JULY

54. Liberty is the one thing you cannot have unless you are willing to give it to others. William Allen White.

55. The history of free men is never really written by chance but by choice. Dwight D. Eisenhower.

56. The lost opportunities we most regret are opportunities for loving. Charles Wagner.

57. It isn't what we think of God that makes us somebody, but it is what God thinks of us. Louis L. Mann.

58. Great tranquility of heart hath he that careth neither for praises nor faultfinding men. Thomas a Kempis.

59. There is no reproach to a bad man's badness like the goodness of a good man. A. M. Fairbairn.

60. Almost everyone knows the difference between right and wrong, but some just hate to make decisions. *Arkansas Baptist.*

61. Before you flare up at anyone's faults, take time to count ten—ten faults of your own. *The Link.*

AUGUST

62. It is in the shrine of the heart that Christ draws near to win our love. Henry Lazarus.

63. Character is determined by a person's moment of commitment when he chooses his star out of a sky of stars. Arthur Miller.

64. We should defend our neighbor, speak well of him, and put the best construction on everything. Martin Luther.

65. If a care is too small to be turned into a prayer, it is too small to be made into a burden. *Decision.*

66. Christ is in the center, the focal point toward which all the lines of perspective move. *Eternity.*

67. In the permissive society the only thing prohibited is prohibitions. John R. W. Stott.

68. What a person is he achieves through the cause that he makes his own. Karl Jaspers.

SEPTEMBER

69. A man never reveals his own character more vividly than when he is portraying the character of another. Jean Paul Richter.

70. In the long run we come closer to God in common worship than in closet worship. Evelyn Underhill.

71. Love is only love when the gift of ourselves is given for the purpose of making our loved one a better person. J. C. Willke.

72. The crisis of self-surrender must always be regarded as the vital turning point of the religious life. William James.

73. The faith that is afraid to think is unbelief in the mask of piety. Gerhard Ebeling.

74. A straight line is the shortest in morals as in mathematics. Maria Edgeworth.

75. Want of enterprise and lack of guts are not Christian virtues. J. H. Oldham.

76. Man must be disappointed with the lesser things of life before he can comprehend the full value of the greater. Edward Bulwer-Lytton.

OCTOBER

77. Purity of heart is to will one thing. Sören Kierkegaard.

78. Even in our loftiest pursuits we are not delivered from life's most basic needs. Ernest T. Campbell.

79. Revival is an experience in the Church, while evangelism is an expression of that experience. Paul S. Rees.

80. All which you are unable to give possesses you. André Gide.

81. Those are our best friends in whose presence we are able to be our best selves. Charles W. Kohler.

82. The final joy is not how fascinating God is but how fascinating we are to him. David A. Redding.

83. The sons of God look on transitory things with the left eye and with the right behold the things of heaven. Thomas a Kempis.

84. Evangelism is the outflow and the overflow of the inflow of the Spirit in a normal New Testament church. Vance Havner.

NOVEMBER

85. The brook would lose its song if we removed the rocks. *Reader's Digest*.

86. Love in practice is a harsh and terrible thing compared with love in dreams. Fëdor Dostoevski.

87. If the Dream is to be American, it must be for everyone. Thomas W. Georges, Jr.

88. Let us thank God that he has made it possible for us to give something back to him. William C. Skeath.

89. Thanksgiving Day can be either a national holiday or a spiritual experience, and if we so desire it can be both. C. Emanuel Carlson.

90. Every day is Thanksgiving if we are really living. Richard Braunstein.

91. If we can't be thankful for what we receive, we should be thankful for what we escape. Arnold H. Glascow.

DECEMBER

92. With most people lovability is not absent but merely undiscovered.

93. Life is a long lesson in humility. James M. Barrie.

94. The man who is wedded to his time will soon be a widower. Elton Trueblood.

95. Blessed is the season that engages the whole world in a conspiracy of love. Hamilton Wright Mabie.

96. Christmas began in the heart of God and is completed only when it reaches the heart of man. *The War Cry.*

97. Christmas is not a date; it is a state of mind. Mary Ellen Chase.

98. To know Christ is not to speculate about the mode of his incarnation but to know his saving benefits. Philip Melanchthon.

99. Life is always difficult in proportion to its intensity and reality. Edward Howard Griggs.

100. Let us not look back in anger, nor forward in fear, but around us in awareness. James Thurber.

SECTION II. Vital Themes for Vital Preaching

1. **Topic: Aftermath of Christmas**
TEXT: Luke 2:17.

Does the fact that the New Year follows Christmas say anything to you? It is the poetic thought that because of the significance of the Christmas event there is hope and the possibility for a new beginning. In a very real sense old things have passed away, and God in Christ is making all things new. It is in the light that we examine the reactions of those related to the events of the first Christmas. In them perhaps we shall see ourselves.

I. There were the shepherds. (1) When the angels returned to heaven they hastened to Bethlehem to find Mary, Joseph, and the Babe in the manger. They spread the good news as to the meaning of this Child. Throughout the village they shared the news with all whom they met.

(2) Then they returned to their work. They resumed the common chore of tending their flocks, but they would never be the same again, for they were continuously glorifying and praising God. A sense of the nearness of God transformed their work as it will do ours.

II. There was Mary. (1) Hearing the words of the shepherds she "kept all these things and pondered them in her heart" (Luke 2:19). Literally, she set side by side for comparison the things she had heard. To the words of Gabriel nine months before she now added the words and praise of the angels over the fields near Bethlehem.

(2) Someone has suggested that Mary may have kept a Baby Book. Why not? Whether or not she did, she certainly kept one in her heart! These events were the real and mighty acts of God as he acted for man's salvation.

(3) Shall we soon forget the events of Christmas? Or shall we also set them side by side in our hearts for meditation and incentive to serve the Lord? We have so many more: Jesus' sinless life, atoning death, mighty resurrection, his living reign and promised return. All of these things are involved in salvation history.

III. There were those of Bethlehem who heard. (See Luke 2:18.) (1) They were astonished at such strange words, but nothing more. The event of the ages took place right under their noses, but they only wondered momentarily and evidently, ignored it.

(2) Is Christ to you just some mythical Santa Claus and nothing more? Are the events of Christmas only toys to be opened on Christmas morning, played with, and soon forgotten? If so, then for you the day is not the gladdest but the saddest day of your life. For you came so near to life and, yet, are so far away. The greatest story ever told about the greatest life ever lived is not some plaything, some fairy tale to be enjoyed for a moment and then dismissed.—Herschel H. Hobbs in *The Baptist Hour.*

2. **Topic: Oneness in the Body** (Week

of Prayer for Church Unity, January 18–25)

Certain concrete realities are inseparably related to the evangelical renaissance now dawning, and whose dawn offers the one real hope for the churches of Christendom to give visible expression to a relationship that is truly "ecumenical."

I. The first reality is new men and women, who, having committed themselves to Christ as Savior and being possessed by him as Lord, give contemporary relevancy to what is involved in the Pauline affirmation: "To me to live is Christ."

(1) This God-man, Christ-man relationship is a reality that goes beyond the status obtained by baptism and confirmation, beyond participation in Holy Communion, and beyond loyalty to church tradition, creeds and structures, however important these may be.

(2) At the core of being truly "Christian" is Christ's personal presence in daily life, accompanied by "gifts of the Spirit"—charisms of diverse kinds by which Christ's men and women are equipped for service.

II. The second reality needed for true ecumenism is visible unity. There is no room in real Christianity for individualism. Christians are members of community called the Church.

(1) Whether "church" means for Christ's disciples a local congregation or a world-wide fellowship, it is incumbent upon them to give fully visible, but not necessarily institutional, expression to the New Testament significance of oneness in Christ.

(2) Across all boundaries of culture and race, of nationalism and churchism, of catholicism and pentecostalism, whatever be their sincerely held differences of opinion and practice, visible Christian unity is an absolute imperative for all persons whose ultimate allegiance is to Jesus Christ. It is their Christian responsibility to give effective expression to this unity in social gatherings, in worship, and in cooperative action.

(3) This does not necessarily involve agreement on all matters, nor the realization of unified church structures. The Church as "the community of all those for whom Jesus Christ is Lord" dare not identify its ultimate objective as organizational, structural oneness, thereby making ecclesiastical union the supreme ecumenical goal. No, let the Church be the Church.

(4) When is the Church "in very deed the Church"? The church's communal selfhood as the diversified Body of Christ is realized when its members see themselves as Christ's servants whose role it is, despite their differences, to be fellow workers for the Kingdom of God, that is, for the reign of God in every facet of human existence. The Church is for the Kingdom. The institutional church as such may be destined to disappear.

III. There is the reality of cooperative action on the road. To live for the Kingdom, churches and their members must walk and act together. They must become a pilgrim fellowship of love and concern, inspired by a wilderness faith, responsive to Christ's timeless mandate, "Follow me." It is their privilege and responsibility to cooperate in all forms of activity that express his loving concern for people and that conduce to human welfare in all its facets.—John A. Mackay in *World Vision Magazine*.

3. Topic: What It Means to Be a Christian

I. It means that, to the extent I am Christian, my dedication, my allegiance, my loyalty is to Christ. To be Christian is to abide in him.

II. It means that my life is lived for and with him in the here and now, in the world. Christianity is living Christ —I in him and he in me—now.

III. In terms of Monday, Tuesday, Wednesday, eating, drinking, making a living, raising children, paying taxes, and making debts—what does this mean? It means that he who is Christian has his life centered in, devoted to, and lived for Christ, for Christianity, and for godly principles in this present world. For such a person, money is not made for his own pleasure; children are not conceived for his own passion; security is not sought for his own protection; and reputation is not made for his own expediency.—Bruce Evans.

4. Topic: Man's Greatest Discovery
TEXT: Matt. 16:15–17.
I. Who Jesus Christ is. (1) He is the incarnate Son of God, the extension of God on the human scene. (2) He was also the atoning Savior. Jesus gave his life on the Cross. (3) He is the resurrected, living Lord. He lives today.
II. How men meet him. (1) They meet him most often in natural confrontation. (2) Sometimes men meet him when they are in the depths of despair. (3) Sometimes men meet him when they are fiercely opposing him.
III. What he does for men. (1) His first wish is to save. (2) He gives you a new spirit. The Biblical-theological expression is that he puts his spirit within you, and he gives with this new spirit a new purpose, a new rulership to life. (3) He satisfies. The better word is, he enables. Jesus Christ enables a person with wisdom and encouragement within his natural capacities. He enables us to be and do that which will please God. He gives faith for prayer and power for Christian witness and work. He is the enabling presence in us.—Paul P. Fryhling.

5. Topic: The Dimensions of the Gospel
TEXT: John 3:16.
I. "God so loved the world." There is the *breadth* of the Gospel. Jesus is speaking about the world of men, the world of human beings created in God's own spiritual image. His love encompasses all men: good and bad, rich and poor, educated and ignorant; men of all colors, all races, all classes.
II. "He gave his only begotten Son." There is the *depth* of the Gospel. This shows how deeply God loved the world. It makes known the high estimate of value he placed on human souls. It indicates the extent to which he was willing to go to save all sinners, even the worst.
III. "That whosoever believeth on him." There is the *height* of the Gospel. To believe on Jesus Christ is to have faith in him. Faith is an upward-looking experience, a lifting up of our hearts and minds to God in Christ. For, when we believe in Christ, we believe in God who sent him to be the Savior of men.
IV. "Should not perish, but have everlasting life." There is the *length* of the Gospel. This is the promise of the Gospel: a life that shall endless be. It was preached by Jesus and it was demonstrated by him. He triumphed over death and the grave, and brought life and immortality to light in the Gospel. He tasted death for every man and came back from the valley of the shadow to say: "Because I live, ye, too, shall live."—Rhodes Thompson.

6. Topic: The Fears of Love (Valentine's Day)
TEXT: I John 4:18.
I. We fear love because we are afraid we are going to be fooled. Trust is making ourselves terribly vulnerable, and yet trust is a necessary ingredient of love.
II. We fear love because we are afraid to be foolish. It seems foolish to show our emotions. It is better to be a little detached, a bit unconcerned. Love seems so foolish in so many ways. When your love is unconditioned by what the other person does, when you give without demanding in return, when you love when a person is obviously not lovable, that seems so foolish.
III. We fear love because we are afraid to feel! When you are willing to be a "feeling person," you are bound to be hurt. While many of us think we are afraid of not being loved, the fear that most of us have is loving. Because to love is to feel deeply, to commit oneself without any guarantee, and to give

oneself. Love is always an act of faith and it is always a risk. Most of us know our own feelings; we can rehearse our wounds and our disappointments. Have we ever really entered into another's life so that we can sense how they feel? Can we see from the other person's point of view?—Charles A. McClain, Jr.

7. Topic: The Church of the Open Door (Brotherhood Sunday)
TEXT: II Chron. 29:3.

I. The Church today must open her doors to the poor and downcast. The Church has been interested only in the cultured, educated, and refined people who could dress nicely and add prestige to the Church. We neglect the poor, the working class, and the dispossessed.

II. The doors of the Church must be open to the church's neighborhood. Many churches have an absentee membership, and they could not care less what the neighborhood is like around the church. Many of these churches are totally oblivious to the immediate needs and problems of the area in which the church is located.

III. The doors of the Church need to be open to all races, for Jesus said that his house was to be a house of prayer for all people. It is a tragic fact that the last bastion of racial prejudice and racism is the Church. We cannot have segregation in schools, public places, hotels, or restaurants. The only place where we can be racist today is in our churches. The sad fact is that many of us are just that.—John R. Brokhoff.

8. Topic: On Being Holy
SCRIPTURE: II Cor. 6:14-7:1.

I. We may test our understanding of holiness by applying it to Jesus, whom the New Testament writers regard as God's holy one *par excellence*. (See Mark 1:24, Luke 1:35, Acts 3:14.) A review of the Gospels reveals virtually nothing at all about Jesus' personal morality or his devotional life. And as for Jewish ritual holiness, Jesus views much of it as a sham. (See Mark 7:1-8.) In fact, he deliberately breaks the laws of ritual purity ("touch nothing unclean") by stretching out his hand to the poor leper and by associating with prostitutes and sinners.

II. In what sense is he God's holy one? He is God's chosen, God's anointed, he who fulfills his divine mission. I Peter 2:9 reminds us that, as followers of Jesus Christ, we too are "a chosen race, a royal priesthood, a holy nation, God's own people," that we may declare his wonderful deeds. All of this is to say that to be holy means fundamentally, not to achieve a certain moral or religious status, but to carry out our mission in the world.—Lewis S. Hay in *The Presbyterian Outlook*.

9. Topic: God Speaks to the Generation Gap
TEXT: Mic. 6:6-8.

We who are older and the young must find some basis for communication if the gap between us is not to grow into even more tragic proportions. And the Church, if it is faithful to its reconciling mission, ought to be a place where mutual understanding and communication can begin. Which is why both young and old might listen again to those familiar lines in the prophecy of Micah.

I. The first accent in this little prophecy, "to do justice," is addressed more directly to those of us who are older. For this is what has inflamed the young, the blatant injustices in a world we have made for the young and are handing on to them.

II. The second accent in the prophecy is addressed more directly to the young: "What does the Lord require of you but to love kindness." For all the sensitivity among the young to social injustice, many of them give little evidence of "loving kindness," of compassion, for anyone except the blacks and the poverty-stricken. They have forgotten that the people who make up the typical parish church—for all their hypocrisy and blindness to the injustices around them—are people, too, fearful of change, precisely the ones who are most threatened by loss of security. They are the neighbors to be loved, too.

III. The third accent in the prophecy is addressed equally to both generations: "Walk humbly with your God."

(1) If we are both to be aware of the arrogant rightness of our views, then we need to walk humbly with our God, subjecting our views and assumptions and prescriptions for change to his judging Word. For any change in the direction of social justice is full of ambiguities.

(2) An answer will have to be found, but either way, there is not absolute right. Some people are going to get hurt. The ambiguities abound. No matter what the problem. Decisions will be agonizing. But the recognition that there is no absolute "right" is a step in the direction of "walking humbly with your God."—Edmund A. Steimle.

10. Topic: What If We Follow Christ?
TEXT: Mark 8:27–38.
What would happen if we seriously proposed to follow Christ?

I. He would lead us into adventure. He may lead us into areas we have never tried before, cause us to do things we have never done before. Maybe we'd teach a Sunday School class, counsel a youth group, visit for our church.

II. If we follow him, Christ will take us into strange paths. He is always ahead of us, this Christ of ours. Hebrews says that he is the pioneer and perfecter of our faith. We have not yet caught up to him. We have not yet learned to live by his way of love.

III. "Follow me," says Jesus, and, if we do, we shall never stand still. Just as we get bogged down in some comfortable little rut, he comes along and says: "Move on!"

IV. "Follow me," says Christ, and, if you do, you choose a lonely road. (1) For Christ does not walk the way of the crowds. He does not take the easy paths. He calls us to a cross. (2) It will never be the popular way to follow this Man carrying a cross. But it is the only way to blessedness.

V. If we follow Christ we may not be sure where we will go but we are sure who will go with us! He will not always lead us to comfort, but always to joy. We may not win every battle, but the ultimate victory will be ours because it is his. Beyond the Cross, in the plan of God, there is the Resurrection.
—Donald B. Strobe.

11. Topic: Proof of God's Love (Lent)
TEXT: I John 4:10.
We are living in a day of doubt, when everyone wants proof and needs assurance of love. Here is proof of God's love.

I. Because he thinks about us all the time.

II. Because he has planned for us.

III. Because he warns us all through the Bible, saying, "Be ready, pray, and watch."

IV. Because he has invited us to share all good things with him.

V. Because he has provided for us.

VI. Because he never leaves us alone.

VII. Because he is willing to forgive us.—W. B. Bingham in *Western Recorder*.

12. Topic: When Jesus Spoke (Lent)
I. The words of Jesus made powerful impact on the Master's hearers because of the newness of his declarations.

II. The teachings of Jesus arrested the attention of his listeners because his words on delivery were obviously verified and valid.

III. The words of Jesus were tremendously forceful with the people because those who heard him knew that the words he spoke were embodied in his person.

IV. The words of Jesus astonished his generation because what he said was so vividly related to the people's lives and the events and questions of the day.—*The Methodist Christian Advocate.*

13. Topic: Hill of Three Crosses (Lent)
Scripture: Luke 23:39–46.
I. The first word from the hill of the crosses came from the thief in rebellion. (1) The thief is related to all who have joined the rebellion against God. The rebellious thief is a symbol for all who have rejected God. (2) The thief in rebellion died in his sin, choosing eternal damnation, while a way of escape and everlasting life was no further away than the central cross.

II. Look at the cross on the other side of Jesus. This is the cross of repentance. (1) The cross of repentance holds the thief who died to his sin. There is no bitterness here. No questions asked. No demands made. Only a request for forgiveness and to be remembered. (2) To repent means to change your mind. It means to look at things, and to think about things, in a new way. It means to think about things the way God wants us to think about them. (3) God, sending his Son in the likeness of sinful flesh, condemned sin in the flesh. Jesus broke into time and canceled out the effects of sin so that it might no longer have dominion over man.

III. The central cross demands our attention. This is the cross of redemption, and the One who died for sin. (1) Perhaps no human mind can grasp the implications of the Cross and God's word of redemption through Christ, but God's word, with the help of the Holy Spirit, will lead us to understand the principle of the Cross and of redemption. (2) Someone had to break the chain and stop the flow of sin if man was to have eternal life and have fellowship with God. This was, and remains, the work of Christ.—Willis E. Dewberry.

14. Topic: Calvary Today (Passion Sunday)
The way to Calvary today is not a vague, undefined, tired old path that has little challenge. It is charted and marked with the tensions and tempests of our times. Calvary is reached today only by those who endure without malice the inevitable crosses we confront on so many hills these days.

I. Let there be a crucifixion of forms of prejudice that rip the flesh of human dignity and decency, and let there be a resurrection of the spirit of spiritual oneness, brother to brother, soul to soul, man to man.

II. Let there be a crucifixion of forms of hatred that produce more and more hatred, and let there be a resurrection of Christian love that helps us "love the unloved" for Jesus' sake.

III. Let there be a crucifixion of the smug spirit of imagined superiority that breeds disdain and contempt for one another, and let there be a resurrection of that balance that makes all men equal in the sight of God.

IV. Let there be a crucifixion of that spirit of greed that spawns mounting materialism, and let there be a resurrection of a true charity that is not only willing but happy to share in a spirit of Christian togetherness.

V. Let there be a crucifixion of hostility that seeks to "right the wrongs of the past" by any and all forms of violence, and let there be a resurrection of a forgive-and-forget attitude that declares, "The past is past; this is a new day; let's make the most of it in a constructive, positive manner."

VI. Let there be a crucifixion of cynicism about motives of our fellowmen, and let there be a resurrection of trust and fellowship, two powerful forces in human relationships.—William E. Chamberlain in *War Cry.*

15. Topic: The Glory of Going a Little Farther (Palm Sunday)
Text: Matt. 26:39.
I. "He went a little farther" than his fellow Hebrews, that devout race, whose conception of God was the highest and holiest known to man, which made them a peculiar people, chosen of

God, through whom he spoke, not only to their race but to the whole world.

II. "He went a little farther" than his parents, Mary and Joseph, whose spiritual life and family devotion were of such high quality that Jesus was thoroughly prepared for the manhood God intended and for the unique mission for which he came into this world.

III. "He went a little farther" than his disciples, men who had left all to follow him and to devote themselves to the work of his Kingdom.

IV. "He went a little farther" than all the angels. He left his celestial home and all the company of heaven, and came to this earth in the form of the Babe of Bethlehem. He became bone of our bone and flesh of our flesh. He renounced his heavenly royalty and identified himself with common man.

V. "He went a little farther" than all mankind. He became obedient unto death, even the death of the cross.

VI. "He went a little farther" in his obedience to the will of God.

VII. "He went a little farther" in his love for mankind than any other human being.

VIII. "He went a little farther"—no one knows just how far he went to achieve our salvation.

IX. "And he went a little farther" and was not only obedient unto the Cross, but also subjected himself to death and the resurrection.—George Hunter Hall.

16. Topic: The Man Who Missed Easter

Text: John 20:24, 26.

It is the story of Thomas, the man who missed the first Easter, and then found it one week later.

I. Why did he miss it? Because he didn't believe it, even though it happened right before his eyes, or very nearly so.

II. In many ways he had the temperament of a skeptic. He was quick to say: show me, prove it, seeing is believing.

III. Thomas was not a hopeless case. Skepticism is not necessarily disastrous. Faith can conquer unbelief.

IV. You might expect that God would turn his back on the man who is always demanding proof even while he is surrounded by it. Why should the Almighty bother about such little men who insult him by posing their stupid questions? God is different. Just because he is so big he can stoop to the level of little men. Because God is God he can go to the trouble of dealing with skeptics, on their terms, and make believers out of them.

V. Jesus does the same thing to unbelievers today. He shows them the scars of the Cross. There is no other cure for skepticism.—Peter Eldersveld.

17. Topic: Ten Commandments for Husbands and Wives (National Family Week)

Text: I Cor. 13.

I. Thou shalt understand what marriage really is.

II. Thou shalt accept each other for what each is.

III. Thou shalt talk things through.

IV. Thou shalt trust one another.

V. Thou shalt forgive one another.

VI. Thou shalt develop a sense of humor.

VII. Thou shalt be loyal to one another.

VIII. Thou shalt take the positive approach.

IX. Thou shalt cultivate thy romance.

X. Thou shalt make thine a Christian marriage.

18. Topic: Be's that Don't Sting (Festival of the Christian Home)

Text: Eph. 4:32.

I. *Be sensible*. God has given each one of us a brain, and he expects us to use it. Life is not a "bed of roses" and neither is marriage. Being sensible means that we look at life objectively and realistically.

II. *Be diplomatic*. A happy home is one where the members of the family exercise tact and judgment in their relationship with one another.

III. *Be loving*. Marriage is only real when the flame called love is kept burning.

IV. *Be devout*. To be our best selves we need the power of God in our lives. Bitterness and prolonged anger cannot breathe in a healthy atmosphere refined by prayer and worship.—George L. Earnshaw, Jr.

19. Topic: Faith and Health
TEXT: Ps. 103:3.

I. Believe in life and the words of Christ, "I am come that ye may have life and have it to the full." Believe that you can get well.

II. Have a meaning and purpose in life. In Christ I find life's meaning.

III. Recognize the healing forces of life. The universe is upon the side of life. Out of the universe life came, and life is sustained by the great eternal forces around us.

IV. Pray with trust and confidence thinking of the answer you really desire.

V. Trust and cooperate with your physician, psychologist, psychiatrist, minister, or healer as the case may be.

VI. Have a high bright horizon in your view. Expect great things from God and accept great things from God.—Frank A. Court.

20. Topic: Six Tests of Love
TEXT: I Cor. 13:2.

I. Do you get exasperated easily? A brain storm on little provocation? Point of ignition easily fired? Rather proud when saying: "My temper got the better of me"?

II. Do you throw your weight around? Vaunt yourself, get a swelled head, have a constant eye on the mirror; like to be "I am Sir Oracle"?

III. Are you impatient? Get bored with slow minds? Resentful, ironic, sarcastic; say devastating things that hurt and burn?

IV. Are you always on the make? "I want mine." "What's in it for me?" "A man's got to look after himself."

V. Have you a taste for dirt? Like to hear bad news or harmful gossip?

VI. Do you give up on some people? Say: "I'm through with her. She doesn't appreciate kindness"?—James W. Clarke.

21. Topic: Tyrannies that Thwart Discipleship
SCRIPTURE: Matt. 4:1–11.

I. The *ego* overemphasizes I, me, and mine. It is that which makes us measure issues, projects, causes, peoples, even God by their effect upon *our* hopes, *our* plans, *our* profit, and *our* security.

II. *Things*—money, clothes, houses, furniture, food, automobiles—all the material paraphernalia of existence dominate our thoughts, not memories, or laughter, not sunlight, or music, or love—only things. "To have" concerns us a great deal more than "to be."

III. *People* exercise a disturbing lordship over our consciousness. What they think of us agitates us more than what God thinks of us.—Albert E. Day in *Discipline and Discovery*.

22. Topic: Ascension Affirmations (Ascension Sunday)
TEXT: Acts 1:9–11.

I. The Ascension to "the right hand of God" is the vindication of the life and teaching of Jesus. It tells us that what he represented on earth is identified with the Power that controls the universe and human history. It expresses the truth that what we see in him is the ultimate Sovereign Reality.

II. The Ascension is a declaration that Jesus Christ reigns everywhere. Since he is "at the right hand of God" and since God is omnipresent, the sovereignty of Christ is universal.

III. The Ascension affirms that Jesus Christ is Lord of the future. It is fundamental insight of the faith that "the Kingdom, the Power and the Glory" belong to the God who was manifested in Christ and that "he must reign until he has put all things under his feet."—*Pulpit Digest*.

23. Topic: Revitalizing Pentecost
SCRIPTURE: Acts 2:1–13, 41–42.

I. Persons must be united in their desire for the Holy Spirit.

II. Persons should meet together regularly for prayer and for sharing their faith.

III. Persons must wait upon the Holy Spirit and receive him when he comes.

IV. Persons should be sensitive to the leadership of the Holy Spirit.—William H. Likins.

24. Topic: Christ's Appeal to Youth

I. Christ appeals to young people because of their need for love. Everyone needs love, but the need is accentuated in the experience of youth. They cover this need up rather effectively because they are so afraid they won't be loved. But the need is there.

II. Christ appeals to young people because of their need for forgiveness. I do not know of any group of individuals who get more uptight about their imperfection.

III. Christ appeals to young people's need for meaning in life. The thing that makes Christ appealing to young people is that he can bring meaning and joy and hope, even in a world like ours. They are attracted by a God who came into this imperfect world and lived in it and brought meaning and hope where there is imperfection and sin.—Kenneth Chafin.

25. Topic: Faith in an Age of Science
TEXT: John 14:9.

Christianity supplies a firm foundation for science in several ways.

I. It insists that nature is a revelation of God.

II. Christianity says that man was created in God's image and therefore man has the ability to understand God's world.

III. Christianity says that man is the ruler of nature and not the other way around. God said man should subdue the earth and have dominion over creation.

IV. Christianity says that God the Creator is a God of order and design who created nature with order and design.—John Primus.

26. Topic: The Nation's Need (Independence Sunday)
TEXT: Prov. 14:34.

I. Dependence upon the power of God. (See II Chron. 14:11.)

II. Determination in the worship of God.

III. Dedication to the Word of God.—C. Reuben Anderson.

27. Topic: The Beauty of the People of God
TEXT: Ps. 90:17.

I. The Church is the people of God, and the beauty of the people of God is in their commitment to his will.

II. The beauty of the people of God is in their compassion.

III. Have you noticed how this verse about the beauty of God is closely related to "the work of our hands"? God will establish and bless the work of our hands.—Jerome J. Hevey.

28. Topic: Gospel Affirmations

The gospel of Christ has three central affirmations.

I. The character of God. We believe that the character and purpose of God have been definitively revealed in Jesus Christ as they have been revealed nowhere else.

II. The dignity of man. The real dignity of man consists in the fact that he is God's creature; man is made with an unbreakable relationship to God.

III. The reconciliation between God and man. It can be summed up in two terms: God's grace and our faith. God in his grace comes to us in our need, and our response to his grace must be a response of faith.—Chester A. Pennington.

29. Topic: Marks of an Effective Ministry
SCRIPTURE: Eph. 4:1–7, 11–24.

I. The first mark of an effective ministry is teamwork. There is cooperative work for all Christians to do.

II. A second mark of an effective ministry is building a warm Christian fellowship, placing central into the life of the Church our Lord's commandments of love, practicing the cohesiveness and durability of God's love.

III. Another mark of an effective ministry is holding central the main purpose of the Church.

IV. Still another essential mark of an effective ministry on the part of both pastor and people is an abiding consciousness of God's presence and power.—Bernard N. King in *Clergy Journal*.

30. Topic: Forever

I. We can believe something that is forever. The two great constants are God and Jesus Christ. They will not change, nor will they fail you now or at the end. (See Deut. 33:27; Heb. 1:12.)

II. We can do something which is forever. The deed of love which seeks no recognition, wants no reward, and put no one under obligation lives forever.

III. We can possess something forever. The treasures of heaven are imperishable. They can be kept forever. They are beyond the destructive power of moth, rust, thieves, financial crises, and death.

IV. We can be something forever. The New Testament says that we who have accepted Jesus Christ as Savior and Lord are now living in an eternal dimension. Eternal life is ours now. (See John 17:3.)—Chevis Horne.

31. Topic: Being Good Is Not Enough

TEXT: Matt. 22:37–40.

I. The Christian life is oriented with God. It is a life tuned in to God. This has been the Christian experience that has little or nothing to do with morality.

II. If you love God, if you are one with him, you have gone beyond morality, which is constantly saying what's right and what's wrong, what you ought to and ought not to do.

III. To love the unlovable, to forgive the unforgivable—that is not morality, that is a gift from God. It is a position reached only by those who know God's love.

IV. Christianity goes far beyond morality because we have a "cause," a mission to the world. We are called to transform the world, to bring men to Christ, to baptize all nations in the name of the Father, the Son, and the Holy Spirit, to bring men to know, love, and serve God as revealed in Christ.

V. A Christian is not a "good guy" trying to get other guys to be good. He is a person with a vision of God, who has seen a vision of a world that can be—a world of love, a world in tune with God, a world to bring to pass—a man with a vision and a mission.—K. J. Campbell.

32. Topic: The Good Shepherd

SCRIPTURE: Ps. 23.

Have you ever noticed how the 23rd Psalm was fulfilled in the person of our Lord Jesus Christ? In the book of Psalms we have a historic past, a spiritual present, and a prophetic future. Our Lord said, "I am the good shepherd."

I. You shall not want rest (Matt. 11:28).

II. You shall not want drink (John 7:37).

III. You shall not lack forgiveness (Matt. 9:6).

IV. You shall not lack guidance (John 14:6).

V. You shall not lack companionship (Matt. 28:20).

VI. You shall not lack comfort (John 14:16).

VII. You shall not lack food (John 6:35).

VII. You shall not lack joy (John 15:11).

IX. You shall not lack anything in this life (John 14:14; Matt. 6:33).

X. You shall not lack anything in eternity (John 14:2–3).—Roy W. Gustafson in *Decision*.

33. Topic: Belief Is Not Enough

Many people contend that Christian Faith is to be measured or determined by one's belief. This is unfortunate, even tragic.

I. Belief without commitment, for instance, is a player who doesn't enter the game, but sits on the sidelines to cheer or to criticize, whatever his disposition may be.

II. Belief without sacrifice is a religion that stands apart, uninvolved, indifferent, therefore futile.

III. Belief without response is a soul looking back over its shoulder.

IV. Belief without participation in life, all of life, is to reduce oneself to a foolish caricature, an otherworldly creature in a world which demands action now.

V. The trouble with the "merely believing" religion is that it is unconfirmed, always defensive, "threatened," and negative. Its energies are spent defending a position or in resisting the strange, the alien, the new. Lacking confirmation through the positive response of faith, therefore having no experimental proof of its own reality, it breeds frustration and insecurity, conflict and confusion.

VI. Faith is a simple response to what God is doing in history and to what God has done in Christ. It involves obedience to the immediate need which God set before us.—Paul L. Clem in *The Birmingham District Bulletin.*

34. Topic: We, Too, Face Goliath

Text: I Sam. 17:45.

I. Each of us has our Goliaths. That strong temptation to justify our prejudices, to seek an excuse not to attempt the best, to rationalize our actions which do not measure up to God's standards, to overlook our own faults and shortcomings but criticize those of others, to neglect to show love to our neighbor in concrete ways, to explain away our habits and attitudes.

II. All of these need to be slain by the devastating blow of the slingshot of disciplined faithfulness in everyday tasks.

III. So many of us are not willing to be disciplined and faithful in the small things; we wait for the big opportunity to come. David's preparation for killing the giant was made during his days of faithfulness in watching and protecting his sheep. His daily practice with the sling, his daily trust in his God, his daily living in his presence, his daily realization that he and his people belonged to God and that God watched over them prepared him to succeed when the big challenge came.
—Walter L. Dosch.

35. Topic: The Church in Social Relations

Text: Acts 10:34.

I. Whatever the issues in the whole problem of social relations, the Church *must stand as mediator and prophet.*

II. The Church *has to speak out.* One of the biggest sins of the Church is that of saying nothing. It should be possible—sometimes it is, often it is not —for the Church to act as mediator in controversies. If the Church has been fair, has been impartial, has applied the principles of Jesus equally, it may be possible to be mediator.

III. The Church *needs to attack where necessary.* What and who is better prepared, more appropriately, more fully and completely commanded to speak out against wrong than the Church?

IV. The Church *needs to bind up wounds* where it is possible to bind up wounds.

V. Whatever the controversy, the Church, if it is to be faithful to its Master, has to be active in all the fields where men live, and this includes social relations. However, it must *act for the same reasons* he did, because it is sent and because the Spirit of the Lord is there.

VI. The Church is *called to be a liberator.* But in doing so it has to be the Church for all because the Gospel is for all.—Don R. Boyd.

36. Topic: The Value of Contentment
TEXT: Phil. 4:11.
I. "Study to be quiet" (I Thess. 4:11).
II. Have something to look forward to each day.
III. Have something to look up to.
IV. Appreciate the present.—Robert W. Frank.

37. Topic: True Religion
SCRIPTURE: Acts 17:16-23.
I. True religion is not a pie in which we put whatever ingredients we choose until it tastes just right to us, or, more often than not, produces spiritual indigestion.
II. True religion is not a stew in which we drop a pinch of this or that until we have what seems to us to be the exact combination to make us happy and content.
III. True religion is not a machine for which we assemble a great collection of cogs and wheels, put them together, and hope it will run.
IV. True religion is a tree that has life and growth and unity and roots which go down deep, drawing their power from the constant activity of God, the Creator.—George Gerald Parker.

38. Topic: The Christian's Social Obligations
TEXT: Matt. 6:10.
What is the will of God for mankind? We believe it is revealed by Jesus Christ. Certain moral principles taught by our Lord bear directly upon economics:
I. That we esteem every man as a being of infinite worth, a child of God, a soul for whom Christ died.
II. That we accept all men as our brothers and seek justice for them.
III. That we obey the law of the family, which is the rule of love, wherein the strong serve and defend the weak.
IV. That we seek the Kingdom of God, giving top priority to the claims of truth, justice, mercy, and holiness.
V. That we regard our possessions and skills, talents and earnings, as gifts of God to be used in obedience to God.
VI. That we view our daily work as a vocation, an offering unto God; that our work serve a worthy human need; and that we refrain from any employment that undercuts what a Christlike God would have done for mankind.—Everett W. Palmer.

39. Topic: Living by the Law of God
SCRIPTURE: Luke 10:25-37.
Why does Jesus give us the two commandments?
I. Because we need an ideal to beckon us on, a goal that lies beyond us or we will cease to grow.
II. Because we need a norm by which to judge our moral obligations.
III. Because they point us to the Gospel, to Jesus himself who commands us to love, who forgives us when we fail, who helps us as we strive to do better, and who uses us in spite of our repeated failures, but can use us to the fullest only if we do recognize our failures and look to him for forgiveness.—Ernest Trice Thompson in *The Presbyterian Outlook*.

40. Topic: Exclusiveness (World Communion Sunday)
TEXT: I Cor. 12:13.
Exclusiveness is not a popular characteristic for a person or an institution to be accused of in our enlightened culture. We have come to think of exclusiveness as antisocial, undemocratic, demoralizing. But without exclusiveness few human accomplishments would have been possible.
I. Jesus was exclusive. The effectiveness of his short ministry depended on his concentration on a narrow, confined, limited area and people. Jesus did not try to convert the whole world personally.
II. It would be a mistake for any of us in the Christian Church to claim that the Church is no longer exclusive. Our entire religious heritage has depended on exclusiveness. Those Old

Testament heroes, who now appear so narrow and restricted and segregated, practiced an isolationism that saved their religious faith. The restrictions of social contract between the Israelites and the Egyptians produced a single-minded Moses in a foreign land. The repudiation of alien values kept the Israelites faithful to the temple worship and the ancient code of behavior. Prohibitions and separations brought forth a Jeremiah and an Isaiah. And it is this same kind of exclusiveness today that Christians must practice to promote the faith.

III. It is a frightening and often demoralizing experience, however, to be a part of a group or an institution or a nation which has allowed exclusiveness to become discrimination because of superficial differences. St. Paul has said the last word to us on the subject of exclusiveness in Gal. 3:27-28, and his teaching must be our guide for all time.—Richard S. Knight.

41. Topic: What Do You Mean You Are Not a Minister? (Laymen's Sunday)

TEXT: I Pet. 2:7.

Every Christian is called to witness as part of the *laos,* the people of God.

I. Roadblocks to the ministry of the laity. (1) The clericalism of the priestly establishment has shunted laymen to a siding for their particular functioning in the Church. (2) The lethargy of the laity in leaving it to the paid professional in the Church.

II. Advantages of the ministry of the laity. (1) The layman does not suffer under the stigma of being a professional clergyman. (2) Laymen are more often closer to common life than the clergy. (3) There is a freshness to the nonprofessional which the professional may well have lost. (4) The early Church thrived on such a ministry of the *laos.*

III. Our common ministry. (1) Peter said you are a royal priesthood. He was saying that the Christian witness of every person is important in the ministry of the Church. (2) The Apostle says that you are a part of a holy nation. (3) Peter says to you of the *laos,* you are indeed God's People. There are not varying classes of citizenship in the Kingdom of God. (4) You don't have to "go into the ministry" to have a ministry as a Christian. If you accept that, perhaps you will move from the area of critical spectator to enthusiastic participant in the ministry to which we have all been called in Christ.—Hoover Rupert.

42. Topic: Why a Social Creed for the Churches? (World Order Sunday)

SCRIPTURE: Gen. 3:14-24.

The purpose of the social creed of the Church is threefold in character.

I. It seeks to unite profound religious beliefs in God and man with the problems men wrestle with from day to day. It is an attempt to hold the light of God's truth, as we understand it, so that men may see what their problems really are and perhaps find new ways to solve them. It is an attempt to bring into terse, compact form a statement of the sins of society and to call upon Christians to repudiate them.

II. A social creed is an attempt to get an increasing number of men and women consecrated to the solution of common problems in the light of Christian ethics. It does not have "blueprints" for solutions, but it does indicate needs and creates faith in the possibility of finding a solution. It asks men like us to work out our own salvation in fear and trembling. It asks us to live responsibly, as to God, in all that we say, think, and do.

III. A social creed reminds us that the Christian witness must be lifted within business, industry, and the professions, as well as in labor and society in general, if the Christian ethic is to get off the printed page and walk up and down as a force and power in Christian thought and life.—Harold A. Bosley.

43. Topic: Questions Facing Youth (Youth Sunday)

I. What career am I going to follow? What is the vocation I am meant for? How will my life be used most effectively?

II. Am I growing successfully in self-reliance, maturing as one should toward self-responsibility?

III. Choice of life companion. Who will this be? What ideals and standards shall I look for? How shall I really be prepared for marriage?

IV. What are my own beliefs and philosophy about life? What does existence mean to me? In response to all that I am taught and all that I experience, what do I believe?—*The Methodist Christian Advocate.*

44. Topic: Formula for a Full Life

I. *Something to live on*—food and all other material assets which sustain us physically.

II. *Someone to live with*—our families and our friends, those clusters of significant others in our lives and those cheering sections of our souls, who enable us to fill in our own identities by stretching us toward significant communities.

III. *Something to live by*—a faith by which we align ourselves with creative and redemptive powers.

IV. *Something to live for*—a cause or purpose in devotion to which we experience a feeling of being in touch with the supreme context in which we rightly belong.—Melvin E. Wheatley, Jr.

45. Topic: Jesus' Conditions of Stewardship (Stewardship Day)

TEXT: Mark 8:34.

I. The "want," the deep-seated desire leaping from the depths of the human heart to become one with him.

II. Disregarding one's self gives us the picture of a quick and total throwing overboard of the practices and things of self to make room for the compulsion of the Christ.

III. The acceptance of responsibility, differing with different people, but none the less real, and involving at all times sacrifice.

IV. The responsibility for following even unto death. Too often the last three words are the only ones that make any impression. But the challenge is for us to reach, through prayer and confidence in the love of God, such relationship with the Father that our life shall reflect the loving, merciful God to a broken world.—James Allen Kestle.

46. Topic: Thanksgiving Every Day (Thanksgiving Sunday)

TEXT: I Thess. 5:16–18.

I. How is it possible for anyone to live in a continuous spirit of thanksgiving? By a continual surrender of life's experiences and situations over to the will of God. Surrender is not just an act; it is an attitude. When we are saved, we surrender our sins; when we are sanctified, we surrender our selves; but after those crises there is a life to be lived, and if life is to be filled with thanksgiving, there must be a continual surrender of life's situations over to God's will.

II. By surrendering the situation, the problem, the experience over to God's will, will mean that you can go on your way released from the foreboding and frustration and the festering of a problem hugged too tightly in the heart where it hampers and hinders the enjoyment and fulfillment of life. It is still your problem, of course, but God is now working on it. And that is what makes the difference between bitterness and blessedness, between resentment and rejoicing, between frustration and fulfillment, between thanklessness and thankfulness in any life.

III. Anyone who lives in such an attitude of surrender and trust not only can but will rejoice evermore and in everything give thanks. And that is what real Thanksgiving—any day and every day—is all about.—William Fisher.

47. Topic: This I Believe

I. I believe in the revealed religion of Jesus Christ.

II. I believe in his revelation because men who have followed him have found themselves in the presence of God.

III. I believe in Christ's revelation because those who have taken him seriously have found new life.

IV. I believe in his revelation because through him men have found the truth that made them free.

V. I believe in Christ's revelation of God because in him men have found joy and peace and faith, making them able for all things.

VI. I believe in his revelation because he speaks with divine authority. He saves us from the "tyranny of the self"—from saying, "I think," "I hope," "It seems to me."—George Gerald Parker.

48. Topic: Can the Gospel Save the World? (Advent)

From the very first days of the Church, confidence has been the Christians' watchword. What were the grounds of this confidence?

I. It rested on faith in God. They believed that God had created the world and that it belonged to him. They believed that God had a purpose for the world. When they proclaimed the Gospel of God's Kingdom to the world, they proclaimed it not as the bright idea of clever men but as the truth of God.

II. Their confidence rested on an experience of Jesus Christ that had changed their lives. He took them as they were. But they were drawn to want to be like him. And in the end the change in them was so profound that they even faced the kind of death that he faced, rather than be unlike him. They were changed people, different from what they had been before.

III. They had an awareness of the Spirit of God in their midst. St. Paul talks about the fellowship of the Holy Ghost. He means a community held together by the Holy Spirit. It was a community of friendship, a community of forgiveness, and a community of unselfishness.

IV. It was a community without distinctions. The alienation between men was reconciled and the unity of God's family restored. This was a new community capable of embracing the whole world.—Charles H. Buck, Jr.

49. Topic: John's Certainties (Advent)

SCRIPTURE: Matt. 3:1–11; 11:2–6; 14:1–12.

I. He was sure of his *preparation*.
II. He was sure of his *mission*.
III. He was sure of his *message*.— Robert F. Shelby, Jr.

50. Topic: The Star of Bethlehem (Advent)

TEXT: Num. 24:17.

Jesus Christ is the Star of Bethlehem, the Light of the world. Not only are there Old Testament prophetic references to Christ as a star, but in the New Testament this designation is further applied to him. (See Rev. 16:22.)

I. *A star is a source of guidance.* The stars have often been used as guiding beacons in the sky. Our text refers to the Star of Bethlehem that guided the Wise Men to the place in Bethlehem where the Christ-Child was.

II. *A star is a symbol of government.* The "star out of Jacob" can have reference to none other than the Lord Jesus Christ who will one day come to rule and to reign. He waits to rule on the throne of every man's heart.

III. *A star is a sign of grace.* The Wise Men embraced the gift of God "that bringeth salvation." We are encouraged to look to Christ, the Star of Bethlehem, for guidance and direction for our lives. We are reminded to accept Christ that his grace may be shed abroad in our lives.—C. Reuben Anderson.

51. Topic: The Glory of His Coming (Christmas)

TEXT: Isa. 9:6.

I. The glory of his advent. (1) He came in the glory of his humanity. He did not come as one isolated or apart from us, but as "Emmanuel"—God with us. (2) He was born of Mary, but begotten of the Holy Ghost. Without the virgin birth there is no sinless Savior, and without a sinless Savior no answer to human sin. (3) He was a Son given. So we see the glory of his deity. He was ever with God as the eternal Son, yet he came out of eternity as God's gift.

II. The glory of his attributes. (1) The name "Wonderful Counselor" speaks of his infinite wisdom. (2) The name "The mighty God" tells of his infinite power. (3) The name "The everlasting Father" is suggestive of his infinite love. (4) The name "The Prince of Peace" reflects his infinite redemption.

III. The glory of his accession. The One who came as the Babe of Bethlehem is coming back as the King of kings and Lord of lords. In that day he will be given the throne of his father David, and he shall judge with equity and justice.—Stephen F. Olford.

52. Topic: The Future Belongs to God

TEXT: Deut. 29:29.

By "secret things" the ancient writer means "the future." No one has any foreknowledge of what will happen in the New Year. We cannot safely predict what will take place in our own life or in the lives of loved ones even tomorrow. But God has revealed the laws of life, and we are at liberty and able to live by them.

I. This means that any apprehension we feel in our approach to the New Year, while it is understandable, is futile, a waste of energy.

II. Our first and foremost task in the New Year is to live in the light of what God has revealed. We don't know enough to solve all the problems of the world, but we do know enough to be patient and kind within our families, in dealing with people in everyday relations, starting now.

III. To do today's duty well, doing what we can where we are and in terms of what we know, is always the best preparation for any unknown tomorrow.

IV. To trust God for the unknown future is the surest way to live calmly today.

V. To have present experiences of God's grace and guidance is the surest foundation for hope as we face the unknown future.—J. Francis F. Peak.

SECTION III. Resources for Lenten and Easter Services

SERMON SUGGESTIONS

Topic: Four Things Jesus Could Not Do

I. The first was at Nazareth. He returned home and doubtless hoped that it would be a great occasion. Of all the helpless and hopeless in Galilee, he knew the blind and crippled and worried persons of Nazareth best. He had the power and will to relieve them. But he did no mighty work there because of their unbelief. (See Matt. 13:58.)

II. The second was in the Upper Room before Christ was taken from his disciples. It was his last moments with them. His heart was full, and he so desired to communicate to them his thoughts and feelings. But all he could say was: "I have yet many things to say to you, but you cannot bear them now" (John 16:12, RSV).

III. The third was overlooking Jerusalem. At the start of the last week on earth, Jesus climbed the hill above the city. The final clash with the Establishment was inevitable and deadly. With a great burden of having failed, our Lord wept, and in weeping he cried: "O Jerusalem, Jerusalem, killing the prophets. . . . How often would I have gathered your children together as a hen gathers her brood . . . and you would not" (Matt. 23:27).

IV. The fourth was at the Cross. The people there who passed by, jeering, cried out: "You who would destroy the temple and build it in three days, save yourself! If you are the Son of God, come down from the cross" (Matt. 27:40). The watchers made sport of him, and he remained where he had been fastened.—John Hunter in *The United Church Observer.*

Topic: Calvary: The Divine Paradox
TEXT: II Cor. 5:19.

I. When Jesus went to his cross it was God suffering for the sins of the world, God bearing human sin, God making his gesture of love to sinful man, God exposing sin but expiating it. What Jesus did on the Cross was done by God in him. It meant that the innermost secret of the heart of God is love which yearns to redeem and will go through death and Hell for that redemption.

II. The strange paradox of Calvary is that a cruel and unjust crime committed by a man has elevated and dignified man's sense of his essential worth and potentiality.

III. The Cross, where man is at his worst, has made man believe in his best! In the light of the Cross, trouble, suffering, despair, and tragedy are transmuted into triumph through Christ.

IV. The deeper the paradox is that the Cross was a crushing defeat of righteousness, and yet it was the greatest victory righteousness ever won.

V. The Cross stands on the frontier of the temporal and eternal world as a symbol of unshaken faith in the final

RESOURCES FOR LENTEN AND EASTER SERVICES

victory of God. It removes the fear of ultimate extinction.—George B. Smith.

Topic: Frame of Reference

The Cross has a threefold frame of reference that spells out the meaning of the death of Jesus Christ in God's plan for the salvation of sinful men.

I. It was the final and ultimate revelation of God's divine love. God's love was characterized by sacrifice, suffering, and death. He spared not his own Son, and his Son offered himself as an oblation and a substitute for sinners.

II. The Cross was the measure of the divine judgment on sin. It brought death to the Son of God. Men everywhere like to pretend that death is just a normal part of the natural order; they resist the ugly fact that it is the inevitable, just, and logical consequence of sin. Calvary is no less than God's judgment on sin.

III. The Cross is the ground of pardon and forgiveness. There and there alone the sinner finds forgiveness for guilt, release from sin's penalty, and deliverance from its power. It is this that brings hope to the heart of man.—*Christianity Today.*

Topic: Look to the Cross

I. The Cross reveals the extent of Christ's commitment. (1) The Cross showed the extent of Jesus' devotion to God for the redeeming of the world. (2) Jesus demonstrated the ideal extent of commitment: his own life presented, given, sacrificed to God for man's salvation. (3) Jesus' commitment was gladly made. (4) Christ's dedication was unshakable. (5) Christ's commitment meant that he would go even the road of the Cross, bearing this tremendous burden.

II. The Cross is the greatest evidence and expression of God's love. (1) The Cross is the mightiest testimony to the love of God for mankind. (2) The Cross reveals God's love for man in the great grace of the reconciliation he effected there and in the indescribable suffering he endured in the Cross because of the sins of men.

III. The Cross holds the answers to our deepest questions. Among these are the following. (1) Why do men suffer when they have done no wrong to bring on their suffering? (2) What will overcome the power of sin in the world's life and in individual men's lives? (3) What is the best use of personal life?—*The Methodist Christian Advocate.*

Topic: On Trial

SCRIPTURE: John 18:12–19:16.

Jesus is still in the courtroom. The evidence has been presented to the judge.

I. He is accused of treason and sedition; his response is that he simply loves his country's enemies as much as he loves his country's friends, and that his ultimate loyalty is to God alone.

II. He is accused of disturbing the peace; his response is that the peace was an enforced burden upon the poor and the oppressed, and that the peace needed to be disturbed.

III. He is accused of blasphemy; his response is that to bring God into secular life is to enthrone him in his rightful Kingdom.—Robert W. Wingard.

Topic: What the Resurrection Meant

I. The Resurrection meant that Christ was God of very God. He was what he claimed to be. Christ was Deity in the flesh.

II. It meant that God had accepted Christ's atoning work on the Cross, which was necessary to our salvation.

III. It assures mankind of a righteous judgment.

IV. It guarantees that our bodies also will be raised.

V. It means that death is abolished.—Billy Graham in *Peace with God.*

Topic: The Easter Event

I. This event speaks to us of authentic life, but we are preoccupied with making a living.

II. This Event speaks to us of life

today, but we see the present chaos as too large to be dealt with.

III. This Event speaks to us of life in the future, but we would rather restore the familiar patterns of the past.

IV. This Event speaks to us of faith, but we are more at home with what can be measured and programed.

V. This Event speaks to us of hope, but we limp along on wishful thinking.

VI. This Event speaks to us of love, but we prefer our stance of indifference.—Robert E. Deckert.

ILLUSTRATIONS

PASSWORD. Our world is full of crosses—celluloid and gold, ruby-encrusted, extruded aluminum. It is too filled with religious crosses, but too empty of the crosses upon which man is willing to be hanged in the name of justice and love. "Father forgive them, for they know not what they do." If the Crucified were to look out upon our world today and see us pitted against one another as violently as we are, his words might very well be the same. Humility may save us. Its source is the Suffering Servant who became the Risen Servant. Resurrection, not grief, is our password. The way, though it leads through death, leads to happiness. The tree of sorrow turns into a tree of life. That's both the possibility and the promise of Christ-community, and it's welcome information for all the commonwealth of men.—James W. Angell in *Put Your Arm around the City.*

VOLUNTARY ENLISTMENT. The Cross is not an affliction which life throws our way and which we cannot avoid. The Cross means taking up a burden that, except for the compulsion of God's love, we would never touch. It means doing something unselfishly for others for the glory of God. The Cross is not something we are drafted into; it is something we take up by voluntary enlistment. The Cross is not an ornament to be worn around the neck; it is an attitude to be carried in the heart.—Donald B. Strobe.

BASIS OF BELIEF. They said that if he would come down from the Cross, they would believe that he was the Son of God. It is precisely because he did not come down from the Cross that we believe he is the Son of God.—William Booth.

JUDGMENT OF HISTORY. If you had seen Pilate on the marble steps of his palace, and you had seen Jesus, pale and wan and weak, and you had been asked, "Which name will last?" would you have said "Jesus"? Would you really? Wouldn't you have said: "Don't be silly. Pilate is the representative of the all-powerful might of Rome. This man is the leader of an insignificant sect. He is a carpenter himself. His followers have no power. They were customs' clerks and fishermen, and they have all run away. Don't be silly, if one name lasts, it will be that of Pilate. He represents imperial Rome." But history has judged between them. You would never have heard of Pilate had it not been for Jesus.—Leslie D. Weatherhead in *Over His Own Signature.*

TORTURING QUESTION. In the last year of my imprisonment in one of Hitler's ill-famed concentration camps, at Dachau, a gallows was transferred from the general camp into the courtyard of the "Bunker," the prison inside the camp. And the upper part of this gallows was visible through the barred window of my solitary confinement cell. How often has this gallows induced me to pray for my comrades who were hanged on it, and how often every day I had to control myself when this idea arose: if these people pull me out of my place here to that gallows I shall shout at them: "You criminals, you murderers, wait and see. There is a God in heaven and he will show you!" And then the torturing question: What would have happened if Jesus, when they nailed him to his gallows, to the

Cross, had spoken like this and had cursed his enemies? Nothing would have happened; only there would be no Gospel, no Christian Church, for there would be no Gospel, no message of great joy. He would have prayed against his enemies, not for them, and would have died against them, not for them.—Martin Niemoeller.

OUR JERUSALEM. Life holds for us all the Jerusalem road, over which our unwilling feet must go. We cannot hope to match the dauntless spirit with which Jesus took that road. But we can, if we will, approximate it. A disciple is not above his master; but he can, if he purposes, follow where his master leads. We cannot hope to escape the Jerusalems of life, nor should we deceive ourselves that we can evade or escape the long hard road without betraying our finer instincts.—J. D. Jones.

A BISHOP'S CONFESSION. A famous French bishop once told this story to his congregation. Three university students of Paris were walking along the road one Good Friday afternoon. They noticed crowds going to the churches to make their confessions. The young men began discussing the whole matter of people worshiping in churches and said that it was but a survival of some old superstition. Suddenly two of the students turned to the third, who was the leader among them, and said, "Will you go into the church and tell the priest there what we have been saying to each other?" "Sure, I will," he said, and went in. He stood in line for some time until at length he reached the confessional booth and then said to the priest, "Father, I have come here merely to tell you that Christianity is a dying institution and that religion is a superstition." The priest came out of his booth and looked at the young man keenly and said, "Why did you come here, my son, to tell me this?" The youth told him of his conversation with his companions. The priest listened carefully, then said, "All right, I want you to do one thing for me before you go. You accepted the challenge of your friends and came here; now accept my challenge to you. Walk up to the chancel and you will find there a large wooden cross, and on it a figure of Jesus crucified. I want you to stand before that cross and say these words, 'Jesus died for me, and I don't care.'" The student was puzzled, but to save face, agreed and then went and did as he had been told. Returning, he said to the priest, "I have done it." "Do it once more," said the priest. "After all, it means nothing to you." He went back and looked at the cross for some time and then finally stammered, "Jesus died for me, and I don't care." He returned to the priest and again reported, "I have done it; I am going now." The priest stopped him, "Once more—just once more, and you can go." The young man walked up to the chancel and looked at the cross again and to the figure upon it. He stood there for a long time, but said nothing. This time he returned more slowly and quietly asked, "Father, can I make my confession now?" The bishop concluded the story with these words, "And, my dear people, that young man was myself."—Daniel T. Niles in *Preaching the Gospel of the Resurrection.*

CRUCIAL QUESTION. The Christian belief in the Resurrection is fundamentally the conviction that Jesus Christ in his expectation of a great creative act of divine intervention was not deceived, that his faith was vindicated, that the power of evil has in principle been broken, and that the new age of God is here. This is the question of the Resurrection, a crucial question upon which every serious man must make up his mind. It is not a matter of proof but of faith. Yet this is not an altogether esoteric belief wholly lacking confirmation in the world without, for we may reasonably ask the secular historian to agree that the coming of Jesus Christ marks the watershed in human history.—Nathaniel Micklem.

THE CHURCH ON THE THIRD DAY On a table in the sanctuary there were two lists for people to sign. One was headed "We need . . ."; the other "We have to share. . . ." No one signed the first list. Fifty families signed the second, listing everything from home and food to firewood and labor. Some of those who signed the second list had lost virtually everything they had except the things they listed to share.—Joel D. McDavid.

POETRY

LENT'S JOURNEY

This is a pilgrimage we make
When coins of golden thoughts are spent,
A pilgrimage for other's sake
Upon the thoroughfare of Lent;

A journey in the sandal prints
Where His disciples one time trod
Toward Calvary where dawning glints
Shown on the resurrection God;

A journey through the market place
Where loving deeds each day afford
The joy of seeing in each face
The glory of the risen Lord.

—Harold A. Schulz. Reprinted by permission.

PENITENCE

She poured the spikenard on his feet
And knelt in grief and shame
To voice the burdened guilt with tears
For words she could not name.

Lord, I too kneel with broken speech
On penitential knee.
Heal, as of old, that my words sing,
A spikenard poured for thee.

—Inez Brasier in *The War Cry*. Reprinted by permission.

MAUNDY THURSDAY

On such a night as this, when the young moon
Swings silver-crescented in the Spring sky,
With all her stars in court;
And tall elms stretch their reaching branches up,
Secret with swelling buds,
And water gurgles somewhere in the dark,
Triumphant over its ice chrysalis—
I walk through the old magic of the equinox
With pulses stirring, toward the lighted cross,
The organ hymning, and the sad Last Supper;
And I know—
That Jesus looked up at the same slight moon,
And felt the stir of rising sap
And smelled the sweet leaves waiting—
And did not want to die.

—Frances Gettelman in *P. E. O. Record*. Reprinted by permission.

STEPS

The steps to immortality
Are steep.
Remember dark Gethsemane
And weep.

A cross to bend a weary back,
Despair.
A nail to break a healing hand.
His prayer.

And empty tomb grown warm with sun.
His voice.
The victory over death is won—
Rejoice!

—Raynette Forister. Reprinted by permission.

HIS HANDS

A newborn infant's hands
  Curled at his gentle mother's loving breast;

She held her baby close,
  Then laid him in a manger bed to rest.

Slim fingered, boyish hands
  In calm and unimpassioned discourse raised,
Impressed the Temple priests,
  And all who saw and heard him stood amazed.

A Man's strong, soothing hands
  Restored the blind and stilled the raging sea;
The dead were made to live—
  And then he came to his Gethsemane.

Nail-pierced, his bloodied hands
  Hung limp and cold on Calvary's tragic tree,
For Christ, our Lord, had died
  For all the world, and mortals such as we.

—Ralph Mitchell Crosby. Reprinted by permission.

I, TOO, AROSE

When Jesus rose on Easter morn
  He did not rise alone;
For all the ransomed Heaven-born
  Ordained to flank his throne
Arose in him that Eastertide
  Eternal praise to give—
For, as in Adam all had died,
  In Christ all now should live.

Yes, even I was in that throng
  Whose number none can count;
I, too, shall sing the victors' song
  On Zion's glorious mount.
Our Second Adam, Christ our King,
  Had conquered all my foes;
Now, resurrected, I can sing,
  In him I, too, arose!

—Harrison Palmer in *Christianity Today*. Reprinted by permission.

PRAYERS

TRANSFORMING POWER. In this beautiful season when your hand, O Lord, touches our earth to create a panorama of color across the landscape, touch our lives with the transforming power of your Spirit.

While some of us have to eat our bread alone, unite our lives, through Christ and his Church, with the lives of all mankind. May we discover the meaning of your greatest gift, your Son Jesus Christ.

Let us learn the joy of your miracles. You have given us the miracle of life and brotherhood and service. You have given us the miracle of healing for hurt bodies and minds and reconciliation for fractured relationships. You have given us the miracle of the Savior. Thank you, Lord. Accept our songs of adoration and prayers of praise.—Bruce E. Mills.

SOUL TRAINING. Father of our spirits, we turn now to you for strength and peace. Keep us, please, from offering the same drivel, the same disappointments, the same sins, the small tokens of praise. All too often we ply you with a quantity of prayers, with little serious intent or effort to put our own house in order. Let us know, now, that it takes much practice and diligent labor for the training of a soul and that we will never be spiritually competent unless there be good foundations for our spiritual home. Forgive us, Lord, for words we offer in prayer just now that mean nothing at all, words that have no serious intention, words that place us at the center of life and make us forget how deeply we need you. Search us deeply, O God, in these holy days of Lent and show us the great glory of him who lived so faithfully, for we know that he alone can show us our best selves.—Kenneth Watson.

PRAYER. O Lord our God, we know that we cannot escape that cross on which thy Son was sacrificed for the sin of the world, for it stands right in the middle of everything; it is the unavoidable cross; it confronts us at every turn of the way. But we must confess that we would try to avoid it if we could, for it is so painfully personal; it tells us the truth about ourselves, the awful truth which we hate to admit. O give us the grace to make that confession, no matter how much it hurts, for we know that otherwise we can never learn the truth of our salvation. And bring the people of this suffering world face to face with the truth of that cross: the truth about their sin and the truth about their Savior. Let them find in his suffering the answer to theirs. Constrain them to deny themselves, to take up his cross and to follow him.—Peter Eldersveld.

FOR MAUNDY THURSDAY. O God, our Father, take us back this night to that little upper room where Jesus met to keep the Passover with his disciples on the eve of his death. Open the eyes and ears of our minds that the words that were spoken and the events that transpired there may bring life to our fainting hearts. As the Lord of heaven and earth girds himself with a towel to wash the feet of his followers, may we learn the lesson that humble service is the lot of those who would be great in thy kingdom. As the Master warns that one of us is a traitor, may we, like the apostles of old, look deep within and say, "Is it I?" and then realize with true penitence that each one of us has played the role of Judas more than once in his life. And then, as the voice of Jesus is lifted up in prayer for us that we may be in the world as his hands and feet, may our souls bow down to receive that holy commission.

There is much in common, O God, between that little upper room and this large one. There were ordinary men faced with a task too great for them, and here, too, are ordinary men and women with neither the strength nor the wisdom to deal with life unaided. But there was thy real presence in Christ, ready to overcome their ignorance with thy wisdom and their weakness with thy power; and here, too, is thy real presence still in sacrament and in contrite heart. Let the Spirit of Christ enfold us and make us one in him, that we may go forth from this place with faith and hope and with high resolve to be in our world as the apostles were in theirs. Take the vows and the covenant here made by all of us, whether for the first time or after many times, and cement them with thy faithfulness, that this hour may be for each one here a commencement, the beginning of a new life so closely entwined with thine that we shall never be apart from thee again.—Nathaniel M. Guptill in *Contemporary Pastoral Prayers for the Christian Year*.

SECTION IV. Resources for Communion Services

SERMON SUGGESTIONS

Topic: Why Are We Here?
SCRIPTURE: Eph. 3.
We have come to give God our best, to praise him, enjoy him, and share his fellowship. In return we receive the best. These are our blessings.

I. We receive strength to face anything. We may have entered weak, but we depart strong.

II. We have a new understanding of life. Too much of our thinking has been on the human plane. The issues of the day, the political unrest, the social revolution which is upon us, and our economic dilemmas have us running in circles. But here we add the third dimension. We reach up to understand God, to receive his directives for our lives.

III. We know God's love. Could anything be more dramatically portrayed than God's gift of his Son as we remember it in this service? Here is the answer to cynicism; here is God's cure for loneliness.

IV. We share an unending fellowship. We are filled with all the fullness of God.—Charles A. Platt.

Topic: The Sacramental Dinner Table
TEXT: Luke 14:12–14.
Jesus chose two everyday, physical acts, washing and eating, for the two supreme signs of our faith. Why did Jesus choose eating as the seal of his presence with us and the pledge of his final victory?

I. He chose to signify his life and death with a bite of bread because eating is vitally necessary. So is divine grace, though we don't always recognize the fact.

II. Eating is a necessity repeated each day; when you break bread at home you continue the Sacrament we celebrate at the table of Holy Communion, or conversely, when you commune with Christ and your fellow Christians in church you fulfill the purpose of your daily eating. Every meal is holy.

III. Eating is enjoyable for its own sake. Some daily necessities, like getting up in the morning, are painful. But almost everyone loves to eat. Today many of us carefully ignore Jesus' emphasis on joy in faith—more's the pity.

IV. Eating is a family affair. That's why hospitality is sacred. When you invite someone to your table, you are inviting him to be, for a while, a member of your family.

V. Perhaps these are the principal reasons for Jesus' making a dinner party the central act of Christian worship. What we do at Holy Communion continues and intensifies what we do every time we eat.—Andrew W. Blackwood, Jr.

Topic: The Table that Circles the Globe
I would like to focus upon a table that circles the globe. (a) This table was thrust into orbit, not by a mighty

rocket but by a divine command. The command was remembered by some of the disciples who heard the Son of God give it. The eternally powerful thrust was in the word, "Go ye therefore." The direction was in two things. First, there was baptism. Second, there was the table of remembrance in the words, "Teaching them to observe all things whatsoever I have commanded you." As Jesus had broken the bread and poured out the cup he had said, "This do, in remembrance of me."

(b) Right after the commission was given the observance of the table began to encircle the world as the disciples preached first in Jerusalem, then in Judea, then in Samaria, then in Antioch, then in Galatia, then in Rome. Then it was extended to the uttermost part of the world. Today the table is set wherever God's people are ready to commemorate the sacrifice of Christ upon the cross. This table circles the globe. Two things have happened wherever this table has been set.

I. When this table of remembrance comes, darkness, hate, and death are replaced by light, love, and life. This has happened in every city and hamlet where the gospel of Christ has been received.

II. The future always looks thrilling from the vantage point of the table. (1) Apart from the communion promise, "Till he come," tomorrow is always dark. At the table there is the knowledge that God has loved man into redemption at the price of the Cross. History's culmination is in the return of the Savior to receive all who have become part of his body.

(2) As we sit at the table, the impetus to give the table an even wider circle and to have even more friends moving out of darkness into light and sitting with us ought to be strong. Jesus commanded that his truth be taught everywhere. Until the day of his return, we who are his disciples must not falter or turn back. We must keep the message expanding.—Jackson Wilcox.

Topic: Great Day in the Morning (World Communion Sunday)

What does it signify to celebrate the Lord's Supper around the world today?

I. Does it mean that the morning has come for all? The morning never comes to all the world at once. We come rather in the hope that as the morning light throughout this day finally comes to all the earth, God's morning for his children shall move around the earth, too, until men rise out of the darkness or sleep which has encompassed them.

II. Are we here today because our mission is accomplished? Because the world has become Christian? Far from it. In Asia it is still only 2 to 3 percent who are Christian and in Africa about 12 percent.

III. We are here rather because we know that something of great significance has been accomplished. It is this: the Christian Church has taken root around the world. That's only the beginning, but it is a necessary beginning. We are here today because when some people would say it is the beginning of the end of our hopes, we reply, it is only the end of the beginning.—Gene E. Bartlett.

Topic: The Sacrament of Life

I. Holy Communion is a sacrament of life, a sign of the Holy Community. Christ is present in all humanity. He comes to all humanity in loving redemption.

II. Christ already has offered the elements: his body and his blood, for the sins of the world. "I shall draw all men unto myself, when I am lifted up from the earth" (John 12:32).

III. World Communion is a pre-enactment of that time when "all in heaven and on earth (shall be) brought into a unity in Christ" (Eph. 1:10).—Winburn T. Thomas in *Monday Morning*.

Topic: Communion Meditation

Bread and wine are the stuff of creation itself—the seed, the wheatfield, and the vine. In them is symbolized and actualized the work of man's hand—the planting, the tending, the harvesting, the mill, and the winepress. By them bodies live, and around them men communicate and feed. Finally, bread and wine are the very flesh and blood of our Lord Jesus Christ, who is the Word made flesh.

Yet there is more. The bread at this high and holy table is broken and the cup is given as a sacrifice, revealing that it is God's very nature to suffer for us—even to die for us. The God who gives the seed to the sower and sets the vine upon earth that men may have food and drink for their bodies is also the God who offers his own body as bread and wine that men may have eternal food for their souls.

And yet there is even more. There is a Last Supper that omens Christ's death and sacrifice upon the Cross; but there is also the first Lord's Supper when in an upper room the disciples eat the bread and drink the cup in the name of Jesus. This bread we break, this wine we drink is ever and always to be received in the joy of Easter, for it is the food of the resurrection.—Arnold Kenseth in *The United Church Herald*.

ILLUSTRATIONS

RENEWAL. For several weeks a missionary-teacher and his students had been traveling from village to village in India preaching the Gospel. The hunger and sickness of the people haunted him and he became depressed. A feeling of hopelessness captured his mind and heart. He thought that if the next villagers were to ask, "Where is hope for us?" he would be compelled to reply, "I have no word of hope."

In the next village, just before the service began, one of the Christian men there sent his son to get a coconut. When he brought it, the father threw it on a rock, breaking it into many pieces. He passed the broken pieces to each person, saying, "Take, eat." This became Holy Communion.

The missionary's spirit was renewed. Out of their poverty of earthly things they shared the riches of heaven. Their physical conditions seemed hopeless; but they belonged to Christ, and their hope was in him.—W. Aubrey Alsobrook.

RIGOROUS DEMAND. One of the possible reasons why there is some contemporary disaffection for worship is not that people think it is meaningless, but because they are beginning to get some sense of how rigorous it is to mean the things one says and does in the sacrament.—James T. Burtchaell.

THIS DO IN REMEMBRANCE. A Scottish girl who had little education and who worked long hours was asked by a kirk-session member why she wished to be received and confirmed as a member. She answered that it was because she wanted to be able to take Holy Communion. The church official asked, "Why do you wish to do this?" "Because," she said falteringly, "because it was the last thing he asked of his friends."—David A. MacLennan.

TIES OF LOVE. At the Table of the Lord we have loving fellowship with the spirits of just men and women made perfect. Since we know that our loved ones have trusted in him, and have gone home to abide with him, we know that, when we come close to him, we draw near to them, and they to us, bound together with ties of love that grow stronger with the passing days and years.—Andrew W. Blackwood.

PRAYERS

IN THIS HOLY HOUR. Our praise can only breathe itself in prayer as we gather round these sacred symbols of the love divine that stooped to share our sharpest pang, our bitterest tear, the amazing grace so freely offered to us.

O Christ, in the hush of this holy hour may we have real communion with thee. May we feel thy mystic presence, nearer to us than breathing, closer than hands and feet. May its spell linger upon us as we go forth to walk the common ways of men as thou didst walk in Galilee.

Fulfill in us thy parting promise, "Peace I leave with you; my peace I give to you; not as the world gives do I give to you," as we fulfill thy last request: "Do this in remembrance of me."—Frank Halliday Ferris.

FOR COMFORT AND STRENGTH. We do thank thee, our heavenly Father, that at thy call and thy gracious invitation we are privileged to come together this day. We thank thee for thy faithfulness; we ask only that thou wilt make us faithful to thee. We thank thee for the glory of thy perfect character, and wilt thou strengthen in us the things that make for character. We praise thee for the wonderful friendliness with which thou hast come to us, giving thy love in Jesus Christ. Wilt thou teach us to return our love to thee.

On this sacred day when we meet at the Table of our Lord with thee, wilt thou bring home to the heart of each person a vivid sense of thy presence. Wilt thou bring into the spirit of each one thy wonderful blessings. May this be a time of new comfort and new strength, a time when peace dwells truly in our spirits because we know that in thy keeping all is well.

Wilt thou especially bless those who are sick and all whose hearts are heavy because of concern. Wilt thou be with those whose spirits are deeply disturbed because of troubles, because of complications that seem beyond our easy mastery. Grant that even in the midst of difficulty, we may find the light of spiritual peace and victory.

We ask that thou wilt bless richly this Church. May its life of prayer be constant and deep, may its eagerness for deeds of service and kindliness and helpfulness be a means of contributing to the ongoing of the good life of this community and our world. Wilt thou be with thy people everywhere and grant that the light that is truly the light of men may shine with brightness and effectiveness and strength in our day.—Lowell M. Atkinson.

DRAW NEAR TO US. Gracious Lord, by the love with which thou didst draw near to thy disciples as they went to Emmaus and talked together of thy Passion: draw near and join thyself to us, who reason of holy things, and give us, as we can bear it, the knowledge of thy mysteries.

By the mercy with which at first their eyes were holden that they should not know thee, be merciful to those who are slow of heart to believe.

By the blessing wherewith thou didst manifest thyself to thy disciples in the breaking of bread, let every act of thine whether in the world of nature or of grace, be to us as a sacrament, opening the eyes of our faith, that we may know thee.

By the power whereby thou didst vanish out of their sight, that their faith in the mystery of thy resurrection might be increased, strengthen and confirm this faith in us.—*Prayers for the Christian Year.*

SECTION V. Resources for Funeral Services

SERMON SUGGESTIONS

Topic: No Night There
SCRIPTURE: Rev. 21:22–25.

For Christ the grave had not been a conclusion but a conduit. Already he was standing on the other side, saying, "Come, there is no night here." As the Seer brings this last scene to a close, he accentuates the delineating characteristics of the Eternal Society. They may be listed under four headings.

I. The first of which might be termed no failure. The power of success is very great. Its privileges are vast. But the principle of success is limited. A man must see where he is going. Better, he needs to see the end from the beginning. So, in the Eternal City there shall be light! By it the nations shall walk and unto it the kings of the earth shall bring their glory (21:24). The good men have done, and there has been some, will be seen for what it is—and without shadow.

II. The Eternal City will include no frustration. In frustration lies the source of much evil. The solution is to remove the frustration. This, John declares, the Eternal City does. Its gates are never shut by day and there is no night (21:25).

III. The Eternal City will encompass no falsehood. The shadows of evil are very real. What we truly are at best, shall be known. The imitation, whether it be the false life or the false faith, will not endure. It can stand neither the test of time nor of eternity.

IV. The Eternal City will harbor no famine. Starvation, which has in all times and places been a curse to stare man in the face, is topped by only one thing—food. So John seized upon this basic need in life and used it to forward his purposes. Through the center of the Eternal City would flow "the river of the water of life." It would bear its refreshing streams to the trees along the bank which would be for the feeding of the people. To an affluent society with refrigerators, freezers, and nearby supermarkets these words have only remote and symbolic meaning. But to John's first readers they meant life.
—*The Watchman-Examiner.*

Topic: Victory over Death
SCRIPTURE: I Cor. 15:55–58.

If we are to gain the victory over death we must learn to use it as a minister for good.

I. For when we see death for what it is we will know that we are to be victors over it and not victims of it. Death sets a goal to life, gives it bounds, something definite, measurable, and tangible.

II. Death can be used to make the common things of life add to our living, help us keep all things in their proper perspective.

III. Death is the great deliverer for the child of God. To us who are left behind, left here to go on for a while longer, certainly the going of a loved one is a crushing blow. But to the child of God who is called into the Eternal Presence it is deliverance.—J. M. Gibbs in *The Methodist Christian Advocate.*

Topic: Walking through the Valley

SCRIPTURE: I Cor. 15:51-58 (PHILLIPS).

What are some of the constructive attitudes you can take toward death?

I. Begin to think of death as a beginning, not an end.

II. The second constructive way of facing grief is to trust in your heavenly Father that he will work things out for the best.

III. In order to face sorrow with confidence and assurance, you must in your own mind and heart convince yourself of the resurrection.—Roy T. Sublette.

Topic: The Splendor of Eternal Life

SCRIPTURE: Matt. 28:1-10.

I. Jesus shows us that personality continues after death.

II. Jesus shows us that we have a new and recognizable body.

III. Jesus reveals that contact is maintained between this world and the next.

IV. Jesus reveals that the way we live here sets the tone for the hereafter.—Paul Lambourne Higgins.

Topic: Radical Trust

SCRIPTURE: Ps. 139.

I. This brings us back to the one helpful way by which we might deal with the darkness. It is the response of the psalmist: radical trust. When troubles threaten to overcome us, we are challenged to remember that there is a Creating Power who shares our pain, yet stands above our pain. The night that falls over our lives may appear to be final and complete; yet we are reminded that there is no night that is final to God.

II. Radical trust does not demand that God take away the dark; it recognizes that God is not like us, a prisoner of our darkness. Radical trust does not ignore the fact that in despair we feel completely cut off from the Divine; yet it acknowledges that the Deity loves and sustains us no matter how far we may feel from him.

III. A trust like that of the psalmist frankly admits that in time of grief a person may feel he has lost his faith. It honestly sees the reality of a hell into which persons in this life might descend. It knows that some persons suffer far beyond their due. But in the face of every negative fact, radical trust announces, in the words of another psalmist: "God is my refuge and strength, a very present help in time of trouble."—Andrew J. Good, Jr.

Topic: Shall We Know Each Other in Heaven?

TEXT: I Cor. 2:9-12 (PHILLIPS).

I. We shall know each other in heaven because of its matchless grandeur and glory. The wonders, the beauty, the blessedness of such a place as heaven implies that as believers we shall be consciously aware of its surroundings. And if we are to be able to recognize and appreciate all of its glorious beauty and majesty, we shall, therefore, be able to recognize one another.

II. We shall know one another in heaven because we shall not know less than we know now! We shall certainly know as much in heaven as we know here. What an incentive! What more worthy challenge for the very best Christian education. It requires that we learn all that we can and relate and evaluate our learning in terms of eternity and utility.

III. We shall know one another in heaven because Jesus would have us believe this. (1) In Luke 16:19-31, Jesus tells the story of a rich man, sometimes called Dives, and a beggar named Lazarus. In this story by Jesus, the rich man died and went below into hell. The poor man, Lazarus, also died and went to Abraham's bosom, or what we would call heaven. The rich man, in hell, was able to recognize the place where he was. He was conscious. He knew as much there as he knew upon earth. Moreover, he was able to recognize those in heaven afar off. He spoke of seeing Abraham and Lazarus in heaven or paradise. And he remembered brethren living yet upon the earth. Surely, if we are to recognize people and places to that extent in hell, how much more shall we be able to know one another in heaven.

(2) There is another instance which to me is the most positive and comforting of all. You will find it in I Thess. 4:13-18. It is the description of the return of our Redeemer at the first resurrection. All of the believers who have gone to be with the Lord, Jesus is going to "bring with him." What is Jesus going to bring with him? Undoubtedly their souls—spirits or personalities—the immortal element in man which God breathed into man. Now what is he going to do with those souls? Jesus is going to reunite them with their bodies—to give them a changed, immortal, glorified body like unto his own! "The dead in Christ shall rise first," and soul and body shall be united. Then what? "We which are alive and remain shall be caught up together with them in the clouds, to meet the Lord in the air: and so shall we ever be with the Lord." We are going to meet our loved ones in Christ who have gone on before, and together with them meet the Lord in the air. No wonder the Apostle Paul concludes, in I Thess. 4:13, "Therefore comfort one another with these words."—Wilbert Donald Gough.

ILLUSTRATIONS

LIFE IN CHRIST. Death is something to be met and overcome. And if a Christian is able to rejoice in meeting it, he rejoices because Christ has enabled him to meet it victoriously. It must also be said here that the sharpness of death is most real, not when death comes to oneself, but rather when death comes to those whom one loves. But even in such an experience, victory over death is what the Christian faith offers. The sorrow that accompanies the bereavement of death is an inevitable sorrow, but Christian sorrow is clean; it is not tainted either by bitterness or by despair.

This death of self in the experience of conversion is the key to our victory over death. Paul could say, "For me to live is Christ and to die is gain" (Phil. 1:21)—for when physical death came to him it could not touch him, since he was already dead and the Paul who lived in Christ was already living in him who is death's conqueror. To die was not to die at all but to continue to live in Christ, gaining through physical death the enjoyment of the direct presence.—Daniel T. Niles in *Preaching the Gospel of the Resurrection.*

THE END AND THE BEGINNING. At the funeral service for the poet, Robert Browning, one of those attending was Browning's great friend, the painter, Edmund Burne-Jones. Afterward, Burne-Jones complained that the service was far too somber to express the glory and the optimism for the future which were so characteristic of Browning. The friend said, "I would have given something for a banner or two, and much would I have given if a chorister had come out from the (wings) and rent the air with a trumpet." And that says it precisely—not only for Robert Browning but for every individual for whom Christian hope is strong and real. A funeral is an end; no question about it. But a funeral also is a beginning, for the one who has died in Christ, and for those who remain to carry forward the Christian vision.—John H. Townsend.

SYMPATHY. A little girl came home from a neighbor's house where her little friend had died.

"Why did you go?" questioned her father.

"To comfort her mother," said the child.

"What could you do to comfort her?"
"I climbed into her lap and cried with her."

FROM LIGHT TO LIGHT. The grave is but a covered bridge leading from light to light through a brief darkness.—Henry Wadsworth Longfellow.

IN TIME OF NEED. Our Christian faith has two great words for these times of personal need. One is that of "sympathy," coming to us from two earlier words meaning "with suffering." In other words, we truly sympathize when we enter fully into the sorrows of others and feel their poignant grief and tragic misfortune as our own. The second word is "comfort," likewise coming from two earlier words meaning "together strong." Thus, in sympathy we enter into and in comfort we close ranks around those called upon to walk through affliction and bereavement.—Thomas A. Williams.

INFLUENCE. A young man brought up in a Christian home took no real interest in values related to religion. One day his grandfather died unexpectedly. Soon afterward the young man made his decision for Christ.
"Was it your grandfather's death that did it?" his mother asked.
"No, it was his life," came the answer.—Clara Bernhardt.

CLIMBING IN THE DARK. I was climbing one of the highest of the Alps by means of a tunnel railway. We started our journey by plunging into the tunnel, and we were in thick black darkness for about twenty minutes. Then we stopped. There was a gash in the mountainside, and we alighted from the carriage that we might enjoy this most glorious view. Then we were bundled back again into the carriage, and plunged into the darkness once more, and climbed another stage of the journey. Soon we came to another opening in the mountain, and a still more glorious view was ours. Our third climb was almost vertical, still in the darkness, till at last we reached the top of the mountain where, because of the exceeding brightness of the sun and the brilliance of the snow, we had to veil our faces. When we were climbing we were in the dark; when we were in the dark we were climbing. I think that is an illustration of our own religious experience. We are climbing up toward God. Speaking from my own experience, let me tell you I am always climbing when I am in the dark, and I am always in the dark when I am climbing. We climb in the dark, and God from time to time rewards us with moments of vision and exaltation. Sometimes I rest for a moment that I may behold the glory to which I have attained by the grace of God that has been working in the dark. And I know that the time will come when I shall at last stand where his glory shall blind my eyes.—A. E. Whitman.

LAST BRIEFING. Just before General Eisenhower died I was invited to pay him a visit at Walter Reed Hospital in Washington, D. C. I was told I could stay 30 minutes. When I went in he was wearing his usual big smile. He knew he didn't have long to live.

When the 30 minutes were up he asked me to stay longer and said to me, "Billy, I want you to tell me once again how I can be sure my sins are forgiven and that I'm going to heaven, because nothing else matters now."

I took out my New Testament and read him several Scriptures. I pointed out that we are not going to heaven because of our good works; we're not going because of the money we've given to the church; we are going to heaven totally and completely on the basis of the merits of what Christ did on the cross. Therefore, "Ike" could rest in the comfort that Jesus paid it all. After we had a prayer he said, "Thank you. I'm ready."—Billy Graham in *Decision*.

INTEGRITY OF THE UNIVERSE. The

foundation of my belief in immortality reaches even farther back than the resurrection of Christ. It rests on the very integrity of the universe. This belief in life beyond the grave has persisted through all races, and this conviction is strongest in our healthiest moments and rises out of our noblest emotion, that of love. The Creator has endowed us with power to love, to believe, to hope. These powers are as deep in our nature as the hungers of the body for food and drink and air. Surely the Creator who keeps faith with the appetites of our bodies will not play false with the hungers of our souls.—Ralph W. Sockman.

COMMITTAL. The committal of our souls is not an act reserved for the last hours of our final day. We commit our souls to something every day in every deed. And the quality of that to which we commit ourselves in the end is bound closely to resemble the quality of that to which or to whom we have most consistently committed ourselves on our journeying toward the end. If we seek God's guidance in our deserts of temptation; if we channel God's powers in our Jerusalems of heavy responsibility; if we will to will God's will in our agonizing gardens of uncertainty and confusion and suffering, then out of that pattern of positives will flow our final affirmation.—Melvin E. Wheatley, Jr.

A MOTHER'S MESSAGE. In 1855 Louis Napoleon, then a refugee in the United States, received a letter from his mother, who was in Switzerland. He carried this letter next to his heart throughout the rest of his life, in the days of the Third Empire and amid the reverses of Sedan down to the hour of his death in England. His mother wrote that she was facing an operation which she had no hope of surviving, and that, therefore, she would never see him again in this life. She finished her message to her son with these imperishable words: "Have faith that we shall meet again. It is too necessary not to be true."—Harold Lindsell.

LAST WILL AND TESTAMENT. A minister of the Gospel who died some time ago concluded his last will and testament with this notation to his family: "I desire to bequeath to my children and their families my testimony to the truth of the Gospel of Christ and the principles of the restoration of New Testament Christianity. This heritage of the Christian faith received from my father, and my father's father, and going back through history to the inspired apostles, is infinitely more valuable than any houses or lands, stocks or bonds. I hereby, then, bequeath and devise it to them as the most precious possession I have."—Ross H. Dampier.

LAST OPPORTUNITY. When Rabbi Israel Salanter, the great sage and moralist of nineteenth-century Russia, was critically ill, he sent for one of his friends who was a confirmed atheist and with whom he had often discussed theology. Greatly flattered at being called to the rabbi's deathbed, the atheist asked wonderingly why he, of all the rabbi's many pious colleagues and friends, had been singled out for this honor. "It is quite simple," the sage declared, smiling. "My other friends I confidently expect to see again in the next world. About you I am not so sure, and I did not want to miss this last opportunity of convincing you that you are wrong!"—*The Jewish Digest.*

POETRY

THE HOMING INSTINCT

A wild duck in its flight may briefly pause
At times in barynards where it picks at straws.
But soon it feels deep stirrings, instincts strong
Within its feathered breast that make it long

For some far distant home, as though
  it must
Rise from its easy sustenance and trust
To its heart knowledge to resume the
  role
Of seeker for some brighter, higher
  goal.
So is there in men, too, a whispering,
An instinct in the human soul to wing
Home to eternity, and thus to ease
The hunger only Heaven can appease.

—Dorothy P. Albaugh. Reprinted by permission.

FACING DEATH

Over the Red Sea going,
Tomorrow, or probably Monday;
Over the Red Sea going—
God takes care of his own.

Over the Red Sea blowing,
The way may open on Sunday;
Over the Red Sea blowing—
God makes way for his own.

Be it today or tomorrow
Moses raises his rod,
Stand we ready on this side,
Stands on the other side—God.

Safe is the watery pathway,
No one treads it alone;
Over the Red Sea going—
God takes care of his own.

—Earl L. Douglass in *Christianity Today*. Reprinted by permission.

WHILE DEATH DIVIDES

I walk beside a wall,
So high, so thick, so impregnable
That any effort of mine to destroy it
Would be utterly useless.
It would only tear my futile hands
And break my helpless body.
But I can walk beside it,
So quietly, so shod with calmness and
  with faith,
That perhaps I may hear your voice
  sometimes
Coming over the wall to me—
And then be able to go on
Until there is no wall.

—Eleanor Gerrard in *Christian Advocate*. Reprinted by permission.

TURN AGAIN TO LIFE

If I should die and leave you here
  awhile,
Be not like others, sore undone, who
  keep
Long vigil by the silent dust and weep.
For my sake turn again to life and
  smile,
Nerving thy heart and trembling hand
  to do
That which will comfort other souls
  than mine.
Complete these dear unfinished tasks
  of mine
And I, perchance, may therein comfort
  too.

—Mary Lee Hall. Reprinted by permission.

SECTION VI. Resources for Small Groups

CHALLENGE TO PRAYER GROUPS

Prayer groups are growing throughout the world, both within and outside of the institutional churches. This is good, as Jesus said, "For whenever two or three people come together in my name, I am there, right among them!" (Matt. 8:20).

I believe in small groups. They can be more intimate and challenging as they meet in Christian fellowship to read the Bible, to share each other's thoughts, and to pray together. They do become very close in their fellowship. Here can be a grave danger because they can become a closed fellowship. Jesus will not be fenced in. He had his twelve, and he sent them out two by two.

Prayer groups should be growing groups and will do so only as they meet the challenge of Christ to go into all the world and bring others into the fellowship of Christ and his church. The amoeba would have been useless in God's plan if it had not grown and divided itself.

It should not be necessary to break up a small, intimate fellowship to grow, but each one within must be reaching out to bring others into new fellowship groups. This could bring on revival in our time.

It came to me that if I could start a prayer group of three and if each one of us then would agree to bring three others together, a chain reaction could be started. If this were continued by each individual who comes into the fellowship, bringing three other individuals each month, how many would be in fellowship with Jesus in twelve months? Figure it out: $1 + 3$ equals 4, 4×3 equals 12, 12×3 equals 36, and so on for 12 times would equal 2,125,764.

There are many prayer groups in the world today. If each would start such a chain reaction, with God's blessing, a revival could usher in the Kingdom of heaven on this earth in this generation. Jesus said, "Repent, the kingdom of heaven is at hand. . . . All power is given unto me in heaven and earth. Go ye therefore, and lo, I am with you always" (Matt. 28:18–20).—John G. Ramsay.

FOUR BASIC TYPES OF GROUPS

(1) The task-centered group. Some groups are structured with a job to accomplish, i.e., a committee working on a program or problem. These are leader-directed groups where intimacy and relationships are secondary to accomplishing the job. Members of the group are means to an important end; being related as persons is secondary. Every church must man the institution with its "task groups." Unfortunately, we tend to consume our lay leadership with this kind of group. There is little or no time left for Christ's mission.

(2) The person-centered or growth

group. Persons are of first importance. The purpose is to relate to persons on a feeling basis and not an idea level. It is a persons and not a program group, a sharing and not a telling group, a listening and not a leading group. It is an unstructured, nondirective, high investment, cohesive, intimate fellowship, based on the ability of its members to be psychologically close and to relate on a high level of trust. It is a laboratory of love where persons experience the giving and receiving of acceptance, forgiveness, understanding, and concern. It is a listening group where persons grow to listen with openness and positive interest; with sacrificial involvement; with expectancy so great as to evoke the fullest capacities from each other; with patience grounded in faith in what the person may become; and without judgment, but with deep care and concern.

(3) The biblical or theological study group. Our work indicates that the experiences of listening and being listened to in the (person-centered) groups are essential psychological and spiritual preparation for understanding the Christian faith. In a very real sense, one first discovers the meaning of Christ's love in these groups. Then one is introduced to the meaning of one's experience in biblical and theological study groups. After one has had eighteen months to two years in a listening group, he may then be able and ready to participate in some group study in depth.

(4) The "On Mission" for Christ group. Essential to understanding the "new life in Christ" is the need to experience a call of commitment to him. The Church of the Saviour in Washington, D. C., has been a pioneer in this type of research and study group. They make it most clear that all group life should be preparation for the task of being a servant minister "on mission" for Christ. Their work in this field with twelve mission groups is an exciting story.—Robert A. Edgar in *Pastoral Psychology*.

PROBLEMS OF STARTING A NEW GROUP

(1) *Setting purpose and direction.* Why is the group being established? What do you expect to accomplish through it? This warrants very close attention. The success of the group is measured by how well it accomplishes its purposes. But if the purposes aren't known or clear, how can it ever determine whether it is successful? And the purposes are important in setting up activities, for whatever the group chooses to do must be chosen because it will permit progress toward these goals.

Perhaps, in our hurry, we may list quickly the purpose of an adult study group as to "discuss important topics regarding the Christian life" or, more simply, "to have good meetings." Yet, isn't the important purpose of such a group much deeper than that: to deepen the member's concept of the Christian faith and life? To "discuss a topic" may give people something to talk about, and it does fill the time, but what contribution is the talk making to the fundamental purpose of the group? People who enjoy talking may come away, as they often do, feeling that it was a good meeting because they got an opportunity to say what they wanted to. They may have used the group for their own satisfaction of having an audience rather than as a place to test their own ideas and experiences in order to deepen their understanding.

(2) *Building member's security in the group.* The first concern of a member in a new group is how he is going to be treated by the leader and other members of the group. Do they really care about him? Do they accept him? Or is he ignored and made to feel like a second-rate member or an outsider? Perhaps you are surprised at these questions, especially when they are raised about a church group. But watch yourself! Perhaps all the right words are said to the new person, but does anyone invite him to take part in the dis-

cussion, and then actually listen to him? Instead, is his contribution politely received, but the next comment someone makes demonstrate clearly that what he said was ignored? The way members respond (or fail to respond) to each other is likely to have much effect on how accepted the new member feels as well as on how much that the leader can do. Our actions truly speak louder than words.

(3) *Defining member responsibility.* What is to be expected of the members as they attend the group? What responsibilities will they have? What opportunities will they have? Members need to know what is expected of them so they can begin to accept responsibilities. In an adult church group it may be very easy for a person to attend many meetings without becoming active in his participation. Indeed, he may feel he is getting value from his attendance. But if the deeper purposes are to be achieved, perhaps more must be asked of him. He has the same responsibility as others for sharing his own understandings with the group. And, also, his active participation in the group is necessary so that he, himself, will get more value from it. The group has a right to expect active participation and involvement from the members so that the purposes of the group can be achieved.—David H. Jenkins in *Baptist Leader.*

THE ROLE OF THE GROUP LEADER

(1) He seeks the maximum distribution of leadership among the group members.
(2) He sees that all members of the group have an opportunity to participate in group decisions.
(3) He encourages freedom of communication.
(4) He seeks to increase opportunities for participation.
(5) He attempts to create a non-threatening group climate in which feelings and ideas are accepted.
(6) He conveys feelings of warmth and empathy, thus encouraging others to do likewise.
(7) He sets the tone by paying attention to the contributions of others, perhaps of reflecting what they are saying with, "Let's see if I understand what you mean."
(8) He helps build group-centered (as contrasted with self-centered) contributions by his linking function in which he points to the relationships among various individuals' contributions to the discussion.—Howard J. Clinebell, Jr. in *Mental Health through Christian Community.*

WHY GROUPS FAIL

Home Bible study groups are subject to disease just the same as any other kind of free association of people. There are many reasons why a group may fail. Let me point out a few of the more common ones.

(1) Probably the thing that kills more groups than anything else is the dominance of one person. This person may be completely sincere and fully dedicated. Yet, he can have personality problems that give him difficulties in the personal relationships that develop in the small face-to-face group. He may not have the patience to wait for people, to think through and discuss the issues until they arrive at a mutual understanding. He may be hungry for attention and, therefore, grab the spotlight. He may just like to hear his own voice. Whatever the reason, it will destroy a group any time one person becomes the dominant authority image. For this reason, it is generally a good idea to avoid letting one prominent person become "the leader" of a group.

(2) If a group makes the mistake of allowing nonspiritual side issues to be discussed or gossiped during the session, this mistake will undermine the group and destroy it. The home Bible study

group, to be successful, has to be just that—a Bible study group. This is the primary reason or motivation for people's assembling. This means that the people in the group have to attune themselves to the Word and the spiritual values that are in the Word.

(3) Physical problems in the surroundings or environment in the home can hinder a group. Sometimes people who have small children will offer to host the home Bible study group. Small children can become disruptive and take the morale out of the group. It goes without saying that a home where the Bible study is held should be aired and clean. It should have enough room so as many as a dozen people, at least, can be seated comfortably.

(4) Groups sometime fail because there is no vital outreach. The very premise of the home Bible study group is that the host and members of the group will reach out to nonmembers, encouraging their friends and neighbors to share in the group. If two couples try to start a group and neither of them is involved with other people in the neighborhood, the group has a limitation. If they do not have much communication with other people in the neighborhood, they will need to get out and knock on doors, inviting people. Sometimes the church needs to circularize the neighborhood if the church is actually sponsoring the group. It can almost be said that no group will be successful unless there is definite and planned outreach to the neighborhood. In effect, this really means the group must maintain its purpose of studying the Bible and reaching other people for Christ.

(5) A final reason for group failure is somewhat related to the first one. One of the mostly deadly diseases that can strike a group is when there is no self-determination. This simply means that the group has to set its goals, even if it does no more than simply agree on preset goals. Usually, however, a group will have specific goals which it will set up for itself. It should select the material it is going to study. It should determine the meeting place and the time and other elements that affect it as a group. It must sense its own self-determination if it is going to be successful. The above things, of course, are symptomatic frequently of a lack of basic Christian attitude and outlook. Wherever this kind of thing gets into the life of the church, it will limit it and certainly hinder it.—Medford Jones in *The Lookout.*

DISCUSSION SUGGESTIONS

Topic: The Apostles' Creed
I. The fatherhood of God. Article I: "I believe in God the Father Almighty, maker of heaven and earth."
II. The Son of God. Article II: "And in Jesus, his only begotten Son, our Lord."
III. The Son of Man. Article III: "Who was conceived by the Holy Spirit, born of the Virgin Mary."
IV. The suffering Savior. Article IV: "Suffered under Pontius Pilate, was crucified, dead, and buried; he descended into hell."
V. The conquering Christ. Article V: "The third day he arose again from the dead."
VI. The exalted Lord. Article VI: "He ascended into heaven, and sitteth at the right hand of God the Father."
VII. The heavenly Judge. Article VII: "From thence he shall come to judge the quick and the dead."
VIII. The Holy Spirit. Article VIII: "I believe in the Holy Spirit."
IX. The Christian Church. Article IX: "I believe in the holy catholic Church, the communion of saints."
X. Faith and forgiveness. Article X: "The forgiveness of sins."
XI. The future of our faith. Articles XI and XII: "The resurrection of the body, and the life everlasting."

Topic: Questions Jesus Asked
I. "Are grapes gathered from thorns,

or figs from thistles?" (Matt. 7:16, RSV).
II. "O thou of little faith, wherefore didst thou doubt?" (Matt. 14:31).
III. "He [Jesus] saith unto them, But whom say ye that I am?" (Matt. 16:15).
IV. "How many loaves have ye?" (Mark 6:38).
V. "Whom say the people that I am?" (Luke 9:18).
VI. "What do ye more than others?" (Matt. 5:47).

Topic: Christ Calls All Christians, without Exception, to Be His Witnesses Wherever They Go
I. Preparing to witness. (1) A right spirit within (Ps. 51:10). (2) Public declaration (Mark 1:9). (3) Facing temptation (Mark 1:12–13). (4) Thinking things out (Gal. 1:15–17).
II. Jesus begins to witness. (1) Beginning at home (Luke 4:16). (2) Ministering to mental illness (Mark 1:23). (3) Relieving physical distress (Mark 1:30–31). (4) Encountering misunderstanding (Mark 2:16). (5) Defying convention (Mark 3:5).
III. The apostles begin to witness. (1) Fishermen preferred (Mark 1:17). (2) Good fishing (John 1:40–41). (3) The inner circle of twelve (Mark 3:14). (4) The first mission sent out (Matt. 10:16). (5) The missionaries report (Mark 6:30). (6) Jesus prays for unity (John 17:21).
IV. Some early converts. (1) Nicodemus: a scholarly inquirer (John 3:2–3). (2) A prostitute (Luke 7:47). (3) One leper out of ten (Luke 17:15). (4) A rich man turns back sorrowful (Luke 18:23). (5) Zacchaeus enters joyfully (Luke 19:6). (6) A turncoat apostle: Peter (Luke 22:61–62). (7) A dying criminal (Luke 23:42).
V. The word goes far abroad. (1) From Jerusalem everywhere (Acts 2:5). (2) Southward to Ethiopia (Acts 8:26–27). (3) Northward to Antioch (Acts 11:26). (4) From Antioch everywhere (Acts 13:2). (5) Westward to Greece (Acts 16:9). (6) To Rome in chains (Acts 25:12). (7) The unfettered Word (II Tim. 2:9).
VI. The Word confronts the nation. (1) Crisis to come (Luke 12:56). (2) Herod alarmed (Mark 6:16). (3) Herod defied (Luke 13:32–33). (4) The law revised (Matt. 5:43–44). (5) Values inverted (Luke 6:20–21, 24:25).

Topic: Brotherhood in Christ
I. What churches can do. (1) Make every Sunday and every day a time of examination into their Christian responsibility in race relations and to confess freely their feelings.
(2) Encourage the organization of a committee on social action or Christian social relations.
(a) To make sure that practices of your church in attendance at service, membership, and use of facilities are inclusive of all Christians, regardless of race.
(b) To get the facts about civil rights and to disseminate and discuss them.
(c) To conduct educational projects for effective citizenship such as the achievement of full political rights for all citizens, the mechanics of voting, the problems of local, state, and national government, and international relations and world order.
(4) To discover the community organizations working for interracial good will and civil rights, and to participate in their programs.
(e) To use the resources of the Church to build public opinion for legislation to protect civil rights for all people.
(f) To encourage other groups in the Church, especially those using the home and foreign missions study courses, to carry out action projects for improving race relations.
II. What the individual can do. (1) As a church member find out: (a) What other racial groups live in your community.
(b) What their churches and civic

organizations are doing to build a better community.

(c) What your denomination is doing about race relations.

(d) What your local church is doing about race relations.

(e) What other community agencies are doing to improve race relations and how you can cooperate.

(2) Seek continuously to understand the meaning of being a Christian in race relations when voting, when seeking an office, and when discharging the duties of political office.

(3) Seek to be Christian in business by treating men, regardless of race, as the sons of God in selling, in buying, in employing, in promoting, and in compensating.

(4) Act as a neighbor in the Christian sense: (a) By learning the basic facts about race.

(b) In speech by avoiding generalizations, correct derogatory or incorrect statements based on race.

(c) In urging that every little child have equal opportunity to those things coveted for your own child, including education, recreation, and health.

(d) In refusing to join with others to restrict neighborhoods against any because of race.

Topic: Various Aspects of the Cross of Christ

I. Inner sufferings of Christ.

(1) The loneliness of Christ (John 16:25–31).

(2) Ignorance of men (Luke 23:34).

(3) Mental sufferings of the Master (Matt. 26:36–46).

(4) The injustice of it all (Matt. 26:60–66).

(5) Indifference of men (Luke 23:33–49).

(6) Dark night of the soul (Matt. 15:34).

(7) The broken heart (John 19:18–27).

II. Meaning of Christ's sacrifice.

(1) Life surrendered (John 15:1–11).

(2) Life identified (John 17:1–26).

(3) Life shared (John 1:1–11).

(4) Life dedicated (Mark 10:35–45).

(5) Fellowship of suffering (Matt. 11:25–30).

(6) The magnetism of sacrifice (John 12:37–46).

(7) The cost of love (Luke 2:33–45).

III. The Cross as a living stone.

(1) The Cross as a cornerstone (Acts 4:12).

(2) The Cross as a touchstone (Luke 2:14).

(3) The Cross as a keystone (Eph. 4:16).

(4) The Cross as a steppingstone (John 12:32).

(5) The Cross as a whetstone (Heb. 4:12–14).

(6) The Cross as a hearthstone (I John 4:19).

(7) The Cross as a stumblingstone (I Cor. 1:13).—Titus Lehmenn in *The Clergy Journal.*

Topic: Hope for Life Situations

I. Hope for those who miss the mark.

II. Hope for those who worry.

III. Hope for those who are lonely.

IV. Hope for those who suffer.

V. Hope for those who die.

Topic: The Way of His Passion

I. Samaria: Place of priority (Luke 9:51–62).

II. Perea: Place of prediction (Mark 10:32–34).

III. Bethany: Place of preparation (John 12:1–8).

IV. Gethsemane: Place of prayer (Luke 22:39–46).

V. Gabbatha: Place of public trial (John 9:12–16).

VI. Golgotha: Place of passion (Mark 15:22–39.)—Gerald C. Studer.

SECTION VII. Resources for Preaching on the Church and Youth

REACHING THE NOW GENERATION. Let us examine the kinds of ministries our churches must have if this now generation is to be reached.

First, the church's ministry must be personal rather than institutional. A church is becoming institutionalized when it is more concerned with getting than with giving. A church also becomes institutionalized when it is more concerned with groups than with individuals. Christ looked on his followers as individuals and he reached them individually. Furthermore, it is important for a church to be more concerned with ministry than with activity.

Second, the ministry of the church must be real and not artificial. Young people want things to be concrete. Youth are flocking to various sects seeking reality. Let us show them that reality is found in Christ.

Third, a ministry geared to reach the now generation must be involved and not isolated. We seem to have a false idea of separation. Young people do not want to be spectators; they want to be participants.

Fourth, our ministry must be imaginative, not imitative. Let it be vivid! The Holy Spirit is infinitely original. Every snowflake is different. Every flower is different. Yet, every church service is the same. We need to ask God for some fresh and new ways of saying the same old thing. The Gospel has not changed, but the ways of presenting it have changed. Our ministry must be imaginative.

Finally, our ministry must be courageous and not timid. We must trust young people with significant ministries. We must give them big challenges. Young people do not want a comfortable faith.—Warren Wiersbe.

NARROWING THE GENERATION GAP. What can be done to narrow the generation gap?
1. Accept the people around you as part of the world you live in.
2. Understand that there are other viewpoints beside your own.
3. Communicate your interest in others by how you live.
4. Listen to other people, even the other generation.
5. Be ready to change yourself as much as you expect others to change.
—Cliff Smith.

RESPONSIBILITY TO YOUTH. (1) The Church is responsible to show its young people empathy instead of simply giving them sympathy.

(2) The Church is responsible to provide for its young people leadership and not merely dictatorship.

(3) In providing this leadership, the Church also is responsible to offer preaching that is honest and right rather than that which is entertaining and popular.

(4) The Church is responsible to have patience and not to expect its young people to grow up overnight.

(5) The Church of God owes its

young people appreciation and commendation.—Charles W. Conn.

I BELIEVE IN TEEN-AGERS. I believe in teen-agers because they make mistakes, just as their fathers did.

I believe in teen-agers because they are our future. They start out clean, eagerly. They want to win. They do not want to lose.

I believe in teen-agers because they are growing. They outgrow their clothes, but they also outgrow their childish ideas, habits, and childishness. They are dynamic.

I believe in teen-agers because they are a good investment. I cannot give them much money, but I can give them a lot of love, understanding, and concern.

A teen-ager wakes up when he meets Jesus Christ. Up to that time, his life has been a protected, cloistered one in which the necessities have been provided through no effort of his own. His clothing, food, housing, all have been given to him by conscientious providers known as parents. Now that he has come into the age of decision and maturity of mentality, his horizons can be unlimited.—J. Lester Harnish.

WHAT TURNS YOUTH OFF. They come to the altar in all sincerity and high purpose. They meet God in a very personal and very real way. Then they turn from the altar and assume that now they must give feet to their prayers, they must affirm their affirmations by Christian action out where they live, they must let conviction and confession of faith send them into the cause of Christian concerns. And they find that some adults—perhaps many adults —in their congregation not only don't see this connection, but dismiss youth's enthusiasm for linking up conviction and cause as but youthful idealism which isn't very reality-oriented.—Hoover Rupert in *Michigan Christian Advocate.*

THE VAST MAJORITY. They help fight brush fires, man the rescue lines in times of disaster, serve their country when called upon, build better homes and schools for the underprivileged, plant crops, raise farm animals, lead church groups, maintain camps, pioneer for progress, study and train themselves for the work of the world in many fields. Who are they? They are the countless young people who are not in the news because they aren't committing crimes or creating violence. They are the fine, decent kids, the vast majority of today's youth.—Esther York Burkholder.

BELIEVING IN CHANGE. Wherever we meet a person young or old, who is holding on to what is noble and pure and of good report, we must never, never by any word whatsoever, tend to undermine that faith; never hurt, or cut by cruel cynicism or bitter humor; never, never damp any enthusiasm for what is noble and great by that dreadful phrase: "When I was your age I believed in that too." All that is best in this curious old world of ours has been achieved by agitators and idealists, in the face, nearly always, of experts, but in the end it will always be the idealists that will win. As one thinks of the crucified Lord on the Cross, one knows it. Those who believe that human nature and human conditions can be changed are the only people who are ever likely to change them. Whenever our faith in idealism is gone, we have ceased to believe in goodness; whatever creed we profess, we have ceased to believe in the Christian God. —Dick Sheppard.

SOLUTION FOR DELINQUENCY. When adults realize that every human being, especially the adolescent, hungers for understanding, acceptance, and recognition, many of the problems of delinquency will be on their way to solution.—William Arthur Ward.

CONTINUOUS RENEWAL. If we indoctrinate the young person in an elaborate set of fixed beliefs, we are ensur-

RESOURCES FOR PREACHING ON THE CHURCH AND YOUTH 51

ing his early obsolescence. The alternative is to develop skills, attitudes, habits of mind, and the kinds of knowledge and understanding that will be the instruments of continuous change and growth on the part of the young person. Then we shall have fashioned a system that provides for its own continuous renewal.

All too often we are giving young people cut flowers when we should be teaching them to grow their own plants. We are stuffing their heads with the products of earlier innovation rather than teaching them how to innovate. We think of the mind as a storehouse to be filled rather than as an instrument to be used.—John W. Gardner in *Self-Renewal.*

THEY REACH FOR SKY

They reach for sky, these sudden-growing children,
Their reach grown greater than their roots,
Their need grown greater than their reach.
They cry for room,
This dream-led girl whom time will teach,
This tall half-boy, half-man who heads for outer space
In rocket race.
High question lights their eyes.
May they be taught
To drink from bubbling springs of thought,
And may we stretch our tattered tent of faith to share
With those who breathe sky-newness
And its star-tuned air.

—Maude Rubin in *The Christian.*

I'M IMPORTANT, TOO. The bishop had come to the church for a sermon of dedication. At the close he and the pastor had withdrawn into the study. Several members of the church joined them in conversation.

A boy in the pastor's church membership class approached the door, wanting to speak to the minister. A well-meaning adult said, "You can't go in there. You know the bishop is here, and he is an important man."

The boy replied, "The minister says I am important in the church, too."—W. Ralph Ward.

THE BIG QUESTIONS. Harvey Cox told of one of his students who said, "I dropped out of church when I was thirteen, but in college I found that the only place I could explore the questions that really interest me was in the religion department. I'm in seminary not because I buy the answers religion has given to the big questions, but because here the big questions are at least still asked."

EXPECTATIONS. Modern advertising has created an expectation gap. Young people have been taught to expect instant solution. Young people are expecting the world to be transformed and changed instantly. They do not realize how slowly history moves and how long it takes to change a social condition.—Billy Graham.

BILL OF RIGHTS FOR YOUTH

I. Every teen-ager has the right to the love and security provided by a happy home life. This does not mean the right to "everything money can buy" but, rather, the right to "all the things money cannot buy."

II. Every teen-ager has the right to his elder's faith and trust. Not blind, unquestionable loyalty which says, "My Johnny can do no wrong," but a firm belief in him despite his faltering faith which he may fall back on to help him start building anew, after all else is lost.

III. Every teen-ager has the right to some sort of "guiding hand"—not overbearing and dictatorial, not weak and purposeless—but a strong, firm power which will offer wise and certain counsel guidance; some person whose strength will be based on truth and who will put his wisdom at the teen-ager's command and will understand if the latter occasionally turns instead to the bitter teacher called "experience."

IV. Every teen-ager has the right to an unchangeable code of morals, ethics, and beliefs by which to live his life. He has the right to draw for himself a clearly distinct line between right and wrong and to learn the consequences he must pay for crossing over the line and the sacrifices he must make to stay on the "right" side, and every teen-ager has the right to believe in his God.

V. Every teen-ager has the right to companionship with others his age, to make and build friendships, to laughter, pleasure, and fun, as well as to hard work and responsibility.

VI. Every teen-ager has the right to every possible opportunity that will aid in the fulfillment of all his potential abilities of body, mind, and spirit.

VII. Every teen-ager has the right to know the truth of every phase of life. Yes, to know the truth, and that truth shall make him free.—Linnea Pearson.

PRAYER FOR YOUTH

Be with them as they try to grope their way
Through all the baffling mazes of today.
Assure them they will find, if they but seek.
Give strength, when indecision makes them weak.
Encourage them, whenever faith ebbs low.
Set in their minds the dauntless will to grow.
Be patient with their fumbling toward a goal.
Gird their impulsiveness with self-control.
Let love of God, with its consuming fire,
Burn from their hearts the dross of base desire.
Fill them with discontent, that they may see

There is no lasting joy apart from Thee.
Grant them no peace, until their lives fulfill
Their full design, according to Thy will.

—Gail Brook Burket. Reprinted by permission.

BASIC AIMS OF THE CHURCH. The basic aims for a church youth ministry:
(1) To identify youth with Christ and the Church.
(2) To give youth a working knowledge of the Bible.
(3) To help youth discover themselves.
(4) To give youth a sense of responsibility to their own generation.
(5) To help youth develop a satisfying devotional life.
(6) To help youth face and solve their problems.
(7) To help youth build a set of standards based on Bible convictions.
(8) To give youth an appreciation for the Christian home.
(9) To help youth appreciate the older generation.
(10) To help youth appreciate their country and their heritage as Christian citizens.—Warren Wiersbe.

THE CHURCH AND THE NOW GENERATION. There are several things the Church must do if Christianity is going to come alive in the minds and hearts of the young.
(1) The Church must rediscover Jesus Christ.
(2) The Church must be honest.
(3) The Church must learn both to listen with compassion and understanding and to speak with loving authority. —Claude A. McMillion.

CHOICE OF FRIENDS. Phillips Brooks said if he could choose the associates for a young man, he would select some who were his inferior so that he might learn patience and charity; he would choose more that were the young man's equals so that he would learn the fullness of friendship; and he would choose

RESOURCES FOR PREACHING ON THE CHURCH AND YOUTH

most from among the young man's superiors in order that he might learn humility and growth.

DENUNCIATION. The denunciation of the young is a necessary part of the hygiene of elderly people and greatly assists the circulation of their blood.—Logan Pearsall Smith.

IDEALISM AT HOME. Idealism is not dead among today's teen-agers. It is only looking for a home.—Grace Fletcher in *What's Right with Our Young People.*

HAPPY CHILDREN. Parents were invented to make children happy by giving them something to ignore.—Ogden Nash.

IT'S HARD TO GROW UP. If your boy is puzzling you, he's puzzling himself just as much.

Chances are he's looking for a way his life can have meaning and purpose. And unfortunately, just when he needs all the help and strength and courage and security he can get, he may not yet have found the answer in his faith. Often he would like to. He is searching for something he can "believe on his own."

Your faith can help if it's strong enough. You may find the answers where you worship. Perhaps he'll worship with you. Perhaps he'll find his answer, too.—*Religion in American Life.*

A YOUTH'S RESOLUTIONS

Like Enoch, walk in daily fellowship with my heavenly Father;
Like Job, be patient under all circumstances;
Like Abraham, trust implicitly in God;
Like Joseph, turn my back to all seductive advances;
Like Moses, choose rather to suffer than to enjoy the pleasures of sin for a season;
Like Aaron and Hur, uphold the hands of my pastor and the leaders of my church with my prayers and support;
Like Caleb and Joshua, refuse to be discouraged because of opposition;
Like Gideon, advance even though my friends be few;
Like David, lift up mine eyes unto the hills from whence cometh my help;
Like Daniel, commune with God at all times;
Like Ezra, prepare my heart to seek God;
Like Andrew, strive to lead my brother to Christ;
Like Stephen, manifest a forgiving spirit toward all who seek my hurt;
Like Paul, forget those things which are behind, and press forward.

—Marvin E. Hall.

A YOUTH'S PRAYER

Grant me time
To contemplate
And hesitate—
To tarry long
And sing life's song.

Grant me grace
To be a friend
And not offend—
To be discreet
With all I meet.

Grant me work
To toil the earth
And be of worth—
Enrich the lands
With these my hands.

Grant me tact
To hold my tongue
When I am stung—
To suffer long
When I am wrong.

Grant me power
To trust in thee
And thus be free—

And never cease
To work for peace.

—George L. Earnshaw. Reprinted by permission.

THE LONG AND THE SHORT OF IT. The first Congress on Evangelism in Minneapolis brought some 4,600 delegates to discuss evangelism in today's world. At one point, Keith Miller, the businessman-turned-author, was about to speak, when the ushers hustled out a young man, presumably a student, whose shoulder-length, flowing hair conformed to the style of many of today's young men. Miller, a devout, concerned Christian layman, angrily commented, "They just threw out the man who looks more like Jesus Christ than any man in this auditorium!" The young man with the long hair was promptly readmitted and Billy Graham spent some time with him and apologized for the ushers. The news release made quite a point of the fact that the great Congress on Evangelism wasn't about to separate the clean-shaven from the long-haired. Nor am I! Still, I have my own hang-up: I wish that those who look like Jesus Christ would act more like Jesus Christ! But that is a problem I have with people who wear short hair, too!—Donald B. Strobe.

SIX STAGES OF MAN

First stage: "Daddy, guess I know how to do everything, don't I?" asked the lad of 10.

Second stage: "Well, anyway, I know more than Dad ever knew," said the boy of 20.

Third stage: "I think I know all that's necessary to know," said the young man of 30.

Fourth stage: "What I don't know isn't worth knowing," said the self-important man of 40.

Fifth stage: "There are a few matters, I am sorry to say, that I am really not quite sure about," said the man of 50.

Sixth stage: "I have learned a bit, but not much, since I was born. Knowledge is so vast that one can hardly become wise in a short lifetime," said the man of 60.

IN BEHALF OF PARENTS. These are the people who—within five or six decades—have increased life expectancy by approximately 50 percent, who have eradicated plagues and who—while cutting the working day by a third—have more than doubled per capita output.

These are the people who, building thousands of high schools and colleges, at a cost of billions, have made higher education—once a privilege of the fortunate few—now available to many millions.

These are the people who, without bloodshed, effected in the 1930's a social revolution which in its humane consequences makes the famous French Revolution seem a mere outburst of savagery and the Russian Revolution a political retrogression.

These are the people who established the United Nations, who defeated Hitler, contained Stalin, and made Khrushchev back down. These are the people who, after spending billions in prosecuting a war, gave billions more, so that the world would not plunge into a depression.

These are the people who soared outward into interplanetary space and downward into the atom, releasing for man's use—for good or ill—the energy of the cosmos.

And, while doing all this, they produced a great literature and an exciting architecture; indeed, they stimulated extraordinary experimentation and creativity in all the arts.

It occurs to me that I have overlooked one of their distinctions: They definitely hold the all-time, long-distance, nonstop, major-league, heavyweight-division record for tax and tuition paying, though I expect that in this particular you will outdo them.—Bergen Evans.

SECTION VIII. Evangelism and World Missions

SERMON SUGGESTIONS

Topic: The Message of Evangelism
TEXT: Matt. 9:35–38.

I. Evangelism surpasses the keenest-eyed pessimism; sees farther than the wisest philosophic optimism; does more than the most effective psychologic-determination. Its theme is the breadth of God's love, the many-sidedness of his abundant goodness, perennially fresh and beautiful in its outpoured mercies.

II. Evangelism is a divine and human partnership. It is the universal law of laboring together with Christ. In evangelism we do not work like hirelings, we are sons; we work not for wages, but for an inheritance.

III. Evangelism is cooperation with God. Christ's Kingdom goes forward or is retarded, according to whether or not we are active or negligent. The slightest faltering of the weakest and lowest saint holds back the coming of the Kingdom of Christ.

IV. Evangelism is refreshing to soul and body. Evangelism will kindle our souls, give health and vigor to our bodies, bring pleasure otherwise unknown, overcome lax discipline, conquer a low state of religious living, avoid the reaping of bitter fruits.

V. Evangelism brings rich rewards. It has the reward of success. Evangelism will be rewarded in the Lord of the harvest's commendation and welcome. Evangelism is the program of God. It is written in large letters in the New Testament. It has proven to be the Spirit-selected program of the centuries.—Hyman J. Appelman.

Topic: Revival and Evangelism
TEXT: Hab. 3:2.

The words "revival" and "evangelism" have been used interchangeably by so many for so long that their real distincts have become blurred. But even a brief glance at a dictionary would help one to see that "revival" means to reanimate, to renew, to restore to new life that which is dying or dead. "Evangelism," on the other hand, means announcing, with the purpose of persuasion, the good news of the Gospel.

I. Revival is spiritual renewal of God's people. Evangelism is what a revived church does about its renewal.

II. Revival is God crying to lethargic Christians: "Wake up—and get to work!" Evangelism is an awakened church crying to sinners: "Repent—and be saved!"

III. Revival is getting one's own heart warmed. Evangelism is setting other hearts on fire.

IV. Revival, as Dr. Ralph W. Sockman said, "is not going down the street with a great big drum; revival is going back to Calvary with a great big sob." —William Fisher.

Topic: The Passion of Evangelism
TEXT: Luke 10:1.

The success of the early Church hinged on certain facts.

I. The sense that Jesus Christ through the Holy Spirit was personally leading the movement, the fact that so few were set apart by men to the work of the ministry, but that all had a part in that work. It was a great laymen's movement.

II. Another reason was that the work was so very personal in character. Philip the evangelist gladly got out of the excitement in Samaria and left Peter and John to settle it while he went hundreds of miles to have a hand-to-hand testimony of the power of the Gospel. He knew that to rub shoulders against the shoulders of a man whose spirit is unquenchable is to put new strength and greater intensity and zeal into ourselves.

III. Perhaps of greater value was the fact that these men had a spiritual fellowship with Jesus Christ.

(1) To feel wisely inspired by such a commission, to march forward regardless of consequences for the saving of human hearts, would be sufficient to make any man a hero and if once it is found, it is absolutely irremovable. And this it was that these men experienced.

(2) What is it that gave them their inspiration?

(a) It is the consciousness that in some inscrutable way, under the providence of the eternal will, they are working out a great mission.

(b) If in our time we possess this animation and faith for the cause we have openly espoused to the world about us, and especially the Church, we will be stimulated and intensified.

(c) It must summarize the apostolic messages and traditions which have been handed down by word of mouth as well as by written scripture.—W. Lionel Evans.

Topic: The Way to Salvation

I. Give yourself time to think, to listen to God, and to pray to him.

II. Obey your conscience and admit that your life has not been what it should be. If you cannot honestly make that admission, you are not ready for salvation.

III. Ask God for forgiveness for the wrong you have done. Because God's love is revealed in Jesus Christ and his redeeming work upon earth, pray for forgiveness, "for Christ's sake."

IV. Accept the forgiveness which God is offering you, whether you feel any change come over you or not. Sometimes the sense of release and healing follows later.

V. Start at once to listen for God's voice and obey what you hear.

VI. Teach your conscience the new way by reading from your Bible or Christian literature giving guidance.

VII. Refuse to be discouraged when now and again conscience says, "Watch it! Wrong lane!" You are bound to make mistakes on so new a journey.

VIII. As soon as you feel in doubt, pray and listen for God's voice within you.—*The War Cry.*

Topic: Evangelism in the Early Church

Why was the apostolic church successful in its evangelistic enterprise?

I. The earliest church possessed a transforming message, the Gospel.

II. Evangelism was the most important work of the earliest church.

III. Evangelism was the work of all members of the earliest church.

IV. Evangelism in the early church was supported by a vital worship experience.—C. George Fry.

Topic: Mission and Evangelism

I. Mission and evangelism are identical in their origin. Both have their origin in Christ. It is because of and as the result of the life, death, and resurrection of Christ that the Church is engaged in mission and evangelism.

II. Mission and evangelism are identical in their instrumentality. The Church is the instrument through which God has chosen to fulfill both mission and evangelism.

III. Mission and evangelism are identical in their goal, the fulfillment of God's purpose for mankind.—The United Presbyterian Church.

Topic: Missions Education in Your Church

I. What is missions education? Missions education is that aspect of Christian education which seeks to create within the individual the ability and desire to be personally responsive to the great commission of our Lord Jesus Christ.

Failure to recognize missions education as an essential and integral part of Christian education is to weaken and render incomplete this vital part of our church's ministry.

II. Why have missions education? Human nature functions on a priority system based on values. One student of human development declared: "Things can get snarled up if a person does not rank-order things in terms of his own priority system. A man's priority system lies at the root of his motivational system and reveals more about him than anything else. When we understand what a man values, we can predict with fair accuracy how he will behave." Missions education is essential to developing values and determining relationships that are pleasing and acceptable to our heavenly Father.

III. Where does missions education begin? Missions education begins with the acceptance of this objective of Christian education: "Our aim is to lead each individual to enter into God's purpose for creation by sharing his Christian faith with the world. This involves confronting him with the claims of the Gospel in such a way that he will accept his role as an ambassador for Christ and actively support the cause of missions. The Church should confront him with opportunities to share in its missionary activities and to suggest ways of individual outreach, such as those found in civic, business, and social relationships, and the possibility of missionary endeavor as a vocation. Sharing his Christian faith with the world also includes the development of an adequate Christian social ethic." —L. Ted Johnson.

Topic: The Christian Communicator

SCRIPTURE: II Cor. 5:11–20, RSV.

Eugene Nida says that the Christian communicator has three characteristics.

I. He is absolutely courageous.

II. He is indescribably, indefinably, unexplainably contented. The environment can be nauseating, but he has the peace which passes all understanding.

III. He is always in hot water. Unless a Christian is absolutely courageous in standing up to conflict, unless he has that inner peace because in the middle of the storm he has what he needs, and unless he is in trouble with the *status quo* because he is speaking the truth, he is not communicating the Gospel.

Topic: The Nineveh Road

The Christian missionary enterprise is constantly being scrutinized, evaluated, and criticized. This is as it should be. It is also often ignored. And this is not all right. I want to tell you in a straightforward manner the three reasons why I am interested in the mission movement of the Church and why I think it is integral to the Christian faith and ministry.

I. The first reason is that the Bible tells us to be missionary-minded. I am being *biblically accurate* when I support missions. And the Bible is our book of authority. It alone tells us who we are, what we are doing here on earth, and where we are going. Throughout the Bible one hears of missions.

II. The second reason why I hold that the mission enterprise is valid and that the Nineveh Road of missions is the highway on which we must travel, is that it is *philosophically accountable*. What do I mean by this? It seems that the religion we call Christianity is one of concern for others. It speaks of kindness. It preaches love, and love, by its very nature, seeks to extend itself. Love would unite everything under its sovereign rule. It is universal and all-inclusive.

III. The third reason which validates the missionary program of the Church is that the world needs something. Not only are we biblically accurate and philosophically accountable, but we are doing what is *practically acceptable* when we engage in such avenues of outreach. Missions tell men who they are, what they are doing as pilgrims on earth, and where they are going. The message of the Church does not teach men to live serenely, but it helps them live peaceably, and this is something that all men in Toledo, Tibet, and Timbuktu need and want. Missions is predicated on the fallen and frail nature of man from which stance I have never seen a single man depart in perfection. God knew that the people of Nineveh didn't know, so to speak, their right hand from their left. He sent Jonah for this reason. Missions help people.—James W. King.

Topic: Sharing the Gospel

I. Sharing the Gospel demands the use of Bible content.
II. Sharing the Gospel demands that the Bible be correctly interpreted.
III. Sharing the Gospel demands that the content of the witnessing be cast against the total theological perspective of the Bible.
IV. Sharing the Gospel demands an understanding of the person to whom witness is given.
V. Sharing the Gospel demands that the witnessing be framed in attractive language.
VI. Sharing the Gospel demands that the witness be presented with effective speech.—H. C. Brown, Jr.

Topic: Why Missionaries Are Missionaries

TEXT: Mark 16:14–18.

I. I have heard it suggested that missionaries go because they personally like to travel or they anticipate servants and comforts in the Congo or in India. This is nonsense. In this day of rapid transportation and credit installment excursions, anyone can travel who really wants to make the effort.

II. I have heard it suggested that missionaries want to feel useful. All of us do. And there are many ways of being useful. Judson could have had a great ministry as a preacher. Schweitzer could have been useful as a theologian or a musician. But there is more than just wanting to be useful.

III. I have heard it suggested that missionaries go out of a desire to do humane service. But this is hardly reasonable. Both government and private industry offer fine careers for people who may be deeply interested in foreign service. There is more.

IV. There is no way of explaining missionary motivation except by going back 2,000 years and listening to the direct command of the Savior of men.

(1) The eleven disciples were together having a meal. They were restless, impatient, hesitant to believe. It was a disturbed, argumentative atmosphere. Then as silently and as quickly as on the other occasions, suddenly Jesus was there. He reasoned with them and told them not to be unbelieving, but to have faith.

(2) Then Jesus turned to a positive command and said, "Go ye into all the world, and preach the gospel to every creature." That was it! And the reason for commissioning was as plain and simple as the command itself. After the command, Jesus promised some special protection and powers for the messengers who would go.

Here is the reason for missionary going and missionary giving. It is a direct command from the risen Master. There must be no disobedience. This is a direct order in a personal relationship.—Jackson Wilcox.

ILLUSTRATIONS

CONTAGION. Conversion is a profound change in character and life followed by an outer change which corresponds to that inner change. Producing changed character is the business of Christianity. When it can no longer produce conversion, it has lost its right to be called Christian. For Christianity is not merely a conception. If a church is not evangelistic, it will soon not be evangelical.—E. Stanley Jones.

NEVER INVITED. Dr. Dan Poling was minister of the great Marble Collegiate Church, New York. At every service he made an appeal, for he thought there must be at least one in need of help. A distinguished-looking man stopped him in the aisle and said cynically, "What can you do for me?" "Nothing," said the minister, "but I know Somebody who can. Come and talk with me." After three meetings he told Dr. Poling: "Years ago I made a promise that I would attend church once a week. But how does it happen that until last Sunday night I was never invited to do anything about it?"—E. J. Webb.

A CODE FOR CHRISTIANS

1. A regular attendance at all divine services.
2. A daily and prayerful reading of the Bible.
3. An exercise of the habit of daily prayer.
4. A frequent self-examination.
5. A daily exercise of our faith in Christ Jesus.
6. A loyal service in the cause of our blessed Savior.
7. Cultivation of a true love for our fellowmen.
8. A daily expression of our loyalty to the Son of God.
9. A daily testimony of our hope in the Lord Jesus.
10. An encouraging of the young people to live a consecrated life.
11. A willing participation in all the plans of the church.
12. A steady purpose to win souls for the Kingdom of God.
13. A systematic and generous giving for the support of the church.
14. A daily expression of our thanksgiving to God in all things.
15. A realization of the abiding presence of Christ.

—*The Lutheran.*

SALVATION

Salvation is a species of well-being.
It differs from prosperity in being compatible with meager provisions.
It differs from happiness in its relatively greater independence of circumstance and its compatibility with other moods than euphoria.
It differs from health in being compatible with relatively more extensive and persistent weakness and incapacity.
It differs from resourcefulness of craft, strategy, and potency in not depending upon one's ability to contrive it.
It differs from security in being compatible with physical hazard, emotional stress, and marital privation.
In biblical terms, it is a confidence consisting in trust of the God who is known in the fulfillment of his promises of presence and succor, and in the persistence of his demand of fidelity to himself, to be expressed in trusting, the resource of his presence as adequate to this present and any future. Those who trust in this fashion are set free to consult the welfare of their neighbor and obliged to seek justice for all and the vindication of the oppressed.
It differs from smugness in being answerable to and dependent upon another's appraisal.
It differs from contentment in being answerable to another's expectation.
It differs from passive dependency in that free, responsible decision is implicit in the notion of salvation.
It differs from stoic autoarchy, serenity, and apathy in being compatible with the possibility of unreserved allegiance to another, in affirming solidarity with other selves in one's ambit,

and in allowing the possibility of legitimate claims upon one's interest.

It differs from Aristotelian theory or contemplation in being impossible of merely private or individual realization.

It differs from Buddhist enlightenment in being impossible of realization at the cost of indifference to other selves.

It differs from Taoist compliance in its refusal to endorse or acquiesce in all that is present and actual.

It consists in a confidence whose ground-tone is joy, deriving from a sense of worth in the esteem of another who is good and able, whose interest evokes nothing which threatens that in which one's true worth is defined.

The character of that worth is such that acceptance of this appraisal of one's value as a self obliges one to acknowledge solidarity with and concern for all other selves as being of the same worth, and to commit oneself to the implementation of the salvation (thus defined) of all men.

In New Testament terms, it is summarily described as seeing in the figure of Jesus the evidence as well as the character of divine solicitude, the evidence and character of human worth; and as the venture of entrusting oneself to that One whose appraisal, demand, and support of all selves is exhibited in the character, career, and vindication of Jesus of Nazareth.—Stuart D. Currie.

PERSPECTIVE. Maybe once upon a time we could think of a missionary as a superior soul from Canada the good or America the beautiful going to set the poor heathen right. But no more. We've seen the burned-out ghettos. We've seen the rural slums. We've seen the stupidity and greed that killed Lake Erie. No longer can we labor under the illusion that God is our great white father and Jesus Christ wears red, white and blue.—Leighton Ford in *The United Church Observer*.

IMPERATIVE. If you are a Christian, you simply respond to two commands: Come! and Go! You cannot select one without the other. Just as you come to Christ, to worship, to hear the Word, to receive the sacraments, so you go into the world as a disciple of Christ. You are sent. Wherever you are tomorrow morning, there is the Church's mission. You represent the Church's Lord. What you say, and do, and are in the world makes you a missionary—whether you stay here or go abroad, whether you talk much about Christ and your church or not. Unless we manage to shed our Christian faith at the church door as we put on our overcoat, we are missionaries. The only question is whether we are good ones or bad ones. —David H. C. Read.

FOREIGNERS

I thought that foreign children
Lived far across the sea
Until I got a letter
From a boy in Italy.
"Dear little foreign friend," it said
As plainly as could be.
Now I wonder which is "foreign"—
The other child or me?

—Edith Blair. Reprinted by permission.

LIGHT REACHES OUT. A visitor was preaching to a little congregation in the heart of a jungle in the Congo. Speaking of the power of light, he asked his hearers: "When you have a little light or fire in your house, what happens when you open the door? Does the darkness rush in and put out the flame, or does the light reach out to penetrate the blackness outside?" This was language they understood, and they nodded appreciatively.

As I heard this illustration, my mind jumped to the laser beam and its marvelous uses. It cuts the hardest substance known to man, penetrates the darkest depths of ocean floors, opens doors, measures distance, welds tissues in a healing process, and performs other miracles. Though I cannot comprehend this form of light, I accept it. I find myself one in understanding and worship with the tribespeople who nod in appreciative affirmation for the Light of life.—Sadie Wilson Tillman in *The Upper Room.*

MORE THAN A MAP

This map is not a map to me,
But mountains, rivers, lake, and sea,
People sad and people gay,
Little children at their play,
Folks with feelings like my own
And some place they call their home.
Their skin may black or yellow be,
But brothers and sisters are all to me—
Members of God's great family.

—Minnie B. Wilkins. Reprinted by permission.

INFLUENCE. In the country of India, where the vast majority of the people are Hindus, only 2 percent of the population is Christian. And yet the fact is that the Christian faith has exerted far more influence in India than this statistic indicates.

To illustrate this far-reaching influence, the Christians in India tell of an orthodox Hindu judge, before whom a Christian was asked to give testimony during a court case. The Christian, so the story goes, asked for a Bible on which he might take his oath of truth, but no Bible could be found in the courtroom.

At this point the Hindu judge reached into his own pocket and drew out a New Testament. "Here," he said. "Use mine."—*Task Force.*

INNER MOTIVE. The member of a missionary society offers that additional dimension which might be called the plus of Christian faith. Technical assistance can be given by any qualified person, but better material conditions bring about profound changes in ordinary human existence. These changes can be very unsettling unless they take place against a background of strong spiritual convictions. The missionary today needs the same technical and professional qualifications as all the other people giving technical assistance. But in addition he has a far more difficult yet even more rewarding task of reinforcing these new techniques with an inner motive and conviction which alone can give point and purpose to progress and development.—Elizabeth II.

HEALING

No mortal mind can comprehend the vastness
Of healing service rendered in His name.
Christ's ministry of help through all the ages
Imbued with love divine is still the same.

To bind the wounds, to render aid and comfort,
To lift the fallen and to cure the ill,
The Great Physician works through many channels,
And miracles are wrought in healing still.

—Della Adams Leitner. Reprinted by permission.

WILL HE DARE. There hangs in our manse a picture by the French artist, Vibert, called, "The Return of the Missionary." As you study it, you will see its seven figures represent the Church.

The setting is the richly appointed drawing room of a cardinal of the Church. The background is a large tapestry hanging on the wall, depicting Christ being taken down from the Cross. "Remember that," the artist seems to say. In the center of the group sits the missionary, lean, scarred, poorly clothed, and pointing to a nail-wound in his wrist.

What is the response? One fat ecclesiastic sips tea. He further serves his belly-god and communes with his little dog on the floor by his chair. Two others tell funny stories. Another, immaculately dressed, gazes at the missionary in sheer amazement. He can hardly believe that such a thing as a crucifixion can happen. Nor does it in his cloistered world! A fifth figure, a young cardinal with a cup in one hand and a cigarette in the other, closes his eyes and naps. Not interested! But there is one more—a young man with a strong, fine, concerned face. He looks at the missionary, listens to his word, thinks on his wound, and seems to be saying, "Do I dare go and do what he has done in making the Crucified known, or will I become as these others, secure, indifferent, unconcerned for others?"—Harrison Ray Anderson in *The Presbyterian Outlook.*

ACT OF FELLOWSHIP. The Christian mission is not an expedition to claim conquests for an absent sovereign. The Christian mission is an act of fellowship with the Lord who is already there, identified with those who as yet do not know him.—John W. Deschner in *The Christian Mission Today.*

CROSSROADS

Not London, not New York, not Singapore;
No giant fortress, neither feverish mart:
The crossroads of the world forevermore?
The human heart.
—Amy S. Bridgman.

BORN WARRIORS. The early missionaries were born warriors. To them religion was a banner under which to fight. No weak or timid soul could sail the seas to foreign lands and defy dangers and death, unless he carried his religion as a banner under which even death would be a glorious end. To go forth, to cry out, to warn, to save others—these were frightful urgencies of the soul already saved.—Pearl S. Buck in *The Fighting Angel.*

EACH ONE TEACH ONE. In the early 1930's, the economic depression in the United States was at its height. Dr. Frank Laubach suddenly found his budget cut in half. This meant he would have to drop 12 of his teachers and cut the salaries of all the rest. Calling 400 Moros together, he broke the news to them. "I haven't any more money," he said. "We will have to stop this literacy campaign."

The faces of the men became stern. Most of them were armed with either guns or knives. Dr. Laubach was frankly afraid. Then Kakai Degalangit, a leading Moro chief with penetrating black eyes and a forbidding manner, rose to his feet and said in a loud voice, "This campaign will not stop. It is Lanao's only hope." "What shall we do?" Dr. Laubach asked. Kakai turned his flashing eyes at the other Moros and said, "I'll make everybody who knows how to read teach somebody else—or I'll kill him!" The missionary was taken aback. "That's a new idea in education," he commented awkwardly. "Will you other chiefs back him?" "Yes," they shouted with one accord. "Teach or die in Lanao!" Each one taught. Nobody died. And everyone was happy.

The more Dr. Laubach pondered over the proposal, the more excited he became. Naturally he did not like the slogan, "Teach or Die," so he changed it to "Each One Teach One." He could readily see the manifold values of the method. What could be better for a newly literate person than to share his newfound skill with someone else? It would crystallize all that he had learned. It would give him a feeling of self-respect and train him in the spirit of sharing; furthermore, was this not the key to the problem of illiteracy around the world?—J. T. Seamands in *World Vision Magazine.*

SECTION IX. Children's Stories and Sermons

January 7. The Right Ingredients

Betty, the teen-ager of the family, came bounding through the house with a deep frown on her face. Something was bothering her. Finally it came out.

"Mom, you have always told us that it is wrong to hate. But it is not easy for me to keep from hating Marilyn Jones. You should have heard what she said to a new girl in our room."

In answer, her mother said, "Betty, I know how hard you try to do the right thing and to have the right thoughts. Do you remember what happens when an ingredient is left out of a cake?"

"Sure," Betty laughed. "It falls flat."

"Well," her mother continued, "Marilyn just has not learned the right ingredients for a happy, good life. Hate is an ingredient in her heart, and she suffers and makes others suffer because of it."

Betty was silent, lost in thought. All at once she said, "I see what you mean, mother." She had found the help she needed to conquer her own thoughts and to help Marilyn.—Mary Imogene Harris.

January 14. Footprints (Missionary Day)

Do you remember the exciting scene in the story of Robinson Crusoe when he discovered a footprint in the sand?

I know a still more exciting scene where there appears in the sands of time a single footprint which is more dramatic and thrilling than all the footprints which are found in any mystery story. It is the footprint of a Christian helping another person and following the footprints of Christ.

There are people who have never discovered the footprints of other people. It is as though they lived in a private world, with no one who really has a claim on their concern. May we be enlightened as to who those people are who need us and quick to respond with help.—Ernest Webb.

January 21. Selfish and Selfless Persons

A selfish person is one who thinks first of himself. A selfless person thinks of others before himself. In each one of us is a mixture of these two. In most of us, one overshadows the other.

Can you think of any people who think of others first? Those whom most people think of right away are the missionaries, the doctors, and the ministers who give so much of themselves to others. There are many who work with the poor and the sick, with little thanks and appreciation. These people are working to do God's will on earth, as it is in heaven. It would be wrong for us to think that in order to do his will we must become great missionaries. How we act toward our family and friends makes a difference. We can help mother, be thoughtful of daddy when he's tired, and try to understand when big sister wants to be left alone. If we try to imagine ourselves in another's place, it will be easier to help when we are needed.

Let us each ask ourselves, "Am I a selfish or a selfless person?"—*Family Devotions.*

January 28. What Is Your Name?

My name is John Beverage. You are Elaine, David, Susan, Jim, and Elizabeth. There are so many that I can't name you all, or I'd never get on with my story. The important thing is that each of you has a name.

Why do we have names? The answer is so that we can identify one another. Suppose you had no name. How would your mother and father call you? It would certainly be terrible not to know whether your mother wanted you or your sister to come in from playing.

When you hear the name of someone you know, you always think of something to go with that name. For example, if I mention these names to you older boys and girls—President Eisenhower, Abraham Lincoln, Queen Elizabeth—you think of them as great and good people. If I mention Hitler and Stalin, you think of them as living evil lives. For you younger ones, if I mention mother, father, grandmother, grandfather, you think of someone who loves you very much, and would never knowingly do anything evil. If I mention the giant in "Jack and the Beanstalk" or the wolf in "Little Red Ridinghood," you think of something evil.

All boys and girls, and grown-ups as well, think the same way. They remember things about you whenever they see or hear your name. When you are young, their thoughts are good ones like, "My, what a nice girl she is!" When we become older, we see that people think almost anything about us, but one thing we can be sure of: the thought is connected with our names.

As you grow into manhood and womanhood some of you may become famous and be known throughout the world. Most of you will not become famous though. And yet you will know many people and they will know you. You want them to know you as a fine person. It is important to have people like you, but it is more important to maintain your own self-respect. The only way to do this is by leading the best Christian life that you possibly can. How do you follow this way? There are many ways people may tell that we are Christians:

(1) A Christian believes in God.

(2) He prays every day, not just on Sunday.

(3) He goes to church and church school.

(4) He gives to support the work of God.

(5) He is kind, thoughtful, and considerate of others in school, at play, at home, at work.

If you follow in the footsteps of Jesus and do the things he taught us to do, then you will be a Christian. And once you are a Christian you may be proud of your name. You will have molded your life after that of the greatest person who ever lived. His name was Jesus Christ. What is your name?—John H. Beverage.

February 4. Message to Scouts (Boy Scout Sunday)

Lord Baden-Powell, who founded the Boy Scouts in 1908, died in Kenya, East Africa, on January 8, 1941. After his death, the following letter was found among his papers. It was his final message to the Scouts.

Dear Scouts: If you have ever seen the play, *Peter Pan,* you will remember how the pirate chief was always making his dying speech because he was afraid that possibly when the time came for him to die he might not have time to get it off his chest. It is much the same with me, and so, although I am not at this moment dying, I shall be doing so one of these days and I want to send you a parting word of goodbye.

Remember, it is the last you will ever hear from me, so think it over.

I have had a most happy life, and I want each one of you to have as happy a life, too.

I believe that God put us in this jolly world to be happy and enjoy life. Happiness doesn't come from being rich, nor merely from being successful in your career, nor by self-indulgence. One step toward happiness is to make yourself healthy and strong while you are a boy, so that you can be useful and enjoy life when you are a man.

Nature study will show you how full of beautiful and wonderful things God has made the world for you to enjoy. Be contented with what you have got and make the best of it. Look on the bright side of things instead of looking on the gloomy one.

But the real way to get happiness is by giving out happiness to other people. Try to leave this world a little better than you found it, and when your turn comes to die, you can die happy in feeling that at any rate you have not wasted your time but have done your best. "Be Prepared" in this way to live happy and to die happy. Stick to your Scout Promise always—even after you have ceased to be a boy—and God help you to do it.

February 11. A Modern St. Valentine

"When Valentine died long ago, his friends remembered the love he showed to people," said Mrs. Tower.

"Mother, do you mean there really was a man named Valentine?" exclaimed Robbie.

"Yes, dear. He was a friendly man, but he felt especially sorry for the many people in prisons who are so often forgotten. He would make up little bouquets of flowers to take to these people, who had nobody to tell them that they were loved. The flowers were his message of love to them and for them. When he died his friends started to celebrate his birthday by sending messages of love to each other. Much later the Church declared Valentine a saint, and so we have St. Valentine's Day."

"It's a happy custom," said father, "and that is why it has continued to grow over the years."

Thoughtfully, Mary Ann looked at her father. "Do you think old Mrs. Rankin down the street would be happy if I made her a valentine? She hasn't any grandchildren to say, 'I love you!'"

"And do you know whom I would like to make one for?" The words tumbled out of Robbie. "For our minister. When he came to see me so many times when I was in the hospital it made me feel happy, but I was always afraid to say so."—Marjorie Haynes.

February 18. Billy and Pedro (Race Relations Sunday)

When Billy came in and sat down to supper he took a few mouthfuls, then announced to his family, "There's a new kid in my room at school, and I don't like him."

"Oh, Billy," said mother. "You don't even know him yet."

"What's his name?" asked father.

"It's Pedro. He's from South America. He has thick black hair all slicked down!" (Billy's own hair was light brown and usually stood right up on end.) "Besides, he's polite and his shoes are shined." (Billy wore sneakers to school.) "He's a sissy!" Billy's tone was scornful.

"Not so fast, young fellow," said dad. "You'd better get acquainted with people before you make up your mind about them."

Just then the telephone rang, and so the conversation about Pedro stopped. But the next morning at breakfast mother said, "Billy, I'm going to send you on a treasure hunt today."

Billy's eyes brightened. "After school?" he asked.

"No. In school. I want you to find some buried treasure in Pedro. I want you to find at least three things about him that you really like and tell us at supper." And mother's face grew quite stern as she added, "And if you fail to find those three things, no dessert."

Billy asked, "What's for dessert?"

"I'm not telling you now," said mother, "but it's something you like."

That evening when the family sat

down to supper, after Billy had had a few bites, mother said, "Well, son, did you find any buried treasure in Pedro?"

And Billy looked so funny as he answered "Yes, mother, I really did. Pedro can sing. He can sing better than anybody in our room. And he's kind. When all the rest of us ran into school when the bell rang, Pedro waited for little Jimmy, the second-grader that has the braces on his legs, you know. He can't move fast, and we sort of forget to think about him. But Pedro waited and held the big heavy door for him. Yes, he's kind! And, mother, he's a good sport. We were playing ball. Tom was umpire. Pedro was up at bat, and Tom called a strike. It wasn't a strike. It was a ball and everybody knew it. But he just said it was a strike because he doesn't like Pedro. None of the kids do. Well, Pedro just looked at Tom, a long, long look. I guess maybe he was counting ten. I don't know. Anyhow he looked a long time—then he grinned and said, 'O.K., Tom, you're the umpire.'"

Mother said, "I'm glad you found three things to like—because dessert is strawberry shortcake." And she went out to get it.

After the family had eaten all the shortcake they could hold, there was still some left. Father looked at it and said, "That won't be very good tomorrow. I'll tell you, son, why don't you go down the street and find Pedro and his sister and invite them to come back with you and finish the shortcake?"

So Billy did. And Pedro and his sister came back to Billy's house. After they had finished the shortcake they played games all evening. Billy discovered that Pedro had a wonderful collection of cowboy pictures and Pedro found that Billy had a good stamp collection, and they had a happy evening until it was time for Pedro and his sister to go home and for Billy to start for bed.

He said good-night and started up the stairs, but halfway up he stopped and called down, "Say, mom, isn't it fun to like people?"—Margaret Henrichsen.

February 25. The Target Lincoln Rejected (Brotherhood Week)

When the famed Bardan's Sharpshooters were stationed at Alexandria, Virginia, in the spring of 1861, they often had an important and distinguished visitor. Every few days Abraham Lincoln, President of the United States, came across from Washington to watch the Sharpshooters' target practice.

One day, when the tall gentleman in the high silk hat appeared, the boys in the Union volunteer company had a surprise ready. The visitor stepped up as usual, and, after selecting a rifle, he announced that he was ready to shoot. Then a unique target was run up, especially for him. It represented a human figure, and in large letters it was labeled "Jefferson Davis."

Already the tall man had his rifle half-raised when the range instructor remarked with a laugh, "We'd like to see you take a crack at that, Mr. President."

But Lincoln took one good look at the target and then lowered his rifle. Although he did not voice a single word, on his face appeared an expression of surprise and disappointment, and, more than anything else, sorrow.

Without a word he laid the rifle down and then went off a little distance from the range. There, with folded arms and bowed head, he walked quietly up and down, keeping to himself. For nearly twenty minutes he continued his solitary pacing back and forth.

After a while, he returned to the range. In his absence, the labeled target had been hastily removed and the regular one set up. When he again took his place, he fired several shots, as was his custom, and then departed.

The tall visitor, burdened with his many duties, probably soon forgot the incident. But every soldier in the company long remembered that Abraham Lincoln would not shoot at a target that was supposed to represent Jefferson Davis, President of the Confederate States.—*Sunshine Magazine.*

March 4. Why We Say Grace

"Daddy, why do we pray before we eat?" Andrew raised his bowed head and asked a question that had been bothering his young mind for some time.

Everyone at the table listened repectfully to the old story as daddy explained it to his son.

This custom is as old as eating. Thanksgiving for the food we eat has its roots in the religious instincts of the human race. In the Book of Deuteronomy, Moses speaks to his people about praising the Lord for their food: "And thou shalt eat and be sated, and shalt bless the Lord thy God for the goodly land which he has given thee."

The early Hebrews had a special prayer to be said over each basic food, in addition to the before-meal blessing. The blessing over bread was considered most important. It was a frequent reminder that no human act, however basic to existence, ought to be performed without reference to the Creator.

The early Christians continued the Hebrew custom. "Whatever you eat or drink, or whatsoever you do," St. Paul told his disciples, "do all to the glory of God."

In America, the best-fed nation in the history of the world, a lot of us forget to pray. Who can explain why? In other parts of the world they have to fight for food, or have no money to buy, or find the shelves empty. But few of us like to remember that more than half the people in the world go hungry every night.

A great many Americans have grown away from the idea of being thankful. We forget that there is a Giver of gifts, a Power greater than ourselves.

We need to refocus our perspective of a finer philosophy of life. It will make us enjoy that pause before meals for "Bless us, O Lord, and these thy gifts."

March 11. The Man Who Sang Like a Lark (Lent)

"Once upon a time long ago there lived a man who . . ."

"Had a fairy godmother," sang Peter.

"Wanted only one thing for Christmas," said John.

"No," said father. "Once upon a time there lived a man who sang like a lark, gaily. He sang because he was happy. He sang to praise God. Francis of Assisi saw the same skies and trees, the same rivers and hills that everyone else saw, but he marveled at them all as special and wonderful gifts from God. And so he sang a song about them. He was tired and ill and so nearly blind that he could scarcely see the hillsides covered with olive trees and the shining wheat fields. But he could feel the warmth of the sun, and he could remember clear blue skies. So from his cot he sang: 'Praised be my Lord God with all his creatures; and especially our brother the sun, who brings us the day, and who brings us the light . . .'

"His friends said, 'Listen! The Lark is singing still!' "—Jane Day Mook.

March 18. The Strangler Tree (Lent)

In the Florida Everglades, I saw one of the most unusual trees in the world. It is called the strangler fig. Birds often drop the fig seeds into the branches of other trees, such as the live oak. After the seeds germinate and the plants develop, the roots begin to push down and around the host tree. They finally enmesh the tree so that it dies, and a strangler fig tree stands in its place.

Sin, if given a chance, takes hold of the human heart, choking the good qualities until they give way to the forces of evil. Sometimes we allow our tempers to choke our pleasant dispositions, unkind thoughts to replace the more understanding ones, and a jealous and covetous nature to take over in place of contentment.

By spending some time each day in meditation and prayer and reading God's Word, we strengthen ourselves so that evil will have little or no opportunity to strangle the good qualities.—A. E. Purviance.

March 25. What God Said (Lent)

Henrietta loved to go to church. One Sunday morning while she was making preparations to go, an accident befell her only clean dress and mother told her she would have to remain at home. During the prayer her mother heard childish footfalls coming up the aisle, and in a moment Henrietta slipped into the pew wearing her soiled everyday frock.

On the way home the mother asked her why she had come to church after she had been forbidden to do so, and the child replied, "Well, mother, you've always told me to take all my troubles to God, so after you started for church I went to my room and asked God what he would do if he were in my place, and he said to me, 'Henrietta, you go.'"

April 1. The Baptism of Jesus (Lent)

"Why was Jesus baptized?" ten-year-old Tommy asked his father on the way home from church one Sunday. Tommy's father had to stop and think a minute.

"On the Day of Pentecost, Peter told the crowd to be baptized for the remission of sins," he said, "but Jesus had no sin."

"We are baptized that we may walk in newness of life, but Jesus lived a perfect life.

"We are baptized because we love our Lord, but Jesus demonstrated his love by giving his life.

"We are baptized to enter into the Kingdom of God, but Jesus himself is the king.

"We are baptized to have the answer of a good conscience toward God, but the sinless Son of God had no guilt.

"Jesus was baptized," Tommy's father finally remembered, "to fulfill all righteousness. His baptism demonstrated to God and to us his humility and his willingness to do what pleased God."—Sam Stone in *Devotion*.

April 8. Everyone Needs a Savior (Passion Sunday)

The minister's wife was discussing sin with some juniors. She explained that God could not be holy and overlook sin. Neither could he tolerate it. To be certain they understood, she repeated once more, "Everyone sins."

Bill looked stunned. "Does everyone sin?"

"Yes," she replied.

"Does even your husband sin?"

"Yes."

"Well," he said desperately, "how are we going to get to heaven then?"

We could never be saved from our sins were we dependent upon any human being, no matter how godly. God himself came in the person of his Son, Jesus Christ. He is the sinless one.

We may not be able to understand how Christ can save humanity from its sins, but our part is to accept in faith that Christ died for us.—Iris Weber Martin.

April 15. Leaves of Healing (Palm Sunday)

There is a unique custom in Italy on Palm Sunday, just one week before Easter. On this special day, large bundles of olive leaves are painted gold and silver and then taken to the church to be blessed by the priest. After the mass the olive leaves are handed around the congregation, and anyone who has quarreled takes some of the leaves and gives them to the person with whom he has had a disagreement. This person cannot refuse to accept the blessed leaves because such an act would be an offense against God. In this manner Italians clear their slates of animosities and approach the Easter observance with no hatred in their hearts.

April 22. When the Tide Turns (Easter)

Philip Mickman, an English boy from Yorkshire, swam all the way from France to England. A few people had swum the English Channel before, but Philip was the youngest ever to do it.

It was a terribly hard swim and it took twenty-three hours and forty-eight minutes—that is just twelve minutes short of twice around the clock. But he did it.

It wasn't so bad when the tide was running with him. He got on splendidly.

But after a time the tide turned, and that was another story. The currents in the English Channel are very, very strong. Not only did they make it hard going, but they carried Philip fourteen miles off his course. Think how discouraging that would be.

But Philip didn't say to himself: "Well, it's no good. I'll never get there. It's too hard. I might as well give up." No. He did it.

How? Just by keeping on—keeping on when things were easy and keeping on when the tide turned against him.

There was the time when things were going well with Jesus, when the people waved their arms and pulled down palm branches and welcomed him into the city. You remember that, too. The tide was running with Jesus that day.

Then the tide turned. In only a few hours it turned. And he found himself in the midst of a crowd, and some of the people were those who had cried "Hosanna! Hosanna!" The tide had turned. What did Jesus do? He did what Philip Mickman did in the English Channel—he just kept on. He called on his courage to help, and in the end he won. They took him to the Cross, they put him in a tomb in the garden, but in the end, he won! He rose triumphant over death!

So he knows now exactly how you and I feel when the tide turns against us, and we have to do a very hard thing. His message to you and me, then, is a very simple one that he learned himself as a boy: "Be strong and of good courage!"—Rita F. Snowden. Adapted from *Story-Time Again*.

April 29. Closing the Door

A young man sauntered leisurely one day into the public library. He stood there in the presence of the written record of the accumulated wisdom of the centuries. In that library he could have read the story of man's life and struggles through all history. In that library there were books of history, science, religion, literature, music, and art. There were books to enrich the mind and strengthen the life of any person who was willing to make himself responsive to their message.

But this young man was completely unaware of their claim upon his life. He looked all around and then asked the clerk at the desk: "Where are your funny books?"

The young man's unresponsive spirit closed the door to any possible help that might have come to him that day. He lost his chance for growth and enrichment, not because help was unavailable for him, but rather because he himself was not responsive to its presence.

May 6. What Rubs Off

A research chemist took his son to the laboratory one day. He gave him a piece of pure silver and a piece of pure gold and told him to press them against each other. Then the father placed the pieces of silver and gold under a powerful microscope and had his son look at them. He saw flecks of gold buried in the silver and silver in the gold. Part of each had come off on the other.

"Persons are like this," he told his son. "When you make friends, part of you rubs off on them and part of them on you. What rubs off may be as simple as an expression or mannerism. Or it may be an idea, good or bad, that will influence you from then on."—James O. Whitfield.

May 13. Watch That Temper!

One day a minister was attending a

baseball game beween two high school teams. Seeing a friend of his in the grandstand, he immediately went up to him. The friend was a scout for the Philadelphia Athletics who had been sent to this particular game to watch one of the pitchers. If the lad pitched a good game, the scout was to sign him up to play for the Philadelphia team when he finished college. In the meantime the baseball club would pay him $2,000 a year, meet all his college expenses, and in the summertime let him travel with the team.

Everything went well, and the boy was pitching a fine game until the seventh inning when several players on his team made errors. Then, instead of working harder, the pitcher pulled off his cap, and in utter disgust flung it to the ground, saying: "You can get another pitcher. I am through with you fellows for keeps."

When the scout saw the boy show such a fit of temper, he got up and said good-by to his friend.

"But aren't you going over to sign him up for your team as you said you would?" asked the minister.

"No," replied the scout. "We can't use him. He has a bad temper. In an emergency, when his team needed him, he would let the other players down. We can't use quitters on our team."

In the Bible we are told, "Be kind to one another . . . forgiving one another." How true it is in this world that we can't have everything our own way! All of our friends make mistakes; we make many of them too. But it is the person who is understanding, who is forgiving of others' mistakes, who does not lose his temper regardless of what happens—it is he whom we admire.—John Schott.

May 20. God's Foresight

Would you believe there's a bird that sees underwater better than he does in the air?

There is one, and chances are you've seen him—the common kingfisher. The lens in the kingfisher's eye is egg-shaped. On the retina, where man and most animals have only one sensitive area on which an image can register, the kingfisher has two. The one used for flying is located so the vision of the two eyes doesn't overlap. All he sees as he flies is a flat, two-dimensional picture of things.

When he dives underwater in pursuit of fish, however, the other sensitive area in the retina comes into play, allowing his eyes to focus straight ahead of him for an overlapping image and the same 3-D picture we see with our eyes. In this way, he can do his below-water fishing with accuracy.

Image the foresight of God in equipping a tiny kingfisher with special eyes so he can find food and live. Consider how much more blessed we are that he has given us Christ to help search for spiritual food to live by.—Max L. Batchelder in *The Lookout*.

May 27. Beautiful Hands

There is a story of the three girls whose main thought was to have pretty hands. They bought expensive lotions and spent a great deal of time in making their hands smooth and beautiful. Occasionally they would get together and compare hands, each one hoping that hers were the prettiest. One day as they stood at the foot of a hill a fourth girl came along. She listened to their conversation about their hands and looked at her own which were calloused from work. The three girls looked, too, and laughed in derision. Just then an old lady came by carrying a heavy sack of bundles. She asked if one of the girls would help her carry her load up the hill. The girls with the pretty hands were unwilling to touch the unsightly sack. But the other girl picked up the bundle and started off with the old lady. At the top of the hill the pair stopped and the old lady, now in the form of an angel, took the hands of the girl who had carried the bundles and said: "The prettiest hands are those that help. The prettiest lives are those that serve."—Clyde N. Parker.

June 3. Knowing the Will of God

The biblical faith is not based upon man's confidence that he clearly knows all about the will of God, but rather that all men can know enough of God's will to live better than we live by human wisdom alone—enough to win God's approval.

How, then, shall we seek to fathom the will of God?

First, pray. We can no more know the mind of God by merely thinking about, or talking about God, than we can know the mind of a person by thinking or talking about him. To know a person well we must think with him and talk with him, in intimate companionship. Prayer is fellowship, conversation with God, and attentiveness when God speaks.

Second, discuss the matter with the wisest, noblest, most devout person you know, for God sometimes reveals his will through his closest friends. But do not regard even the wisest person as the infallible spokesman of God.

Third, while you are waiting for God's answer, go on performing your common tasks and fulfilling your everyday duties to the best of your ability. Sometimes it is in the midst of the most unattractive, commonplace duties that God speaks to us most clearly. He spoke to Moses, while Moses tended sheep in a wilderness, calling him to lead Israel out of bondage.

Fourth, if the moment arrives when you simply must act before you are certain of God's will, then act according to the best light you presently have. Do so in the confidence that God honors our best choices and our best work, even when it is imperfect.

Fifth, dare to believe that it is best when sometimes the divine will overrules our will, as when a kindly parent refuses to let his little child play with matches or razor blades. God has dealings with us that are often beyond our understanding and liking, but they are always for our good.

Sixth, once you have acted according to the best light you have, waste no thought or emotion on self-recrimination and regret. If your best seems unsuccessful, remember that some great defeats God gloriously uses in a way that shames and shadows earth's victories.

Remember that cross on a hill?—Harold E. Kohn.

June 10. A Sacrifice Move

On a platform marked off to represent a large chessboard, a game was played in sight of an attentive audience. Instead of little figures of carved ivory or ebony, flesh-and-blood men filled the different positions on the board. The two contestants, seated in a balcony where they could look down and see the whole board at a glance, called out the plays and the chessmen moved.

One of the players seemed especially enthusiastic about the game. He obeyed his cues eagerly, cheered as other men responded to instructions, and entered into the spirit of the occasion thoroughly. Then a sacrifice move was ordered which meant that he would be eliminated from the board. At once his cooperative attitude changed. "Take George," he begged, pointing to a fellow player, "don't take me." The game was enjoyable for him only when he could feel some self-importance.—Elinor Lennen in *Help in Troubled Times*.

June 17. The Isle of Nightingales (Father's Day)

In an autobiography entitled *The Americanization of Edward Bok* the author relates this story about his father. Off the coast of Holland in the North Sea there is a small island along which stretches a dangerous ledge of rocks. More than a century ago the inhabitants of the island looted vessels that were driven ashore there and often murdered the crew. The King of Holland appointed a lawyer to clean up the island. This young man from The Hague was given the title of Mayor-Judge.

The island was a grim place on which

there was not a single tree. One day the Mayor-Judge called together his council and said: "We must have trees. We can make this island a spot of beauty if we will." The council opposed him, saying that trees would not grow in such a windswept place. "Very well," he said, "I will plant them myself." This he did, a hundred the first year and more in the years that followed. Soon the birds came in large numbers. In time people came to study the birds because there were so many of them. Nightingales arrived, too, and eventually it was called the Isle of Nightingales. Artists from various countries came to paint on the island. Said one American artist, "In all the world today there is no more beautiful place."

Early in his experience the lawyer asked a girl from Holland to marry him. In time they raised twelve children. Along the way she said, "While you raise your trees, I will raise our children." One day, when the children were old enough, she said this to them, "Now as you go out into the world I want each of you to take with you the spirit of your father's work, and each of you in his own way and place to do as he has done—make the world a bit more beautiful and better because you have been in it."—V. Carney Hargroves.

June 24. Birds and Men (Nature Sunday)

The rare species of cormorants on the Galapagos Islands have wings but cannot fly. Because they have no enemies and can secure their food on foot, they no longer have any need to fly.

At the other extreme on these islands of fascinating wildlife is a little bird which is the only living creature besides man that can use a tool. The woodpecker finch breaks twigs off trees to use in digging insects from holes. With remarkable skill, this bird selects just the size twig to probe into hiding places that his beak would not reach.

These two types of birds are typical of people. Some have lost the ability to soar into higher spiritual realms by failing to use God-given powers. They feed upon society for material needs, but miss the thrill of expanding their lives in greater knowledge and adventure.

Like the woodpecker finch, many Christians have learned to use tools of learning for personal growth.—Roberta Dillon Williams in *The Upper Room*.

July 1. What the Liberty Bell Says (Independence Sunday)

On the sides of our beloved Liberty Bell which hangs in Independence Hall, Philadelphia, are these words cast on the metal itself: "Proclaim liberty throughout the land and to the inhabitants thereof. . . ."

Who wrote these words? Why are they on the bell?

They came from the Bible (Lev. 25:10).

No better words could be inscribed on this bell, nor could they have come from a better source. For the liberties we cherish in America, so new in the year 1776 when our nation was born, and even today so rare for most of the world's peoples, come not from man but from God. Thus, God's Word furnished us our Liberty Bell liberties and freedoms.

We all know the story of how the Liberty Bell rang out the glad news of a new nation in birth on July 4, 1776, when the brave delegates from the various states signed the Declaration of Independence in Philadelphia.

These delegates to the Continental Congress, who put their names at the bottom of the Declaration of Independence, trusted not so much in their own powers as in God's. America was a weak nation—poor in money, divided in loyalties, and altogether new and daring in her ideas on men's freedom. Could such a bold and untried venture work? Could men really govern themselves, electing their own rulers instead of serving a king?

The delegates believed that the rights and freedom we hold dear come from God and are not given by men; thus nobody had the right to take them away.

In our day, nearly two hundred years after the words were written, it is our task not only to make these freedoms available to every citizen in America but also to help make them possible for all men everywhere. For all men are God's children and entitled to these same rights.—Graham R. Hodges in *Pulpit Digest*.

July 8. What We Do Thoughtlessly

Virginia and Bobbie were playmates. One day Bobbie thought it would be lots of fun to pour water on Virginia's fine new dress. When he saw that Virginia didn't think his trick was funny and that she was about to cry, he immediately was sorry and said hastily: "I apologize! I apologize!" Virginia sobbed: "But I am still wet."

It is easy for us to injure another person. Often it is done thoughtlessly. Sometimes our apology is very superficial. Yet even if we realize the gravity of our act and do feel sorry, it is difficult to bring ourselves to make a real confession. But often a confession cannot undo the harm.—O. E. Krueger in *The Secret Place*.

July 15. Kindness of God's Creatures

Man's record in his dealing with the lower animals is spotted with much cruelty and neglect. We owe it to all creatures of God to treat them with responsible concern. Our whole Christian understanding of creation implies this. Man is the highest animal, endowed with a unique capacity for communion with God and for striving to be like God in his own character and conduct. God has given to us full responsibility for the care and protection of the lower creatures. Any mistreatment or neglect of them is a betrayal of our trust from God.

A little girl's mother overheard her saying in her evening prayers, "Dear God, don't let the little birds be set in Tommy's trap. They won't. They can't. Amen!" Her mother asked, "Betty, why are you so sure that the little birds won't be caught in the trap?" "Because," said Betty triumphantly, "I jumped on the trap and smashed it."

Do you do everything within your power to be a good friend and protector of God's dumb creatures? This is no small thing in the sight of him who loves all living things.—*Forward*.

July 22. Garden Clock

If you asked someone what time it was, and instead of looking at his watch he glanced out into the flower garden and said, "I see by the poppies it is eleven," you would probably be startled. And you would be curious to know how time could be told by flowers.

Flowers are not as accurate as watches, but if you have the right flowers in your garden and if you will watch and study them, you can tell time by your garden clock.

To start you on your way, here are a few of the more common flowers and the times that they generally open their petals or go to sleep. You will soon find many others to add to your list of time tellers.

The gay, bright morning-glories usually open between five and six in the morning. The yellow dandelion, that persists in cropping up in even the best-tended lawns, usually opens its blossoms between seven and eight. The lovely California poppy, like a real lazybones, wakens between ten and eleven each day.

Around noon the morning glories begin to close their blossoms, and about four o'clock the old-fashioned four-o'clocks open. When the sun sets, the wonderful white moonflower bursts into bloom. Right before your eyes the tight bud will begin to loosen, and suddenly the moonflower is blooming for you. As the flower opens, it releases its fragrance just as though someone had pulled the stopper from a bottle of perfume.

Watch the flowers in your garden and see when they open and close. You will be surprised at how accurate a clock a flower garden can be.—Marion Ullmark in *Sunshine Magazine*.

July 29. Two Greedy Men

St. Martin of Tours in one of his journeys caught up with two fellow travelers, one of whom was a greedy, covetous man, the other of whom was a jealous and envious fellow. When he came to leave them, St. Martin said he would grant them a parting wish. It was this: whichever of the two would make a wish first would have his fulfilled and the other would get exactly double what the first had wished. The two men were stumped. The greedy man wanted his wish, but he also wanted the double portion. The envious man desired his wish, but he could not stand the thought of the other getting twice as much as himself. Therefore neither was willing to make a wish. Finally, the greedy man seized the other by the throat and threatened to choke him to death unless he made a wish. Whereupon the envious man, to escape being choked, said with a wry smile: "All right, I'll make a wish. I ask to be made blind in my left eye." At that, he lost sight of his eye, and the other fellow went blind in both eyes.—Ralph W. Sockman.

August 5. Lesson from the Airline Pilots

Many of you have been passengers on commercial airliners or have gone to the airport to see them come and go. I am sure you have noticed the official-looking briefcases that the pilot and copilot carry. Sometimes the pilots call these cases their "brains."

In these cases is a lot of information —weather charts, company operation rules, government regulations, details about airports, and other useful data. Now a pilot is a highly trained man and knows how to fly a plane; yet he would not think of being without this important case. As he directs the big plane he would be uneasy without it.

We are God's highest creation—able to think, plan, act, and do many wonderful things. Because we are so able, many people think they can do everything and anything on their own. They feel so self-sufficient that they seldom go to church or Sunday School, they fail to study the Bible, and many times they refuse to acknowledge God as their heavenly Father or Jesus as Savior and Lord. When they get into a difficult spot they have nothing to turn to for help, and they usually fail and hurt others as they go down.

The Christian ought to be at least as wise as the airplane pilot, always prepared for emergencies in the ways of life, using every available help for straight, safe living. Next time you go to the airport, look for the pilot and the information case he calls his "brains."—Lloyd N. Whyte.

August 12. Holding an Elephant

For generations, wide-eyed youngsters have watched with awe as circus trainers and handlers control huge elephants making them perform all kinds of chores. Then each beast stands quietly as a ring is snapped around his leg, with a chain leading to a wooden stake driven into the ground. The elephant could easily pull up the stake and run away, but he never does.

What the youngsters don't know is that the elephant is held, not by the chain, but by something that happened to him when he was very young. While he was still just a baby, a chain he could not break was fastened to a big stake he could not pull up. At first he pulled and pulled to be free, but he found over and over again that he couldn't, so he soon stopped trying to get free. Eventually he got so big that he could pull up the stake, but by that time he had been convinced that he could not be free, so he spends the rest of his life chained up by a habit too powerful to break.

We, too, can be influenced for life by our habits. That's why you should make very sure you learn them in Sunday School and church.—Max L. Batchelder in *The Lookout*.

August 19. Passing the Test

A lad, answering an advertisement for a helper in a hardware store, received the job. When he reported for work next day, he was taken to a dark, dusty attic where he was given the job of separating a large box of bolts, nuts, nails, screws, washers, and other odds and ends. It was a tedious job, but the boy stuck to it. Halfway through the box, he discovered a wadded-up piece of paper, which he almost discarded. But then he began to unfold it, and to his amazement he found that it was a five-dollar bill. Immediately he left his job and reported his discovery to the owner of the store.

"You may keep it, son," replied the owner. "You've passed the test."

"But what do you mean?" he asked.

"I hid the bill in the box and sent you up to sort that stuff as a test. Three other boys before you failed it. Now I know that I can trust you at the cash register, so you will work down here from now on."—John W. Wade in *The Lookout*.

August 26. The King's Lesson

Once upon a time there was a wise old king who ruled over a people who always expected others to get things done for them. And so the king, feeling rather vexed about this, thought it was about time he taught them a lesson.

On one of his highways there was a notoriously narrow stretch of road. Late one night the king went there alone, and he dug a hole right in the middle of the narrow road. Having done this, he took a leather pouch from under his cloak and dropped it in the hole and covered it with a large stone.

The following morning a farmer came trundling along in his cart, and, noticing the stone—and with much grumbling on account of the stupidity of the fellow who had placed it there—just managed to scrape past it.

Next came one of the king's soldiers. He, his head held proudly aloft, didn't see the stone at all, and went sprawling against it.

And so it went on from day to day. The stone remained where it was, and nobody made any attempt to move it.

At last, the king summoned his people to meet him at the spot where he had placed the stone. There, in their presence, he moved the stone, and from the hole which it covered he took out the leather pouch to which there was attached a piece of paper with the words "To him who moves the stone" written on it. The king loosened the thong of the leather pouch, and from it he emptied glittering pieces of pure gold!

"My people," said the wise old king, "let this be a lesson to you. Never expect others to do for you what you cannot be troubled to do for yourselves."—G. E. Breeze in *The British Weekly*.

September 2. The Hands of Labor (Labor Sunday)

The Roman Emperor Domitian set upon establishing his kingdom, and he wanted to be sure that nothing endangered it. But he heard a rumor that troubled him. News came that there were still living in Palestine relatives of Jesus, descendants of the royal house of David. He was terrified at the news.

Domitian ordered that these relatives of Jesus be brought to him, and they were summoned to the palace. They were simple men, and the power of the emperor coupled with the beauty of the place all but robbed them of speech. The emperor confronted them, asking about their claims to his kingdom.

Fearfully the men related that they were grandsons of Judas, one of Jesus' brothers. Together they possessed an estate valued at only 9,000 denarii, less than $2,000, which they cultivated themselves. Domitian listened intently, but he did not believe them.

Then one of the farmers displayed his calloused, work-scarred hands. Seeing them, the emperor finally believed that these men had no thoughts of usurping his throne. Their only claim to royalty was as sons of God in the heavenly kingdom.—Doris Harris in *The War Cry.*

September 9. The Touch of Greatness

Men will go long distances to visit some place which is famous because some famous person lived there. Men will pay large sums of money for some quite ordinary thing which has become extraordinary because it once belonged to some famous person. The human mind and the human heart are always fascinated by contact with greatness.

Every time we enter a church and worship there, we are putting ourselves in touch with the saints and the heroes and the prophets and the martyrs. We can say to ourselves: "I belong to that fellowship to which those who loved and died for their faith in every age and generation belonged."

When we sit at the sacrament, we can say to ourselves: "I am doing exactly what Jesus did with his disciples in the upper room long ago."

For the Christian this contact with greatness is even more universal. We live in the world which is the work of God. The men and women among whom we live and move are the children of God. The world in which we live is the handiwork of God. Everywhere we go, we can say: "Here is God."—William Barclay.

September 16. Hearing God Speak

Some years ago a great scientist got the idea that sounds of various kinds—instrumental music, singing, speeches—could be sent out into the air and could then be picked out of the air again 50, 100, or 1,000 miles away. This idea gave us the radio.

As you know, there are many programs going on in this church auditorium this morning, but we don't hear them. We are not tuned in to them. Even if we had a score of radios here we wouldn't hear these various sounds unless we were tuned in. If we were tuned in, we might hear another church service, a news broadcast, or a concert.

Now let us leave this age of the radio and travel back in history over many centuries to a man named Moses who was taking care of his herd of cattle on a hillside to the east of Egypt. He had been born of Hebrew parents in Egypt but had made his escape from that country. He knew that many of his countrymen were still living there and that life for them was desperately hard. He often thought about their hardships and felt genuinely sorry for them. He probably prayed for them frequently. This day as he watched his herd he heard God speaking to him and telling him to go back to Egypt to organize his countrymen and bring them to a new homeland. Now it is probable that Moses' cattle heard no unusual sounds that day as they grazed. Apparently the Midianite herdsmen who were tending their flocks nearby heard nothing. God was speaking, but only Moses heard, and he heard because he only was tuned in to hear the voice of God.

Now let us travel in imagination across the centuries again, and come down nearer to our own. We arrive at a time when a few families were coming into this community, the first to make their homes here. They built houses for themselves and stables for their few animals. Then they said among themselves, "We should have another building, one where we could meet together on Sundays to tune in to God." They didn't use that term, because it was in the days before the radio was invented, but that's what they meant. They knew that it would be easier to hear God speaking to them when they met together for that purpose.

When one year had gone by since they opened their church, they decided that they should mark that anniversary in a special way. Such celebrations have been kept up across the years since, and today we are celebrating another of those anniversaries. That is fitting and proper, for the life of any community finds a milestone in the opening of a church—a place where men and women, and boys and girls can join together in public worship to tune in to God.

Having tuned in to him on Sunday, we are more likely to keep tuned in during the rest of the week. Then when we sit down to a meal which contains food from the ends of the earth, we think of God's goodness and care for us; when we view a sunset or a forest aglow with autumn colors, we think of the glory of God; and when we go about our daily tasks in the home or the school, we think of them as God's work.

Jesus had something to say on this subject on one occasion. For obvious reasons, he didn't use the illustration of the radio. He pictured one's life as a house with a door which might be opened or closed. And he said, "Behold, I stand at the door and knock; if any one hears my voice and opens the door, I will come in."—Lorne J. Henry.

September 23. Neighbors

Neighbors are a very important part of our living. They help us make a community. They often become close friends. They lend a helping hand when needed, and they provide us with an opportunity to be helpful.

Yes, we neighbors occasionally cause each other some concern, perhaps distress, when we fail to accept responsibility for being a neighbor. And at times we want to be alone, both individually and as a family. But together we and those who live near us make up our neighborhood and, if our neighborhood is to be a place where we feel a sense of belonging and acceptance, then each must fulfill his responsibility to the others.

What is true of our neighborhood is true of the world. We have responsibilities to people in Asia, Africa, China, India, and Europe. We must accept our responsibilities joyously. To have true neighbors, in our community and in the world, we must be true neighbors.— Charles V. Lee in *Family Devotions*.

September 30. Confession of a Witch Doctor

High in the mountains of Guatemala, a small country in Central America about the size of our state of Ohio, live three million people. Most of them are descendants of the Maya Indians, a proud and highly civilized group of people. Many of them live in the mountains much as their kinsmen have lived for hundreds of years. They still dress in colorful costumes, speak a little-known language, grow their own food, and go barefooted.

Families are large, and in almost every household there is a small baby being carried papoose-fashion on the mother's back. Many of the people still worship the ancient gods. Even today one may see their sacred mountains with sacred and magic campsites on them. One mountain we visited had fourteen magic spots on it. A magic spot is one that a witch doctor has picked out by a funny-shaped rock or by a strangely twisted tree. A wide bare spot is made by leveling the ground and by sweeping it clean and bare. At one end a small stone shrine is often put up by placing a few rocks on top of each other. Here the sacred fire is kindled, and here the witch doctor—who is priest, doctor, and judge—often goes to sacrifice a chicken. On the edge of these magic spots are many chicken feathers. But the center of the magic spot is kept clean and swept, with not even a footprint on it.

The witch doctor, for a gift or for money, will take a chicken to the magic spot, light smoky candles, pray strange prayers, and sacrifice the chicken on the crude stone altar in order to try to get a better crop for somebody, or to heal a sick child, or to get revenge. The witch doctor is an important man and is feared by many. He wears a great black coat with jewels and pins and a black cap trimmed in red. He chants strange songs.

One witch doctor not long ago heard about Jesus, his love and his way of life. He became unhappy over his old way of life and saw that the Jesus way was much better. Yet, he did not want to give up the importance and the security of his position as a witch doctor.

Gradually, through his contacts with Christian missionaries and through his own prayers and thoughts, he came to see that the only way for his future was the Jesus way. And he made the great confession that has marked Christians down through the centuries: "Jesus Christ is Lord" and "Jesus Christ is Lord of my life."

This former witch doctor found a joy and a happiness in the Jesus way of life that he had not known before. He began telling his friends of the Jesus way and encouraging them to make the great Christian confession and choice.

Now, you and I are not witch doctors in a picturesque faraway land, but we will be expected someday to make the great confession that all Christians make. Through our experience at home and in many ways in the Sunday School and church, we are being prepared to choose the Jesus way of living. Almost every day we can take part in it. Jesus said, "As you wish that men would do to you, do so to them." Love your mother and father and be kind, helpful, and cheerful to others. As we do these things each day, we shall be making real preparation to confess, as the witch doctor confessed, "Truly Jesus is the Lord of my life and him truly will I serve."—Grover Wilson.

October 7. Helping a Brother (World Communion Sunday)

Once I planted a vine beside a trellis. How carefully I tended the little sprout, watering it and teaching the tendrils to twine about the slats. Warmed by the strong sun and nourished by the refreshing rain, the vine grew and little by little climbed halfway up the trellis. Then the leaves began to unfold, and in a little while it began to provide cooling shade and became a thing of beauty.

But one dark night there came a storm. The wind blew furiously, and the rain fell in torrents. The next morning, when I looked at the little vine, it was lying prone on the ground, half submerged in muddy water.

Then what did I do? I stooped down and tenderly lifted the fallen vine out of the mire and twined it carefully about the trellis again. In places I fastened its tendrils to the slats with pieces of soft string, and it began to hold up its head once more. Then I watched it grow day by day and observed with pleasure that the vine I had lifted up was taking a fresh hold.

Do I ever think to be as considerate of my fellowmen as I was of that little vine that knew neither pain nor pleasure? Am I as eager to lift up my brother who has fallen?—*Pastor's Round Table.*

October 14. What's in Me for It?

I was once asked to deliver an address to a youth fellowship convention. The topic was, "What's in It for Me?" I came to a rather rigid conclusion. You cannot with reference to any area in your life answer the question "What's in it for me?" apart from asking at the same time a parallel question, "What's in me for it?" For that is what what is in you is for, to respond creatively to life as you encounter it. And so I say to you and to myself exactly what I said to the kids: "There is nothing in anything for any of us but the raw materials out of which to create something for ourselves."

What's in volleyball for you? Volleyball means different things to different people. What's in a volleyball for you cannot be answered apart from what's in you for a volleyball.

What's in prayer for you? Prayer means different things to different people. What's in prayer for you cannot possibly be answered apart from what's in you for prayer?

Life is a gift for which we should be grateful; but the more you get it unwrapped, the more you discover that the gift is a "do it yourself kit" for which we are responsible.

Any promising approach to an understanding of life's meaning, to our attitudes of awe and wonder with which we must always begin, we must add the attitude of gratitude and responsibility.

Christ dealt with life not only as a mystery beyond him and as a gift to him but also as a claim upon him. Standing before the mystery of life, Jesus turned his awe and wonder into faith. Accepting the gift of life, Jesus translated his gratitude and responsibility into humble loving service.—Melvin E. Wheatley, Jr.

October 21. The Hound that Couldn't Make Up His Mind

A hunter took his hound dog with him and went out to hunt bear. Suddenly the dog smelled fresh bear tracks and began to follow its path. Then, just as suddenly, he smelled the warmer trail of deer crossing the bear tracks. The hound now followed the scent of deer. Halfway down the hollow, fresh rabbit tracks entered his nostrils. Now he took off after the rabbit. When the tantalizing smell of chipmunk crossed his path, he began to chase chipmunk. Later that evening, the hunter found his dog excitedly circling a tall reed. At the top was a scared mouse!

We would say: "What a lame-brained hound. I'd get rid of him in a hurry!" And yet, what happens to us when we are faced with on-the-spot decisions? How often have you changed course in mid-stream?

Usually, the things of importance, those things that really count, don't come upon us through an advertisement or TV commercial. We usually discern God's voice as we learn to be open to the real issues of life. We weigh the alternatives and their end results. Many opportunities that seem "golden" at the moment quickly lose their appeal when considered in terms of ten years or a lifetime. The person who is seeking God's will always evaluates the possibilities on the basis of what this means for his life and the lives of others. Goals and achievements that contradict the highest meaning of life, cannot be God's will.—Bernie Wiebe.

October 28. Thinking the Best

Bob and Joe were roommates in the college dorm. They found much in common from the day they first met on the campus. Both were athletes. They had classes together. They became such chums that they were called "campus twins." It was a shock to their friends when their comradeship suddenly came to a dead end. Bob moved to another room and found another roommate.

Little by little the facts became known. Bob had received a twenty-dollar bill from home. He left it on his desk when he went to class. When he returned, the money was gone. Only he and Joe had keys to the room. That evening Joe came back with a new sweater. Bob was certain Joe had stolen the money. Joe flatly denied knowing anything about the money. Bob did not believe him.

Spring came and a dead oak tree was cut down. When it hit the ground two squirrels scampered away. The boys ran to see the hole where the squirrels had a nest and found three baby squirrels snuggling among the leaves. They found something else: a torn and crumpled twenty-dollar bill.—Julius Fischbach.

November 4. Benjamin Franklin's Philosophy

Benjamin Franklin, using Poor Richard, the imaginary maker of his Almanac, as a mouthpiece, taught a philosophy of common sense. In his autobiography, he told a story of a hatter in Philadelphia who desired to place a signboard over his shop. He wrote it down, "John Brown Makes and Sells Hats for Ready Money."

"Oh, dear!" said a friend to whom he showed it. "Cut out 'Makes and.' Nobody cares who makes the hat so long as it is good." Then the sign read, "John Brown Sells Hats for Ready Money."

"Dear me!" exclaimed another friend whom he consulted. "Why, this is an insult to the community! 'Ready Money,' indeed! Strike it out!" The sentence then read, "John Brown Sells Hats."

"Absurd!" cried a third friend, as he burst into roars of laughter. "Do you suppose people will expect you to give hats away? There is no need to say they are for sale! Why 'Sells hats'?"

Again he went to the sign-writer and ordered him to paint the board bearing the simple legend, "John Brown, Hats." The tabloid was complete; that told all that really needed telling.

With such wisdom Jesus agreed when he said that our talk ought to be Yea, yea, and Nay, nay. If we have any honor or character, oaths are not needed to emphasize the truth we have to tell. (See Matt. 5:34-37.)—Robert G. Lee.

November 11. Wishing Is Not Enough (Stewardship Day)

One day I visited Eastman House in Rochester, New York. In its garden is a shallow pool with a fountain. I heard a father explain to his three children about making a wish, then tossing a coin to make it come true. They immediately wanted to do just that.

Two of the children chose a coin from their allowance, but the littlest girl hung back. "But, Daddy, I don't want to spend my money, I want you to give me a nickel to throw in."

The father answered: "But, honey, it won't work that way. You see, it's got to hurt a little!"

She was unconvinced, but I thought how right and wise he was. To wish is not enough. Something of ourself, some effort on our part must implement the desire to give.—Mildred Fredericks in *Guideposts*.

November 18. Thank You (Thanksgiving Sunday)

There is a phrase which is not used as often as it ought to be—just two little words, "thank you." We can say it in many different ways, and every language has its own special phrase for "thank you." Do you ever stop to think just how important these words are?

A newspaper published a letter that had been received by an old lady. She lived alone, had few friends, and did not get much mail, but one day to her surprise a letter arrived written in a very neat hand. It was from a boy of sixteen, crippled by infantile paralysis, who lived nearby. This is what he wrote: "Thank you for the beautiful flowers you have had in your garden this summer. The sight of them has cheered me very much."

What a lovely gesture of gratitude! Not only did the boy find pleasure in watching a pretty garden, tended by the old lady, but more important, he remembered to say "thank you" for the blessing he had received. How many of us would do that?

St. Luke records the healing of ten lepers by Jesus as "he was passing between Samaria and Galilee." Nine of the lepers were so overjoyed by the cure that they hurried to tell the good news to their friends, but they forgot to thank their Healer. Only one of the ten returned to Jesus to say "thank you," and St. Luke tells us that he was a stranger.

There are some people who forget to say "thank you" even though they have received a blessing. There are others who never want to say "thank you." Many people take for granted the joyous benefits which God so graciously provides. What a wonderful difference saying "thank you" makes! The blessings of this world are many and come to us in different ways. Do not accept them as a matter of right. We should glorify God and remember to say "thank you" every day for his love and care, like St. Paul, "Always and for everything giving thanks to God."—Stanley Barratt.

November 25. The Star and the Seal

The symbol of the six-pointed star (Mogen David) which appears on some of the paper currency of the United States is there because the founders of our country were all pious men, familiar with the Old Testament. All of our first money, from the years 1793 to 1820, contained stars of six points. This was because of the trials and tribulations of the United States at its conception. In fact, Benjamin Franklin, who was one of three designated as a committee to draw up a design for the Great Seal of the United States, suggested for the reverse side of the seal a scene of Moses leading the Jews across the Red Sea in their exodus from Egypt.—William H. Sternberg.

December 2. The Legend of the Glowworm (Advent)

There is a lovely legend concerning the glowworm. This tiny little creature —so the legend goes—was present at the first Christmas. It saw the star in the sky. It saw the shepherds who adored the Christ Child. It saw the Magi who came with their magnificent gifts. The glowworm wondered if it, too, might go to the manger and perhaps even bring a little gift.

At that time the little glowworm was a very ordinary insect. Yet it felt the glory and thrill of the first Christmas. So it uncovered a seed of grain that it had hidden against a bad day. This was its one treasure. The little creature would give it to the Christ Child. Laboriously the glowworm made its way, pushing, carrying, pulling, and dragging the grain for the Christ Child.

At last the glowworm arrived at the manger where the Babe was lying. Mary and Joseph stood nearby. The glowworm was so small that the human eye could hardly see it. But the Baby Jesus saw it; and, as the glowworm made one supreme effort and pushed its treasure into his infant hand, a loving smile appeared upon the Baby's face. A tiny hand reached out—or so it seemed— and touched the little creature. Immediately, the glowworm began to glow with happiness in response to the Christ Child's love. It has been glowing ever since, the legend affirms, a perpetual witness to the glory of the touch of Christ.—Lowell M. Atkinson.

December 9. Face into the Storm (Advent)

Among my foul-weather friends I cherish the black-capped chickadee as one of the most companionable. When the first hints of autumn chill the air and fair-weather birds flee to more comfortable climes, the chickadee remains. And when I saunter through a cedar clump, reading tracks—tales of animal adventures of the night before—a chickadee is sure to carol a cherubic welcome. From cedar bough and spruce branch, from balsam twig and birch limb, on the sunniest days or in the most merciless storm of snow or sleet, all winter long the chickadee's cheerful chant rings out.

One reason why the black-capped chickadee can survive hard Northern winters is that it has the good sense to face into the wind. Like the feathers of all the birds, a chickadee's feathers lie pointing tailward. If the bird turns its back on winter winds, snow will blow in amidst the feathers, carrying the raw and bitter cold next to the body where it can nip at the black cap's warmth and finally freeze it to death. But when a chickadee faces into the wind, snow flurries are stopped by the close matting of its feathers, which hold in body warmth and fend off savage weather. A black-capped chickadee endures the winter by facing the storm.—Harold E. Kohn.

December 16. For Whom the Bells Toll (Advent)

According to an old legend the bells in the town cathedral would begin to ring only when someone brought to the altar a sacrifice uncontaminated by selfish motives. Each year at Christmas time the people of the town brought their gifts, hoping to hear the tolling of the bells for the first time. But decades passed and no sound was heard from the bell tower.

Then one Christmas a young lad was bringing his gifts to the church—a bag of grain and a few small coins he had labored a year to save. But as he made his way to the church he discovered some little birds that were starving. After pondering the problem, he poured out the grain for them. Later he met a blind beggar. Once more the struggle went on within his heart, but finally he dropped the coins into the poor man's cup.

Arriving at the cathedral, he made his way to the altar, embarrassed because he had nothing left to give. Then his hand touched an apple he had in his pocket—his lunch for the day. Without a moment's hesitation he placed it on the altar amid the great amounts of money and jewelry others had given. Then as he moved away, the bells began to peal out a joyous melody, for this little one had learned what his elders had not: God requires a man to do justly, to love mercy, and to walk humbly with him.—John W. Wade in *The Lookout*.

December 23. The Best Gift (Christmas)

What is the best gift you ever received? Better still, what is the best gift you ever gave? Perhaps you will recall that in each instance, the best gift was one that was tied with the heartstrings of the giver, one that included a part of self.

A little girl who had no money to spend gave her mother several small boxes tied with bright ribbons. Each contained a slip of paper on which was printed a simple message: "Good for two flowerbed weedings." "Good for two floor scrubbings." "Good for two errands." Such gifts are a giving of self, and how much joy they bring to both the giver and the receiver!

It is obvious that the Wise Men gave first of themselves. They made the long journey themselves rather than sending their gifts. When they arrived at their destination, they fell down and worshiped the Christ child, and then presented their gifts. If you would give Christ the best gift, make the long journey of complete submission to him, worship him, then give of your treasures to him.—Wanda Fulton in *Devotion*.

December 30. The Man at the Center of History

Kathy came home from school with a frown on her face. "Mother, today at school we learned that some man, I've forgotten his name, lived in 120 B.C., and I remember dad saying that Moses lived in one thousand something B.C. But what does B.C. mean?"

Mother explained that B.C. are letters standing for the words "Before Christ." "But let's ask daddy at devotions," she suggested.

Dad explained it this way. "The birth of Jesus divides all history," he said. "All time that came before Jesus was born is called B.C. and all since then is called A.D."

"I know what A.D. means," said John. "It comes from the Latin words 'Anno Domini,' meaning 'In the year of our Lord.' We put it in front of the date."

"Jesus came in the center of history," dad said, "and he must come in the center of our lives if he is to change them as he has changed the reckoning of time."

"Of course, people are divided about who Jesus was," said mother. "We must show by our lives who he is, that he is our Lord and Savior. And he is this when we put him at the center of our attention and our lives."—Fred Morris.

SECTION X. Sermon Outlines and Homiletic and Worship Aids for Fifty-two Weeks

SUNDAY: JANUARY SEVENTH

MORNING SERVICE

Topic: **The Gospel Drama**
SCRIPTURE: Luke 15:11–32.
Act. I. The Virtue of Sin: The Story of the Younger Son. (1) This title pertains to the pathway all human beings take and the redemption possible. For the younger brother is all of us. His story is not only a record of a wasted youth; it is also a hymn to freedom. It is the record of a human being longing to be a self, an individual; a person traversing the road which God makes possible with the glorious gift of freedom.

(2) We see him first seeking his independence, his freedom. "Give me the share of property that falls to me." This is not a whine; it's a request to become a self—to establish his own individual personality, to become a man. And so he did. Yet what a contemporary and eternal picture; the self undirected turns against itself. Unbridled freedom becomes license; we become our own gods.

(3) The scene changes. "He squandered." "He began to be in want." Is there a more trenchant picture of the experience of man?

(4) The younger son went further. "He came to himself." This is the virtue of his sin. The recognition of his need took an over-all view and saw that becoming a self curiously leads to self-glorification. He is a dramatic example of the paradoxical warping of the freedom which man is given and needs. Yet when he came to himself he was on the road back.

(5) This recognition of need led inevitably to his repentance. "Father, I have sinned." This is the vital part of salvation: to come to oneself, to recognize the thwarted use of freedom, the license of unbridled freedom of self, the separation from the Father.

Act II. The Sin of Virtue: The Story of the Elder Brother. (1) His sins were not the gross sins of immorality; they were the drawing-room sins which so easily beset us all.

(2) He was self-righteous, smug. Ready to condemn, proud. "God, I thank thee that I am not like other men." Self-satisfied. Proud of his virtue and anxious to point a finger at his brother.

(3) He was selfish. The fatted calf was a symbol of all for which he had labored. His goods were his proudest possession. His position had been theatened. He was looking out for Number One. He could have little concern for anyone. He had lived near the father,

yet curiously enough was further away than his brother.

(4) He was unforgiving. At least the younger son recognized the need of forgiveness. The elder brother neither saw his sin nor had the capacity to forgive.

Act III. The Prodigal Father. (1) Here is both the climax and the denouement of the story and of the Gospel. The key to understanding the parable and life itself lies in the prodigal love of the father. Love was given in superabundance to his sons. After all, this is the point of the story as Jesus told it.

(2) The father gave the freedom. He encouraged the younger brother to become an individual. He didn't ask what the son would do. He bestowed the independence fully.

(3) Yet, while his son "was yet a distance," the father ran to meet him, ready to accept the repentant, full of mercy, compassionate. He went to him and enfolded him in his arms, meeting face to face, reaching out, loving.

(4) The father's love was prodigal enough for both sons. One was loved because he did not see; one was loved because he did. The love was enough for both. This is the assuaging balm of forgiveness which is the father's greatest characteristic. Both sons have been lost. In a real way, both had been found.

(5) The forgiving love of the father brings this gospel drama to the climax at the end of Act III. Nor is there a moral at the end, nor an application to be made. For this dramatic parable is the drama of the entire Gospel. The production goes on still, on the stage of life. You and I are among the players.—Ronald E. Sleeth.

Worship Aids

CALL TO WORSHIP. "Know therefore that the Lord thy God, he is God, the faithful God, which keepeth covenant and mercy with them that love him and keep his commandments to a thousand generations." Deut. 7:9.

INVOCATION. Blot out, we humbly beseech thee, O Lord, our past transgression; forgive our negligence and ignorance; help us to amend our mistakes and to repair our misunderstanding; and so uplift our hearts in new love and dedication that we may be unburdened from the grief and shame of past faithlessness, and go forth to serve thee with renewed courage and devotion.

OFFERTORY SENTENCE. "Walk in love, as Christ also hath loved us, and hath given himself for us as an offering and sacrifice to God." Eph. 5:2.

OFFERTORY PRAYER. Our heavenly Father, may thy Kingdom be uppermost in our minds, our hearts, and our lives. Accept our gifts and with them the rededication of all that we are and have to thy greater glory.

PRAYER. O God of grace, grant us forgiveness of our sins and imperfections. Help us to forget the failures of the past, cherishing only the wisdom and humility which they have taught us. Inspire us with new hopes and new purposes. Deepen in our hearts a love of what is true and a passion for what is good, and make us wise to see and eager to live the life that is life indeed. Show us the solemn meaning of our common days and the holy purpose for which they are given.

As thou hast blessed us hitherto, still lead us, still admonish us; and whether our life lie in the shadows or on the uplands, make us conscious of thy gracious companionship. Whatever light may shine or darkness fall, keep us in the fellowship of those who trust and obey thee in the love and service of Jesus Christ.—Thomas Eakin.

Illustrations

FACING THE FUTURE. You face the future calmly, not because you foresee what it will be, but because you know your Master will be there. Since today

SUNDAY: JANUARY SEVENTH

he lights up all shadows and overthrows all obstacles, surely he will do the same tomorrow with new obscurities and new difficulties.—Phillippe Vernier.

A FATHER'S DECISION. Many centuries ago there was a lawgiver named Zaleucus who is said to have written a code of laws for the Lacrians, a tribe of people in Asia Minor. Zaleucus wanted his laws to be wise and just; and since many of the problems of his people were caused by drunkenness, he decreed that any man who was found drunk should be punished by having his eyes plucked out.

Zaleucus, however, did not bargain for what happened next. The first man to be charged with drunkenness and brought before him for judgment was his own son.

What a problem confronted the lawgiver! Would his justice be carried out at the expense of his son's sight? Or would mercy triumph over justice, and leave Zaleucus open to a charge of favoritism?

Finally Zaleucus made his decision. His son should give one eye, and in place of the other, Zaleucus would give one of his own.—Ross Dampier in *Devotion*.

THE SINGLE-HEARTED. Only the single-hearted are happy. For only the single-hearted man has a clear direction, a clear goal. The man who wants only a bit of God always finds God to be only a brake, an impediment, a pain. But he who wants God wholly learns that he is the source of power that gives man verve and freedom; following him is the most joyful thing in the world.—Helmut Thielicke in *The Waiting Father*.

Sermon Suggestions

THE PATIENT GOD. Text: Rom. 15:5. Why does God pay no attention to our noisy little clocks and marked-up calendars, our schedules and timesheets? (1) Because quality takes time, and he won't sacrifice excellence for speed. (2) Because permanent results are only achieved by the slow pace of righteousness and love. (3) Because he is growing souls and not rabbits, and that requires time. (4) Because he holds the winning hand. Like a strong man he is secure and unruffled in his strength and patient because he knows what the outcome will be.—Angus J. MacQueen in *The United Church Observer*.

HOW TO FINISH WHAT WE START. Text: Luke 9:62. (1) We are able to finish what we start when we count the cost before we begin. (2) We are able to finish what we start when our motives are strong to the degree of intensity that is necessary to be able to finish what we start. (4) We are able to finish what we start when God approves of what we have begun.—Robert W. Burns.

EVENING SERVICE

Topic: Divine Guidance
TEXT: Acts 16:6-8.
There are three kinds of divine guidance, as typified in our text. (a) Negative guidance, as when St. Paul was stopped going north or south. (b) General guidance, as when St. Paul was directed westward. (c) Special guidance, as when St. Paul was called to Macedonia.

I. *Negative guidance*. All sorts of things happen to us in life that we cannot understand. But if we are Christians we have got to believe that God allows nothing to happen to us that cannot be turned to good and to his purpose. God makes all things work together for good to those who love him.

II. *General guidance*. (1) St. Paul, stopped from going north or south, was directed westward. He didn't know why at the time, but westward he went. God doesn't tell us beforehand what the future holds for us. We have to live by faith and not by sight, and faith means trusting God and going ahead, step by step.

(2) General guidance means that

God shows us the right direction but not the destination. It often means that we have got just to plod on.

III. *Special guidance.* There are times in life when we all need special guidance from God. But it is not always easy to get it. Unless we are and have been faithfully following God's general guidance for our life, we are not likely to get special miracles of guidance in emergencies. Special divine guidance is for the prepared mind and heart—for those who learn the spiritual language of God, who live in close communion with him. St. Paul could never have been the great Christian he was, nor have accomplished the great work he did, without becoming a man who so trusted in God that he could go forward always, even in the dark, being confident that God was guiding him aright.—H. V. Martin.

SUNDAY: JANUARY FOURTEENTH

MORNING SERVICE

Topic: Making Common Cause for Christ

I. Christian churchmanship today in its own way must say, "Reservations, please." (1) A friend once asked a noted author how he found time to write. The reply came back, "I didn't find it, I took it." That's what we have to do for the important things. We will see that this time, this energy, and this money is reserved, spoken for in advance.

(2) Even a glance at our lives will remind us that we have to do this in other realms. There are priorities. If you want to enjoy the facilities and utilities offered your home by living in a modern city, you have to make commitments to receive the service. There are priorities less obvious, but even more real. If you want to have a family life that has richness and depth, it will make some claims upon you. We must see that there are times and experiences reserved for the family.

(3) Does it not follow that in the Christian life a test of the decision you make about Christ is whether you reserve the time, the resources, and the energy to serve his cause? If you really say to Christ, "Yes, I will follow," there is a sense in which he replies, "Your reservations, please." Your following will mean little unless it touches your time and your resources.

II. Churchmanship today requires another phrase, "Call out the reserves." (1) Those reserves are tremendous. Most business institutions have a practice of publishing their reserves so that everyone may know that they are stable and secure. But we have never even been able to list the reserves in terms of service and strength that are in the Church of Christ. But this we know: Much of it has not yet been used or even awakened.

(2) Any man or woman who has cared enough about Christ some time in his life to ask to become a part of his Church is an untapped reserve. The seed of service is in him. No small part of our churchmanship today is to help this great reserve of people, who have put one foot in the Church but no more, come all the rest of the way in until at last they move toward the center of the experience and the service to be rendered.

III. There is a third phrase from our common speech which ought to be before consecrated Christian churchmen these days: "Danger, construction ahead."

(1) Have we gone beyond the note of daring and danger in being a Christian? Sometimes we can only answer, Yes, we have. We have settled down to being very respectable, very commonplace, very dead level. Yet, there is something in the heart of all of us, if

SUNDAY: JANUARY FOURTEENTH 87

there is a spark of life in us, that responds to the challenge that says, Come, dare something with me.

(2) Christ came a long time ago with a word like that. Have we heard it so often that it has lost its urgency? The call is to sacrifice, to the giving of ourselves. Many a person who thinks he is waiting until he feels like it will never feel like it until he makes his decision and gets into the Christian cause. George Eliot causes one of her characters to say, "We Florentines live scrupulously in order that we may spend splendidly." It is the splendid giving of ourselves in response to an hour like this which is the mark of a churchmanship for this hour. The sign is very clear, "Danger, construction ahead." But that's the kind of hour that makes the Christian cause so wonderfully important, even exciting.

IV. The fourth phrase is, "Unconditional surrender." This is the center of the Christian experience. A famous tightrope walker from France came to this country at the close of the last century. After winning much fame by his spectacular feats, he announced that he would walk a tightrope across Niagara Falls. He asked for volunteers because he wanted to carry a young man on his shoulders. The young man who volunteered and was accepted has told the story of his training. The one thing Blondin said to him over and over was this: "Remember, my will is supreme. You must not resist me in any way. I must be completely in command." So, they practiced over and over that this discipline might be learned. The crossing was successfully made. That young man who volunteered later became a Christian, one of the early members of the Christian Endeavor movement. Many times he told this story to young people, because he said that it was here he learned the lesson of his life. Christ says to a man: My will must be supreme. You must not resist but surrender that I may make your true life.—Gene E. Bartlett.

Worship Aids

CALL TO WORSHIP. "Make a joyful noise unto the Lord, all ye lands. Serve the Lord with gladness: come before his presence with singing. Enter into his gates with thanksgiving, and into his courts with praise: be thankful unto him, and bless his name." Ps. 100: 1–2, 4.

INVOCATION. Almighty and merciful God, who hast created us for thy service and glory: we confess in thy holy presence that we have broken thy commandments and sinned against thee. We have offended by our deeds, by our thoughts, and by the sinful impulses and desires of our hearts. In the greatness of thy love shed abroad in us a holy sorrow for all our transgressions and make our wills obedient to thy perfect love revealed in Christ Jesus our Lord and Savior.

OFFERTORY SENTENCE. "Unto whomsoever much is given, of him shall be much required: and to whom men have committed much, of him they will ask the more." Luke 12:48.

OFFERTORY. Our Father, take us with all of our failures and develop us after thine own heart. Give us more of the mind of the Master, more of his spirit of compassion, and more of his sacrificial and loving heart.

PRAYER. God our Father, who in Christ art the Savior of the world: we remember with gratitude all messengers of thy Word who through stormy seas and perilous paths brought the Gospel to our fathers. Without this precious heritage we could not this hour rejoice in the gift of thy life and love. Bestow upon us strength and courage that our faith and deeds may become a consistent witness unto all who watch our ways. May those who love thee not be persuaded by thy truth and those who know thee not find in Christ life's deepest thirst satisfied. Impart to us the world-wide vision of the Spirit which belongs to thy disciples.

O God, whose Spirit calls us to serve in thy Kingdom: we utter our praise for the work of our missionaries in many lands. We are grateful that through them our devotion to thee may bear fruit. Be especially near to those who because of persecution are suffering imprisonment or hardship. By thy grace let the upheavals and confusions of the peoples in our time become a means unto the furtherance of the Gospel of him who loved us and gave himself for us.—Samuel J. Schmiechen.

Illustrations

AN ARMY EN ROUTE. The Church was never designed as a comfort station. It was never intended to be a mere haven of rest, a social unit, a camaraderie of like-minded souls, or even a fortress. The Church is an army en route. Jesus said, "I have not come to bring peace, but a sword." The classic stance of a Christian is not a man scampering for security, or cowering for protection, or crouching in defense, or even rising to resist. Rather it is a man striding ahead, moving out in the name of the triumphant Christ.—*Decision.*

LEADERSHIP. The Church must lead not only in religion, but in life. It must minister not only to the spirit, but to the whole man, the whole community. It must be into the revolutionary waves that will sweep the world relevant as well as reverent.—Charles H. Percy.

Sermon Suggestions

UNDERSTANDING THE BIBLE. (1) Read the Bible in the light of God's revelation in Christ. (2) Read the Bible with a readiness to hear what it says. (3) Read the Bible to hear what new truth the Holy Spirit would today say to us. (4) Read the Bible with a readiness not only to hear but also to do the will of God.—Ernest Trice Thompson.

DEATH HATH NO DOMINION. When the body of Jesus was buried in Joseph's tomb, the cause for which he lived and for which he died seemed even to his own disciples to have suffered final defeat, but before many days passed that influence of Jesus was much more powerful and widespread than it had ever been before. (1) Repeatedly he has been buried in partisan prejudices and in bitter theological disputes, but he has come to life again in lives transformed, like Paul and Augustine and Francis. (2) Again and again he has been buried in deadly formalism, but he has come to life again in music that set men marching toward the Kingdom of God, in poetry that restored something of the lost radiance, in lives made better by his presence. (3) More than once he has been buried in churches which have forgotten his spirit and overlooked his message, but in every such hour one might have said, "He is not here, he is risen and goeth before you into a world created anew by the power of his spirit." —Raymond C. Brooks.

EVENING SERVICE

Topic: Toward a More Effective Church

TEXT: John 14:13.

I. The effectiveness of the Church depends on its vision of God. (1) If a stranger who knew nothing of Christianity, though understanding our language, wandered into one of our churches on a Sunday and stayed for a service, what sort of picture would be suggested to his mind of the God we worship?

(2) How can our church services convey a sense of greatness and majesty of God if our own view of him is small and mean? Do we ever think of him as the psalmists thought of him, majestic in his creative artistry, wonderful in his providential care?

II. The effectiveness of the Church

SUNDAY: JANUARY TWENTY-FIRST

depends on its belief in the uniqueness of the Gospel, on the strength of its conviction that "there is none other name under heaven given among men by which we must be saved."

(1) The Christian faith is unique, unique in its demands upon the human conscience, unique in what it offers to sinful men. The uniqueness of the Gospel is in Christ himself, in what he was, what he did, and what he does still. We cannot enter into fullness of living until we meet with him, and he sets us free.

(2) If the Gospel is unique, if it is true that God has given him a name that is above every name, then everyone has the right to hear it, and to have the opportunity of saying "Yes" or "No" to Christ. A Church that is sure of the uniqueness of the Gospel will be under constraint to make it known.

III. The effectiveness of the Church depends on its readiness to use its spiritual resources. (1) How far is the Church as you know it held back by lack of imagination, prejudice, conservatism, timidity, unwillingness to put Christ's promise to the test?

(2) Evidence is not lacking that great things begin to happen when Christ is taken at his word.

(3) I am not pleading for any particular strategy. Only that we should be more ready to attempt great things for God, trusting in the mighty power of his Spirit. He is calling his Church to a greater effectiveness.—Wilfred Salmon.

SUNDAY: JANUARY TWENTY-FIRST

MORNING SERVICE

Topic: Who Am I?

TEXTS: Gen. 2:7; I John 3:2.

Against the backdrop of Scripture—or within its framework—let us meet the inquiring, often plaintive, voice of today's person who asks, "Who am I?" Who, what, and why is this person he calls *himself*? What is man, after all?

I. *A personal-sensitive being.* (1) The child best demonstrates that the human being is a personal-sensitive individual, sensitive to all things around and, for the child at least, especially the good things.

(2) Why does a young person have those ambitions, goals, and desires? Because God has put something in man that is often impatient with the present status of things. Youth's ambitions, imagination, and achievements are indicative of his divine creaturehood.

(3) The adult has achievement drives, too. The father is anxious to have a satisfactory income in order to provide for his family. The mother is anxious to provide for the needs of the family and to keep them whole and happy. These are times when man as a personal-sensitive being must make a judgment with himself and decide to what extent God may want him to fulfill his purposes within his capacities and time, and let the greater goals be achieved by others.

(4) Man is also a social being. He must live in harmony, hopefully, with those around him. He is always a part of a community, beginning with the family and the kinfolk; then it enlarges to the neighborhood around him, then the village, town, or city, and on to the nation and the world.

(5) Who are you? You are a personal-sensitive being, sensitive to the people around you and to your place among those people. You are a being of creative purposefulness, and you cannot rest if there is something more or greater which you can possibly accomplish.

II. *A physical-psychological being.*
(1) Gen. 2:7 is the majestic statement of the fact that man as an animate being, composed of the same

chemicals, minerals, and fluids that are common on this earth, is a personality inbreathed by deity.

(2) As a physical being, man follows the same principles in all animate life for reproduction, for provision, for nurture and sustenance, and for protection against that which would destroy. The biologist tells us how the seed germinates and produces "the first blade, then the ear, then the full corn appears," whether that seed is for a plant or a tree or the "seed" for an animate organism within the womb of the female being of the species. As it does so it soon ceases to be just an embryo; after a few weeks it has become a recognizable form, and then as more weeks and months go by that form becomes an amazing likeness of its parents.

(3) Now why did a protrusion grow on this part or that part of the embryo, here to become an arm, there a leg, etc.? Why did these things thus develop? The biologist tells us accurately how it is done, but why each cell does what it does and when to proceed to the next step, why this ever began neither the biologist nor the geneticist assays to tell us.

(4) Why then does each cell do what it does? God has fed the code into it. It may not be without point that these life-producing elements are acids. Perhaps there may be an electrolytic process as well as an electronic. Whatever the process, that mini-microscopic computer advises the cell how to develop, what proteins to make, and what to do with them. Thus the control of our bodies through chemical reaction takes place.

(5) The concept becomes somewhat awesome when it is suggested that not only the body, its form, color, strength, and so on are thus directed, but even the mind, the emotions, and the attitudes may be so influenced and "programmed." We have unlocked at least some doors to the language of life that cannot be ignored in honestly seeking to understand the doctrine of man. The genes determine to some meaningful extent what we do and what we are. The behavioral sciences hold the greatest power potential yet, and the biological revolution may prove to be greater than the industrial revolution of the late nineteenth and early twentieth centuries or the technological and nuclear revolutions of more recent decades.

(6) While the geneticist has begun to know the language of life, he also knows that the key to life is deeper than anything he has yet discovered. What, for example, set the blueprint by which these mechanisms function? Who set it? If it were purely by chance, how could its delicate balance so long have been maintained?

(7) The credo of creation points up the mystery and puts the key where it belongs—and many scientists readily concur—in the hand of God. "So God formed man out of the . . ." chemicals, minerals, and fluids, the common stuff of earth; "and God breathed into . . ." that organic form the genius of human life which thinks, invents, organizes, communicates, and all the rest. God made the amazing physical-psychological being that he is.

III. *A spiritual-immortal being.* Look again at those words in Gen. 1:27 and 2:7: "Then the Lord God said, 'Let us make man in our image.'" "So God formed man out of the dust of the ground and breathed into his nostrils the breath of life, and man became a living being." Between these two, man's greatness and nobility are established.

(1) What is the "image of God"? It is the human spirit as we know it and as we have not yet fully understood it.

(a) The image of God in man includes his personality, that "real self" which experiences the joys, the love, affection, and satisfaction of purpose, as well as the hurts of loss, hate, or sorrow.

(b) That image includes man's intellect—the ability to gather information, to store it away in the brain, and to call upon it when he desires it or

SUNDAY: JANUARY TWENTY-FIRST

needs it for comprehension or in making a value judgment or initiating communication or invention.

(c) The image of God includes will—the ability to take the value judgment and act upon it, either positively by saying yes to going the way that judgment points or by saying no and going in another direction because of certain other desires that he wants to fulfill. It is this decision-making prerogative, freely operative, which, from the human side, makes man a sinner or a saint, an unresponsive unbeliever or a God-accepted believer.

(d) The image of God speaks of immortality—the desire within every person for ongoing life. This sense of infinity in man is part of the hallmark, the fingerprint to God, in humanity. It is doubtless significant that the Greeks called man by the word *Anthropos,* from which we get the word anthropology, the study of man. Anthropos means "the up-looking one." Man is a bi-ped that looks physically forward and upward; but more than that, he is a spiritual being that looks up toward God. Despite man's often blatant degeneracy, the indelible mark of his spiritual heritage and hope is clearly discernible.

(2) This is the doctrine of man: created by and for God, willfully sinning against God, redeemed and regenerated by God, ultimately fulfilled in and with God for eternity. Whether the source of reference is the Scripture or man as a person in his environment or the inner structure and nature of the human spirit, one comes inevitably to the conclusion stated so succinctly by St. Augustine, "We are made by thee, and our souls are restless, O God, until they rest in thee."—Paul P. Fryhling.

Worship Aids

CALL TO WORSHIP. "The Lord is exalted; for he dwelleth on high: he hath filled Zion with judgment and righteousness. And wisdom and knowledge shall be the stability of thy times, and strength of salvation: the fear of the Lord is his treasure." Isa. 33:5–6.

INVOCATION. Lord God Almighty, holy and eternal Father, who dwellest in the high and lofty place, with him also that is of a humble and contrite spirit: we come before thee, beseeching thee to cleanse us by the grace of thy Holy Spirit, that we may give praise to thee, now and forever.

OFFERTORY. Our Father, may we who have seen thy providential hand in all the experiences of our lives seek to possess such greatness of mind and spirit that we shall be enabled to offer these gifts with an unselfish joyfulness.

OFFERTORY SENTENCE. "If thou draw out thy soul to the hungry, and satisfy the afflicted soul; then shall thy light rise in obscurity, and thy darkness be as the noonday." Isa. 58:10.

PRAYER. In these days of tension when life is pulled taut as a bowstring, we turn to thee, our heavenly Father, seeking refreshment and reinvigoration, renewal and recreation. We know that with thy help we can bring to fruition every hope, aspiration, and task of life. Help us, O God, to put our smallness aside, to lose ourselves in others and their needs, to forgive the hurts that are often thoughtlessly inflicted upon us, and to return good for evil.

Help us to strive and struggle to bring peace back into the realm of human experience in the knowledge that there will be peace without when there is peace within. Help us to restore faith in life and certitude in religion. May we put Christ at the center of everything that we are and do, recognizing that when he is at life's center we can become the channels of thy power. We offer this prayer out of the limited experience which is ours, lifting it unto thee who art the ultimate experience. —Chester E. Hodgson.

Illustrations

QUESTION. A standard test given to all astronauts includes the question, "Who am I?" and the candidate is required to give twenty answers to that question. John H. Glenn recalls that the first few answers were easy: "I am a man; I am a Marine; I am a flier; I am an officer." But, he says, "when I got down near the end of the list, it was not easy to figure out just who I am."

EXPERIENCING GRACE. Grace strikes us when our disgust for our own being, our own indifference, our weakness, our hostility, and our lack of direction and composure have become intolerable to us. Sometimes, at that moment, a wave of light breaks into our darkness and it is as though a voice were saying, "You are accepted." You are accepted, accepted by that which is greater than you. Simply accept the fact that you are accepted! If that happens to us, we experience grace.—Paul Tillich in *The Shaking of the Foundations.*

Sermon Suggestions

ON ACCEPTING YOURSELF. Text: Gen. 1:27. (1) Accept yourself—the real you—knowing that you are a wonderful creation, made to love and to be loved, to labor, to create, to achieve, to forgive, to trust. (2) Accept yourself—the real you—knowing that no apology is needed for who you are or what you are, for God made you to be loving and to be free. (3) Accept yourself—the real you—in the circumstances in which you find yourself, knowing that God will labor with you to be your best where you are. (4) Accept yourself—the real you—knowing that you are never alone, that God is the ground of your being, involved in all that you do and concerned in every affair of your life. (5) Accept yourself—the real you—knowing that you are a lovable creature and that you can be set free from all that makes you unloving.—Wallace Fridy in *The Sanctuary.*

BACKING OUR FAITH WITH OUR BRAINS. Text: Matt. 22:37. (1) God's judgment is upon the evil mind. (2) God's method of transforming a person's life comes through the renewing of the mind. (See Isa. 55:6–7.) (3) There are certain benefits that God brings to the life when one's mind is committed to him. (a) The committed mind knows the will of God. (See Rom. 12:2.) (b) Besides knowing the will of God you will know the peace of God. (See Isa. 26:3–4.) (c) The committed mind will be sound. (See II Tim. 1:7.)—Walter L. Dosch.

EVENING SERVICE

Topic: But There Is Judgment
SCRIPTURE: Gen. 18:23–25.

I. At our peril we forget the inevitability of divine judgment. (1) Ours is a moral universe, and God will not be mocked. The folks of Sodom never bothered their heads about God's judgment. They sinned to their hearts' delight and basked in immorality.

(2) We fool ourselves if we hide under the sentimental picture of "Gentle Jesus, meek and mild," forgetting that the entire New Testament reveals Jesus in all his majestic greatness as Lord and Judge.

II. The inevitability of divine judgment should drive us not to despair but, like Abraham, to urgent, earnest intercessory prayer.

(1) Abraham knew that Sodom deserved punishment, as our world does today. But he was tortured by the thought of the righteous being destroyed along with the wicked.

(2) Yet how right he was in pouring forth himself in earnest persevering prayer. For hours he pled with God for the people whom he himself had sought to help. And his prayers were not in vain.

III. How blessed we are if we share Abraham's certainty of God's righteous character. Abraham, you see, shuddered at the thought of the righteous in Sodom being slaughtered along with the sinful, and he was convinced that God must share his feelings. From his own poor conscience, he lifted his eyes to the great, holy God, whose moral nature was infinitely grander and nobler than his own. "Shall not the Judge of all the earth do right?" Our cause for confidence is even greater. "He who has seen me," says Jesus, "has seen the Father." Righteous love is indeed on the throne of the universe.—Charles S. Morrice.

SUNDAY: JANUARY TWENTY-EIGHTH

MORNING SERVICE

Topic: **Faith and Freedom under God.**
TEXT: Gal. 5:1.

We are in the midst of revolution. Ferment, revolt, and rebellion are undeniably the characteristics of our times. This is the tension in which we live. Where do we take our stand? How are we reacting?

I. We must really listen to the issues that are being raised. (1) The scribes and Pharisees refused to listen to Jesus. He came to them with the truth that would have liberated them from their error and brought them to God and eternal life. They did not like what they were hearing, so they silenced his voice by crucifixion.

(2) Is anybody listening today? Are we listening? Surely not all rebel voices are speaking the truth. Some are vomiting filth that can only be sourced in the Devil himself. Many protest voices are motivated by sheer sensualism and self-centeredness. But we must keep on listening, discerning as best we can truth from error. By remaining sensitive to the truth, we will repent when sin and hypocrisy are exposed in us; we will be willing to change when change is needed; we will do what is right where injustice prevails; and we will provide enlightened opinion leadership within the circles of our influence. We must listen to the voices that are now being raised, for we know not when nor from where the voice of truth will be speaking.

II. We must live by established principles. These are difficult days in which we live. Time and again we are confronted with the necessity of making a decision. How do we stand fast in this kind of a world? The principles that brought us to faith and freedom under God have not changed.

(1) There must be a personal commitment to Jesus Christ as personal Savior. What does this mean? It means we are cleansed, pardoned, and set free from the guilt of all past sins by the virtue of God's grace and not our own works, no matter how good they may appear. God's grace is in Jesus Christ, crucified and risen. When our eyes are opened to behold this wondrous love and by faith, we respond to him and accept him as Savior. Then and only then do we come into the glorious liberty of the children of God.

(2) Lest your commitment to Jesus Christ becomes too subjective and becomes sentimentalized, too easily molded and adapted to the accepted life styles which are typical of the seventies, remember that you are committed to Jesus Christ as he is revealed in the Scriptures. The most memorable and the most important legacy for freedom was Luther's declaration: "My conscience is captive to the word of God. Here I stand, I cannot do otherwise."

(3) A Christian is called by God to live as a man for others. This is the "universal priesthood of all believers." This affirms, not only that each Christian believer had freedom to pray to God directly, through Jesus Christ himself, but also to serve others through love. The clergy has no corner on God when it comes to intercessory prayer,

and surely when one intercedes on behalf of another at the throne of grace, he is performing the function of a priest.

(4) As Christian freedom is not license to do as I please in the indulgence of my flesh, so Christian freedom is not freedom to do as I please irrespective of the good of my neighbor. (See Gal. 5:13.) Love cannot exploit a neighbor for selfish or personal reasons. Our faith and freedom under God is established by our commitment to Jesus Christ as personal Savior, our serious acceptance of the Scriptural norm, our obedience to God's call to live as a man for others and to live in obedience to God's will. —Walter L. Dosch.

Worship Aids

CALL TO WORSHIP. "Let us search and try our ways, and turn again to the Lord. Let us lift up our heart with our hands unto God in the heavens." Lam. 3:40–41.

INVOCATION. Almighty God, Fountain of all good, kindle in us insight and aspiration, that this hour of prayer may be a moment of time lived in eternity. Open our ears that we may hear. Soften our hearts that we may receive thy truth. Reveal thyself to us here that we may learn to find thee everywhere.

OFFERTORY SENTENCE. "What shall I render unto the Lord for all his benefits toward me? I will pay my vows unto the Lord now in the presence of all his people." Ps. 116:12–14.

OFFERTORY PRAYER. We give thee thanks, O Father, that through our tithes and offerings thou dost give us an opportunity to illuminate the dimness of the future and to glorify our present life with the word of him who is the Light of the world.

PRAYER. O God, so much of our worship is taken up with talking about thee! In these moments we are talking with thee. We bring thee more than words of praise; we offer thee our lives to be cleansed of evil and self-conceit.

May we live the abundant and eternal life of which Jesus is the pattern and the giver. When the pressure of opinion draws us into conformity may we adhere to the truth. When ease lures us may we be strong. When sorrow comes and disappointment confronts us may we face them with valor that is free from self-pity and frenzy. When the tides of doubt or disillusionment sweep about us may we cling to the cords of faith we have tested until they greaten to a strand that cannot be broken.

We pray not for ourselves alone. We offer our petitions for those whose poverty dulls their spiritual hunger; for those who suffer from injustice and are barred from opportunity; for those in whose homes selfishness and indifference have banished love and fidelity. Mindful of the brave struggle many are making, we beseech thee to grant them the courage to overcome hardship, the integrity that survives sneers, and the goodwill that can prevail over hostility.

May the spirit of Jesus quicken in men's lives such righteousness, such loving concern, and such glad trust in thee that thou canst once again look on thy handiwork and see that it is good.—Harold L. Bowman.

Illustrations

APATHY AND CYNICISM. I have a profound personal conviction that, if we are brought to a disaster through an atomic cataclysm, it will not be through the machinations of evil men but by the apathy and cynicism of men of goodwill. For apathy and cynicism are at bottom simply manifestations of unbelief, unbelief which takes the form of a refusal to confront the desperate chaos of the world.—Carey B. Joynt.

CHANGE OF CLIMATE. What you are

SUNDAY: JANUARY TWENTY-EIGHTH

doing when you are really listening is putting your hand quietly in the other man's life and feeling gently along the rim of his soul until you come to a crack, some frustration, some problem, or anguish you sense he may or may not be totally conscious of. As you are listening, you are loving this person and accepting him just as he is. The magic of this kind of concern is that you will often find your conversation moving imperceptibly from the general surface talk of the world situation, the weather, into the intimate world of families and of hopes, of his life and yours. This change of climate sometimes takes place in a very short time in a listening atmosphere of concern and trust.—Keith Miller in *The Taste of New Wine*.

Sermon Suggestions

DENYING YOURSELF. (1) Deny yourself the luxury of pettiness. (2) Deny yourself the luxury of pessimism. (3) Deny yourself the luxury of self-pity. (4) Deny yourself the luxury of uncontrolled anger.—William Arthur Ward.

WHERE FREEDOM ENDS AND LICENSE BEGINS. Text: Gal. 5:13. (1) Freedom becomes license when we hurt others. "Use not liberty for an occasion for the flesh, but by love serve one another," Paul admonishes his hearers. (2) Freedom ends and license begins when we fail to postpone immediate gratification for a higher good. (3) Freedom lapses into license unless we are willing to couple our actions with responsibility to others.—Lloyd J. Salazar.

THE ENEMY WITHIN. Scripture: Rom. 7:7-25. (1) Our enemy is within ourselves. (2) This enemy tricks us into believing that our enemy is without. (3) If we conquer the "enemy within," we discover that the "enemy without" is our brother.—Levon G. King.

EVENING SERVICE

Topic: An Unworthy Question

TEXT: "What shall we have therefore?" Matt. 19:27.

We are perhaps surprised—even a little disgusted—that Peter put this question to his Lord. Those who follow Christ for what they get out of it cannot be ideal disciples. "Rice" Christians are not good Christians.

(a) Criticism is held somewhat in check, however, by the fact that the Master did not reproach Peter. He took the apostle's question seriously and vouchsafed a clear and definite answer. "Every one that hath forsaken houses, or brethren for my name's sake, shall receive an hundredfold."

(b) The Lord Jesus does not discourage his disciples from rejoicing in their rich heritage. There is no sin in calling attention to the credit side of the Christian balance sheet.

(c) There are profits which a Christian man must forego: there are pleasures in which no Christian may indulge. Self-denial is an inescapable condition of the Christian life. But it is meet, right, and our bounden duty to bear witness to the fact that Christ bestows "an hundredfold" more than he demands.

I. One of the blessings which the Lord imparts to his faithful followers is the certainty that good will ultimately triumph over evil.

(1) Peter is assured that there will be a regeneration, that the "Son of man shall sit in the throne of his glory," and that "ye also shall sit upon twelve thrones, judging the twelve tribes of Israel." This is not the place to discuss all the implications of the promise, but it is beyond all question that victory will crown the sacrifice offered by the Lamb of God, and the lesser sacrifices required of his servants will not be in vain.

(2) Amid the abounding alarms and excursions of the present day, the Christian, believing his Lord, can never be utterly cast down. "He must reign."

II. It is not only in relation to the world at large but also in the experience of the individual that the credit side of the Christian balance sheet becomes real and operative. "Lo, I am with you always," said the Master. "It shall be given you in that same hour what ye shall speak" is his abiding promise. In small affairs, as well as in times of crisis, we have had abundant evidence of guidance from on high.

III. God, who directs us with his eye, sometimes bestows his promised bounties through human channels.

(1) The Christian fellowship is often the medium of blessings and inspirations which only Zion's children know.

(2) The "great cloud of witnesses" is not a figment of the imagination; the "communion of saints" is not a mystical unreality. "The fellowship of the prophets" is one of God's good gifts to all who serve him. No other fellowship on earth can compare with that of the friends of Jesus.

IV. "What shall we have therefore?" (1) Christ's answer to Peter may be summed up in words which guarantee solid joys and lasting pleasure to every Christian soul. The three great things are his: faith, which outlives every conceivable woe and disaster; hope, which lives and sings; and love, which never fails.

(2) There is only one way to life which is life indeed. The joys which know no end can be found only in him who is "the way, the truth, and the life." What we give up for his sake is not worthy to be compared with what we gain in him.

(3) We are glad that Peter asked his unworthy question, after all.—Norman E. Dando.

SUNDAY: FEBRUARY FOURTH

MORNING SERVICE

Topic: "I Am the Way"
TEXT: John 14:6.

I. *How Christ is the Way.* (1) Christ is the Way because he teaches us how to know God. It is in Christ that we know God, by reading about him in his holy Word. When Jesus took upon him our flesh and died for our sins, he gave us liberty and boldness to enter into the Holiest by his own blood, by a new and living way, a lawful way for the sinner to the Father. The Incarnation was not enough without the Crucifixion. So Jesus is infinitely greater than the Bible. Just as there is more in the sun than in the moon and the stars, more in the face than in the portrait of it, so there is more in Jesus than in any revelation of him in his Word.

(2) Christ is the Way not only because he died for us, but also because he resurrected and went to intercede for us in heaven. An intercessor is one who acts between two parties or two individuals. Christ is God and Man, and he makes our imperfect prayers acceptable unto God, and so we ask "for the sake of" or "through Jesus Christ our Lord." It is "by him that we have access to the Father."

II. *How are we to follow this Way?* This Way like every other way has its own peculiar characteristics.

(1) It is the Way of faith and not of sight. We cannot see God by our visual aid; indeed, we cannot visibly see heaven or hell. We must believe in them by faith. Those who choose the way of faith go out each day with the Cross in their hearts, saying, "By this sign, conquer." They know that the things of faith last and that faith abides.

(2) It is the Way of holiness and obedience. (a) Christianity is to triumph, not by its dogmas or its doctrines or its creeds, but rather by the characters which it produces. Men may misunderstand our doctrines, ignore our dogmas, and refute our creeds, but they cannot misinterpret or be deceived by

SUNDAY: FEBRUARY FOURTH

the flame of holiness which burns within the Christian and spreads itself in a noble character going about doing good.

(b) Obedience to God means service for God. Christ came "to minister," and because of his great example of obedience he could descend so low as to wash the dirty feet of his disciples, forgive a prostitute her manifold sins, and receive and bless little children, acts which were so alien and foreign to his day and age.

(3) It is the Way of love. This means that we must try and do the hardest thing of all, namely, to love our enemies. Christ could do this with those who spat on him. Following his example, Lazarus has forgiven many a hateful and intolerable Dives. The rich man in the parable could have built a bridge by the Way of love to fill in the great social gulf between them, but he did not have the essential materials of sympathy, pity, and compassion to build such a bridge.

III. *Companions of the Way.* (1) We must band together as useful, practical Christians, seeking to do good in every way. We Christians are very much like a bunch of keys. If you look at such a bunch you will notice that they are a variety, with different sizes and various shapes. We Christians are the same. Keys are kept together by a ring. So if we follow him who is the Way, we shall be bound together by the ring of love.

(2) Remember, the worst enemy of keys is rust, and is not that the worst enemy of the Christian? By rust in the life of the Christian I mean, of course, laziness. The Apostle warns us not to be weary in well-doing. Amos the prophet cries, "Woe to them that are at ease in Zion." Lazy Christians are the greatest hindrance to the advancement of Christ's gospel in the world today. But the key's best friend is a drop of oil, and how true is this of the Christian also, for his best friend is the oil of the Spirit.—Albert Ashbden Hughes.

Worship Aids

CALL TO WORSHIP. "Oh that men would praise the Lord for his goodness, and for his wonderful works to the children of men! For he satisfieth the longing soul, and filleth the hungry soul with goodness." Ps. 107:8–9.

INVOCATION. O heavenly Father, who hast given us a true faith and a sure hope: help us, we pray thee, to live as those who believe and trust in the communion of saints, the forgiveness of sins, and the resurrection to life everlasting; and strengthen this faith and hope in us all the days of our life.

OFFERTORY SENTENCE. "Take heed what ye hear: with what measure ye mete, it shall be measured to you: and unto you that hear shall more be given." Mark 4:24.

OFFERTORY PRAYER. O God, who hast given us thy Son to be an example and a help to our weakness in following the path that leadeth unto life, grant us so to be his disciples that we may walk in his footsteps.

PRAYER. Almighty and most gracious God, Giver of every good and perfect gift, we bow our heads and lift our hearts to thee in gratitude for thy many great gifts:

For the gift of life and the ability to enjoy it and use it in thy service; for the gifts of faith, freedom, and fellowship, through which we come to know thee and love thee, we give thee thanks.

For the gift of thy Son, our Lord and Master Jesus Christ, whom we would learn to love and to serve more perfectly, we praise and bless thee, Father of us all.

For this mighty and mysterious universe in which we live and for the good earth which provides us with all our bodily needs, we raise our voices in thanksgiving.

For the world within, deeper than we dare to look, higher than we care to climb; for the great kingdom of the mind and the silent spaces of the soul, we come before thee with thankful hearts.

For the truth which makes us free and for the vision without which we would perish, we offer thee our prayer of thanksgiving in the name and spirit of him who gave himself for us, even Jesus Christ our Lord.—John H. Gregg.

Illustrations

THE WORK OF THE SAVIOR. The Savior works mightily every day, drawing men to religion, persuading them to virtue, teaching them about immortality, quickening their thirst for heavenly things, revealing the knowledge of the Father, inspiring strength in the face of death, manifesting himself to each.—St. Athanasius.

ROAD MAP. If we think of life as a journey and consider it to be the opportunity for getting from where we are to where we want to be, we will have a working rule that provides us with both a purpose and expanding possibilities for our lives.—Fred P. Corson.

Sermon Suggestions

JESUS' "GO" MOVEMENT. Scripture: Matt. 28:16-20. (1) Go—into the world. (2) Go—preach the Gospel by example. (3) Go—by Christ to your neighbor. (4) Go—be what you are called to become.—Duane A. Kofahl.

CHRIST: THE ONLY HOPE. (1) What he is. (2) What he taught. (3) What he did. (4) What he promises.—W. Douglas Hudgins.

EVENING SERVICE

Topic: Salvation through Christ
SCRIPTURE: Rom. 7:24-25.
I. The first step to freedom from our selfishness and sin is to have faith in Christ. (1) That does not mean we immediately understand and accept all the doctrines of the Christian religion. Theological ideas, like the Incarnation and Eternal Judgment, can wait until we are further advanced in the Christian life. We begin with Jesus.

(2) The human heart responds naturally to Christ. His heroic qualities appeal to the heroism in our youth. His concern for those who are in need calls forth a response from all who are discouraged. His message of the Kingdom catches the enthusiasm of all who are seeking for a way by which this tired world can be given new life and hope.

II. After confessing that we believe in Christ and that we have faith in him, one more step is necessary. We are called upon to commit our lives to his keeping. We bring him our talents and our weaknesses, our hopes and our disappointments. We ask him to forgive all that is unworthy and to bless our abilities and our strength during the days which are ahead.

(1) No experience of faith is complete without this act of surrender. After all, it was the self which was the root of our trouble. By our surrender of self, we turn over to Christ all that we are and allow him to make of us whatever it is his will to make.

(2) The text implies that the road to salvation through Christ is an upward path. It is an escape from a prison in which we often seemed destined to serve a life sentence. The direction is upward, and the guidance of Christ is sufficient for every step of the journey.

(3) It is possible for you to have a similar experience. It does not matter what you have done, what motives have dominated your life, or what sordid thoughts have sullied your mind! If you are willing to believe in Christ and to surrender your life to him, you can know the joy of salvation.—G. Ernest Thomas.

SUNDAY: FEBRUARY ELEVENTH

MORNING SERVICE

Topic: The God of All (Race Relations Sunday)

Text: Rom. 3:29.

We must keep reminding ourselves that God is the God not of one nation alone, that he has no favorites, is no respecter of persons or nationalities. His love and grace reach out to all mankind. He is concerned about all. He is the God of all. Let us dwell on three things.

I. Our common humanity. (1) Paul says all alike have sinned. We all share a sinful nature. Selfishness, pride, jealousy know no frontiers. So do love and kindliness, courage and gallantry, joy and hope, as well as disappointment, sorrow, and death.

(2) We all come from the same creative Hand. We are all God's creatures, rich and poor, learned and unlearned, black or white. Beneath all surface differences God made us alike. To be a man means to be a fellowman.

II. God's gifts have never been limited to any one race. (1) "Do you suppose that God is the God of the Jews alone?" The world owes much to the Jew—in art, music, philosophy, science, and the like. And in the realm of religion his contribution has been outstanding. The world's Savior was a Jew. That, however, should not blind us to the fact that the gifts of God have not been confined to that particular people.

(2) Different people have different gifts. Thank God, we don't live in a monotonous, dead-level world. While, however, we are conscious of our own gifts we should not be blind to the gifts of others, nor should we make of our own a pedestal for pride. Rather should we receive them with humility and gratitude and use them responsibly.

III. The third thing is the fact and significance of the Cross. "Christ died for all." It was this fact before which, when once admitted, all distinctions, national and other, vanished.

(1) The Cross is the great leveler. It puts us all on the same footing. In its presence and his presence who died on it, there is neither Jew nor Greek. All are one. He has broken down the walls of partition. The Cross strikes out "nationality" and writes in its place "humanity." Christ died for all.

(2) "Do you suppose that God is the God of the Jews alone?" Is he not the God of Gentiles also? Certainly, of Gentiles also, of everybody. Humanity at bottom is one. God's gifts are not the monopoly of any particular race or people. The gospel with the Cross at its heart is a world-wide gospel, for all who have faith.—A. Stanley Hill.

Worship Aids

CALL TO WORSHIP. "Now in Christ Jesus ye who sometimes were far off are made nigh by the blood of Christ. For he is of our peace, who hath made both one, and hath broken down the middle wall of partition between us. Now therefore ye are no more strangers and foreigners, but fellowcitizens with the saints and of the household of God." Eph. 2:13-14, 19.

INVOCATION. Almighty God, our heavenly Father, we lift up our hearts to thee, invoking thy blessing upon our worship. Thou hast made us one in our need of thee, one in our yearning for a strength beyond the self, one in our quest for the peace which passeth all understanding. Cleanse our hearts and open our minds that thy truth may enter our lives, to the glory of thy Son, Jesus Christ our Lord.

OFFERTORY SENTENCE. "Whatsoever ye would that men should do to you, do ye even so to them: for this is the law and the prophets." Matt. 7:12.

OFFERTORY PRAYER. O thou who art the Father of all, may we live as thy children and brothers of all whom thou hast made to dwell upon the face of the earth that thy kindness may be born in our hearts.

PRAYER. Eternal God, our Father, amidst the clang of confusion in this day, life sometimes seems too much for us. Often we slip from tested highways into the swamp of disillusionment and despair. Our cherished dreams for peace and goodness that have lured us into high adventure are only partly realized. The noble heights of vision for personal achievement and a better world have been unscaled and, at times, even our sight grows dim.

When such moods are upon us, dear Father, we turn with greater thankfulness to this sanctuary where the sense of thy unfailing presence is made fresh and vivid. We are grateful for the renewal of our sinking spirits, and we rejoice that here assurance is again made strong in the joy of mercy and forgiveness. We thank thee for trustworthy guidance as we set our feet once more upon the sure way and for corrected vision as we discern life in proper and wholesome perspective.

Thy love is complete and abiding, and we pray that thou wilt help us to use the strength and resources given to us here to understand others and to minister to their need.—Charles B. Tupper.

Illustrations

THE WAY. The glory of the early Church, feeling the fresh breezes of his spirit, was in the abolition of the problem of race. Here men of diverse backgrounds—proud friends and kinsmen of the Caesars and humble denizens of the back alleys of the cities of the empire—found in Christ a common gathering place which raised them to the level of a new, blessed relationship. Perhaps some poor slave in Philippi picked up a letter one night to read it to a gathering of the disinherited of the city. By the flickering light in a simple room he came to the close of the letter, sealed in an affection of brotherhood. These were the words that humble assembly heard: "All the saints salute you, chiefly they that are of Caesar's household." They found their answer to the problem of race in him who says, "I am the Way." In the beleaguered catacombs, in modest upper rooms, during the treasured hour around the table of the Lord, the early Christians wiped away their differences of race, awed a world with their devotion to all men, snapped the fascination which old Rome held over them.—Gardner C. Taylor.

LOVE AND STRENGTH. Without love he who is strong becomes a law for the weak, and the law makes those who are weak even weaker. It drives them into rebellion or indifference. Strength without love destroys first others, then itself. For love is not something that may be added to strength; it is an element of strength. For love is not an irrelevant emotion; it is the blood of life. Strength without love leads to separation, to control of the weak. Love reunites what is separated; it participates in what is weak, and God participates in our weakness and gives us strength by his participation.—Paul Tillich.

Sermon Suggestions

HUMANITY ONE IN CHRIST. Text: Col. 3:11. In Jesus Christ there cannot be (1) race distinction (Greek and Jew), (2) culture distinction (Barbarian and Scythian), (3) social end economic distinction (bond and free), or (4) sex distinction (male and female). —E. Stanley Jones.

THE BLOOD WE SHARE. Text: Acts 17:26. (1) The biblical emphasis on the fundamental unity of mankind forces us to reconsider the familiar idea of sharply distinct races within mankind. (2) The biblical emphasis on the fundamental unity of mankind is the basis for the fact of the universality of sin, the fact that all men are and all men have been sinners. (3) The biblical teaching of the essential unity of mankind is the foundation for the whole important concept of "the neighbor" in the New Testament.—John Primus.

EVENING SERVICE

Topic: Jesus Looks Great in Black

The Christian life is Jesus Christ doing his own thing in me—not me trying to do my thing. By his own power and will he has brought me into the family. What has this done for me?

I. I know who I am. I'm a son of God. I'm one of the brothers of Jesus Christ.

(1) And the beautiful thing is that this hasn't negated my blackness. If anything, it has confirmed it. God's intention is to live his life through my redeemed blackness.

(2) Since I am a member of the royal family of God, I can go out and face the world with a completely different attitude. I am secure in who I am: a black man in whom God is living. I no longer have to be ashamed. Black is beautiful, but it is a lot more beautiful since Jesus Christ is living through it. This is the discovery black people need to make today: Jesus looks great in black.

II. Not only do I know who I am, I know what I've got. (1) The Bible tells me that I am a joint heir with Jesus Christ. This means that, with Jesus Christ, I will inherit everything that God has. The Bible says that I am a partaker with Jesus Christ of every spiritual gift in heavenly places, which makes me the richest person in all the world. I don't mean this in terms of dollars and cents but in terms of the spiritual wealth that it takes to make a man a man.

(2) What makes a man a real man is his ability to love, his ability to be at peace, his ability to be patient, his ability to be temperate, his ability to have mercy—his ability to have all the "fruit of the Spirit" that we read about in the fifth chapter of Galatians.

(3) Because now that I am connected with Jesus Christ, I have a sense of security, not only as to who I am but what I have, a sense that God guides my destiny. Therefore, I can deal with my brother, both black and white, with a sense of security. I can fight injustice without having to worry about the repercussions. I can love my enemy without having to worry about being taken.

III. The Bible tells me, that I am seated together with Jesus Christ in the heavenly places (Eph. 1:20), which puts me on the highest social level in all the world. I don't have to break my neck to belong to any particular social group, because I am already on as high a level as you can get.

(1) I must be involved in the struggle for justice whether it concerns a white man or a black man. If a black man's rights are being denied, I must be committed to his fight because it is a matter of the Kingdom of God. If a white man's rights are being denied, I must stand against my black brother in order to rectify that wrong because it is a matter of the Kingdom of God.

(2) My attitude toward my neighbor is: Because Jesus Christ is alive in me, all I ask is to love you. Whether you love me back or not is unimportant. I can now derive enough love from the life of Jesus Christ to be able to survive without your love. But what I do ask for is the privilege of loving you.—Tom Skinner.

SUNDAY: FEBRUARY EIGHTEENTH

MORNING SERVICE

Topic: The Church and Civil Rights (Brotherhood Week)

The entire racial rights program of the churches appears to be predicated on the conviction that the time has come to make full use of the power inherent in the corporate church as a social institution.

Several pertinent responses to the racial right crusade of the churches are now in order.

I. The objectives of the churches—to achieve civil rights and justice for every person of whatever color or racial background in every nook and corner of our land—deserve the enthusiastic support of every Christian.

II. Christian citizens, like all other types of citizens in our land, should work for appropriate legislation against racial discrimination. Laws have their distinctive functions—political functions—to perform in every organized society.

III. The means that the churches as corporate bodies propose to use to reach these goals should be critically scrutinized and evaluated in accordance with the basic tenets of our Christian faith. It would be a fatal error for any Christian church to refuse to hear members who question the validity and prudence of the means it is using to achieve racial justice or to equate the dissent of its members with disloyalty to the Church or with opposition to racial equality itself.

IV. In the crusade for racial justice, so little emphasis is laid by the churches on spiritual means and so much on secular means that we should ask whether many churchmen must now be thought of as belonging to that group Jesus referred to as "men of violence," who are determined to take the Kingdom of God by force.

(1) Have we forgotten what the prophet said to Zerubbabel in the name of God, "Not by might, nor by power, but by my Spirit, says the Lord" (Zech. 4:6)?

(2) The Kingdom of God cannot be established on earth by human resources alone—not by social engineering, legislation, the use and manipulation of economic power, group pressures, or armies and wars, even to perform in an organized society. The Kingdom of God can be established only by the power of the Spirit of God working upon, within, and through the hearts of men.

V. The distinctive role of the organized church in society is to be the instrument of God whereby human beings may find the inner, spiritual resources and motivations—the moral and ethical convictions, constraints and restraints, and undergirdings—necessary for their striving, each in his own sphere, to become instruments for building a Christian society. The Church, therefore, is engaged in the fundamental spiritual work of the world. If it fails to perform its unique, distinctive work, all other institutions ultimately fail. If it allows itself to become just one more institution among others in society, using primarily secular means, it betrays its divine trust and is disloyal to the people who look to it for aid in finding spiritual resources for living.

VI. If and when the Church embarks upon campaigns that necessitate its using primarily legal coercion and economic and group pressures in order to compel its members to treat their fellowmen justly, it has already failed in its central purpose: to make Christians who love their fellowmen voluntarily, from inner compulsion and desire. Every church member is the extended church in action in the particular spot in the social order where he lives. When he fails, it is not so much the Church's failing as his failing the

SUNDAY: FEBRUARY EIGHTEENTH

Church: his failing to live up to his teaching, his professions, his promises; his failing to maintain his spiritual disciplines.

VII. Many observers have commented on the churches' launching and carrying on their crusade for racial justice with Pentecostal zeal. But it should be remembered that the zeal at Pentecost was inspired by the Holy Spirit, not for bringing secular pressures upon people, but for proclaiming the Gospel to them, for beseeching them to give the redemptive love of God a chance to change their hearts. The human heart is the perennial target of all the Church's efforts. Unless the hearts of men can be radically changed, the campaign against racial injustice and all other forms of evil will ultimately fail.—Ilion T. Jones.

Worship Aids

CALL TO WORSHIP. "Hereby perceive we the love of God, because he laid down his life for us: and we ought to lay down our lives for the brethren. Let us not love in word, neither in tongue; but in deed and in truth." I John 3:16, 18.

INVOCATION. Most merciful Father, we have done little to forward thy Kingdom in this world, to establish the brotherhood of men and love as the law of life. We have suffered our own fortunes to blind us or our pains to embitter us. We have forgotten that whatsoever is done to one of the least of thy brethren is done unto thee. Pardon our shortcomings; forgive our past neglect. Give us a simple and a single heart intent on pleasing thee. Help us in all our seeking to seek first thy Kingdom and thy righteousness, that we may be blessed with the full measure of thy blessing. And make us to come, as came thy Son Jesus Christ, not to be ministered unto, but to minister.

OFFERTORY SENTENCE. "Verily I say unto you, Inasmuch as ye have done it unto one of the least of these my brethren, ye have done it unto me." Matt. 25:40.

OFFERTORY PRAYER. O thou Source of all light, open our blind eyes to see the beauty of the world as thy gift, and grant us the will and wisdom to do our part in bringing thy light into dark places.

PRAYER. O God, in whose family not one child is forgotten, grant that we may be Christians with a world vision. It is written that thy children shall come from the east and the west, the north and the south, and shall sit down together in thy Kingdom. Help us to hasten the day when that will happen. Make us dissatisfied with any arrangement that degrades and divides the peoples of the world.

Help us to be living witnesses of thy love and power. Forgive us for representing thee so poorly in this hour of the world's agony. We have been doubters instead of doers, watchers instead of workers, hearers instead of helpers.

Exend thy mercy, O God, to all whose days are filled with pain and sorrow. Strengthen all who give themselves to the ministry of healing that the sad anthem of suffering may not drown out the glad chorus of praise from the earth. Give to all teachers the joy of bringing light and liberty to the minds of youth. Grant to all leaders of the nations wisdom, fairness, self-restraint, and the ability to see what their decisions do to the little peoples of the world. For those who serve on distant shores, let the stars of Christian hope outshine the present darkness and the threat of war. —Cecil R. Findley.

Illustrations

LIFE'S LESSON. Life has taught me that active loving saves one from the morbid preoccupation with the shortcomings of society and the waywardness of men. There is only one way in which one can endure man's inhumanity to man and that is to try, in one's own self, to exemplify man's humanity to man.—Alan Paton in *Saturday Review*.

ANSWERED ANEW. The spirit which lies behind our observance of Brotherhood Week is as old as our civilization. It goes back to the answer given to the first man who asked, "Am I my brother's keeper?" Through thousands of years there have been many noble answers to this same question, answers which bravely affirm that all men—of all religions, of all colors, of all languages—are in fact brothers, that no man can live alone. But in every age it must be answered anew. We live in a period in which the question has a new sharpness and a new edge, because there are new forces in the world which divide and threaten men, forces which work to lock each man within the prison of his own mind, which make friend distrust friend, nation distrust nation. In the face of these forces it is imperative that we heroically by word and deed give voice to our faith: that every man is indeed his brother's keeper, that no human being in the world can escape his spiritual involvement in what happens to any other human being, that no man, in the troubled sea of mankind, can be an island. It is the purpose of Brotherhood Week to inspire us to give an answer for our time, with an eloquence never before heard.—Dwight D. Eisenhower.

Sermon Suggestions

CARING ENOUGH. Text: Gal. 6:2. (1) Care enough to be aware. (2) Care enough to feel. (3) Care enough to individualize. (4) Care enough to give. —Steve Wesson in *Evangel*.

HOW TO DESTROY PREJUDICE. (1) Be a loyal Christian. (2) Be a good neighbor. (3) Refuse to spread lies and rumors about people of a different race or religion. (4) Keep your children's minds free of prejudice. (5) Realize that men must be evaluated as individuals, not as members of groups.—William C. Kernan.

CHRISTIAN SENSITIVITY. (1) To be sensitive to people, we must be open to experiences with people. (2) Christians need to be sensitive to human need, not only the needs they see around them but the great problems and needs of the family man. (3) Christians need to be sensitive to sin. (4) Christians need to be sensitive to the divine will.—Myron R. Chartier.

EVENING SERVICE

Topic: To Heal the Split
TEXT: Col. 1:17.

"Split" is a familiar word. The scientist talks of the "split atom," the psychologist of the "split personality," the social service worker of the "split home," the sociologist of the "split community," the political scientist of the "split government," the geographer of the "split world," and the ecumenic of the "split church."

The urgent need: a supreme and universal persuasive which men will accept and live by, so that instead of a split there will be unity.

I. Paul flatly declared to the Christians of Colossae that in Christ "all things hold together." Moffatt's translation is that in Christ "all things cohere." He is center of the human universe by which order and integration can be secured: the core unity by which all discords can be resolved. All things in heaven and earth are to be held together in him.

II. Paul's affirmation is the correspondent conviction of the Christian Church over the centuries. Her liege cry, now as then: "There is none other name under heaven given among men, whereby we must be saved" (Acts 4:12).

(1) Many have lost faith in alliances, government, education, arms, commerce, and even the Church as a

unifying force, but few have lost faith in Christ.

(2) They do not follow him, but they believe in him. They are convinced that if his spirit and mind ruled, nobilities long dead would rise from their graves, aspirations long withered would assume fresh bloom, and harmonies long muted would break into symphonic sound.

III. This we should never forget. In art, science, philosophy, history, and religion there is the principle of parallelism: that which appears in one century reappears in another. The idea, the issue, the deed of a thousand years ago bobs up in the life of today. Art has its recurring subject, science its recurring problem, philosophy its recurring idea, history its recurring event, and religion its recurring text.

(1) In all of those fields there is what has been described as "the eternal recurrence of the similar." That is, in all but one—the field of personality. There has been no recurring Christ.

(2) Many great, good, and brilliant men have preceded and succeeded him, but none has ever paralleled him. The schools of culture, the wisdom of teaching, the ancient and new religions, the fruitful civilizations of 2,000 years have never been able to reproduce him. He defies comparison.

(3) When we brood deeply upon it, we realize that in him all differences can be resolved, all ruptures healed. He and he alone can meet and defeat the terrifying events of this time and close the gaping chasms which threaten to swallow our civilization.

IV. How does he unify? By his sheer moral power. Justin Martyr declared him to be "The Spermatic Word"—the concentrated, creative, vital energy from which new life comes. This truth is exemplified in human experience. The disciples were so ordinary. Hallmark of the commonplace stamped on them. By his power welded into an association that defied the greatest government of the world and poured new life into the veins of a sated and wearied age. The same story repeated a thousand times.
—James W. Clarke.

SUNDAY: FEBRUARY TWENTY-FIFTH

MORNING SERVICE

Topic: God's Workmanship
TEXT: Eph. 2:10 (RSV).

Many have found the contemplation of God's handiwork interesting, instructive, inspiring. In the mineral, vegetable, and animal kingdoms, no less than in the stellar system, God's works attest his wisdom, skill, power, and love.

(a) To Paul the greatest interest and importance attaches to the re-creation of human lives that had been debauched, deformed, all but destroyed by sin. To him such work seemed to involve, not only mystery and marvel, but miracle! The transformation of a marred, maimed, mutilated soul into the resuscitation of a dead body. Yet he affirmed not only that those of far-off lands and ages had opportunity to observe and experience such revolutionary change.

(b) Often the thoughtful have been moved to wonder, and question, as to the explanation. Some have inclined to attribute it to accident, or fortuitous circumstance of chance, or human wisdom, or power and skill. This Paul vigorously denied. He would go further and affirm that such wonders are skillfully designed and wrought, and that God is the designer and artificer.

(c) The text indicates a product, a purpose, and a plan of God. These I am asking you to consider.

I. Think first of the product, namely, a rescued, redeemed, regenerated human life. It is made clear that the individuals in question had been not merely defective or diseased, but dead. Moreover, they were not merely resuscitated; they were re-created, made new creatures of a higher order.

(1) The question naturally arises as to the explanation. Paul's answer is clear. "We are his workmanship." "It is he that made us, and we are his; we are his people, and the sheep of his pasture." The Fourth Gospel declared that such "were born, not of blood nor of the will of the flesh nor of the will of man, but of God."

(2) In proof we require no evidence other than the product. Its very nature is a convincing demonstration of its divine origin. Think of the saintliest man or woman you have known, and your reason will assure you that the origin is not natural but supernatural. When we behold a human life at its highest and holiest, we are impelled to exclaim with the psalmist: "Thou hast made him little less than God, and dost crown him with glory and honor."

(3) The saint is not merely a resuscitated sinner; but is a renewed, refined, regenerated being. Paul wrote the Corinthians: "If any one is in Christ, he is a new creation." Such has been born anew; born from above!

(4) Paul was a new man. His aspirations, aims, and activities were entirely different. He wrote to the Philippians: "Whatever gain I had, I counted as loss for the sake of Christ." It is so with all who yield themselves unresistingly and unreservedly to the will of God. Jesus represented God as saying of the returned Prodigal: "It was fitting to make merry and be glad, for this your brother was dead, and is alive; he was lost, and is found."

(5) Note the further fact affirmed by Paul that God's re-creative work was effected "in Christ Jesus." That phrase recurs many times in Paul's writings. It is meaningful.

II. Next we face the question of purpose. Why did God re-create sinners of old? Why does he re-create sinners now? The apostle's answer is crystal clear.

(1) His general statement is: "For good works." This accords perfectly with his statement to Titus concerning Christ: "Who gave himself for us to redeem us from all iniquity and to purify for himself a people of his own who are zealous for good deeds." Paul also urged Timothy to teach believers "to do good, to be rich in good deeds, liberal and generous." Two purposes are involved in this urgency. Good works are helpful to both beneficiary and benefactor.

(2) When you do good to another, you gladden, strengthen, and enrich him. All about us are men, women, and young people weary, weak, wretched whom we can help. Most of us know from experience that often a very simple act, or utterance, or smile, will help and hearten!

(3) To fail of good works is to fail of the purpose for which you were given being! If this be recognized, you should be interested in some specific forms of good works which are included in God's plans for us.

(a) On the list I place first an item which Jesus specifically named. One day a group asked him: "'What must we do, to be doing the work of God?' Jesus answered them, 'This is the work of God, that you believe in him whom he has sent.'"

(b) A second form of good works magnified by the New Testament writers is witnessing. It is well known that the primary dependence of the Lord for the making of disciples is human witnessing.

III. The last clause has been misunderstood by many. In the King James Version it reads: "Which God hath before ordained that we should walk in them." Some have supposed that word, ordained, implies a sovereign decree to which conformity is compulsory. But no such implications are in the word. Several modern versions substitute the word prepared for the word ordained. There is no intimation of compulsion or constraint. What is affirmed is that each Christian faces the opportunity, the possibility, of realizing in his experience the purpose for which he was rescued and renewed. This assurance is based upon the facts of the divine purpose and plan.

(1) It is heartening to know that God, the all-wise, all-powerful, all-loving Father, with exact and exhaustive knowledge of your possibilities and limitations, and of the circumstances under which you live and labor, has formulated a plan by which you may accomplish the good works which constitute your intended mission in this life.

(2) Your course, and the consequences, will be self-determined. You can make your life fruitful in good works or you can expend your energies in evil works. You can assure for yourself God's favor, or you can assure for yourself his disfavor. The result will be determined by your aims, activities, accomplishments. It is true that no one is saved by good works, but it is equally clear that Christians are saved for good works, and to fail of such activities is to fail of the purpose for which one was rescued and renewed.—Leroy Dean Anderson.

Worship Aids

CALL TO WORSHIP. "Bless the Lord, O my soul: and all that is within me, bless his holy name." Ps. 103:1.

INVOCATION. Almighty and everlasting God, whom the heaven of heavens cannot contain, much less the temples which our hands have builded, but who are ever nigh unto the humble and the contrite: grant thy Holy Spirit, we beseech thee, to us who are here assembled; that cleansed and illumined by thy grace, we may worthily show forth thy praise, meekly learn thy word, render due thanks for thy mercies, and obtain a gracious answer to our prayers.

OFFERTORY SENTENCE. "If there be first a willing mind, it is accepted according to that which a man hath, and not according to that which he hath not." II Cor. 8:12.

OFFERTORY PRAYER. O Lord, upon whose constant giving we depend every day, teach us how to spend and be spent for others that we may gain the true good things of life by losing every selfish trait.

PRAYER. Eternal God, we praise and bless thee for the revelation of thy glory in the face of Jesus Christ, who, being rich, for our sakes became poor and laid down his life that we might have life and have it abundantly. Develop in us, we beseech thee, his vision, that we may see those things that belong to our peace. Develop in us his understanding and compassion, that we may help one another and live with all men in charity and goodwill. Develop in us his devotion to thy Kingdom, that we may discover the meaning and the true glory of life. Develop in us his faith in thee, that we may not be overwhelmed by any disaster but may live bravely and creatively.

O God, most merciful and gracious, forgive us all that is past and grant that we, becoming true followers of Christ, may be used of thee to promote the welfare and progress of mankind.—Ernest Fremont Tittle.

Illustrations

DISCOVERY. The greatest discovery I made in life was that God was probably right when I thought him to be wrong.—Reuben A. Torrey.

CALAMITY. God has not left us alone. His indifference to our fate would be the most terrifying of all calamities.—Earl L. Douglass.

Sermon Suggestions

TOGETHER WITH GOD. Text: I Cor. 3:9. (1) Togetherness with God is a partnership of love. (2) Togetherness with God is a stewardship of life. (3) Togetherness with God is a fellowship of light.—Stephen F. Olford.

MISTAKES. (1) Why are mistakes made? Someone did not know, someone did not think, or someone did not care. (2) How may mistakes be avoided? To know what you are doing, to think while you are doing it, and really to care whether or not it is done right. (3) When mistakes happen it is not too hard to forgive the person who did not know or too difficult to excuse the one who did not think, but it is hard to forgive and excuse one who made a mistake because he just did not care.

EVENING SERVICE

Topic: Unanswered Prayer
TEXT: I Sam. 28:15.

I. Is it possible that sometimes our prayer is not answered because it was not genuine, was not really meant? There is such a thing as what the New Testament calls "double-mindedness." We put one purpose into our prayer while we organize our life round another, and it is the second that comes out on top every time.

II. Is it possible that someone else's prayer goes unanswered because of my failure to rise to some duty or opportunity?

(1) Consider the case of Ananias. Saul is blind and helpless; he prays for help and sees in a vision someone laying hands on him and restoring his sight. At the other end of Damascus Ananias is commissioned to do just this, but hesitates. Had he finally refused, then, so far as he was concerned, Saul's prayer would have gone unanswered. We may generalize and say that A prays for B; C is in contact with B, and, though he knows nothing of it, would regret it if he knew, by his failure in that setting the prayer of A is left without an answer.

(2) It may well be that more than once someone has prayed and, because of a failure on my part, he has been left with the problem of why so legitimate a prayer should be in vain. For we are all members of the household of God, and it is one of the laws of that household that the needs of one of its members are normally met, not by direct intervention on the Father's part, but by some action of another member.

III. Is it too daring a thought that the problem that should exercise us is not why God does answer our prayers, but why we do not answer his?

(1) If you ask what can possibly be meant by God praying to us, I would remind you of those words put into his mouth by the psalmist: "O that my people would listen to me, that Israel would walk in my ways!"

(2) Did not Jesus lament over Jerusalem as the city that would not listen to him? He stands at the door and knocks, but we do not open, so he has to turn away. How often has the inner voice been silenced, the prompting of the Spirit been suppressed, the call of Christ been disobeyed!—E. L. Allen.

SUNDAY: MARCH FOURTH

MORNING SERVICE

Topic: Biblical Basis for Evangelism

I. *Motivation for evangelism.* (1) We are motivated by the very *atmosphere* of the biblical message. The word for "evangel" or the "gospel" and its derivatives is found 103 times in the New Testament.

(2) The primary evangelistic *activity* of a New Testament man is observed in the life of the pre-eminent missionary evangelist, the Apostle Paul. When one thinks of the geographic area covered and the number of people reached by that man within the brief time span he had to do it, it is utterly a miracle.

(3) We are motivated by the *com-*

mand of our Lord to evangelism. The well-known great commission in Matt. 28 says to us, "Go therefore and make disciples of all nations." Evangelism is intrinsic and essential to God's plan of redemption, and we are moved not because of our wishes but because of our Lord's command.

(4) We discover in the Bible that we are motivated by our own *experience*. Something happens to the person who meets Jesus Christ. When that experience is genuine, the person himself becomes an evangelist. There really can be no evangelism unless the person has experienced what he is talking about. It is absolutely necessary to experience forgiveness and assurance before a person can evangelize.

(5) The Bible reveals that we are motivated by the *work of the Spirit* within us. (See Acts 1:8.)

II. *Message of evangelism.* That message is uniquely centered in a person, an action, and a proclamation.

(1) It is centered in a *person,* our Lord Christ. Jesus Christ is not only the proclaimer of the way of truth, he is also the way and the truth. He is the content of the message of evangelism.

(2) The message is centered in an action that is related to that Person. At one of the resurrection appearances our Lord spoke the words of Luke 24:44–49. He clearly revealed that the Old Testament Scriptures pointed to his suffering, death, and resurrection. One cannot divorce the person from the action. The two are tied together. The two become the central issue of the Gospel—the good news.

(3) The message is a proclamation. One cannot divorce the person and action from the actual communication of that story. Men and women are lost apart from a knowledge of Jesus Christ and his work for them. (See II Cor. 4:3.) The work of Jesus Christ has become the bridge between a holy God and a sinning people. But God needs communicators. That is a necessary part of the message. (See II Cor. 5:20.)

III. *Mode of evangelism.* (1) Not only must we be concerned about the simplicity of the language with which we proclaim the good news, but we must also be reminded that what is to be told is simply the story of what Christ has done for us. (See I Cor. 1:17, 2:2; Gal. 6:14.)

(2) The transforming work that takes place in human experience is not dependent upon the abilities of the witness, but upon his simply relating the story of Christ's work.

IV. *Method of evangelism.* When we look at the method of evangelism in the Bible it is certainly not antiquarian. It is highly relevant.

(1) The primary method is the method of *incarnation.* (See John 20: 21.) The redemptive work of our Lord demanded that he identify himself with mankind. The only possible evangelism that can take place is when we are willing to identify ourselves with the men of the world.

(2) Those of us who have been concerned about evangelism usually are strongly concerned about *proclamation.* We believe so firmly in proclamation that we tend to proclaim our message from a distance. We forget the demand of involvement. When preaching is used in evangelism it must always be supplemented by other methods. If it is not, we miss the incarnational aspect. (See I Cor. 9:9–23.)—Gordan G. Johnson.

Worship Aids

CALL TO WORSHIP. "The kingdoms of this world are become the kingdom of our Lord, and of his Christ; and he shall reign for ever and ever." Rev. 11:15.

INVOCATION. Eternal God, in whom we live and move and have our being, whose face is hidden from us by our sins and whose mercy we forget in the blindness of our hearts: cleanse us, we beseech thee, from all our offenses and deliver us from proud thoughts and vain desires, that with lowliness and meekness we may draw near to thee, confessing our faults, confiding in thy grace, and finding in thee our refuge and our strength.

OFFERTORY SENTENCE. "Give unto the Lord, O ye kindreds of the people, give unto the Lord glory and strength. Give unto the Lord the glory due unto his name: bring an offering, and come into his courts." Ps. 96:7–8.

OFFERTORY PRAYER. Open our eyes that we may see thy goodness, O Father; our hearts that we may be grateful for thy mercies; our lips that we may show forth thy praise; and our hands that we may give these offerings according to thy wish and desire.

PRAYER. Our Father, through thy dear Son Jesus Christ we come to thee, with no merit of our own, but miserable sinners saved by the love and grace of our Savior. We plead with thee, O Father, that whatever cup there is that we must drink, thou wilt be with us and help us. Thou hast never laid any cross upon us, but what Christ will bear it with us. Many a tie has been separated, but may the tie that binds us to our Savior never be separated. There is no road over which we may tread, our Father, but what he will go with us all the way. So help us, that while we live we may go a little farther into the deep recesses of our own souls and search them. If we find there that which is not pleasing in thy sight, give us divine grace to remove it. Then, our Father, place within us thy Spirit, thy holy Spirit, thine everlasting Word, that we may be strengthened, comforted, sustained. Help us to go onward and upward to him that loved us and gave himself for us.—I. W. Gernert.

Illustrations

THE GOSPEL AND THE WORLD. Describe the world in the blackest tones you can, paint its mistakes and its sins in hues that run red like blood, tick off the minutes that we have left to save our civilization until there are only a few left, and the Gospel is still great enough and powerful enough and surprising enough to transform this world from what it is to what it ought to be, to make it a fit abiding place for men and women and especially for little children. The world is not too much for the Gospel of Jesus Christ.—Ben M. Herbster in *United Church Herald*.

TOO TOPICAL. During World War II Eivind Berggrav, the Bishop of Oslo, was put into prison. At first he was allowed to have his Bible and to send a short letter to his wife each week. When he wrote to her one day in 1942, he said: "The gospel lesson for yesterday was remarkable. It contained that passage, 'I am come to set the captive free, to bring freedom to the oppressed.'" The bishop's wife was called before the chief of the Gestapo police and told that her husband was henceforth forbidden to quote from the Holy Scriptures. "The Bible is much too topical," the chief said.—Robert W. Olewiler in *These Times*.

Sermon Suggestions

MORE THAN MEETS THE EYE. Text: II Cor. 4:18 (PHILLIPS). (1) There is more than meets the eye in the Church. (2) There is more than meets the eye in your daily work. (3) There is more than meets the eye in love. (4) There is more than meets the eye in life itself. (5) There is more than meets the eye in a worship service.—Don R. Boyd.

CHARACTERISTICS OF GREAT PREACHING. (1) Preaching must be supported by thorough and thoughtful preparation. (2) Preaching should be done with enthusiasm, as if the preacher himself believed in it. (3) Preaching should be imaginative. (4) Preaching should start where the people are. (5) Preaching should be easy to understand.—Robert Cleveland Holland.

SUNDAY: MARCH ELEVENTH

EVENING SERVICE

Topic: A New-Time Religion

What may be some of the characteristics of the new-style religion?

I. Christianity will recover some of its lost warmth. (1) The new-time religion will recapture something of the joyous spirit of the old-time religion. Present-day religion has lost a kind of power that blessed the early Church—the power to bring a light to the eyes, a song to the heart, and a shout to the lips.

(2) The new-time religion will have a revived sense of warmth—a fellowship of the genuinely concerned, songs that will be spirited and sung with full voice, prayers that will speak of a man talking directly with God, a movement and involvement of all worshipers that will restore a fresh vitality to the common life of Christians.

II. A new-time religion will be marked by the fact that people will know what they believe and why they believe it.

(1) It will be characterized by foundations of belief that have been dug deeply and laid solidly. The dull-grays of neutrality will be set aside, and the blazing colors of positive convictions will stand forth.

(2) The new-time religion will lead a man toward satisfying answers to life's basic questions: Who am I? Why am I living? What is the purpose of my existence?

(3) The new-time religion, for so long out in the wilderness of "death-of-god" theologies, will come into being with a recovery of convictions, a mature theology biblically rooted. And with it will come a fresh commitment and a new sense of purpose for the individual and for society.

III. The new-time religion will become transcendental. That is to say, it will restore to our faith the awesome sense of the Mysterium Tremendum—the power of the transcendent God, the force of the mystical and the strength of the spiritual. The new-time religion will get back to the unique function of religion—to hold up before men the glory, the power, the majesty, and the mystery of God.

IV. The new-time religion will bring a new consciousness of the spirit of God in our midst, the Holy Spirit breaking forth new truth among us. We will know and feel a new awareness—an awareness unknown before in experience to so many of us.

(1) The Holy Spirit! Operative in the individual and in history. God tirelessly active, involved in the experiences of the person and in the event of history.

(2) The new-time religion will look with gratitude to the old-time religion and draw forth much of value from it. But it will know that God has not yet spoken the final word. We will honor and revere the saints who have gone before us.

(3) Those who believe in God the Father, and in his Son, Jesus Christ our Lord, and in the Holy Spirit, can look forward to the years ahead in the confident and sure hope that God has yet more truth to break forth among us.—Charles L. Copenhaver.

SUNDAY: MARCH ELEVENTH

MORNING SERVICE

Topic: Not Ashamed of the Gospel (Lent)

TEXT: Rom. 1:16 (GOODSPEED).

I. The truth at the heart of the Gospel alone makes sense of things. It makes life's sums come out right.

(1) The Gospel is veritably God's-spell, incredibly good news, for it weaves a spell of meaning and purpose about life. It gathers the fragmentariness of

much of our living up into a luminous, spiritual pattern. There is a metaphysic, a way of thought, in the Gospel, which undergirds life.

(2) The word "gospel" is not synonymous with creed, doctrine, religion, or church, although it has to do with these terms. It is, Paul tells us, "God's power for the salvation of everyone who has faith." It has to do specifically with the radiant proclamation of what God, the Creator-Redeemer, has done for men in Jesus Christ.

(3) The Gospel-utterance of the first Christians consisted of a brief body of momentous events: Jesus Christ had come; he had lived, suffered, died, and risen from the dead. In this mighty deed of the living God, salvation appeared for men.

(4) What a sublime process of events is gathered up in the Apostles' Creed: "And in Jesus Christ his only Son our Lord, who was . . . born of the Virgin Mary, suffered under Pontius Pilate, was crucified, dead, and buried, . . . the third day he rose. . . ." Notice how the verbs in this great declaration of faith are vibrant with motion and meaning, as they declare the mighty works of the living God. Truly, the Gospel of Jesus Christ puts a dynamic and creative truth at the center of our lives and bids us live day by day in the light of it.

II. Notice what that Gospel has accomplished in retrieving the God-given-and-implanted dignity of man's soul.

(1) It had been in the world only a brief span of years when Paul wrote his letter to Rome. Yet it had already flung a new glory over the face of the earth. The Greek and Roman worlds, with all their vaunted power and culture, were sunk in moral and intellectual decay.

(2) Then came Jesus Christ and the Gospel and Church which bear his name. For the first time, a sated and weary humanity lifted its eyes in hope. Its muddied bloodstream received an inoculation of new hope. A divine elixir stirred the human soul.

(3) The Gospel of Jesus Christ is nothing less than a quarry, out of which were dug the elements that went into the making of a Christian civilization, itself a new emergent. It is the ethic of reverence for human personality, as it was taught and lived out by Jesus.

III. The Gospel of our Lord Jesus Christ marks the one sane and realistic approach to our many world problems.

(1) Just look at a few of them. (a) What is to hold in leash the bristling nationalism of the hour, this modern insanity that one's own nation is an end in itself and not an integral part of humanity? The answer lies in a larger, global outlook, and that is a chimera apart from the Christian Gospel.

(b) Look at the problem of racism and its hatred for those of another race, color, and nationality. What other agency than the Gospel of Jesus Christ can change hatred to love and understanding in the human heart?

(c) Who cares enough about human beings to abolish our foul-smelling slums and to redistribute the necessities of life on the basis of need rather than profit? The Christian man, of course!

(2) In a world where injustices and cruelties have been meted out to millions of the innocent in the name of "expediency," the crying need is for Christians who know that the Gospel of their Lord marks the only sane and realistic approach to the solution of world problems.

IV. One more reason why I am not ashamed of the Gospel is the transformations it works in the lives of people when it lays hold on them.

(1) Listen again to what the Apostle is saying: The Gospel is "God's power for the salvation of everyone who has faith." That is the one condition on which it can release its joy and power in your life. If you really want it, you must avail yourself of that power of God by means of life-giving and creative faith, and that gift of faith God gives to those that ask him.

(2) We aren't offered a creed for the swallowing, nor a mere set of doctrines. We are offered Life, a Person,

SUNDAY: MARCH ELEVENTH

One in whom the redeeming love of the Father is gathered up, One who wants to be our Friend, Master, and Savior.

(3) This Gospel of Jesus Christ is not good advice. That can be gotten out of any book on psychology. The Gospel is Good News—"God's power," says Paul, "for the salvation of everyone who has faith."—Aaron N. Meckel.

Worship Aids

CALL TO WORSHIP. "I will praise the Lord according to his righteousness: and will sing praise to the name of the Lord most high." Ps. 7:17.

INVOCATION. Our heavenly Father, who by thy love hast made us, and through thy love hast kept us, and in thy love wouldst make us perfect: we humbly confess that we have not loved thee with all our heart and soul and mind and strength, and that we have not loved one another as Christ hath loved us. Thy life is within our souls, but our selfishness has hindered thee. We have not lived by faith. We have resisted thy spirit. We have neglected thine inspirations. Forgive what we have been; help us to amend what we are; and in thy spirit direct what we shall be; that thou mayest come into the full glory of thy creation, in us and in all men.

OFFERTORY SENTENCE. "Give, and it shall be given unto you; good measure, pressed down, and shaken together, and running over." Luke 6:38.

OFFERTORY PRAYER. Our heavenly Father, help us to remember that though Christ does offer his companionship, yet to us belongs the decision as to whether or not we will follow him. May we through these gifts and our witness share with all the world the blessedness that comes to us through thy grace.

PRAYER. Eternal and Heavenly Father, there is no one word to use for all of us. We bow our hearts before thee, each a little world in himself, each with heavy regrets and high hopes of his own, each with a prayer that no other will even utter, each with praise no one else can offer.

If we are wearied, strengthen us; if we are proud, humble us; if we are perplexed, enlighten us; if we are torn by inner strife, heal us; if we are lost in meaningless activities, gird our wills with thy purpose; if we are discouraged by our families, hearten us by thy merciful compassion; if we have sinned, teach us how to repent; if we have been sinned against, teach us how to forgive; if we are selfish, deepen our love of thee and of man, that we may cast away our self-concern; if we are censorious, silence our tongues until our hearts learn how to understand; if we have tried in vain to pray, grant us patience to wait in silence for thy voice. Whatever our wilderness may be, lead us by some Sinai to the promised land; whatever Gethsemane we have entered, disclose to us thy will that we may act with deliberate courage and unhesitating faith; whatever heavenly vision thou hast granted us to fulfill in earthly labor, endow us with untiring strength and endurance, that we may complete the task to which thou hast called us with integrity of soul and steadfastness of purpose, to the glory of God and the redemption of the world.—Samuel H. Miller.

Illustrations

AT WORSHIP. Here may the faithful find salvation and the careless be awakened. Here may the doubting find faith and the anxious be encouraged. Here may the tempted find help and the sorrowful comfort. Here may the weary find rest and the strong be renewed. Here may the aged find consolation and the young be inspired.—*Book of Common Worship.*

THE PATH HE MADE. Jesus finished what he set out to do. We follow in the path he made across the rough unknown sea of suffering and death.—Theodore P. Ferris.

Sermon Suggestions

THIEVES OF THE CROSS. Text: Luke 14:27. (1) Worldly and unbelieving friends will cause one to lose his cross if their influence is effective. (2) Worldly and unbelieving relatives can exert unholy influences on the believer, causing him to lay down his cross. (3) Worldliness and sin will automatically take the cross from any person who allows these elements any place in his life. (4) Traditional religion is a robber of spirituality. (5) Indifference and unconcern, or being at ease in Zion, will take away your cross.—Walter P. Atkinson in *Evangel*.

YOU DO MATTER. Text: Rom. 12:3. (1) You do matter to God. (2) You matter to other people. (3) You do matter because of what you can do.—Homer J. R. Elford.

EVENING SERVICE

Topic: Joy in Worship
TEXT: Ps. 122:1.

The author of Ps. 122 recalls the joy with which he received the invitation of his friends and neighbors to join in the pilgrimage to Jerusalem to take part in one of the great festivals of the Temple. Then the psalmist proceeds to suggest three elements in a normal service of worship, three reasons for going to church. Each of these three elements ought to contribute something to the joy of worship.

I. *Praise.* (1) The Jewish joy in worship was the joy of thanksgiving to God on account of all that he had done for his people in delivering them from peril and danger of every kind. This was particularly true of the joy of the Jewish festivals. The Feast of the Passover, for example, kept the people in joyful remembrance of the deliverance of their forefathers from the hands of the Egyptians.

(2) With even greater reason than the ancient people of Israel, the Christian Church—the new Israel—can rejoice on account of what God has done. His promises have been fulfilled in the events centered round the Incarnation, the Resurrection, and the Ascension of Jesus Christ. It is little wonder that the early Christians gave expression to their joy in revitalized worship.

II. *Prayer.* (1) Of course, praise and prayer overlap. Many hymns take the form of prayer to God for help and guidance. On the other hand, as Origen stated many centuries ago, "Public prayer should open with thanksgiving." It is, however, intercessory prayer—prayer on behalf of others—that is chiefly suggested by the psalmist.

(2) As Christians, we dare not limit the possibilities that are inherent in believing prayer, for ourselves and for others.

III. *Instruction.* (1) We come to church to learn more about God's judgment, about God's laws, and about God's will for our lives. As we read the Bible we can hear God speaking to us. In every sermon, however poor and stammering it may be, we are brought face to face with the living God through Jesus Christ.

(2) Instruction is there, but there should also be something more. Every sermon should present to us some challenge from Jesus Christ and some inspiration for nobler living. The Word of God comes to us in order that Christ's joy may be in us and that our joy may be complete.—William C. Morrice.

SUNDAY: MARCH EIGHTEENTH

MORNING SERVICE

Topic: What Faith Jesus Had! (Lent)

I. *In his belief in himself.* (1) He was of so poor a family that he was born in a manger. He was born amid such times that he was quickly taken to Egypt to escape the slaughter, ordered by Herod, of the infants. Then to come back to Nazareth, such a wretched place that people had come to say, "Can there any good thing come out of Nazareth?" There to stand at the side of his carpenter father and for years to be his mother's only helper when Joseph died. Such an ordinary family that later his critics had contempt for this local Boy from such a family! (See Matt. 13:54–57.)

(2) Against all that, Jesus kept saying: "Such as I am, I mean much to God. Such as I am, I am important in making this world different." (See John 12:27.)

II. *In his belief in his fellowman.* (1) Look at him selecting his followers, selecting fishermen mending their nets; a hated taxgatherer; a woman of the streets; two women, one of whom not much of a housekeeper. Had he not any sense at all? You needed someone with entree at court, someone with "pull" where it counted, a high priest, a Herod with a king's influence. Yet here was Jesus choosing such common kind.

(2) What were they worth when the pressures came on? Look at Peter denying him with oaths. Look at Judas betraying him for what would now be only about $50. Yes, when the time came all the disciples forsook him and fled. Yet what faith Jesus kept in them in his last hours. (See John 15:16; 17:9–10.)

III. *In his belief in his methods.* (1) His world was full of tramping armies. It was a time of naked power. Imagine the impact of that on his mind. In every settlement were Zealots, Jewish nationalists, ready to take sword and drive out the Romans. It would be hard for a Jewish lad not to feel his blood race and some night at a secret conclave swear before God that he would someday shed Roman blood. What other course offered any hope?

(2) That Jesus was led to consider such means we know from the temptations. But Jesus put all that behind him. If men would not come to his side from simple love of God, he would not have them. If the Kingdom could not win on its merits, well and good.

IV. *In his belief in his God.* (1) Jesus believed in God as the all-loving Father of all men. But see where that had brought him—to this cross where the nails tore his flesh; where thorns put blood into his eyes; to the point where he was all alone. If this God was Father, why did he allow this to happen?

(2) Is not it over this matter of God's love that we often stumble? If God is a god of love, why does he allow this to happen to this good man or that good woman? Yes, it is here we are vulnerable, when life does not turn out the way we believe it ought to for the good people. The answer of Jesus is: "You can trust God as your Father, no matter what appearances may be to the contrary."—Arthur Organ.

Worship Aids

CALL TO WORSHIP. "Thy word is a lamp unto my feet, and a light unto my path. I have sworn, and I will perform it, that I will keep thy righteous judgments. Quicken me, O Lord, according unto thy word." Ps. 119:105–107.

INVOCATION. O Lord God, who hast left unto us thy Holy Word to be a lamp unto our feet and a light unto our path: give unto us all thy Holy Spirit, we humbly pray thee, that out of the same Word we may learn what is thy blessed will, and frame our lives in all holy obedience to the same, to thine honor and glory and the increase of our faith.

OFFERTORY SENTENCE. "Therefore, as ye abound in every thing, in faith, and utterance, and knowledge, and in all diligence, and in your love to us, see that ye abound in this grace also." II Cor. 8:7.

OFFERTORY PRAYER. O Father of our Lord Jesus Christ, we dedicate these offerings to the fellowship of him, whom to know aright is life eternal.

PRAYER. Eternal God, Creator of the world, Sustainer of life, Lord of history, and Father of our spirits, thou art great beyond our power fully to know or comprehend; the oceans of thy love and wisdom are great and our ships of understanding are small, yet sail upon them we would, in humble awe and simple need.

We bless thee for both the ordinary and the extraordinary mercies of our lives. We give thee thanks for all our creature comforts: food to eat, work to do, the medicine of friendship, the healing of love, the goodly fellowships of community, college, and church; our share of morning and of night, of labor and of rest, of health and sickness of life—and yea of death.

Hear us as we pray for our own needs: the courage to face the inmost issues of our lives, to acknowledge the fears that haunt us; our need to forgive and to be forgiven; our need for light and life and truth; our need for deliverance from both the root and the flower of the evil consequences of even our highest and best efforts.

Even as we pray for ourselves we remember those who stand in special need, those who stand in dark and difficult places, those who face the brokenness of our common life and are most deeply hurt and scarred by it. O God, our help in ages past, our hope for years to come, thou whose faith and hope and love the long centuries have not dimmed, create in us, too, faith and hope and love.—Joseph F. King.

Illustrations

THE COST OF DEDICATION. In Irving Stone's biographical novel, *The Agony and the Ecstasy*, Bertoldo, the master sculptor, speaks to the young, aspiring Michelangelo. "Dedication is expensive," he says. "It will cost you your life." Michelangelo, with great insight, replies, "What else is life for?"

ESSENTIAL INGREDIENT. Faith is that characteristic of life that keeps a person going on, when stopping would be convenient; it keeps a person looking up, when he feels like looking down; it keeps a person hoping, when hopelessness invades his heart. Faith must be the last thing to go, for when it is gone, living is futile.—C. Neil Strait.

Sermon Suggestions

CHRISTIAN CHALLENGE. (1) The challenge of the Scriptures. (See Heb. 4:12.) (2) The challenge of the Spirit. (See John 16:8.) (3) The challenge of the saints. Christian people are commissioned to be witnesses to Christ and, therefore, to challenge a sinful world to reckon with the fact of Jesus, the Son of God. (4) The challenge of the seasons. No thoughtful person can think through the calendar of the year without being challenged by such events as Christmas, Easter, and so on.—Stephen F. Olford.

WHAT JESUS BORROWED. Text: Matt. 8:20. Jesus was the great borrower of history. (1) He borrowed a barn to be born in. (2) He borrowed a boat to preach from. (3) He borrowed a colt to ride into Jerusalem. (4) He borrowed an upper room in which to eat the Passover supper. (5) He borrowed a tomb to be buried in.—J. Wallace Hamilton.

EVENING SERVICE

Topic: Rich Toward God
Scripture: Luke 12:13-21; Matt. 6:19-21.

Why should we lay up treasure in heaven instead of treasure on earth? Jesus gives us four reasons:

I. Earthly treasure is transient. Some of it perishes (moth, rust); some of it we lose (through thieves or, it may be, the stock market); in the end we leave it all behind. Heavenly treasure, on the other hand, is permanent; we may enjoy it here and hereafter.

II. Earthly treasure steals our hearts, for "where your treasure is, there will your heart be also." In Jewish psychology the heart was not only the seat of the emotions but also that of the intellect and will. One's treasure engrosses his affections, commands his thoughts, and determines his purpose. If a man lives for money or for wealth it affects his whole inner life, colors all he thinks and does.

III. Earthly treasure blinds our vision. What Jesus means to say is this: If we recognize that God's Kingdom and his righteousness are the highest moral value in life, then we have clear moral vision, we can distinguish between good and evil, we are walking in the light. On the other hand, if our real treasure is on earth, then feeling, emotions, intellect, and will are all affected; our moral vision is impaired, our moral judgments are distorted, conscience is no longer a safe guide, we are walking in the darkness.

IV. It is impossible to serve God and mammon. (1) In Jesus' day mammon was a morally neutral term and meant wealth or riches or money. Jesus said they must put either God or mammon first. No man can serve God and money, for both claim the whole man. We must choose, therefore, which we will serve, which we are going to put first.

(2) But though we cannot serve God and money, we can serve God with money. One of the best ways in which a man with business talents can serve God is to make money, to make it honestly and fairly, in a business that serves the economy, and then to use his money for the glory of God and the good of mankind.—Ernest Trice Thompson in *The Presbyterian Outlook*.

SUNDAY: MARCH TWENTY-FIFTH

MORNING SERVICE

Topic: Citizens of Eternity (Lent)
Text: Eccles. 3:11.

I. May I suggest that one distinguishing mark of a divine nature of man is that he is capable of thinking?

(1) Descartes, the French philosopher, claimed this to be the thing that marked out man as in possession of a soul—of a real self that set him high above the brute of the field. "Cogito ergo sum"—"I think, therefore I am," said Descartes. This is a faculty that no other creature on earth possesses.

(2) Man is capable of thinking God's thoughts. He is able to think of his own existence and actions. He is able to comprehend the universe in its vastness. And while this may show up his own littleness, it also shows him as something greater than the universe.

II. Another distinguishing mark is that man has a conscience. Man has a sense of right and wrong, and while this sense may vary in different individuals —it may be higher with some and lower with others—it is there as a mark of man's divine nature. I know that in some people conscience is very primitive and undeveloped, that others for a time are able to silence or ignore the voice of conscience; but it is there all the time, and there are moments in the best and worst of men when they sorrow over their misdeeds.

III. The really distinguishing thing that marks a man out as a soul is his sense of need that nothing on this earth can fully satisfy. God created man in his own image, and he set eternity in his heart. That is why we can find no rest or abiding satisfaction here on earth; that is why we are strangers and pilgrims here as all our fathers were.

IV. Man's sense of need to worship and pray marks him out as belonging to a higher order than things earthly and temporal.

(1) The ancient Greeks called man by the word "anthropos," a word which means the upward-looking one. Man finds something within him that prompts him to lift his face to God.

(2) Prayer is the hallmark of divinity stamped upon our poor humanity. When we pray, when we go up to God's house to worship, then we are taking heaven and earth to witness that we are men and women made in God's own image and destined to share his companionship throughout endless ages.—Tom Calvert.

Worship Aids

CALL TO WORSHIP. "We have thought of thy lovingkindness, O God, in the midst of thy temple. According to thy name, O God, so is thy praise unto the ends of the earth." Ps. 48: 9–10.

INVOCATION. O God, who makest thyself known both in the stillness and in the hurry of life: come to us as we seek to come to thee, in this place of prayer. In music, word, and song lift our hearts to thee, and so purify our thoughts and strengthen our resolves that we shall go forth into the world of tomorrow, confident that thou art with us.

OFFERTORY SENTENCE. "Lay up for yourselves treasures in heaven: for where your treasure is, there will your heart be also." Matt. 6: 20–21.

OFFERTORY PRAYER. Awaken us to the claims of thy holy will, O God, and stir us with a passion for thy Kingdom, that we may respond at this time with our gifts and also with our lives.

PRAYER. O thou Spirit of the living God, unseen yet everywhere, do thou find some open door into the quiet of our souls. As thou dost come, may we let thy presence work a redeeming difference in us.

We confess that too commonly we have loved darkness rather than light. We have deliberately chosen evil in the face of good. We have surrendered to the enticements of the world and rejected the imperishable values of the spirit. We have been poor soil in which thy truth could grow, and we have given weak expression to thy way of life. The coming of thy Kingdom tarries long because of our slothfulness. As we now surrender ourselves to thee, do thou take new possession of us that under thy leadership a better chapter may be written in our lives' story.

May we come to know the folly of becoming so busy and overscheduled that our inner lives go uncared for and become filled with worthless things when they could be managed as a priceless possession where the best is to be established and nurtured.

Let thy possession of us lead us to abhor a life that is without purpose and an outlook that does not comprehend service. Challenge us today with the possibility that waits on our doorsill, to equip the Church better to feed the souls of men.

May this hour of worship bring us so close to Jesus that, seeing the contrast between his depth and our shallowness, we may be done with lesser things, and rising up and following him, may someone's sorrow be lessened, someone's burden lightened, someone's appreciations refined, someone's temptations con-

SUNDAY: MARCH TWENTY-FIFTH

quered, someone's spiritual companionship made vital.—Russell Van Alen.

Illustrations

LOOKING UP. Two women while driving across a lonely section of country encountered tire trouble. The rear tire of their car went flat.

When they had stopped the car and alighted, one of them said: "This is a fine state of affairs. Oh, for an angel now."

"Here I am," shouted a voice from above them.

The women both looked up, and, sure enough, a man—a telephone lineman—was climbing down the pole on which he had been at work. He helped them change the tire, and his parting words to them as they started to drive away were, "When in trouble, look up."

COMMON WORSHIP. Every Sunday as we worship, we are surrounded by the saints of the ages, by the children of the present, and by fellow Christians with as wide a variety of problems and needs as there are human beings. And all of us are here to praise God with joy; to confess our shortcomings and our need for more than ourselves; to gain instruction and inspiration, and plunge into life with new resolve.—David B. Watermulder.

GRAVE OMISSION. The dominant note of modern British philosophy is quite opposed to all forms of religious belief. Most modern philosophers miss no opportunity in their writings and in their broadcasts to discredit the claims of religion and of the Christian faith in particular. Those who do this are brilliant men, and they are sincere in their search for truth. Yet in their attempts to reduce the whole of experience to knowledgeable human terms they seem to have made one grave omission: they have overlooked themselves! In their desire to give a naturalistic interpretation of life and experience they have failed to realize that they are only rational, intelligent beings themselves because behind them is the infinite greater reason and intelligence of God. —Raymond J. Jones.

Sermon Suggestions

NEW TESTAMENT LIFE. Text: Matt. 6:20. There is something different in the life revealed in the New Testament. There we find people sustained: (1) By a faith that is unshakable. (2) By a fellowship that is enduring. (3) By a peace that baffles understanding.—Harry H. Wiggins.

SOURCES OF HOPE AND CONFIDENCE. Scripture: Ps. 61. (1) "I will abide" (v. 4). (2) "I will trust" (v. 4). (3) "I will pray" (v. 2). (4) "I will sing" (v. 8).—C. Reuben Anderson.

EVENING SERVICE

Topic: Christian Life in a Time of Change

We live in a new time. Every generation feels that way about itself, but this time it is true! Only superlatives can get at the facts, only exaggerations are true. Never before in the long history of human affairs has mankind had to make so many profound decisions in so short a time. That is the overwhelming fact about our technological time. Never before has a great society been within grasp. Never has disaster been so threatening. Never have problems been so complex and solutions so baffling. Never has a new society been so desperately needed. Never have the alternatives been so striking.

Several responses to all this technological change are possible.

I. We could cling to the past. Religious people are especially enticed by this option. Christianity believes in a world that cannot be shaken. The Gospel declares Jesus Christ as the same yesterday, today, and tomorrow. Hence we tend to ignore change, or resist it, or deny it.

II. We might seize every new thing

as panacea and consider every change as progress, as though it were an escalator taking us ever upward and onward.

III. We might give up in frightened resignation. (See Luke 21:25-26, NEB.) Such default would betray our basic Christian commitment to live by faith.

IV. It is exactly when the unchangeable things are known to change that the power of God becomes most available to men. Then they must live by faith or not at all. When the good earth is no longer good, when the human power to destroy exceeds the divine power to create, when birth can be controlled and death postponed and the genetic nature of human nature be deliberately managed, when men can make and change things which heretofore we felt were God's province only, when all the certainties of the past are shaken and the whole stability of the established order is threatened, and everything once secure is infected with change—then we do indeed live by faith, or we fall with everything fallen.—Robert H. Hamill. Abridged from *Plenty and Trouble* (Nashville, Abingdon Press, 1971).

SUNDAY: APRIL FIRST

MORNING SERVICE

Topic: What Is Christianity All About? (Lent)

TEXT: Col. 1:3-5.

I. *Faith in Christ Jesus.* (1) Faith is the starting point. No one is a Christian without faith. (See Heb. 11:6.) Here is a company of people who have heard the Gospel from the lips of his colleague, Epaphras, and who have turned to Christ and placed faith in him.

(2) Faith is a simple word that can mean a lot of things, and in fact, in this letter, at least three aspects of faith are mentioned.

(a) There is the inheritance of faith, the body of Christian truth which these Colossian believers are counseled to adhere to in the face of false teaching. (See Col. 1:23.)

(b) There is faith as the response of an individual to the call of Christ—the act of commitment. The Gospel comes to us with our name on it. The Gospel tells us of God's great love, and all that Christ has done for us, and all that he can mean to us as Savior, Redeemer, Lord, Master, Friend, Counselor, Guide, Life. Faith lays hold upon all this and draws the blessings and benefits of Christ as we come to know "the grace of God in truth" (Col. 1:6).

(c) Faith is also a way of living, a new outlook, a distinctive life-style. And so the Christian lives by faith; he walks by faith; he meets every situation that comes to him in faith. His faith grows; it is tested and one day will be rewarded.

II. *Love for God's people.* Paul moves on to talk about the expression of faith. (1) How do you know that you are a Christian? How do you test your belief? Paul gives us an answer here. We know the reality of our faith by the quality of our love. Normally it is love to God, but here it is love for our fellow Christians.

(2) How would you define love in this context? (a) Love, when it is lived out, should make it easier for other people to believe in God.

(b) Substitute for love the word care. "You shall care for your neighbor as you care for yourself." "Well," said Jesus, "here's a test. Love the Lord thy God; care for his honor and glory, and care for your neighbor as you care for yourself."

(3) It was said in a later generation of the Church, "See how these Christians love one another." Not a cynical

comment, as it has become today, but a plain statement of observable, tangible fact. Love is an action to be performed.

III. *A hope laid up in heaven.* (1) Paul is thankful to be able to record that these Christian believers at Colossae have a hope that is laid up in heaven.

(2) Hope is faith that stretches itself in its outlook to the future and finds that future to be one of confidence and assurance and certainty, not because of anything in us, nor because we are naturally optimistic about the future.

(3) The writer of Heb. 6:19–20 has in mind that curtain separating time and eternity, the seen from the unseen, the tangible from the intangible. Hope penetrates the barrier, pierces the curtain, and sets itself in the presence of God. Hope, as the anchor, pulls us irresistibly forward, because Jesus our forerunner has entered through that veil and now lives in the presence of God, and he is the guarantor of the promises of God. He is the ground of our hope.—Ralph P. Martin in *The Standard*.

Worship Aids

CALL TO WORSHIP. "Come unto me, all ye that labor and are heavy laden, and I will give you rest. Take my yoke upon you, and learn of me; for I am meek and lowly in heart: and ye shall find rest unto your souls." Matt. 11:28–29.

INVOCATION. Eternal God, in whom we live and move and have our being, whose face is hidden from us by our sins and whose mercy we forget in the blindness of our hearts: cleanse us, we beseech thee, from all our offenses and deliver us from proud thoughts and vain desires, that with lowliness and meekness we may draw near to thee, confessing our faults, confiding in thy grace, and finding in thee our refuge and our strength.

OFFERTORY SENTENCE. "Give unto the Lord the glory due unto his name: bring an offering, and come before him." I Chron. 16:29.

OFFERTORY PRAYER. Dear Lord, as we travel the highways of life give us a generous and sympathetic spirit for all people in all circumstances of life.

PRAYER. Our Father in heaven, we thank thee for writing a book for us, by inspiring devout men in ages past, which has the correct answers to life's most perplexing problems. We thank thee for preserving it for us through persecutions and indifference and for giving it to us in a language that we can understand. May we never regard the Bible as a mere ornament in our homes to impress others, but as thy special word to us. Let it be "a lamp unto our feet and a light unto our path." May we search it daily that we may become "wise unto salvation through faith which is in Christ Jesus." Help us to find in thy Book the comfort we need in our sorrows, the guidance we need in our confusion, the faith we need to overcome all doubt, and the hope we need when life seems to have lost all meaning. Direct us through thy Word to see how weak and sinful is our life and how great is thy love that is ready to forgive us for Jesus' sake. May we through daily and consecrated study of the Holy Scriptures learn to know thee better, to love and serve thee more, and to trust thee fully for time and for eternity.—Armin C. Oldsen.

Illustrations

UNTIL SURRENDER. The claims of our Lord set a man against himself, I discover. They split him down the middle. They make him schizoid. Once he faces up to the claims of Christ he is divided, he is at war, until surrender. He can never be justified by what he does: his new gadgets, his nursery rhyme creeds, his one-eyed philosophies, his mud-pie civilization, his kindergarten councils. He can be justified only in himself, and his justification begins only when he is a man of peace, and his peace comes only when he surrenders to the Source of peace against which he fights.—Carlyle Marney in *Peace! Peace!*

WHERE THE WAY BEGINS. We think we must climb to a certain height of goodness before we can reach God. But he says not "At the end of the way you may find me"; he says "I am the Way; I am the road under your feet, the road that begins just as low down as you happen to be." If we are in a hole, the Way begins in the hole. The moment we set our feet in the same direction as his, we are walking with God.—Helen Wodehous.

Sermon Suggestions

GOD'S FORMULA. God has made his formula for church extension clear. We must have these four ingredients: (1) Increased spiritual vision. (2) Greater spiritual vigor. (3) More obedience in Christian giving. (4) More dedicated personnel.—Luther Grubb.

SOME MARKS OF THE CHRISTIAN. Text: Gal. 6:17. (1) The birth mark. (See John 3:3.) (2) The water mark. (See Rom. 6:4.) (3) The knee mark. (4) The collar mark. (See Matt. 29:30.)—Herman E. Rowlett.

EVENING SERVICE

Topic: The Supreme Incentive
TEXT: II Cor. 5:14.
I. The love of Christ was perfect in its expression. The quality of love is revealed by its expression. (1) As it manifests itself in conduct or action it declares itself whether it is only a superficial emotion, a mere whim, a sudden impulse, or a profound and permanent direction of the mind and heart.

(2) Judged by all these tests the love of Christ proved itself unique and sublime. For the salvation of mankind he gave not a part but the whole of his being. He saw the tragedy of humanity, its fate concentrated and summed up in its sin, and his death was the answer to that tragedy.

II. The love of Jesus was unlimited in its scope. (1) All exclusion of nations or faces from the benefits of the Gospel and of civilization are bound to fail. Missions are not an accident of the life of the Church. They are not an accretion to Christian activity. They are of the essence of the Gospel.

(2) The death of Christ, as Paul saw, was the means by which God was to reconcile all things to himself, whether they were things on earth or things in heaven. That gives us the measure of the scope of the love of Christ.

III. The love of Christ was sublime in its purpose. (1) The purpose of anything is that which it aims at, what it seeks to accomplish. That is expressed with perfect clarity by the apostle when he says, "That they who live should no longer live unto themselves."

(2) By the necessities of life we are all compelled to think of ourselves. That is at once legitimate and reasonable. But what is legitimate and reasonable may become a passion, an obsession, perhaps a mania, and everything beyond ourselves be ignored or forgotten.

(3) What we need is the reversal of this enthronement of selfishness, and that is to live for him who for our sakes died and rose again. That is living for others, a true altruism which gives personal service for our fellows.

IV. This love constrains us. (1) Christ's love is a compelling power. "Constrains" is a strong word, and in the original means holds us like a vise. We are held; we cannot do otherwise. We are under complete restraint and constraint, under pressure of an infinite obligation. Love in its supreme expression always takes this form.

(2) By looking unto Jesus the Church is to find its power. To do things in the

moral as in the physical world we need power, and in that higher region nothing compels but love. It gives power, and looking unto him who is the Author and Finisher of our faith we shall always be enabled to say, "I can do all things through him that strengthens me."—Joseph Shillinglaw.

SUNDAY: APRIL EIGHTH

MORNING SERVICE

Topic: The Crucial Hour (Passion Sunday)

TEXT: Luke 22:53.

In Jesus' life it had always been "my hour." Once he spoke with caution and reserve: "Mine hour is not yet come." Another time, the Gospel writer called it "his hour." But now everything seemed to be in reverse; the tables were turned, as we are apt to say. Jesus faced these temple officials and the other rabble and said: "This is your hour." How could this be?

I. It was their hour because they were about to be seen for what they were. (1) For three years Jesus' work among his people had been marked by kindness, mercy, and sympathetic concern for all, especially the helpless. Yet his overtures of love and the sincerity of his motives were met with ignorant superstition, cold indifference, or the heated opposition of religious respectability.

(2) As the days passed, it was clear that the rolling momentum of this wave of passion had to break sometime. Or, to change the metaphor, inevitably the festering sore must discharge. Things were mounting toward a climax. Jesus had done everything for these people—he had taught, healed, blessed, and pleaded with them—everything short of making the ultimate sacrifice.

(3) Now it was their move. And in this final act the people—people similar to you and me—were to show the world with staggering frightfulness what human nature can stoop to do.

(4) We cannot go on hiding what we are. The crucial time comes when we are confronted with the Lord of life whom we cannot avoid, whom we cannot beat down, and who will not close his eyes to the exceeding sinfulness of sin, and we are forced to stand in confusion and nakedness before him. It is the moment of life or death. "This is your hour."

II. It was their hour because they were forced to fight him on their own ground.

(1) Up to this time in his ministry it had always been the very opposite. They had tried to meet him on his ground, but the results were always confusion and embarrassment on their part.

(2) After Gethsemane Jesus moved on a different level. He was now held and undergirded by the vast security of the Father's will. And those who tried to lure him into a battle on their ground experienced the maddening frustration of their own sorry hour.

III. It was their hour because their old order was about to be shattered by the new.

(1) What was uppermost in their minds in this hour? This Jesus had been a thorn in their flesh—he flouted the Jewish law; he accused religious people of hypocrisy; he was too fond of sinners and social outcasts; he made church folk feel uncomfortable and gave them an uneasy conscience. Therefore, the most expedient thing to do was to get rid of him. After all, their God was safely institutionalized within the framework of a Law, but this Man had let God loose and was upsetting things in a sweeping fashion. Put him to death and then all will be over and done with, they hoped.

(2) But these enemies of Jesus discovered that the battle they were fight-

ing was not limited to an hour. It turned out to be a moral and spiritual encounter, and such a struggle is not between today and tomorrow, but between today and forever, because the eternal God is involved in it. They could rub Jesus out by their own methods in three short hours, but within three days they were to discover that God is beyond death in a realm where hate cannot live and envy cannot work. Calvary was their hour, but this ugly strategy came smash up against God's order of love, and love was to win the day.

(3) Were it not for that love, it would have been their hour in the most dreadful sense—the hour of everlasting death. But when love goes as far as it can in meeting sin, the painful encounter takes the shape of a Cross, and what in man's hands spells death, in God's hands proclaims life, victory, and hope. —Donald Macleod.

Worship Aids

CALL TO WORSHIP. "Worthy is the Lamb that was slain to receive power, and riches, and wisdom, and strength, and honor, and glory, and blessing." Rev. 5:12.

INVOCATION. Almighty God, the Giver and Lord of life: we bless and praise thee for thy merciful keeping and gracious care, for all the gifts of thy providence and grace, and for all the blessings which manifest thy Fatherhood. We thank thee for the faith which sustains us, the hopes which inspire us, and the light by which we daily walk. We thank thee for Jesus Christ, who, by the life he lived, the temptations he conquered, the gospel he taught, and the Cross he bore, has brought us nigh to thee and closer to one another.

OFFERTORY SENTENCE. "If any man will come after me [saith Jesus], let him deny himself, and take up his cross daily, and follow me." Luke 9:23.

OFFERTORY PRAYER. Our Father, help us this day to remember that we do not live in our own strength but that thou art our help, and that from thee cometh even these gifts which we consecrate in Christ's name.

PRAYER. O God, who hast redeemed us through the mystery of the Cross: we bow before thee in reverent gratitude for the revelation of thy love declared in Jesus Christ. We praise thee that he shared our common life and humbled himself and became obedient unto death, even the death of the Cross. We bless thee that he bore our griefs, carried our sorrows, and triumphed over sin and death. We glorify thee that through his perfect and sufficient sacrifice on the Cross there is pardon for the penitent, power to overcome for the faithful, and transformed life for all who truly turn to him.

Give us grace to yield ourselves in glad surrender to the Lord Jesus. May we share his spirit of obedience to thy will, his consecration to the welfare of humanity, and his passion that the Kingdom may come and thy will be done on earth as it is in heaven. So may Christ dwell in our hearts and reign there as our divine Redeemer.— Carl A. Glover.

Illustrations

BATTLE CRY. One man visited Gethsemane. He was sure he would come away chastened, submissive, surrendered, but his thoughts turned to the words of Jesus, "Arise, let us be going" —going to meet the betrayal, the rejection, the accusation, the spittle, the cross. And he said, "I came away from Gethsemane, not depressed into submission, but with a battle cry sounding in my heart."—Charles A. McClain, Jr.

CONSEQUENCES

If there were no calamity, there would be no courage.

If there were no stress, there would be no strength.

If there were no suffering, there would be no sympathy.
If there were no cross, there would be no Christ!

—Harry Emerson Fosdick.

Sermon Suggestions

THE MEANING OF THE CRUCIFIXION. What did it mean for our Lord? Crucifixion means (1) forgiveness, (2) concern, (3) compassion, (4) separation, (5) sacrifice, and (6) death.—John Merck.

A WORD FROM THE SENTENCED. Listen to the last known words of this man sentenced to death beside Jesus. (1) A word of wonder. "Jesus [Lord]" is the word. (2) A word of willingness. "Remember me" pleads this malefactor. (3) A word of witness. "When you come into your kingdom." A dying man dying with Jesus witnesses to his endless life.—J. Roy McComb.

EVENING SERVICE

Topic: Yoked to Christ
TEXT: Matt. 11:28–30.
Every life has its yoke because every life has its work and its burden. This metaphor was so common that all who heard Jesus understood its varied implications.

I. In those days some people wore certain types of yokes with which to carry burdens. Cattle also had yokes with which to pull loads. The Romans put some rebellious tribes, which they conquered, under the yoke until they became submissive. Those who heard our Lord speak these words must have felt that they were addressed directly to them.

II. A yoke not only is linked to a burden, but it becomes a part of the burden. Here and in two other places Jesus refers to the burdens the people bear. In Matt. 23:4 and Luke 11:46 he condemns the legal, Pharisaic ordinances which made religion intolerable to the people. Peter, in Acts 15:10, rebukes the traditional religious demands as an unbearable yoke. Men wanted peace of heart and peace with God, but they could not get it struggling to carry the obligations of a religion of works. Jesus offered them a new burden which was as light as love; he offered them another yoke which was easy; it did not chafe and irk and gall the spirit as did the demands of the law.

III. A yoke was also an instrument of labor. Every man is a servant of someone or something. Jesus said that whoever sinned was a slave of sin (John 8:34). He called them here to yoke-service with him. The yoke of Jesus was the will of his Father. He always wore it and never worked without it (John 8:29). He urged the weary to work in a new yoke and experience a new service which would bring rest, not weariness, to their spirits.

IV. Almost always a yoke implied a union of partnership. A yoke of oxen meant a pair. To take a yoke was to join oneself to another. Here was an offer to become a partner in life's struggle with the Lord of life! Here was a companionship that would dissolve loneliness and reward them with a knowledge of God himself. But better than being with the Lord is the privilege of becoming like him. We take on the characteristics of those with whom we live.

V. A yoke almost always implied that two of a kind were in the yoke. The Scripture forbids joining the unlike in labor (Deut. 22:10). To be a yokefellow with Christ, then, is to become like him. For Christ to take us into his yoke is to assure our transformation; we will become like him as we labor with him and learn of him.—John T. Wallace.

SUNDAY: APRIL FIFTEENTH

MORNING SERVICE

Topic: Beyond Courage (Palm Sunday)

Text: Luke 9:51.

I. The behavior of Jesus on the first Palm Sunday suggests his faith that, when things look blackest, the possibilities are greatest.

(1) When Jesus rode into Jerusalem, he was under no illusions. He knew that what he stood for was not popular. He knew also that it was the key to a better future and that the possibilities in the situation were incalculable. He was confident that, if for the moment he lost his gamble for the heart of the world, he would win it in the end. He could have saved his own life. The Cross was not inevitable. He could have refused it. Instead of going into Jerusalem, he might have returned to Nazareth or Capernaum and thereafter led a comfortable and respectable existence. But he chose to enter Jerusalem, to pass down its main street, through the Garden of Gethsemane, through the judgment hall of Pilate, on out at the other end to die on a cross between two thieves with a prayer for forgiveness on his lips.

(2) It took something beyond courage for Jesus to volunteer for God's sake to set himself against the ugliness and evil of his time. It took faith that, when things look blackest, the possibilities with God are greatest. In the light of history that faith was abundantly justified.

II. The future belongs to those who believe that life is moving toward a purposeful destiny even when the world seems to be going nowhere.

(1) When Jesus "set his face stedfastly to go to Jerusalem," he stood in the tradition of the prophets, believing that God is lord of history. He sensed, as Shakespeare did, "the soul of the wide world, dreaming on things to come." He spoke incessantly of the Kingdom of God, as if it were the goal of everything. As he saw it, no matter how things seem, a man is either for or against the Kingdom, and therein lies the meaning of his life.

(2) If we are going to take the dark future that lies before us and turn it into an Easter dawn, we shall have to understand with the historian, Charles A. Beard, that "the world is not just a bog in which men trample themselves in the mire and die, but something magnificent is going on here. And the challenge to human intelligence is that of making the finest and the best in our heritage prevail." You cannot get courage out of a vacuum or heroism out of nothingness. Courage and heroism like unto that of Jesus require faith that under God "something magnificent is going on here," and we were meant to be part of it.

III. The future belongs to those who see and trust the best things in the worst times.

(1) When Jesus "set his face stedfastly to go to Jerusalem," he went in the faith that the best things in life have their roots in God.

(a) Truth might seem very feeble as a weapon for dealing with the temple police and goodness not very forceful beside men bearing swords, but truth would last.

(b) Love might appear altogether helpless before a mob shouting, "Crucify him," but love would last. Jesus bowed before the evil power of Caiaphas, and Caiaphas condemned him. But history condemned Caiaphas, and gave the future to Jesus. The Romans condemned Jesus to the shame of a rugged cross, but history shamed the Romans and glorified the cross. The noblest things are not so feeble as they seem. They are mighty with the strength of God.

(2) I know these are discouraging

days and the future seems frightfully black. Nevertheless, once long ago, a Man of faith and courage, with the light of God in his eyes, looked squarely into a black future and "set his face stedfastly to Jerusalem."—Harold Blake Walker.

Worship Aids

CALL TO WORSHIP. "Sing unto the Lord, sing psalms unto him. Glory ye in his holy name: let the heart of them rejoice that seek the Lord." Ps. 105: 2–3.

INVOCATION. Great God and Father of mankind, we would make way for thee in our own lives that we may make our own way with thee in thy world. May grateful memories of thy past goodness give us confidence in facing the dark mysteries of the future. Illumine our insights with love that we may not deceive ourselves by believing too little but that we may count on the best until we bring it to pass. Make us equal to our high trusts, reverent in the use of freedom, just in the exercise of power, generous in the protection of weakness. Guide the wayward, comfort the sick, and console the mourning. Have mercy for our sins, and fit us for the life everlasting.—Ralph W. Sockman.

OFFERTORY SENTENCE. "Prepare ye the way of the Lord, make straight in the desert a highway for our God." Isa. 40:3.

OFFERTORY PRAYER. As thy faithful disciples blessed thy coming, O Christ, and spread their garments in the way, covering it with palm branches, may we be ready to lay at thy feet all that we have and are, and to bless thee, O thou who comest in the name of the Lord.

PRAYER. O thou who hast made us for thyself, whose Son has taught us the high reaches of prayer, and whose love restricts our willfulness and forgives our sinfulness when we are penitent, we turn to thee in the quiet of the sanctuary for the benediction of thy presence.

Breathe on us, Breath of God,
Fill us with life anew,
That we may love what thou dost love,
And do what thou wouldst do.

Take from our minds the strain and stress of these days which are trembling between good and evil. Let the ordered and beautiful peace of thy nearness flood our souls. Restore unto us the joy of thy salvation. Make us wholly thine, united and held together by the sacred bonds of the Christian family.

We pray that thou wilt bring us closer to some of the eternal verities of the passion story: our Lord's determination to go to Jerusalem, counting the cost, his loneliness in a friendless and cruel city; his deliberate choice of the way of the Cross; his final disposition of prayer, "Not as I will, but as thou wilt"; and his commitment of heart, body, mind, and soul to God: "Father, into thy hands I commit my spirit."

And we pray that thou wilt increase in us the longing to grow in grace and truth, to be more and more like the blessed Son of God, to gain some of his courage and compassion, to face life's crises as he did, and to go about dying with his certainty of the sustaining power and the steady love of God.—Herbert Beecher Hudnut.

Illustrations

CHRIST ENTERS JERUSALEM. Nothing in his ministry was more deeply considered than this entry into Jerusalem, and nothing required of those who saw it greater seriousness and discernment. Here he presented himself to the assembled nation in character, bringing to the front what he counted significant. He was born to be a king, but a king whose authority rests not on compulsion but on his power to persuade the minds of men, and a king not parted from his people by the wide world of circumstance but sharing their privations and their lowliness; and he maintained that a kingdom founded thus would spread from sea to sea, and would last from age to age.—W. M. MacGregor.

SERVANT OF SERVANTS. "Christ in you" is not a gorgeously robed aristocrat, arrayed in purple and fine linen and gold and pearls, but it is a lowly, peasant Carpenter, horny-handed, truth-telling, a Servant of servants, seeking always the lowest seats in the synagogues and feasts, condescending to wash the disciples' feet. They wanted to make the "Christ in you" a king one day, but he wouldn't be a king, save of men's hearts.—S. L. Brengle.

Sermon Suggestions

ALONE BUT NEVER LONELY. Texts: John 16:32. The greatest Man who ever lived was often alone: "He was alone praying" (Luke 9:18). "Ye shall leave me alone," he told his disciples (John 16:32). He "departed into a solitary place" (Mark 1:35). (1) He was alone in the wilderness when he fasted for 40 days and faced the assaults of the Devil. His only companions were the wild beasts. (2) He was alone on the mountainside. He had no place to lay his head, he tells us. He left the city to find his resting place on the hillside under the stars. We read: "Every man went unto his own house. Jesus went unto the mount of Olives" (John 7:53; 8:1). The contrast is most impressive. (3) Alone in the Garden of Gethsemane, "his sweat was as it were great drops of blood falling down to the ground" (Luke 22:44). As he agonized in prayer his chosen companions were asleep. (4) Alone on the Cross, he endured scoffing and pain while he bore the sins of the world. There his loneliness reached its climax as he cried, "My God, my God, why hast thou forsaken me?" (Matt. 27:46). (5) He was alone in temptation, alone in sorrow, alone in sufferings. No man was ever more alone. He lived and died alone, the lonely, solitary Man. (6) Having experienced such loneliness, he knows exactly how we feel. He is, therefore, able to sympathize with us in our loneliness. How it helps us to have fellowship with Someone who has borne the same burden we bear! His perfect sympathy irradiates our lives with joy. (7) To the words, "Ye shall leave me alone," Jesus added, "Yet I am not alone, because the Father is with me" (John 16:32). The fellowship between Father and Son was the sweetest communion seen anywhere on this earth. Such fellowship strengthened him.—Gordon Chilvers.

WHEN IS ENOUGH ENOUGH? (1) When has one forgiven enough? (2) When has one prayed enough? (3) When has one studied God's word enough? (4) When has one given enough of his resources to God? (5) When has one grown enough as a Christian?—James N. Metts, Jr.

EVENING SERVICE

Topic: Meanings Defined by the Cross

For a long time in Christian history the quest was to define the meaning of the Cross.

I. So there arose the traditional theories of the atonement. (1) There was the ransom theory (Irenaeus, Origen, Augustine, and others), which held that the death of Jesus was a payment to Satan to obtain the release of mankind from hell, where man was sentenced for the sin of Adam.

(2) In the eleventh century Anselm, in his satisfaction theory, the first systematic theological statement of the atonement, interpreted that Christ's death met God's requirements of punishment of man for his sins.

(3) There was also the moral influence theory (Abelard), which set forth that Christ's death moves man to moral transformation, thus making him acceptable to God.

(4) A more modern view of the Cross is that Christ's suffering reveals the suffering God experiences because of the sins of the world.

(5) Preceding all of these ideas is

Paul's declaration, "God was in Christ reconciling the world to himself" (II Cor. 5:19). Paul stressed not how or why but what God had wrought through Christ, acknowledging the overwhelming place of the Cross in the work of Christ: "But far be it from me to glory except in the cross of our Lord Jesus Christ" (Gal. 6:14, RSV).

II. We should always be seeking to find the meaning of the Cross, and we should appreciate and apply the rich insights about the Cross which our fathers in the faith have passed on to us. But the need now is not so much for the defining of the meaning of the Cross as it is for the understanding and accepting by mankind of the meanings which have been defined by the Cross.

(1) The Cross defined that Jesus is greater than all the powers that oppose him.

(2) The Cross made it clear forever that persons are precious to Christ.

(3) The Cross defined for all time that the principle of sacrifice and the role of suffering are the means by which one most powerfully manifests his dedication to the saving of people and the furthering of the Kingdom of God in the world.—*The Methodist Christian Advocate.*

SUNDAY: APRIL TWENTY-SECOND

MORNING SERVICE

Topic: Tears for a Time of Joy (Easter)

SCRIPTURE: John 20:11-18.

The angels and Jesus asked Mary Magdalene on Easter morning, "Woman, why are you weeping?" She explained that she was weeping because she could not find the body of Jesus. These were tears of sorrow. But when Jesus revealed himself to her, her tears turned to tears of joy as she exclaimed, "Rabboni," meaning "Teacher." Her day began with tears but ended with smiles. This is in contrast to last Sunday, *Palmarum,* when the day began with smiles but ended in tears. Easter makes us shed tears of joy. As in the case of Mary, tears of sorrow are transformed into tears of joy.

I. As Mary was asked on the first Easter, "Woman, why are you weeping?" so we are asked on this Easter Sunday why we weep tears of joy.

(1) These tears of joy result from the victory Christ won over death. We cannot appreciate this victory until we realize the horror and finality of death.

(2) Death is man's worst enemy. Death takes away the meaning of life. If death is the ultimate, life is absurd. Then, we can say with Paul, "Let us eat, drink, and be merry, for tomorrow we die."

(3) It took God to gain the victory over death. God caught death on the Cross in the person of Christ. There was a cosmic battle between life and death. When Jesus died, the strife was o'er and the battle was won. The paradox of the situation was that God used Jesus' death to defeat death. When Jesus came out of the tomb under the power of God, death instead of swallowing up everything as in the past was now itself swallowed up by the grace of God. Never was there a victory like this.

(4) Easter, therefore, is a day for the blowing of trumpets, the singing of alleluias, the crashing of cymbals, and the beating of victory drums.

(5) This victory has personal implications. It means that a Christian funeral has a note of triumph about it. Of course, the body is dead, but because of the resurrection we know the soul, spirit, or psyche of the departed is alive with Christ. There is no need to feel sorry for the deceased. He is more alive than we are.

II. On this Easter day, why are you weeping tears of joy? The Christian answers, "Because of the assurance of the truth the resurrection brings."

(1) The resurrection assures us that Jesus is the Christ, Lord and Savior. If there had been no resurrection, Jesus would have been just a man. Indeed, he would have been considered a martyr to a good cause, but that is all. Now we know for sure that Jesus was more than an ordinary man. True, he was all man, but he was a God-man. On Easter you are sure that this Jesus of the Cross was the very Son of God whose death was a vicarious sacrifice for the sin of the world. Because of the resurrection, we know he shares in the Godhead and is worthy of our worship, devotion, and our very lives.

(2) Easter assures us that good will ultimately overcomes all opposition. Sometimes we wonder whether good is as strong as evil. Easter assures us that life will outlast death. Truth is greater than lies. Love is stronger than hatred. The righteous will finally succeed, and the wicked will come to nought.

III. Why tears of joy on Easter? (1) The resurrection comforts us with the knowledge that we have a living Christ here and now. This was the good news for Mary Magdalene. She came to the tomb which she expected to be filled with a dead body. The empty tomb meant to her only that Jesus' body was stolen. Then Jesus came to her and called her by name. At once she saw him alive and rejoiced.

(2) We too can rejoice that Jesus is alive, for it means that we have a living Christ who knows our very name. You are that important, that valuable. It shows his interest and concern in you and what happens to you.

(3) We have a living Christ right now to forgive us. We need forgiveness daily. Without this forgiveness, we get farther and farther apart from Christ. Life gets tied up, and our minds and hearts get into knots of tension. Christ daily comes to us upon our invitation and forgives us and by this forgiveness brings us life and freedom to live as a person.

(4) This living Christ who came to life again on Easter comforts us by his presence. He comes to us and asks our help. Christ asks us this Easter Sunday to be his witnesses. He wants us to go to all the world and tell the good news that death has been conquered, that truth is eternal, that he is really alive forevermore.—John R. Brokhoff.

Worship Aids

CALL TO WORSHIP. "Blessed be the God and Father of our Lord Jesus Christ, which according to his abundant mercy hath begotten us again unto a lively hope by the resurrection of Jesus Christ from the dead, to an inheritance incorruptible, and undefiled, and that fadeth not away, reserved in heaven for you." I Pet. 1:3-4.

INVOCATION. Eternal and ever-blessed God, grant this day light to the minds that hunger for the truth and peace to the hearts which yearn for rest. Grant strength to those who have hard tasks to do and power to those who have sore temptations to face. Grant unto us within this place to find the secret of thy presence and to go forth from it in the strength of the Lord.

OFFERTORY SENTENCE. "Give unto the Lord the glory due unto his name: bring an offering, and come before him: worship the Lord in the beauty of holiness." I Chron. 16:29.

OFFERTORY PRAYER. O God, thou Giver of all good gifts, in gratitude we bring our gifts on this day of joyous worship. Refine them, we pray thee, in the mint of thy divine purpose, and use them to the end that thy Kingdom may come and thy will be done on earth as it is in heaven.

PRAYER. Lord God, our heavenly Father, we know that thou art even now looking upon us with eyes of understanding and compassion, more eager to bless our lives than we to ask thy blessing. We turn to thee with earnest prayer that a channel may be opened into thy grace through which we may receive thy love.

We come into thy presence with happy and glad remembrance of times past when thou hast dealt with us according to thine infinite wisdom and mercy for our own good. Especially we thank thee for the glorious life of deliverance thou hast given us through Jesus Christ, for the light that has come into our lives through the opening of the Holy Scriptures, for the glory that has been given to our daily existence through our life of prayer when each day we speak with thee. We thank thee for the way our lives today are strengthened by these glad experiences of yesterday, for the hope thou dost give the morrow because thou art steadfast and dependable in thy compassionate character. Thy righteousness is unchanging from day to day, from generation unto generation, and thy presence as our living God is the mighty foundation on which we can surely rest our hopes. We ask that thou wilt lift us above the vicissitudes of the current events of our earthly life. Grant that we may find a higher hope and a deeper foundation for our assurance in the unchanging wonder of thy character of goodness and love and wisdom and strength. As we rest our lives in thy care and in thy keeping, may we know in our heart of hearts that all is well.—Lowell M. Atkinson.

Illustration

THE SEPULCHRE AND THE SUN. The women "came unto the sepulchre at the rising of the sun." It is hard to imagine any more vivid contrast than that. The sepulchre—death, dampness, darkness, imprisonment, life cramped into something from which it cannot extricate itself. And on the other hand, the rising sun—brightness, life, vividness, power, mystery, beauty, glory! Sometimes it seems as though this life were a race between the sepulchre and the rising sun, and that the sepulchre had a good head start and was sometimes winning the race. The sepulchres of life are so easy to find, so hard to miss, so easy to describe; the finalities, the places where you bury not only the people you love but the things you have dreamed about and felt you had to give up because they had been snatched away from you. Why, the sepulchres mark the way of life all along! And we say, Well, if life is a race between the sepulchre and the rising sun, the sepulchres are bound to win out. The rising sun, on the other hand, is much more difficult to describe, infinitely more mysterious, alive, renewing; much harder to get one's hands on, but life-giving, life-renewing!—Theodore P. Ferris in *The Pulpit*.

Sermon Suggestions

WHAT THE ANGEL MIGHT HAVE SAID. Text: Matt. 28:6 (RSV). (1) Suppose the angel had said to the women at the tomb, "He is not here"—only that. They would have faced nothing but broken promises and an empty tomb. (2) Suppose he had said: "He is not here. His body has been removed." Then they would have searched in vain until their aromatic spices had lost their fragrance. (3) Suppose he had said: "He is not here. His body has been stolen." Then fearing the approach of Roman soldiers, the women would have fled to avoid entanglement in conspiracy. (4) But when the angel said, "He is not here: for he is risen," the whole picture was changed.—Fred B. Wyand.

THE PROCLAMATION OF THE EASTER ANGEL. Scripture: Luke 24:1-12. (1) The Easter Angel calls from our hearts the confirmation of the fact that God is God of life and death. (2) The proclamation of the Easter Angel is our assurance that our waiting is not in vain, because we live already in eternity. (3) The proclamation of the Easter Angel gives to life dimensions we have not yet experienced.—Harry N. Huxhold.

EASTER IS TODAY. Easter happened once, long ago, at a definite time and place, but there is something timeless about Easter, not bound by the calendar or by pages of ancient history. Easter is today. (1) Easter is trust in God's victory over the doom of this world. (2) Easter is faith in God's justice over the injustices of this life. (3) Easter is joy, always, in spite of every weakness toward despair. This is the Christian encounter with life. This is Christian inheritance. This is resurrection today and hope for the world to come.—Herbert M. Barrall.

EVENING SERVICE

Topic: Easter: Our Commencement Day

TEXT: Mark 16:2.

In the light of the sacred records, let us think of Easter as a God-given time for new beginnings.

I. Let us consider our common worship. (1) As members of God's redeemed family we ought to think of worship as our most vital and wonderful experience here on earth. In this respect Easter ought to serve as a new beginning.

(2) Ever since the first Easter Day, under the guidance of the Holy Spirit, Christian worship has taken on new dimensions of breadth and height. We sing about our Redeemer and about his claim to rule over land and sea, the world around. In his name we utter our prayers and meet with him in loving fellowship at the altar or the communion table. There we live with him in heavenly places and rejoice to believe in the communion of saints, including the whole redeemed family of God, both on earth and in heaven.

II. Easter should mark a new beginning of Christian preaching. (1) As believers in Christ we ought never to ignore or make light of the Cross with its God-given power to save, to bless, to transform. But we who think of the Gospel as centering around the day of the Cross ought also to remember that in its fullness and glory the Gospel of redeeming and transforming power began to win recruits for Christ largely after the first Easter day.

(2) We ought to preach and teach chiefly in the present tense. Much as we ought to exult in the Christ of Yesterday and in the Christ of Tomorrow—the Christ of the Cross and the Christ of the Crown—there is a sense in which we ought mainly to preach about him as the Christ of Today, the Christ of the Church and of Christian experience here and now.

III. Easter ought to stand out on the Christian calendar as a day of new beginnings in Christlike living.

IV. Easter as our commencement day marks the beginning of Christian service.

V. Easter as our commencement day ought to fill our hearts with Christian hope. We who believe in the living Christ can sing and pray, as well as preach and serve, with peace and joy, in the blessed assurance that God's Kingdom will come and that his will is to be done, through the blessed fulfillment of all the promises about the Kingdom, which is "righteousness, and peace, and joy in the Holy Spirit."—Andrew W. Blackwood.

SUNDAY: APRIL TWENTY-NINTH

MORNING SERVICE

Topic: The Heart of Our Message (Orthodox Easter)

Scripture: Luke 15:11-32.

The heart of the Easter message is optimistic, because it deals with God's answer to our human predicament. Yet the pessimism of sin is there, too.

I. God offers us a gift—the gift of eternal life. (1) This eternal life is a now thing. Just as you can experience death in the now, you can experience life in the now. It starts now, and it goes on forever. It is a growing, never-ending experience. No one can ever take it away from you. It involves both this life and the life to come.

(2) This eternal life is a God quality of life that comes from knowing that your sins are forgiven and you are restored to be what God originally created you to be. This is a gift freely given. It is not based on your own merit, for whereas you have earned the wages of your sin, God's eternal life is yours simply for the receiving.

(3) This free gift of eternal life doesn't for a moment minimize all the good works that you might have been doing and that you aspire to do. This is simply saying that there is no way you can buy your way into God's favor. When you have genuinely experienced God's free gift of eternal life, you then will want to respond by doing things that bring glory to him. God's salvation, eternal life, is designed to free you from sin.

(4) True freedom is only to be found in Jesus Christ. His free gift is eternal life, which then enables you to live within the limitations of this world with a sense of direction and purpose. True freedom is not a life without restraint. True freedom is learning to live within restraint in a way that will glorify God and bring happiness to your fellowmen.

II. The good news of Easter is the fact of justification—that because of God's act in Jesus Christ your sins can be removed as far as the East is from the West, making you just as if you had never sinned. The great fact of Easter is the fact of sanctification—that the outgrowth of your justification is the work of the Spirit of God in your life, continually perfecting you as you grow in the knowledge and love of Jesus Christ. He made it all possible. He is your Savior and must be your Lord.

III. The Easter message is a story of tension—the pessimism of sin being vacuumed up by the optimism of eternal life in Jesus Christ. This pessimism of the wages of sin being death is best summarized in Christ's story which can bear two titles.

(1) It is the story of the prodigal son who, restless in his father's home, asked for his inheritance. He took off into a distant country. He had friends as long as he had money to spend on wine, women, and song. But his money ran out, and so did his friends. The prodigal ended up eating the slop he was supposed to serve to the pigs—a despicable thing for a Jewish lad. The wages of sin is death.

(2) But the optimism of the Easter message is also best summarized in this same story which can be called the story of the loving father, whose heart was broken by his son's rebellion. He stood, day in and day out, on the hillside, watching, yearning for the return of his wayward boy. The day came that the son returned, hoping only to be treated as a servant in the house of his father, knowing he had thrown away his birthright. But the father was still there, faithfullly scanning the horizon. His face was probably creased with the years that had gone by. His hair most likely was whitened by concern and age. And on that fateful day he saw his son in the distance. He rushed forward to

meet him.—John A. Huffman, Jr., in *Christian Life*.

Worship Aids

CALL TO WORSHIP. "God hath exalted him, and given him a name which is above every name: that at the name of Jesus every knee should bow, of things in heaven, and things in earth, and things under the earth; and that every tongue should confess that Jesus Christ is Lord, to the glory of God the Father." Phil. 2:9–11.

INVOCATION. O thou who hast granted us the light of thy truth and hast made thy way known to us so plainly in the revelation of thy Word: we pray today for all those who seek to bring wisdom to thy human children, remembering especially all those in the schools of our land. We pray for teachers that they may be granted thy wisdom, for students that they may be diligent to learn, for all who administer our schools that with patient skill they may lead the way so that the schools may be a firm foundation to what is good in America and may increase themselves in strength. Do thou grant to all of us an understanding of thy will, that above the confusion and fog of our modern life there may come to us a revelation of what is right and what is wrong. Grant us wisdom that when we know what is right we may walk in that path.—Robert W. Burns.

OFFERTORY SENTENCE. "Every good gift and every perfect gift is from above, and cometh down from the Father of lights." Jas. 1:17.

OFFERTORY PRAYER. Cleanse and accept these our gifts, O God, and may they be used according to thy will to redeem, restore, and renew the ministries within thy Kingdom.

PRAYER. Heavenly Father, we thank thee we are called to be children of the light. Even though we have been children of the darkness, and have loved the ways of error rather than of truth, and of sin rather than of holiness, thou art calling us to the light of eternal day. We would answer thy call in penitence, and we would return to thee like wayward children who are coming home again. We do not ask to lose the sense of our shame, but we ask to taste the sweetness of thy forgiveness. We do not ask to forget our rebelliousness, but we ask to be assured that we are reconciled to thee. We would sit at thy table and receive the bread of life. We would worship at thy feet and receive the baptism of the Holy Spirit. We would stand before thee with our feet shod with the shoes of readiness, willing to go out on errands of Christian love and service. If we are inclined to frivolity may we become inclined to be serious and reverent. If we are heedless may we become fired with heavenly ambition and spiritual devotion. Redeem us from the littleness of selfishness and lift us into the blessed communion of our fellowmen. Give us a wide and generous outlook upon human affairs. Endow us with the sympathy that rejoices with them who are rejoicing and that weeps with them that weep. If thou art leading us through the gloom of adversity may we find that even the clouds drop fatness. If thou art leading us through the green pastures and by the still waters, may we recognize the presence of the great Shepherd and may our joys be sanctified. Hallow all our experiences, we humbly pray thee, and may we all become branches in the vine of our Lord. —John Henry Jowett.

Illustrations

BOWING DOWN. In the last chapter of Fëdor Dostoevski's novel, *The Possessed*, the author has Stepan Trofimovitch declare: "The essential condition of human existence is that men should always be able to bow down before something infinitely great. If men are deprived of this, they cannot go on living, they will die of despair."

SUNDAY: APRIL TWENTY-NINTH

ROOT OF VIRTUE. A vital religion is the root of virtue. What a man believes about God and the moral government of the universe is bound to affect his conduct. A noble creed makes for noble living. Low thoughts on the meaning and value of life produce low actions. A vague and formless faith operates in the direction of a vague and irresolute character. The moral life is not self-sufficient. Goodness is a flower whose roots strike deep into the soil of belief. Disregard the roots and the flower withers and dies.—Robert J. McCracken.

Sermon Suggestions

THE VIEW FROM THE SUMMIT. There is such a difference in the mood between Easter Sunday and the Sunday that follows that sometimes you might wonder if you were in the same church. On Easter Sunday there is always a great congregation; there are the beautiful lilies that grace the altar; there is an atmosphere of high anticipation. That is mostly gone on the Sunday after Easter. Easter Sunday was a mountaintop experience for those people in Jerusalem. On Easter Sunday they stood at the summit and viewed life from that lofty vantage point. But it didn't last for them, just as the joy and excitement and beauty of our own Easter observance does not last as long as we wish that it might. (1) Apparently no one is allowed to remain at the summit. We are not permitted to take up permanent residence there. There are occasions in a man's life when he feels as if somehow he has been lifted up into seventh heaven. It may be the inspiration of great music. It may be the fellowship of kindred spirits. It may be the total and self-giving love of another person. It may be some spiritual insight which suddenly comes alive for us and illuminates the scene like a powerful light that is turned on in a dark room. As I say, sometimes we can explain it; at other times there doesn't seem to be any apparent explanation. We wake up in the morning and the sun is shining and suddenly it is sheer bliss just to be alive. We have all had such experiences at one time or another. But it is never permanent. For some reason of its own, life does not permit us to take up residence at the summit. (2) There is always something of the summit that remains with him. We retain something of the inspiration for those days when life must be lived at sea level. That is what happened after the first Easter. It was a mountaintop experience for those disciples who saw Jesus and knew that he was alive. They were not permitted to remain at the summit, but something from the summit remained with them. (3) The important thing about the summit is always the view. The view from the summit shows us two things: it shows us life as it is, and it also shows us life as it will be! There is only one place where you can see life as it is, and life as it will be. You have to see it from the summit. Easter is a summit from which we can catch a view of life as it is and life as God intends it to be. —Clarence J. Forsberg.

CAUGHT BETWEEN SHOCK AND ASSURANCE. Text: Luke 24:32 (ABS). (1) The Emmaus road fellowship reminds us that life is in constant tension between shock and assurance. (2) The Emmaus story suggests that Jesus has the ability to make sense out of things. (3) This record of an Easter afternoon walk says that to wake to the Resurrection hope is to feel the agony of coming alive. (4) This Easter afternoon scene reminds us that the secret of vital Christian experience must be shared to be fully real.—Hoover Rupert.

EVENING SERVICE

Topic: The Life of Faith and Doubt (National Christian College Day)
TEXT: Rom. 12:3.
There are several relationships between faith and doubt that the Christian may possibly maintain and not just

the one alleged relationship where they mutually exclude each other. Let us consider some of these relationships.

I. It would be tragic if a Christian could entertain no doubts at all. For, plainly, there are times when it would be unchristian not to doubt.

(1) What Paul is primarily concerned about is personal knowledge or insight, the kind of insight whereby we know ourselves as we are known. The knowledge he has in mind comes from looking into ourselves intensively and arriving at a better understanding of those motives that prompt our actions, those personal drives that bring our ambitions alive. He is asking us to develop that kind of sober judgment that would enable us to see through the facade surrounding our actions, our words, and our thoughts. He is claiming that it is unchristian not to doubt some of the visions of our personal grandeur.

(2) Though Paul is speaking about the knowledge of oneself alone, there is here, I am sure, a principle that can be enlarged to apply to the act of obtaining all knowledge. For in obtaining all of our knowledge we must be critical in our judgments. In order to do this, the Christian must at times doubt the knowledge he presently has.

II. There are times when the Christian must simply say: "I don't know." In such instances he does not need to doubt nor exercise faith. He simply suspends judgment.

(1) According to Paul, claims about our self-knowledge should not be exaggerated. The ability to say, "I don't know," should stem from Christian humility which Paul calls the followers of Christ to possess.

(2) Not only, then, are there times when a Christian must doubt, but there are also times when he should say: "I don't know." He experiences the twilight of understanding where doubt and faith give way to humility and even reverent agnosticism.

III. There are times when the Christian should sense the interplay of doubt and faith—times when his life is caught in the grip of the tensions and opposing forces of doubt and faith.

(1) The text speaks to us again. Paul holds that our thinking should proceed according to "the measure of faith" that we have. But that is just the trouble. We are always pretending to have a greater measure of faith than we actually do. As a result, we have allowed the reality of the Christian life to evaporate into an ideal world, which does not exist, where the Christian becomes that clean, pure person who does not dirty his mind with doubt. In that world, he is the acme of perfection. Being perfect, he is unable and unwilling to move through the precarious tensions of faith and doubt. Thus the Christian assumes that his life will be one without problems. Far too many times he regards his life as a sheltered life, the life where every problem is solved.

(2) The unvarnished fact is that the Bible plainly denies this view of the Christian life. The Bible points out the tensions of life—faith and doubt, to mention two such tensions.—Ivan E. Frick.

SUNDAY: MAY SIXTH

MORNING SERVICE

Topic: The Making of Christian Homes (National Family Week)
TEXT: Eph. 5:1.

I. The Christian home must be based on the foundation of absolute and unshakable loyalty within the marriage relationship.

(1) This unique relationship into which a stranger does not intrude is what makes a marriage a success and leads to true happiness. Such unshakable loyalty "pays off," for no other

way has yet been discovered for a man and woman completely to satisfy one another and to fulfill each other's deepest needs. Only thus do they "become one," as they were meant to be. There is no other method of creating permanence, stability, and happiness in a home and family.

(2) In a day when Christian people are recognizing the fact that sex is one of God's good gifts, that it is nothing "dirty" or to be ashamed about at all, but rather one of life's truest blessings —at such a time the commandment, "Thou shalt not commit adultery," is still the best advice for a prospective bride and groom. Adultery, be it physical or spiritual, is still a poison that kills a marriage. One cannot speak or think lightly of something that sooner or later, and almost inevitably, wrecks a family.

II. The Christian home must be controlled by a spirit of loving respect for each person in it as an individual. "The husband," St. Paul writes, "is the head of the wife. As the church is subject to Christ, so let wives also be subject in everything to their husbands." Didn't you women rebel as you listened to these words? How outrageous they sound to modern ears! "Children," he continues, "obey your parents . . . for this is right." Is there a young person anywhere who doesn't hate the sound of this?

(1) What is St. Paul really saying? In a day and age when a woman was her husband's property and when parents were expected to be tyrants, often having the power of life and death over their childreen, and in a social system far different from our own, St. Paul is insisting that the relationship between men and women and between young and old in the home should be one of mutual concern, consideration, and deference. "Be subject to one another out of reverence for Christ," he insists, and this was indeed a revolutionary point of view.

(2) He is telling the men that they should love their wives, not just own them and use them. Likewise, the relationship between parents and children is to be put on an entirely different plane from that which was customary in St. Paul's world. Parents are to be considerate, understanding, long-suffering, patient, and kind.

(3) In our world of increasingly impersonal relationships, where in business and in industry human beings are more and more becoming "interchangeable parts" of the organizational machine, the Christian family ought to be the one place where each person is cherished, respected, and loved for what he or she actually is. The Christian home is the one place where nobody is somebody else's doormat and where all have a place in each other's affection and concern.

(4) In such a Christian family each member will in turn have a real reverence and respect for the welfare and the plans of all.

III. The Christian home should be a place where God is acknowledged and reverenced at all times.

(1) What the New Testament is saying to us as families is that every home must be a kind of church, or it isn't a Christian home or a stable and happy home. The institutional church to which we come on Sunday cannot substitute for the Christian home, nor can it succeed without it. Christianity is a "house" religion, and, as such, it stands or falls.

(2) We sometimes say that "the family that prays together stays together." However, the atmosphere of the home as much as formality of religious observance makes it Christian. The first question to ask is: "Do the people in it live in obedience to Christian teachings and principles and in reverent awareness in all things of the presence of God?"

(3) Ask yourself whether or not your home is a place where people pray, where children are helped to learn how to do this, where God is recognized and talked about and children's questions about him are answered conscientiously,

where work is done, decisions made, and plans are carried out as if you were a family of the children of God.—Edward C. Dahl.

Worship Aids

CALL TO WORSHIP. "Whatsoever things are true, whatsoever things are honest, whatsoever things are just, whatsoever things are pure, whatsoever things are lovely, whatsoever things are of good report; if there be any virtue, and if there be any praise, think on these things." Phil. 4:8.

INVOCATION. O God our Father, Creator of the universe and Giver of all good things: we thank thee for our home on earth and for the joy of living. We praise thee for thy love in Jesus Christ, who came to set things right, who died rejected on the Cross, and who rose triumphant from the dead. Because he lives, we live to praise thee, Father, Son, and Holy Spirit, our God forever.

OFFERTORY SENTENCE. "Greater love hath no man than this, that a man lay down his life for his friends." John 15:13.

OFFERTORY PRAYER. Our Father, help us who claim to be Christians to bring forth fruit consistent with our profession of faith. May these tithes and offerings be so used that others may hear the glad story of thy redeeming love.

PRAYER. O thou eternal God who art the Father of us all, we lift our hearts in the intercession for this our city.

We bless thee for all that makes it a good place in which to live and work. We thank thee for the way in which so many people of such varied national and racial origins live together in mutual appreciation and understanding. We bless thee for our homes in which the simple but fundamental virtues of kindliness and cooperation are nurtured; for the schools in which our youth are trained with knowledge and wisdom for participation in our city's life; for our industries and business concerns which with imagination and drive afford to so many of our people the opportunity to make secure the economic base for the good life; for the multitudes of public officials who serve us with honesty and efficiency; for the private and public institutions which labor to meet our physical, social, and cultural needs; for the charities of the city which minister to the moral and spiritual needs of our people.

But we would also lay before thee, thou great Shepherd of our souls, the unmet needs of our people. We would pray for those who must live under conditions which make the creation and maintenance of real homes distressingly difficult; for the children and young people who are not learning the most important lessons of life; for the multitudes whose work is monotonous, degrading, or uncertain; for those whose life is concerned primarily with the struggle for mere existence or in pursuing false or superficial values; for those who are indifferent to the claims of the Church for the moral and spiritual undergirding of their lives, or whose adherence to their faith is but nominal or formal. We acknowledge before thee with shame and sorrow the deplorable sag in the moral standards of our people both in high places and in low.

O thou who art the Lover of all men, look with compassion upon the multitudes of our city. Arouse within our citizens a new concern for the moral and spiritual welfare of our city. Make of all our churches centers which will radiate goodwill, righteousness, and faith in thee until the city of our pride becomes the city of God.—Kenneth D. Miller.

Illustrations

CHRISTIAN HOME. A young Oriental, a graduate of one of America's finest medical schools, shortly before his return to his homeland was visiting in a Christian home where he had often been a guest during his student days.

"Doctor," said his host, as they sat about the dinner table, "tell us, what has impressed you most about American life during your stay in our country?"

Looking around the family circle of well-loved Christian friends, and without a moment of hesitation, the young doctor replied: "This is the most wonderful thing I have seen in America, this Christian home. We have nothing like it in my country."—Fred W. Hoffman in *Baptist Observer*.

ANALOGY. A growing child is like the young tree, which, sheltered by others that have reached full growth, does not, as yet, require roots that are broad and deep. But, by and by, these defenses will be removed. He will be left to stand alone, enduring and resisting as best he can, while the frosts of the world's selfishness chill his generous sympathies and the tempests of stormy passions assail him as the whirlwind smites the oak. Then he will need those convictions and sentiments which it is now his daily privilege to absorb from his father's example, his mother's instruction, the companionship of his sister, and all the beneficent influences of the early home.—*The Universalist Leader*.

Sermon Suggestions

MAKING YOUR MARRIAGE SECURE. Text: Luke 14:28. The rope of marriage is made up of many individual strands that must be woven together with loving care by husband and wife. Many marriage ropes break simply because these strands have been neglected. Every so often, all of us ought to take another look at these strands and see what we can do to keep them in tiptop shape. (1) The strand called commitment. (2) The strand of honesty. (3) The strand of a loving concern. (4) The strand of grace.—George L. Earnshaw.

A LADDER FOR YOUTH. As you start out in life, you will need five things: (1) A faith to live by. (2) A cause to serve. (3) A fellowship in which that faith can be nourished and through which that cause can be served. (4) A decision to accept that faith, serve that cause, and enter that fellowship. (5) A life dedication to that faith, to that cause, to that fellowship.—E. Stanley Jones.

TEACHING THEM. Text: Matt. 28:20. (1) Consider the teacher as witness. (2) Consider the teacher as interpreter. (3) Consider the teacher as tormentor.—Wesley P. Ford.

EVENING SERVICE

Topic: Raising Children for God's Kingdom

TEXT: Eph. 6:1-2.

Our Christian families are part of God's program of salvation. Parents who raise children to know and fear God's name play a key role in what God is doing in the world. And children who honor their parents are object lessons to friends and neighbors of the reverence and respect we owe to God, who is the Father of us all. Though the commandment Eph. 6 is given to children, the parents' responsibilities are implicit in it.

I. It is our first responsibility to remember that our children belong more to God than to us.

(1) He has high hopes and fine plans for them, and he counts on us to help them be what he wants them to be. We don't own our children. We have them as a trust from God.

(2) As we teach our children the dignity of being human, we teach them to honor God even above us, their parents. We do this best by the way we ourselves honor God.

II. Our second responsibility in helping our children obey God's command is to be sure that we honor our children as persons made for God.

(1) Where do children learn what honor and obedience mean? From our example. Our respect for them is the best way to insure their regard for us.

(2) Some people think children are to be broken like wild horses. But our ultimate aim is to relate to our children, not to ride them. It is their maturity, not our mastery, that we must seek.

III. Our third responsibility is to remind our children that honoring others adds to our own dignity as persons.

(1) This is particularly true of our attitude toward parents. We are so much a part of our parents—their fingerprints are all over us—that what they are cannot be separated from what we have become. Any person who detracts from his parents' dignity—whatever their station in life or however they have treated him—diminishes his own sense of worth.

(2) Can we treat children like people? Yes, by treating them with dignity and preparing them for responsibility.

(3) Always a realist, Paul knows that we parents are as much flawed by sin as our children are. We can easily pervert the commandment that calls for their obedience into a personal power play. Paul's warning is wholesome: our task is not to lord it over our youngsters but to prepare them for their own Christian service.—David A. Hubbard.

SUNDAY: MAY THIRTEENTH

MORNING SERVICE

Topic: The Virtues of a Good Home (Mother's Day)

SCRIPTURE: Matt. 7:7–12.

I. The Christian family is one in which the ideals for living found in the life and teachings of Jesus Christ are accepted, exalted, and exemplified.

(1) Jesus Christ stands at the center of the Christian home. It takes him seriously as the One in whom we find our clearest revelation of the will of God for the life of man. It accepts and seeks to understand and practice the things he stood for, limited only by the understanding and ability of its members.

(2) The Christian home is distinguished by two great facts: (a) It accepts the Christian estimate of life and, therefore, teaches a disciplined attitude toward life. (b) It teaches a standard of values in which love is central.

(3) The Christian estimate of life itself makes us realize that life is not a private possession to take lightly, to treat as we please; it is a gift—a gift of God, a gift brought us through our ancestors and through the tradition of which we are a part. More than a gift, it is a trust. It is something that we must treat reverently; we haven't earned it any more than we have asked for it, yet it is the thread on which are strung all our days and experiences. It comes to us alive with significance for each present moment and pregnant with meaning for the future. Every day is precious because it is from God.

(4) Add to this the Christian estimate of another: any and every other person is a fellow creature of God. We may note the fact that another is different from us in color, nationality, creed, economic means, or professional achievements. Real as such differences are, they are all secondary, if not superficial. We come into this life possessed of certain real properties, the deepest and most important of which is this: we are fellow creatures of the Creative Spirit which we call the Will of God.

(5) We begin by acknowledging that all men are creatures of God; then we are invited to take another tremendous

SUNDAY: MAY THIRTEENTH

step: we are brothers in Christ. We ought so to regard and so to treat each other. This means that we will try to be completely sensitive to the personality of another, to his needs and relationships. It means that we will do everything in our power to give every person we know or come in contact with not only the precious right to freedom but also the encouragement to bring to full fruition the God-given abilities in his own life.

(6) The Christian home is the place where this teaching, this encouragement, can be given best. Tolerance is not a "taught" virtue in the sense of verbal instruction; it is "learned" from the behavior of those we love and trust.

II. The Christian home teaches a standard of values, of right and wrong, of good and bad.

(1) This Jesus surely did! He gave us the Christian estimate of evil in motive and deed. For example, the attitude of covetousness toward the possessions of another or the passionate craving for fame and honor. These are evil because they are disintegrative attitudes; that is, they tend to separate us from other people; they tend to make us dangerous to other people. They create in us the conviction that other people are here primarily for our pleasure, service, and convenience. They cheapen and depersonalize life. That is why they are evil and unchristian.

(2) Then there is the evil of self-righteousness which is the perennial curse of religionists. By self-righteousness we mean the feeling that, because we know the proper religious word, we are the exemplifications of a worthy religious idea; the conviction that by some hook or crook the simple fact that we have been raised in the Christian tradition makes us a worthy representative of that tradition; the feeling that, because we are acquainted with the verbal structure of a lofty religious standard, we have the right to use it in passing judgment upon other people.

(3) Then there is the evil of hatred. Injustice and injury come the way of all of us. The question that we must face is the spirit in which we are going to meet injury and injustice when it is done to us. The way we normally meet it is to get even. That, said Jesus, is an unmitigated evil because it destroys the divine relationship between men who are fellow creatures and brothers in his sight.

(4) The Christian standard of values places in our hands the key to victory over them. It is a small key, but somehow it opens the door we need to the greatest of all virtues—love. Love can be described rather accurately from the point of view of the teachings of Jesus. In his sure hands it does not disappear into the general idea of goodwill. It is far more precise than this.

(a) It is, in fact, a spiritual pilgrimage which begins with an honest recognition of our interdependence with other people.

(b) The Christian concept of love is to accept this interdependence as an open door to the greatest good.

(c) The Christian conception of love is the willingness to share the best that we have and all that we have without thought of restraint or reward and being willing to refine in the fires of life what we think is best.

III. The duty of the Christian home is clear: to place Jesus Christ at the center of our common life, to teach a standard of values central in love. We need not be deterred by the obvious fact that no one of us will ever have the perfect home. But we can proceed with confidence because we have a standard, some notion of the kind of home we want. And we can measure our homes not alone by this standard but also by the test of whether we are better equipped to live in this one world as a result of living in our homes, of whether our children come out of our homes citizens of the world, members of the human family in their own thought and plan as in God's will.—Harold A. Bosley.

Worship Aids

CALL TO WORSHIP. "Both young men, and maidens; old men, and children: let them praise the name of the Lord: for his name alone is excellent; his glory is above the earth and heaven." Ps. 148:12–13.

INVOCATION. O shake the stiffness from our souls, our Father. Cause us to be again as little children, looking at the world with eyes unprejudiced and still unclouded by the films of insecurity, or pride, or hatred of our fellow man. Help us to reinterpret what we see but do not recognize, to reassign the authorship of that to which we sometimes say there is no author, and in the end to live as those who know that thou art both our Origin and Destiny and that, shouldst thou remove thyself from us, we should be ourselves removed.

OFFERTORY SENTENCE. "If ye then, being evil, know how to give good gifts unto your children: how much more shall your heavenly Father give the Holy Spirit to them that ask him?" Luke 11:13.

OFFERTORY PRAYER. Dear God, help us to become unobstructed channels that thy love may flow through us to others and our gifts may be used for the proclamation to all men of thy saving goodness.

PRAYER. Thou hast promised that if with all our hearts we truly seek thee, we shall ever surely find thee. With all our hearts we seek thee now, O thou who art ever seeking us.

We thank thee for thy goodness to us. May we try more consistently to deserve it. We thank thee for treating us better than we deserve. Help us to treat each other in the same way.

We need thy forgiveness. We have done things we ought not to have done. We cannot plead ignorance. We knew what was right and did what we knew was wrong. We need thy cleansing. Deeds unkind, words untrue, thoughts unclean: the stain of these is on us all. When we contrast our moral shabbiness with thy holiness, we are ashamed. Create in us a clean mind, a clean imagination. What in us is dark, illumine; what is low, raise and support.

We need thy reinforcement. We do not ask to escape the sorrows which are part of man's lot. We ask only assurance that in thy divine economy nothing good is lost, that what is excellent as God lives is permanent. We do not ask to be relieved of our share of life's burdens. We ask for strength to bear them without faltering or failing. We do not ask exemption from exacting tasks. We ask for wisdom and skill to do them aright.

We need thy peace. In a troubled, strife-torn world we need a peace that the world cannot bestow. We know that all peace comes from thee and that we cannot find it until we first find thee. But we should not be seeking thee unless thou hadst already found us. What is our prayer but an answer to thy call, a response to the intimations of thy presence around us and within? May the benediction of thy peace enfold us, calm, compose, and quiet us as we lift our prayer to thee in Jesus' name.—Frank Halliday Ferris.

Illustrations

THE WORSHIPING FAMILY. The distinguishing quality of a Christian home is that Jesus Christ is the center, and all its members seek to obey his law of self-denying love. It is the parent's supreme privilege to lead the children to Christ. It cannot be too strongly urged that regular, corporate family worship be practiced as a fundamental part of home life. The family worshiping together receives enduring blessing for itself and is a powerful witness for God in the community. A home whose way of life is that of Jesus Christ would naturally demonstrate the enduring values

SUNDAY: MAY THIRTEENTH

of home life held precious by all nations.—*The Madras Conference.*

IT'S ME. After a carelessly good time in the mud, a small boy came home for dinner. He was a thoroughly dirty mess! Wishing to shame him, his mother said: "Whose boy is this? I don't know of such a dirty boy living in the neighborhood." The little fellow ran up to his mother and burst out: "It's me, mother; it's me, under the dirt!"—David McCarthy in *The Upper Room.*

Sermon Suggestions

A GREAT WOMAN. Scripture: II Kings 4:8–37. (1) The Shunammite was great in hospitality. (See v. 8.) (2) The Shunammite was great in her spiritual understanding. (See vv. 9–10.) (3) The Shunammite was great in her contentment. (See vv. 12–13.) (4) The Shunammite was great in her faith. (See vv. 25–26.)—J. E. DeVore in *Evangel.*

WHAT THE WORLD NEEDS NOW. Scripture: I Cor. 13 (NEB). (1) Love is the indispensable ingredient which makes every other answer viable. (2) Love brings out the best in us and in all men. (3) Love is the only answer that has a future.—Clarence J. Forsberg.

EVENING SERVICE

Topic: A Word to Change Lives

SCRIPTURE: I Cor. 13; II Cor. 5:20–6:10.

I. *Love is constructive.* "Love is patient and kind." Whereas "patient" suggests passivity, "kindness" implies activity. The gentle word, the cheery smile, the gripping handshake, the sympathetic note—these may be constructive expressions of love.

II. *Love is mature.* People are supposed to grow up, not blow up. Yet, some feel that they are God's pets and that they have a right to blow their top now and then. Such love is immature.

III. *Love is enduring.* Love alone remains when all else gives way. Even though its back may be against the wall, it refuses to yield.

IV. *Love is transforming.* (1) Lives are changed when love is accepted from God and shared with others: the child finds security; the careless adolescent girl becomes a loving mother; the indolent teen-aged boy assumes responsibilities; the unfaithful husband gets interested in his own wife and family; the frustrated wife begins to understand the real needs of her husband; the negligent mother rejoices in the privileges of motherhood; the alcoholic finds a new outlet for self-expression; the racial bigot looks upon other races as his brothers; and the scheming businessman becomes a man of Christian ethical standards.

(2) Love transforms us as well as others. Under such conditions love absorbs insults and unjust attacks.

V. Modern man needs to think of love as more than a word. It is infinitely more. It is an act. The word and the act meet at Calvary where God is seen as going all lengths to make himself known to the world in the life, work, and death of Jesus Christ. In that cross you and I may learn more than the need for and the nature of love. We may discover how to express real love to God and our brothers. It is in Jesus Christ that we see the way to and the power of the Great Lover.—William H. Likins.

SUNDAY: MAY TWENTIETH

MORNING SERVICE

Topic: Prayer: The Source of Wisdom
Text: Jas. 1:5.

I. *The deficiency supposed.* "If any lack wisdom." (1) To hear such a suggestion is instantly to be conscious of our lack of this most essential quality. This is often so in the matter of decision. If there is one conscious deficiency at such a time it is the lack of wisdom.

(2) We need it again in dealing with others. We are all so differently made. Some are gifted with tact and patience, with a graciousness of manner that never gives offense. Others are hasty in judgment, impatient in attitude, and tactless in approach. Constantly brought into touch with people, we find they want their own way, and we want our way. They think they know best, and we are sure we know best. What is the priority need? It is wisdom that will persuade us to forget self, walk humbly, and speak graciously.

II. *The direction suggested.* "Let him ask of God." That is what this man of prayer counsels. Often conscious of the deficiency himself, he knew where to seek this most needed gift.

(1) He tells us the way to inquire: "Ask." James directs us to the source of all wisdom, "God." The wisdom we so much need is not of the head, but of the heart. Its source is not on earth, but in heaven.

(2) This we do simply. As a child asks for protection of its parents. As a hungry man appeals for bread. To ask is not to give voice to choice language or to use ambiguous words. It is simply to say what you need.

(3) We must ask sincerely. Nothing wavering. That is, without doubt. Confident that the appeal will not be in vain. Are you in need of wisdom? That which enables you to make the right decisions, to maintain the happiest relationship with others, and solve the particular difficulties of life? Here is the direction suggested: "Ask of God."

(4) We do so, remembering the wealth we may enjoy. "That giveth liberally." James would encourage us to come the way of supply by an assurance of the wealth of the supply. He speaks of the breadth of God's sympathy. He "giveth to all."

(5) Another encouragement for those who "ask of God" is in the welcome they may expect. He "upbraideth not." God mingles no acid with his honeycomb. He might bring many charges against us and each one a true charge. But he is too eager for our temporal and spiritual wealth to mar the welcome gift with the harsh word.

III. *The definite satisfaction.* We note the definite satisfaction: "It shall be given him."

(1) James could speak with certainty, because he himself had been so blessed. On his knees he had asked of God, and God had most graciously supplied his lack. The satisfaction he had enjoyed was something he must share with others. Hence his word of counsel here, particularly for those sorely tried.

(2) Such an occasion, however, is not the only experience in which wisdom is needed. In the whole walk of life it is a constant need. Often we fail to realize the lack, and we wonder why things go against us. Does it not show us the vital necessity of a constant appeal to God?—H. H. Gladstone.

Worship Aids

CALL TO WORSHIP. "Let him that glorieth in this, that he understandeth and knoweth me, that I am the Lord which exercise loving kindness, judgment, and righteousness, in the earth: for in these things I delight, saith the Lord." Jer. 9:24.

SUNDAY: MAY TWENTIETH

INVOCATION. Merciful God, forgive the halting nature of our discipleship. We confess that so little of thy love has reached others through us and that we have borne so lightly wrongs and sufferings that were not our own. We confess that we have cherished the things that divide us from others and that we have made it hard for them to live with us. And we confess that we have been thoughtless in our judgments, hasty in condemnation, grudging in our forgiveness. Forgive us, we beseech thee.

OFFERTORY SENTENCE. "The end of the commandment is charity out of a pure heart." I Tim. 1:5.

OFFERTORY PRAYER. Help us, dear Father, to be cheerful givers of our time, means, talents, and self to the Master that he may use us in the upbuilding of his Kingdom.

PRAYER. Father of us all, forgive our feeble faith which causes us to slink through life afraid and apprehensive. Restore us once again to our birthright. We have sinned as did the Prodigal. We have found no lasting satisfaction in our sin. We are uneasy because of our wasted opportunities. We are cut off from the fellowship of thee and our fellow men who are striving to do thy will.

But we are trying even now to make contact with thee again. May we have the joy of the Prodigal as he sees his father run in love toward him. May we feel thy arms of love circling us and be conscious of thy joy that we have turned to thee again. As we confess our sin, knowing in our own minds the just punishments of slavery to sin which is our due, please hush our speaking with words of love. Call us thy children once again. Clothe us in righteousness; put the sandals of purposive living on our feet; put the ring of service on our finger; restore us to sonship and love and the center of joy and celebration.

We have been lost in self, in things of the world, in worry, in fear, but now we are found of thee.—Alvin D. Johnson.

Illustrations

THE HIGH COST OF INTERCESSORY PRAYER. Alexander Whyte was engaged in prayer for the life of a dying friend, asking that this man be spared for his family and for greater work for God's Kingdom. Suddenly he was interrupted by a Voice, asking: "Are you in real earnest in what you ask, or are you uttering, as usual, just so many idle words? To seal the truth of what you say about the value of his life, will you give a solid proof of your earnestness? Will you consent to transfer to your sick friend half of your remaining years? If you have ten years before you, will you let your friend have five of them?"—Duron Sparks.

ONE SLIGHT CHANGE. A vigorous atheist came upon a framed motto in a bookstore. He bought it and hung it above his daughter's bed. The legend said, "God is nowhere." Unbeknown to her father, the girl was taken to a nearby church school by concerned neighbors. Presently she opened her heart to God's encircling love and confessed her faith in Christ. One night she took the motto out of its frame and made one slight change. She drew a line between two of the letters. The sign as amended read, "God is now here."—Ernest T. Campbell.

Sermon Suggestions

WHY PRAY? Text: I Cor. 14:15 (PHILLIPS). (1) Why pray? Because Jesus prayed and taught his disciples to use the great Lord's Prayer. (2) Why pray? Because we need inner cleansing, dedication, and forgiveness. (3) Why pray? Because our belief in God demands it. (4) Why pray? Because God is personal and real. (5) Why pray? Because we need prayer to complete our life. (6) Why pray? Because prayer is a channel, a contact with God. (7)

Why pray? Because "thou, O God, hast made us for thyself, and our hearts are restless until they find their rest in thee."—Frank A. Court.

THE GREAT MOTIVATOR. Scripture: John 17. In Jesus' prayer are three things that motivated him and can motivate us. (1) Sense of purpose. (See v. 4.) (2) Sense of direction. (See v. 6.) (3) Sense of love. (See vs. 23–24.) —Don Wright.

EVENING SERVICE

Topic: The Touch That Blesses
SCRIPTURE: John 6:1–14.
Here is a text that we cannot escape in our Christian faith: Jesus Christ always stands before us with these words: "Bring them to me." Whatever you have, bring them to me. Let me touch them. Let me handle them. Let me break them. Let me bless them. Let me pray over them. Bring them to me.

I. Bring me your boys. Bring me your poor fish and loaves. It is not much, but bring them to me and let me bless them.

II. Bring me your multitudes. I have compassion on them and I will send them out better fed and no longer hungry, because they have sat before me.

III. Bring me your doubts, as Philip brought his. Bring them to me. Don't deny them. Bring them to me. Express them. Let me know about them. Confess them. Bring me your doubts. Let me touch them.

IV. Bring me your faith. It is not much. It may be tempered with the doubts that were present even in Andrew. "The fish and the loaves," said Andrew, "they are not much among all these people." But bring them to me anyway.

V. Bring them all to Jesus Christ. Let him bless them and send them out again among the multitudes. Today, as 2,000 years ago, if you give to Jesus whatever it is that you have, it will feed the 5,000, and there will be baskets full left over.—Vernon Bigler.

SUNDAY: MAY TWENTY-SEVENTH

MORNING SERVICE

Topic: Pathways to God through the World around Us (Rural Life Sunday)
Suppose we should find ourselves on an island in the Pacific without any Bible to read and had to formulate our idea of God. What would the universe tell us?

I. It is a universe that is alive, growing, expanding, and becoming. Even those who study the far reaches of space believe that the universe is expanding, is growing, and is unfinished. It is a world in which we know our God is alive.

II. As we study God's sixty-seventh Book of the Bible, the great Book of Nature, we discover a world of great beauty and breathtaking views. God could have created a world of dull, ordinary color, but he upset the paint box everywhere, and we think of God as the great celestial artist. No one really has ever been able to reproduce on canvas a gold-tipped sunset or a living dawn as the sun has moved back the curtains of the night.

III. Hush, my soul, and stand still and listen to the music of the universe. In nature there is a glorious chorus of heavenly music we may always hear. Those who study our day tell us that noise, confusion, and disharmony can kill as well as overpopulation, smog, and pollution. Well, God has given us the counteraction for all of this in the music and joy of the great out-of-doors. Ah, step aside from life—sweet music of joy—it was there all of the time, but we didn't take time to listen.

IV. Note that we find the universe

of law and order and great control. The seasons can be charted, the day never varies, and the sun never misses its appointed time. How can man be irreverent in the face of such a cathedral of glory and wonder?

V. Certainly as we turn to nature we also find power. In fact it is our only source of power. Man may know how to release power from the atom or from the coal or utilize the rushing water of a stream, but power in itself is always given. The greatness of man is that he has been able to utilize power and create and build an entirely different kind of a world. From my viewpoint, man's greatest power is his power to create, but it is always power from the universe. There is spiritual power, inner power, the power of thought and mind. There is the closing phrase of the Lord's Prayer, "Thine is the Kingdom and the power and the glory for ever and ever." God's greatest power is revealed not only in the universe but in the dreams, ideals, and hopes of man.

VI. Look at the order of growth and the unity of life. One little snowflake is beautiful, but it takes millions of snowflakes to cover a prairie field or a forest or to create a storm. Life builds upon life.

(1) We are interested in conservation and ecology. Have you ever thought that real conservation is simply preserving the balance of nature and the story of life as we know it? When man cuts down trees, he takes from the atmosphere the oxygen the trees create. As man dries up the marshes and the bogs, he takes away a source of moisture and the balance that is found in the story of nature.

(2) So the God we find in nature is bringing us together in spiritual ties that would enable us to help each other, to live in a world of balance, and to find our place in the long story of growth.

VII. Every sermon should bring us to some definite conclusions.

(1) God is the great artist. Isn't he challenging us to make our life beautiful through our imagination, our desires, and our innermost dreams? It means, too, that here is the story of human relations as God would intend man to live with all mankind in the beauty of understanding, respect, and human dignity.

(2) If God has given us a world of music and harmony, it means that we are challenged to live in harmony with ourselves and others.

(a) A happy person is one who has will, imagination, emotion, and desire all marching to the same celestial music.

(b) Often we need to pray that God will touch the harpstrings of our own life so that they, too, may respond to the music of joy, harmony, and understanding.

(c) Also we cannot only play life's music on the white keys. Sometimes there are black keys, but the joy of life is in using the black keys and the white keys in a music of understanding and joy.

(3) If we find that God is the great scientist of law and order, it means that our life should have the sense of reverence and the desire to fulfill the potential of our possibility and to become more than we are. In a world of law and order there is no place for the wars, race riots, and tumultuous discord that seem to be a part of our day.

(4) If life is power, we do not have to live on the might of our own power, but it challenges us through prayer and worship to open our life to the world of Christ so that we know God as Father and thus truly find and discover our highest self.—Frank A. Court.

Worship Aids

CALL TO WORSHIP. "O come, let us sing unto the Lord: let us make a joyful noise to the rock of our salvation. Let us come before his presence with thanksgiving, and make a joyful noise unto him with psalms." Ps. 95:1-2.

INVOCATION. Almighty God, our heavenly Father, who reignest over all things in thy wisdom, power, and love: we adore thee for thy glory and majesty, and we praise thee for thy grace and truth to us in thy Son our Savior. Grant us the help of thy Holy Spirit, we beseech thee, that we may worship thee in spirit and in truth.

OFFERTORY SENTENCE. "Seek ye first the kingdom of God, and his righteousness, and all these things shall be added unto you." Matt. 6:33.

OFFERTORY PRAYER. Almighty God, may we trust more and more in thy kind providence, and may our submission to thy will be revealed in the deep devotion expressed through these gifts we offer in Christ's name.

PRAYER. Come, O God, as the wind, and drive away the clouds of doubt that so easily beset us.

Come, O God, as the rain, and refresh the hard, dry places of our souls.

Come, O God, as the morning sun, and make plain our path before us.

Come, O God, as the quietness after the storm, that we may be still and know that thou art God.

Holy, holy, holy, Lord God of hosts, heaven and earth are full of the majesty of thy glory. Glory be to thee, O Lord most high. O thou by whose providence the good earth is awakened, we rejoice that once again the flowers appear on the earth and the time of the singing of birds has come. So wilt thou awaken our souls to the claims thou hast upon us and grant that our service to our fellow man may cause him to sing thy praises.

We thank thee for seed time and harvest. We praise thee for the kindly providence which provides for all our needs through the fertility of the soil. We rejoice in the colors of spring, the blessing of water, the growth of the forest, and the riches under the earth. Grant, O God, that we may be good stewards of these resources, so shall generations yet unborn rejoice in thy goodness because we have been faithful in this our day.

Merciful God, we ask thy blessing upon all whose daily occupation is with the things of nature and who do their work open to the sky. We thank thee that thy bounty reaches us through their labor. May they never be so engrossed in nature as to forget nature's God, the God and Father of us all.

As wind and water, sun and rain, spring and winter work together to make life good, so may all the changes of this mortal life bring us closer to thee. And when our day on earth is done and the things of this world fade from our view, then may we behold the King in his beauty, even Jesus Christ our Lord.—Joseph E. McCabe in *Service Book for Ministers*.

Illustrations

TEN COMMANDMENTS OF THE NEW EARTH

I. You shall live in harmony with all the earth and with every living thing.

II. You shall return to the earth all the organic treasures she freely gives you.

III. Do not put greed above duty nor wealth above wonder.

IV. Do not demand useless things or trade for unnecessary things.

V. Every person shall have a fair share of the earth and no more.

VI. You shall fight to protect the earth; it is your home.

VII. Be masters of technology and not its slaves.

VIII. You shall make beautiful and enduring whatever is to be made.

IX. You shall keep faith with future generations and be wise guardians of their inheritance.

X. When all this is done, come together with all your brothers and sisters and sing the joy of earth.

BEYOND SCIENCE. There is a misconception that scientists can establish a complete set of facts and relations about the universe, all neatly proved, and then on this firm basis men can securely establish their personal philosophy, their personal religion, free from doubt and error. Science proves nothing absolutely. On the most vital questions it does not even produce evidence. On the essential and central core of faith, science must of necessity be silent. But its silence will be the silence of humility, not the silence of disdain. Young men, who will formulate the deep thought of the next generation, should lean on science, for it can teach much and it can inspire. But they should not lean where it does not apply. There is cause for much concern for those who follow science blindly.—Vannever Bush.

VISIBLE LOVE. When we work to the glory of God, we are like a flute: silver, polished, and ready for song. When we work to the glory of God, we become as a ladder, willing to bear a burden; like the tree, ready for fruit-bearing; like the net, mended for the glistening fish of the sea; like the craft, shipshape for the journey. Work is love made visible.—*Today.*

Sermon Suggestions

LIVING BY FAITH. Scripture: Heb. 11:1–10. (1) To live by faith is to base our lives on the certainties of God as we live in the midst of much uncertainty (vs. 1–3). The saints of old ("elders") our example. (2) To live by faith is to truly worship God as we live in the midst of much false worship (v. 4). Abel our example. (3) To live by faith is to walk with God as we live in the midst of much ungodliness (vs. 5–6). Enoch our example. (4) To live by faith is to obey God as we live in the midst of much sinfulness (v. 7). Noah our example. (5) To live by faith is to follow God as we live in the midst of much self-centeredness (vv. 8–10). Abraham our example.—Don R. Cooper.

BASES FOR THANKFULNESS. (1) Let us be thankful as inhabitants of this beautiful planet that God has not yet removed us from it for our wanton wickedness. (2) Let us be thankful as citizens of this bountiful land that God has not yet sent us the way of the proud empires of former days. (3) Let us be thankful as Christians in America that God has not yet removed the candlestick of testimony from this portion of his Church. He is still mercifully giving us a chance to serve him mightily by the proper use of the resources he has entrusted to our care.—*Christianity Today.*

EVENING SERVICE

Topic: Reaping Requires Sowing
TEXTS: Matt. 13:3; Gal. 6:9.

Nobody reaps unless somebody sows. We need not be farmers to know that there cannot come a harvest unless someone sows the seed. This is true, not only in the sowing of the seed which produces corn, but also of the sowing of the Word of God which produces Christian men and women.

I. The harvest of souls in the Kingdom of God will no more automatically appear than will the corn in the farmer's field. Both require someone to sow the seed. This gospel of Christ which you and I share has come to us because committed men sowed the Word of God in human hearts. Some of us realize how personal the sowing can be. In a moment of darkness a humble, dedicated soul takes the light of God, and for the first time a person's eyes are opened to the unsearchable riches of Christ. Or a child, through the faithfulness and devotion of a Sunday School teacher, grasped a truth about God, and what was sown, in later years bore fruit, leading to the tremendous discovery that Christ is real. These experiences do not occur, perhaps, as often as we would wish, but they do happen, and the harvest comes because someone sows the seed.

II. If God wants his message to be declared, he must have a man to do it, whether it be a proclamation from the pulpit by the minister or a layman's quiet word in the home, factory, or wherever the Christian meets men. God needs people and uses them to bring others to him. Are you sowing the seed of the Word of God? Are you helping to bring forth a harvest of souls? Jesus once said that the fields were white unto harvest and that the laborers were few. Those who sow the seed of God's truth also are few. Are you one of them, trying by word and deed to make known the Lord? There can be no reaping without sowing.—Frank Barker.

SUNDAY: JUNE THIRD

MORNING SERVICE

Topic: A Tree to Climb
Scripture: Luke 19:1–10.

Do we want to see Jesus? Do we want to see God? Do we want to see that which has so far eluded our physical and mental sight? We can never see that which has always been a stranger to our eyes if we persist in limiting our field of vision to the familiar—to that which greets our eye as we stare blankly ahead down old, nonproductive paths.

Unlike Zacchaeus, with a nearby tree enabling him to see over the crowd, unlike the child with the body-building, skill-challenging tree in the backyard, few of us possess a tree that can be climbed in an instant, a tree with the ability to show us the object of our heart's desire. But the world about us and within us is filled with trees to climb.

I would like to describe this grove of trees available to the modern-day Zacchaeus. From the limbs of one, drawn upward by the challenge, we might figuratively have the experience of Zacchaeus, and we might see Jesus.

I. The challenge of the tree of prayer. If this is to be like the tree of Zacchaeus, our tree of prayer must be a new attempt to climb high. We must not be content with observing our usual heaven-hiding forms. We must investigate every branch of the tree of prayer —climb through the limbs of personal petition, on to intercessory prayer, above to prayers of confession and thanksgiving. We must visit within the branches of morning, noon, and evening prayers, spoken and silent prayers.

II. The tree of study—the tree involving the investigations of new areas of history and research, new experiences and deeper diggings. From its trunk stretch branches too numerous for us but to touch often in passing. But here we have a tree offering the study of the Scriptures, the sciences of man and nature, the biography of self, and the biographies of countless saints and sinners. Here we have the choicest fruits of thought and life. Here we have a tree offering shade and warming summits. Here we have a tree to climb that offers heights for every eager mind and spirit that would attain a view of what now walks hidden.

III. The tree of worship. But how many limbs of its stately form have we known? On the tree of worship, awaiting our visit, are the limbs of public worship, private worship, family worship, morning worship, evening worship; worship in stately cathedrals and in simple chapels; worship under the forest trees and by the waters of the seas; worship beneath the stars and under the sun; worship by glaring modern light or by the soft light of campfire or candle. We can worship in simplicity; we can worship in great and complicated liturgical fashion. We can participate in, lead, observe worship. We can do all these and many more. But if we seek long to know the tree of worship, our eyes may see the blessed sights of Zacchaeus.

IV. The tree of service. Many times

SUNDAY: JUNE THIRD

we have heard about and sometimes have known its branches. Many are the forks on the tree of service. Would we care to travel its heights, we would find service to neighbor, far and near; service to neighbors of all creeds and colors; service to home, to town, to state, to nation; service to God and service to humanity. We would find service of action, of gift, and of love. We would find service that causes us to sit, to stand, to run, to walk; service that causes us to get dirty or to retain sterile cleanliness. On the branches of the tree of service we might see God if, in our journey over its branches, we carry in our hearts great gifts of love.

V. The tree of dedication. And the tree of dedication seems to reach over and intertwine with the branches of all the other trees. For once the lowest branches of the tree of dedication are grasped, one finds he is also suddenly moving about the branches of the other trees. He is experiencing devoted prayer, devoted study, devoted worship, and devoted service. There is no more important tree than the tree of dedication. It seems to bear a great relationship to the tree of Zacchaeus, and to even its lowest limbs we should all aspire if the success of Zacchaeus is the success we desire.—Glenn L. McKee in *Pulpit Digest*.

Worship Aids

CALL TO WORSHIP. "I will praise thee with my whole heart. I will worship toward thy holy temple, and praise thy name for thy lovingkindness." Ps. 138:1–2.

INVOCATION. Almighty and everlasting God, who givest to all who desire it the spirit of grace and supplication, deliver us, O Lord, from all coldness of heart, from all indifferent wandering of the mind, that we may fix our affection upon thee and upon thy service. Fill us with holy, peaceful, and beautiful thoughts, that with steadfast minds and kindled affection we may worship thee in spirit and in truth.

OFFERTORY SENTENCE. "Seeing ye have purified your souls in obeying the truth through the Spirit unto unfeigned love of the brethren, see that ye love one another with a pure heart fervently." I Pet. 1:22.

OFFERTORY PRAYER. Our Father, help us to love thee so well that we shall have all thy Kingdom interests and all thy children at heart.

PRAYER. Thanks be to thee, O Lord our God, who besettest us with goodness and holdest our souls in life. Thou hast given us this world of beauty, perplexity, and wonder; the stately order of the stars above; the shining order of the soul within; light for the eye; the eye for light; and Christ, our eternal Hope. For these thy gifts, and for thy keeping of thy gifts and us thy children, we render thee our praise. Stained, we have come to thee for cleansing, and never hast thou turned away thy face; stricken, thou hast brought us joy, deeper than grief, and stronger; fallen, thou hast raised us up; despairing, thou hast given us new heart; and, in our death, hast opened unto us a door; and lo! it is a way which leadeth unto life. Praise be to thee, O Lord most high.—John Underwood Stephens in *Prayers of the Christian Life*.

Illustrations

DISTORTING VISION. A poultry man in Santa Rosa, California, is making contact lenses for chickens. These lenses, made of molded plastic, fit snugly over a chicken's eyeball. They have one important difference from the contact lenses people wear, however. Instead of improving vision, these lenses distort things, causing poorer eyesight.

The reason? Lens manufacturer Al Shriner explains: "Modern methods of raising chickens cause severe social problems among them, not unlike those experienced by humans in crowded areas of big cities. Chickens on big poultry farms no longer run in fields where they have to scratch and pick for a living, but are confined in cages or crowded houses where food and water are handy."—John H. Townsend.

THREAT OF EDUCATION. We need the solemn reminder that the educated men threaten our existence. The uneducated jungle tribesman of South America or Africa cannot make an atom bomb. At the Nuremberg war crimes trials, Mr. Justice Jackson noted that the worst crimes are committed by the most educated men. He concluded, "Only well-educated and technically competent men can destroy civilization."—Emerson S. Colaw.

Sermon Suggestions

UPWARD AND FORWARD (Ascension Sunday). Text: Acts 1:8–9. (1) The upward look. Catch the pose of those men as they gazed up into heaven with the upward look; I'm sure they held the pose for no little time. If someone had come by them at that moment, he might have scoffed at them and called them stargazers, dreamers, idealists, looking up into heaven when they should be busy on the earth. But remember that one of the most important things in life is to have an upward look, the kind of look that theirs signified. And what did it signify? (a) A finished redemption, for their gaze followed the object of their faith, the only object of faith that has any value—Jesus Christ. (b) A source of power, for from that time prayer was to be made in the name of Jesus. (c) The cause for hope, for the only cause that man can have for real hope, both the man who faces death and the world that must look upon its problems and wonder how it will all come out, is in Christ. (2) The forward movement. The apostles did not only engage in the necessary upward look, but also a forward movement. (a) First of all, to personal development as they were obedient in prayer to God and in meditation. (b) They moved forward in that there was a bit of church administration that needed doing: they had to choose a twelfth apostle. (c) They moved forward in preparation for the enduement of power to become witnesses of Jesus Christ to the ends of the earth.—Paul P. Fryhling.

LIFT YOUR ANCHORS AND SAIL. Text: Ps. 107:23–24. (1) Lift your anchors and sail in the direction of God. (2) Lift your anchors and sail in the direction of a wholesome character. (3) Lift your anchors and sail in the direction of a strong body. (4) Lift your anchors and sail in the direction of a continuous education. (5) Lift your anchors and sail in the direction of a worthy vocation. (6) Lift your anchors and sail in the direction of a lifetime of service to God and your fellowmen.—W. E. Calhoun.

EVENING SERVICE

Topic: With Jesus Christ at a Wedding Feast

TEXT: John 2:11.

I. *The range of his human interests.* (1) Nothing human foreign to him! To attend that feast he must have walked at least six miles. On the way up from the Jordan he would talk with the twelve about the grapes on the vine and the eagle in the air, but never apart from the goodness of God and the desires of men. At the feast he mingled with the guests. "His delights were with the sons of men." To this hour he has not changed. He is "the same yesterday, and today, and for ever." The living Christ!

(2) Behold him as Friend of people and as Believer in marriage. In a day when divorce puts out the fire on many a hearth, learn from him that a Christian wedding means the beginning of joys dear to the heart of God. Why else did our Lord perform the first of his teaching miracles at a wedding? In

all his "training of the twelve" why did he stress marriage more than almost anything else? Through the apostles why did he later use marriage as the favorite symbol of union between himself and the Church as his bride?

II. *The wealth of his practical sympathy.* (1) Sympathy here means putting oneself in the other man's place, looking at the world through his eyes, feeling as he ought to feel, and doing all one can to lead him Godward. Among the myriad needs of earth today, what looms larger than the need to feel sure that God cares, practically? In its upper reaches, such compassion appears throughout the Gospels, not least at Cana.

(2) Today the living Christ rejoices with those who rejoice. He cares when hearts overflow with joys unconfined, when spirits mount up as on angel wings and try to capture the secrets of the stars. He cares far more when he fills two young hearts with holy love, and he waits to bless them at the marriage altar. Not only does he hallow such an hour with his presence and benediction; if the need arises, the Lord stands ready to use the powers of God to keep a shadow from darkening the beginning of a Christian home.

(3) Christ knows that soon or late shadows will come. In a world of sin, where he set his face like a flint on the way that led to Golgotha, he would have you make ready for days of distress. "In all our afflictions he is afflicted, and the angel of his presence shall save us." "When life tumbles in," leaving behind scarcely a wrack that heart holds dear, he will stand by. Never will he seem so tender and so strong as when he goes with you down through the valley of deepening shadows that men call death. He will stand by when you must bid farewell to the one you love more than all else on earth.

III. *The glory of Christ's transforming power.* (1) Glory here means the attractive goodness of God, the outshining of the splendor that we shall behold at the Great White Throne.

(2) Our Lord can even transform persons. He began to do so with the disciples when they believed in him as the Son of God. Through them he started out to change the world. Today he wishes to transform each of you and then employ you as a custodian of superatomic power. Herein lies the secret of all you can accomplish in evangelism at home, in missions beyond the seven seas, or in any other kind of human betterment.—Andrew W. Blackwood.

SUNDAY: JUNE TENTH

MORNING SERVICE

Topic: I Believe in the Church (Pentecost)

TEXT: Eph. 5:25.

I. I believe in the Church because of its power to transform life.

(1) The Church is the one society that is committed to the preaching of the Gospel and the proclamation of the way of Jesus. It is his representative in the world, the organ of his gracious purposes. It has accepted the responsibility of lifting him up that he might draw all men unto himself.

(2) The cynics keep on talking about the impossibility of changing human nature, yet the Church is changing it every day. It transforms both individual lives and our social life. This community is a different place, and a better place, because this Church stands here to direct men to God, to assist them in the worship of God, and thereby to be remade by God.

(3) The Church stands for the highest values yet revealed to man; it is the salt of society, saving it from decay; it is a moral cleansing agent, rebuking evil and purifying the atmosphere by

its ministries. The call of the world is often downhill, but the Church ever points men to the heights. We have inherited this Church; we have benefited by its presence here. Our debt to it is much greater than we commonly acknowledge.

(4) I believe in the Church because of its power to transform life. Do you want such power released into the world? The more like Christ you become, the more you give yourself to his Church, the greater the transforming power God is able to loose among men; for the Church's power to transform is limited only by our willingness to be used, to sacrifice, and to serve on behalf of Jesus Christ.

II. I believe in the Church because it is catholic. We who are Protestants must not be afraid of the word "catholic." It stands for some of the great truths which all true Protestants have cherished.

(1) I believe in the catholic Church because I believe it is Christ's intention that all men and women become his followers, and because I believe it is his intention that the Gospel be applied to all of life. We were meant for life in one household of faith, in one family of God.

(2) The world will never know peace and brotherhood until it takes Christ and his Church seriously, for the Church is the one society summoning men to genuine brotherhood. Christ is the one power who can supply the dynamic which will enable men to achieve that brotherhood.

III. I believe in the Church because it holds before men a demanding and a hard way of life. (1) The function of the Church is never to coddle men; it is to summon them to purity of life and social righteousness. The Church, when it is true to its Founder, does not invite men to a soft and easy existence; it challenges them to put self aside and be consumed in the service of God.

(2) The Christian way is a hard way and, like everything else that is worth while, it will always remain so. I believe in the Church for this very reason—because it holds before men a demanding way of life. To ask for God is to be confronted by stern demands and challenged to noble ends. A large number of those who remain apart from his Church and a large number of those who are within the Church but who do not seem to find joy and peace there, do so because they are not prepared to do justly, to love mercy, and to walk humbly with their God.

(3) The Church exists to offer Jesus Christ to men and women who are too weak to achieve the good life by their own efforts. He can bring new life to men and women like you. No matter who or what you are now, he believes in what you can become.—W. Burton Crowe.

Worship Aids

CALL TO WORSHIP. "Thou wilt keep him in perfect peace, whose mind is stayed on thee: because he trusteth in thee. Trust ye in the Lord for ever: for in the Lord Jehovah is everlasting strength." Isa. 26:3–4.

INVOCATION. Almighty God, who of thy great mercy hast gathered us into thy visible Church: grant that we may not swerve from the purity of thy worship, but may so honor thee both in spirit and in outward form that thy name may be glorified in us and that our fellowship may be with all thy saints in earth and in heaven.

OFFERTORY SENTENCE. "Verily, verily, I say unto you, he that believeth on me, the works that I do shall he do also; and greater works than these shall he do. And whatsoever ye shall ask in my name, that will I do, that the Father may be glorified in the Son." John 14:12–13.

OFFERTORY PRAYER. God of our fathers, dearly do we cherish the blessings which thy Church brings to us and dearly do we covet the privilege of sharing through these gifts the proclaiming of thy Word until all of the earth shall praise thee.

PRAYER. We thank thee, our Father, for the devotion that has kept religion alive in history and led thy Church forward through the centuries. We give thanks for thy living Church, the foundation of which is the faith of men; the walls and pillars, the courage of human hearts; the buttresses, the goodwill that reaches out into the life of humanity; and the arches that overtower its beauty and hold the temple firm, the clasp of brothers hand in hand.

Strengthen this bond of brotherhood and make us one with this vast family of believers who are united in the purpose of serving mankind. Consecrate us in this moment as we remember the valiant Christians who have gone before us—prophets, saints, pioneers, and martyrs. Help us to work as builders of faith's unfinished cathedral, where all people will someday worship thee before the altar of truth and love, and will go out as classes, nations, and races to live together in a harmonious world family.—Robert M. Bartlett.

Illustrations

WINDOWS TO THE WORLD. It really would be a wholesome thing for Christians to describe their churches as "windows to the world." Instead of thinking that our institutions are places of refuge and retreat, we would be advised to regard them as points of entrance to humanity and the world of need. We should assemble within these walls, in other words, to have our vision sharpened and our service well-defined. Here things should come into focus: what the world is like and what God would have us do. Our look ought to be upward and outward; our perspective ought to be expansive.—John H. Townsend.

OBITUARY. Funeral services to be held for Mr. Sunday School at Neglect Funeral Parlor. Officiating will be the venal Dr. Precisely Peaceful of Cloister Cathedral. Burial will be in Concernless Traditionalism Park. Mr. Sunday School, a hardy pioneer, a veteran of many furious campaigns and the evangelistic right arm of the Church, died slowly at the hands of his friends. Elder Busy neglected Mr. Sunday School while holding important meetings to make piously authoritative observations. Preacher Jealous ignored him lest he be larger than the preaching services. Miss Indolent Teacher starved him with pointless pottage. Superintendent Lethargic reduced Mr. Sunday School to a spineless vegetable by taking away his purpose and will to grow. Reminiscence College failed to give him leadership injections while piously educating well-preened shepherds for contented flocks. Mr. Musty Member drowsed near the deathbed and said, "Too bad! One would think someone might have helped poor Mr. Sunday School."—Medford Jones.

Sermon Suggestions

SUGGESTIONS FROM CHURCH HISTORY. A careful study of the record of the Christian Church seems to indicate: (1) Schism based on selfishness, prejudice, hate, or error should be done away with. (2) Elimination of the main historic branches of Christendom is neither desirable nor feasible. (3) Christians should look upon the Church Tree and its branches and beautiful symmetry with love, admiration, and reverence. (4) Additional consolidations and unions should take place within the various denominational families.—Lara Peterson Qualben.

THE HOLY SPIRIT'S COMING. Pentecost as a New Testament feast marks the beginning of this great blessing for us and for all the Church. (1) The Spirit is working toward the proclamation of Christ. (2) The Spirit is working toward the integration of mankind through the Savior. (3) The Spirit is working toward the restoration of the unity that has been lost. (4) The Spirit is working toward the preaching of the Gospel in all parts of the world.—Dick L. Van Halsema in *Decision*.

THAT THEY MAY BE ONE. Text: John 17:11. The church of Christ is not so divided as it appears to be. There are many points of difference. Yet few, if any of these, are on central issues. (1) All of the Christian world uses the same Bible, though the various translations may differ and the emphasis upon how the Bible is to be used may not be the same everywhere. (2) Except for a small minority, all professing Christians conceive of their God as a trinity, Father, Son, and Holy Spirit. (3) All of the churches of the world are founded upon the faith expressed in John 3:16. (4) All teach the forgiveness of sins to the penitent believer. (5) All teach the supremacy of love.—John R. Weinlick.

CHURCH GROWTH. (1) Reach all we can. (2) Teach all we reach. (3) Win all we teach. (4) Conserve all we win.—Richard Laue.

EVENING SERVICE

Topic: On Being Part of a Family (Children's Sunday)

TEXT: Num. 2:34.

I. Being part of a family is one of the most important treasures of our lives. (1) Many things are shaken today, and we should remember that a house divided against itself cannot stand. Probably we must start all over again to learn some fundamental meanings of living together. When we do that, we must start with the home, for it is there that we have the symbol of unity and sharing and mutual responsibility.

(2) Young people are to a great degree what home makes them. Children and young people have a way of catching the habits of their parents and the attitudes of their parents, and they see very quickly what appears to be most important to their parents. An unknown author has written under the heading "Wanted: Parents": (a) Parents who will be as diligent to get their children to church school as they are to get them to weekly school or the dancing class. (b) Parents who are as concerned about the spiritual development of their children as they are about their social standing. (c) Parents who will set the example of making room on Sunday for attendance at a place of worship.

II. Being a part of the family should mean having awakened in us the fact that there are those who need us. This is true, regardless of the ages of the members of the family. All of them, from the new baby to the grandparents, are going through changes and some of them are very rough.

III. Being part of a family should mean being part of a group that through discussion seeks answers to personal and community problems. We should discuss the matter of race. We should discuss problems of government. We should discuss problems of the Church. We should discuss problems of the campus. We should discuss problems of youth and problems of parents. Often too at the dinner table, or any occasion when the family finds itself together, the parents can guide the conversation into areas that will not only encourage participation but will also lift up a standard and will quicken vision.

IV. Being part of a family should mean a place where we have exposure to faith. In the family, children have a right to exposure to faith. It is in the very nature of the Christian home. The first words of the marriage ceremony are a reminder that the couple is in the presence of God to be joined together in marriage and that marriage is instituted of God, regulated by his commandments, and blessed by our Lord Jesus Christ. The couple usually receives the benediction kneeling before God. If they are blessed with a child and bring him for baptism, they promise in dependence on the grace of God to bring him up in the nurture and the admonition of the Lord. The Christian family begins with reminders of responsibility to God. An old hymn reads, "We gather together to ask the Lord's blessing." It's a great thing when a family does it.—Howard C. Scharfe.

SUNDAY: JUNE SEVENTEENTH

MORNING SERVICE

Topic: The Lord, the Giver of Life (Trinity Sunday)

TEXT: "And I believe in the Holy Ghost, the Lord, the Giver of Life." The Nicene Creed.

I. God the Holy Ghost works among men through his inspiration of the Holy Scriptures. The Bible is the record of God's revelation of himself to men. God the Holy Ghost gave to the writers of the Bible the special assistance we call "inspiration" that they might recognize the mighty works of God when they saw them. Christians use the Bible both as history and as a record of God's revelation.

(1) As history, the Bible should be treated as we would any other historical source. It must be examined critically to determine what actually did happen in the period of history now long past. Although the record is not so detailed as we should like it to be, we don't stop being Christians because the authors of nearly twenty centuries ago did not anticipate all the questions we should like answered.

(2) For the Christian the Bible is not only history, but also the inspired record of God's revelation of himself. We know God only as he has revealed himself to us, and the Bible contains the record of that revelation. We prove doctrine from the Bible, and we reject the claim of any doctrine to be necessary to salvation if it cannot be proved from Scripture.

(3) We believe that the Bible is inspired by God the Holy Ghost because we know by experience that it satisfies the spiritual needs of all men of every race and climate. We believe that the Bible is inspired by God the Holy Ghost because we see a difference between the Bible and the sacred books of all other religions. We believe that the Bible is inspired by God the Holy Ghost because we believe the record of the Apostles and Fathers of the Church who were witnesses of the events recorded in the Bible.

II. In the Church we observe God the Holy Ghost working in several ways.

(1) God the Holy Ghost operates in the Church by filling its members with mutual love. Wherever a break has occurred in the unity of the Church there has been a previous breach in mutual love; men have rejected the operation of God the Holy Ghost in their lives.

(2) God the Holy Ghost operates in the Church through the devotion of the great mass of members of the Church. Time and again the history of the Christian Church has shown cases where the devotion of the masses was greater than the misleading errors of the leaders. The faith of the laity has often saved the faith of the Church.

(3) God the Holy Ghost works in his Church in the operation of the councils of the Church which have sat from time to time to define matters of faith or morals. These decisions, since they are in conformity with the Holy Scriptures, are believed to be led by the Holy Ghost.

(4) God the Holy Ghost works through the Church by giving his power to individual members of the Church. This power of God the Holy Ghost is grace. Grace is received through preaching, prayer, meditation, and the performance of works of charity. In every case it is the gift of divine help—a spiritual gift.

(5) God the Holy Ghost operates through human conscience. Conscience is the power to distinguish between right

and wrong. It is conscience which causes us to say, "I ought" or "I ought not." Conscience makes the decision as to what is right or what is wrong, but it is the will which carries out the decision. We ought, therefore, not to confuse conscience with will. God the Holy Ghost communicates to us through our conscience, but the conscience itself is not the voice of God. Conscience is the means whereby we hear the voice of God.

(6) God the Holy Ghost also comes to man through his reason. Reason is the power of judgment; it ought not to be confused with conscience. A man may have great powers of reason, and yet have a perverted conscience. Again a man might have very feeble powers of reason and yet have a really enlightened conscience. We are taught to pray for "godly judgment." Often our judgment calls us to follow the voice of learned people or others in authority, but, should their judgment offend our conscience, we must break away from their authority and remember that we alone are responsible to God for our actions. We must remember that the judgment of others may be wrong. It is God the Holy Ghost who directs our judgment as well as our conscience.—Nelson Waite Rightmyer.

Worship Aids

CALL TO WORSHIP. "Thou art worthy, O Lord, to receive glory and honor and power: for thou hast created all things, and for thy pleasure they are and were created." Rev. 4:11.

INVOCATION. Great is thy name, O Lord, and greatly to be praised, and to be had in reverence of all them that call upon thee. For thou only art God; we are the people of thy pasture and the sheep of thy hand. Therefore we worship and adore thee, Father, Son, and Holy Spirit, ever one God, world without end.

OFFERTORY SENTENCE. "Honor the Lord with thy substance, and with the firstfruits of all thine increase." Prov. 3:9.

OFFERTORY PRAYER. We praise thee, O God, for thy countless blessings and pray that thou wilt accept these gifts of gratitude in Jesus' name.

PRAYER. God our loving Father, we open our lives to thee now that thou mayst enter them and take possession of the souls which thou hast redeemed. Be to us all that thou hast promised to be to thy faithful people. Minister to us as thou seest our needs. In our perplexities let thy light shine upon our path, that we may follow the way of thy purpose. In our troubles be our refuge, that we may find thee as the shadow of a great rock in a weary land. In our temptations speak thy word of forgiveness, that we may not again fall into evil and know the bitterness of shame. In our loneliness be our Companion, in our sorrows give comfort, and in our weakness let thy strength be made perfect. We pray not only for our own lives but for those who are more precious unto us than life itself. We remember all whose joy makes us joyful, but especially we ask thee to help and bless all who bring sadness to our hearts because they are ill or bereaved or depressed or unhappy or passing through times of great stress and anxiety. We remember them in silence before thee. Wilt thou hear these our prayers and the unspoken petitions of our hearts and, when thou hearest, answer and forgive.—A. Leonard Griffith.

Illustrations

ULTIMATE DIFFERENCE. It makes an ultimate difference whether a man looks at the strange enterprise of Jesus with reserve of a sympathetic spectator—this costs nothing, and if the affair gets hot he can bail out in time—or whether he throws his whole existence with this Jesus of Nazareth.—Helmut Thielicke.

COLLAR OF SLAVERY. Among Christians in Africa, there is difficulty in translating the New Testament word for redemption. For the word redemption they have a phrase, "God took our heads out." It goes back to the nineteenth century when slave trading was the vogue. White men invaded African villages and carried off men, women, and children. They put an iron collar around the neck, and a chain ran from one native to the next. They were driven to the coast where Portuguese slave traders put them on boats and shipped them for sale in America. Sometimes a chieftain would see a friend. If he had the money or a jewel, he would buy out of the chain gang. When the price was paid, the captors removed the collar around his neck. He was freed from slavery through the mercy of a friend. In the same way, redemption is God's taking our heads out of the collar of slavery.—John R. Brokhoff.

Sermon Suggestions

WHY WORSHIP? This world can be saved from political chaos and collapse by one thing only, and that is worship. For to worship is (1) to quicken the conscience by the holiness of God, (2) to feed the mind with the truth of God, (3) to purge the imagination by the beauty of God, (4) to open up the heart to the love of God, (5) to devote the will to the purpose of God.—William Temple.

THE CURE FOR THE CHURCH DIVISION. (1) The message of the Church is based on God's wisdom and not man's. Therefore, there is no room for human boasting. (See I Cor. 1:18.) (2) The Church was composed of fairly simple people, and there is not a great deal of room for pride in this. (See I Cor. 1:26.) (3) Spiritually immature people are incapable of dealing with the spiritual problems the Church faces. (See I Cor. 3:1.) (4) We who are followers of Jesus Christ are to be servants and not masters. (See I Cor. 4:1.) (5) Those who endanger the unity of the Church stand in danger of the judgment of God. (See I Cor. 4:5.)—Kenneth Chafin.

EVENING SERVICE

Topic: Jesus and His Heavenly Father (Father's Day)
SCRIPTURE: John 20.
What was it like—this relationship between Jesus and his heavenly Father?

I. Jesus never tired of his heavenly Father's company. He did not just say that he loved God; he proved it by spending as much time with God as he could spare from his divinely appointed labors. The busier he was, the more he insisted on having some time with God in quiet, confiding prayer.

II. Another thing that strikes us is the relaxed familiarity of the relationship. The very fact that Jesus called God Father marked a sharp departure from what the Jews believed about God. To most Jews, God appeared as an awe-inspiring Oriental monarch with a jealous regard for protocol.

III. When Jesus talked about God, he made it clear that he was talking about a Father who is never too busy to listen to his children.

IV. This conviction of God's personal care inspired Jesus to teach his disciples that no concern of theirs was too small for the attention of God.

V. Jesus devoted his whole life to the service of his heavenly Father. We say, "Like father, like son"—sometimes in admiration but usually in contempt. With Jesus, the saying may be reversed: "Like Son, like Father." The disciples came to see the perfection of God mirrored in the face of their Master.

VI. Perhaps the most touchingly human aspect of Jesus' relationship with his heavenly Father was the resistance with which he greeted some of his Father's decisions. If Jesus had accepted every one of them without a moment's hesitation, his Sonship would have lacked reality. He would have been a moral robot rather than the human instrument of our salvation.

VII. The most striking thing about Jesus' relationship with his heavenly Father was his absolute trust in him. Jesus trusted his heavenly Father, and he was not disappointed. The same God who had chosen Jesus to carry out his plan of reconciliation and redemption did not stop short of the fulfillment of his plan but raised Jesus from the dead. The Father vindicated his faithful Son.
—John R. Bodo in *Presbyterian Life*.

SUNDAY: JUNE TWENTY-FOURTH

MORNING SERVICE

Topic: Consider the Rainbows (Nature Sunday)
Text:

Man is born with rainbows in his heart
And you'll never read him unless you consider the rainbows.

—Carl Sandburg.

Let us take a look at the rainbows in the human heart.

I. The rainbow of promise. (1) The newborn child is potentiality—potentiality for good and for evil. As the social psychologists remind us, the newborn child is a candidate for personality. It is not clear what he shall become. In the language of the poet, we know, "that God has mixed in him the rapture and the tears, and scattered through his brain the starry stuff." He has also mixed in him the Old Adam, what theologians called original sin.

(2) Jesus saw enough of evil, felt sharp thrust of it in his own life, to have caused a lesser person to have given up on his faith, but he never ceased to believe that if the gentle impulses of love, mercy, and compassion were cultivated they would ultimately overcome the evil impulses of the heart. He understood human nature. He knew that men were born with rainbows of promise in their hearts. He took twelve common men and challenged them to greatness.

II. The rainbow of endurance in his heart. (1) Man is biologically tough. From the day of birth a "host of enemies is encamped against him." Invisible, microscopic, and submicroscopic enemies, as well as the visible hazards of the environment, dispute the passage with him. And yet he has survived the long ice ages, slings and javelins of enemies, and deadly diseases.

(2) In things spiritual man has shown remarkable endurance. How often in history it appears that he has been beaten down, whipped, but he has always rebounded. His temples and works of art tell us of his spiritual endurance. His ideals and dreams are often beaten down, frustrated, but man returns to pursue his dream with new hope and confidence. The teachings and the dream of the young Galilean who spoke almost twenty centuries ago still live on. Why? Because man is spiritually tough. His ideals and hopes may be dimmed by events, but he does not give up. In matters of spirit as well as of physical endurance, man has the capacity to endure.

(3) Because the spirit of man is dauntless he will live in the faith that the children of this earth have boundless possibilities worth working and sacrificing for, and what eye hath not seen nor ear heard is laid up as a consummation for the sacrifices of this life.

III. The rainbow of aspiration is in his heart. (1) He is rarely satisfied with things as they are. The highest mountains beckon to him. He posts his flags on distant planets and walks among the stars. He is an incorrigible adventurer. He is always standing at some golden

SUNDAY: JUNE TWENTY-FOURTH

gate, key in hand, fumbling a bit at the lock, but eventually the gate opens and he passes through to a new world. His feet are firmly set on a road that leads to a Promised Land.

(2) What is it that keeps the world from going to pieces, life from becoming unbearably harsh and brutal? What is it that keeps the world from surrendering to cynicism and disillusionment? It is the aspiring heart of man. One of the functions of religion is to provide us with goals and dreams. To be sure, they are fleeting, elusive dreams, pulling us forward, forever exceeding our grasp. Man dreams of the Kingdom of God on earth. He knows that God intended men to live together as brothers, and if he does not learn to do this he will surely perish.

IV. The rainbow of reverence and worship adorns his life. That was a remarkable moment in the history of the world when the first man "turned his face from the clod" and cried out to God. Only man can contemplate eternity.

(1) What a wonderful gift, the capacity to see the burning bush. There was mystery in the bush. It should have been consumed by the fire, but it was not. So Moses said, "I will turn aside now, and see this great sight, why the bush is not burnt?" On a memorably beautiful morning such as this the world is a giant burning bush, a world of incomparable beauty and mystery. If one stands still long enough to hear the song of the birds and to behold the beauty of an earth burgeoning with life, he will, like Moses, be compelled to turn aside and contemplate mystery.

(2) To understand the interrelatedness of all life and to know that one is an intricate part of the web of life evokes reverence and awe. It has been given to man alone to endure the pain of his mortality and the capacity to bow down and worship God. His shrines of worship speak to us of man's peculiar endowment.—Charles F. Jacobs.

Worship Aids

CALL TO WORSHIP. "Let all those that put their trust in thee rejoice: let them ever shout for joy because thou defendest them: let them also that love thy name be joyful in thee." Ps. 5:11.

INVOCATION. Most gracious Father, who withholdest no good thing from thy children and in thy providence hast brought us to this day of rest and of the renewal of the soul: we give thee humble and hearty thanks for the world which thou hast prepared and furnished for our dwelling place, for the steadfast righteousness which suffers no evil thing to gain the mastery, for the lives and examples of those who were strangers and pilgrims and found a better inheritance in peace of soul and joy in the Holy Spirit, and above all for the life, teaching, and sacrifice of thy Son our Savior Jesus Christ.

OFFERTORY SENTENCE. "I will freely sacrifice unto thee: I will praise thy name, O Lord; for it is good." Ps. 54:6.

OFFERTORY PRAYER. O heavenly Father, we pray that thy blessings, which are as countless as the stars, may be so used as to bring light and love to thy children everywhere.

PRAYER. Eternal Father of mercy, as we bow before thee this day may it be with thoughtful minds, devoted hearts, and wills in tune with thy holy purposes of justice and love. We would come before thee humbly yet confidently in the name of the Christ who is our Savior, our Shepherd, and our Friend. Turn our minds from every distracting care and interest that we may worship thee in spirit and in truth.

We praise thee for thy majesty and power shown in this great universe, and we thank thee for the many revelations of thy loving care for each one of us. Thou hast made gracious provision for the fulfillment of our every need. We offer our gratitude for every source of inspiration and comfort. For the helpfulness of friends and neighbors, for the loyal devotion of dear ones, for the light of thy holy Word, for the fellowship of the Church, and for the saving friendship of Christ, we magnify thy holy name.

Help us to take a more vigorous, active share in the tasks of this congregation. Give us a new vision of the work of thy Church Universal. Grant still greater strength to those who work to build bridges of understanding and neighborliness in areas of ignorance and prejudice. Bless mightily all who try to advance peace and goodwill among the people of the earth.—James Croswell Perkins.

Illustrations

WRITTEN IN HIS ROSE GARDEN. I accept all that the physicists tell me of this rose that is breaking into bud; it is a system and collocation of electrons, a form of complicated energy, but when I see the rose I am directly conscious of the Power. The rosebud is a soundless, unarticulated word of God to me; it points beyond itself to that which is beyond the grasp of human nature's power.—Nathaniel Micklem in *A Religion for Agnostics*.

THE NEW AND THE OLD. Spring does not waste her force in regrets over last Autumn's frustrated harvests. Mother Earth takes into her vast and transforming heart the defeated and decayed; she makes of them the very soil from which new births may blossom. She substitutes a new access of life for old deaths; she edges out our battle trenches with the gracious green of her grasses. Something like that is always happening in our human world of which we need in our despondent moments to take brave account.—Gaius Glenn Atkins.

SACRIFICE. Reverence for life does not allow the scholar to live for his science alone, even if he is very useful to the community in so doing. It does not permit the artist to exist only for his art, even if he gives inspiration to many by its means. It refuses to let the businessman imagine that he fulfills all legitimate demands in the course of his business activities. It demands from all that they should sacrifice a portion of their own lives for others.—Albert Schweitzer.

Sermon Suggestions

WHERE CHRIST PLACED LIFE'S EMPHASIS. Throughout all of the New Testament there is unanimity of where Christ placed the emphasis, and there is no division as to the life and spirit of Christ and what he did and what he said. (1) Jesus changed the emphasis in religion to the forward look rather than the backward glance. (2) Life with Christ found its meaning and purpose in his fellowship with God. (3) Our Lord placed the emphasis upon faith and action. (4) Our Master placed the emphasis upon the goodness in people. (5) Jesus placed the emphasis on inner control and discipline. (6) Christ placed life's emphasis upon sacrificial service, giving rather than receiving, being a part of life's answer rather than a part of life's problem.—Frank A. Court.

THE SIN OF DOING NOTHING. Scripture: Luke 10:25–37. (1) In any circumstance I can do one of three things: I can do good, I can do harm, or I can do nothing. When I see a man in need, I can either help him, hurt him, or just leave him alone and do nothing. (2) Jesus considers the alternative of doing nothing to be in the same category as to do harm. Think of the parable of the Good Samaritan. There were the thieves who did great harm to a man. There is also the Samaritan who came alone and did a great good to the same man. What did the priest and the Levite do? They did not beat him. They did not take his money, because it was already gone. The beaten man was suffering while they walked by, and they could have helped him, but they did not. In "doing nothing" they did harm to the man that was lying there.—Bernie Wiebe.

EVENING SERVICE

Topic: The Unseen Presence
Text: II Chron. 6:18.
I. *The reality of the Presence.* (1) Once we know the presence of Christ within us nothing will change our faith in that experience. The reality of the Presence is the believer's evidence for his faith, it is the source and maintenance of his spiritual life, and from it come all spiritual blessings. (2) How do we possess this Presence? Technically it is God's gift at our conversion. The Spirit of Christ is born in the believer. But just as human love at courtship and marriage has to give place to something deeper, some quality less dependent on the physical, so of the Spirit. The awareness of the Presence of Christ should grow and deepen over the years.
II. *The Presence lost.* (1) The loss of the Presence is not an infrequent experience. Cowper is not the only man who could cry, "Where is the blessedness I knew when first I saw the Lord?"
(2) What is the New Testament answer to this experience? It is, of course, that nothing, not even God himself, can alter the fact that when we cease to be conscious of the indwelling presence we cease to live the full and joyous life. Life becomes a burden and peace departs from us. Even our worship becomes distasteful to us.
(3) The New Testament answer to the lost presence is that once his Spirit is born in our hearts, it never completely leaves us again. This is surely one aspect of the grace of God. We may lose the consciousness of the Presence, but we should never forget that the Presence within us is the spirit of the Savior, the One who not only died for our redemption, not only able to save to the uttermost but also able to keep to the end.
III. *The Presence restored.* If I have lost the sense of God's presence, how can I get it back? In considering this let us remind ourselves of this fact: there is nothing which gives God greater joy than when his presence is born or restored within the human soul.
(1) If this is so, how can I get it back? There is no set formula. For some it is the renewal of times of prayer and communion; for others it is the revival meeting or the quiet beauty of worship. Yet for others a book or preacher, and it may be that trouble or distress, bereavement and sorrow may be the means of bringing some to this experience. But for many there is another way. It is this: by an act of self-discipline.
(2) By some divine ordinance self-sanctification quickens God's truth in our lives. "And for their sakes I sanctify myself that they also might be sanctified through the truth." Surely the point is this: even the truth of his glorious Gospel was powerless until he had quickened it into life by his own self-sanctification—the giving of himself upon the Cross.—D. H. Reeder.

SUNDAY: JULY FIRST

MORNING SERVICE

Topic: Worthy Heritage and Spiritual Fortitude (Independence Sunday)
Text: Gal. 5:1.
What is so uniquely different about the American way of life?
I. If we were to try to explain it in twenty-five words or less, more than likely we would find ourselves struggling for the proper expression.
(1) Thinking of our American life should thrill us. This land is rich and good. It is abundant in natural re-

sources. It produces crops far beyond what we ourselves can use. It is good because we are concerned that there be a better life for all God's children.

(2) This land is filled with beauty, awe, and majesty. Life can become flat, drab, and meaningless if we lose our sense of awe and wonder. If we look upon the mountain and see only its mineral analysis, if we scan the far horizon of seas and lakes and cannot lose ourselves in rhapsody and song, we have lost that wonderment. What about the sunsets and starry summer skies? The crisp walk in the winter wonderland? Let us not leave it only to the poet and dreamer to exult in the majestic splendor of our land.

(3) America is the land of hallowed shrines—Bunker Hill, Valley Forge, the Washington Monument, New Salem, Mount Rushmore, the *Arizona*.

(4) America is the laughter of little children, the smile of a friend, the needs of a stranger. It is the love of all men for each other, no matter what their station in life, no matter what their color. America is brotherhood. It is heroes, and it is cities, villages, and hamlets. It is all of this and much more.

(5) America is worship. Whether a man stands under the open sky or kneels before the cloistered altar, his whole life, like the needle of a compass, is pointed to God.

II. On a Fourth of July some years ago, an enterprising reporter for a Madison, Wisconsin, newspaper went out on the street with a copy of the Declaration of Independence and interviewed passers-by. He sought the signatures of people who would endorse the views of the Declaration. The reporter approached one hundred and twelve people, of whom only one would sign his name to his basic document that spells out the rights of our people. A hasty glance by most people was enough to call these lines "too radical."

(1) Do we shy away from the doctrine of the Declaration of Independence because many Americans have ceased to believe in its literal and universal truth? Are we getting to the place where we no longer believe that we have a right to free speech and free assembly? Would we brutally stifle peaceful marches for freedom with fire hoses, vicious dogs, clubs, sticks, and stones?

(2) What about free press and speech? Shall we read only what is good for us to know? Are we afraid that those who speak against our high ideals might contaminate us? Sway us? Does this not reflect that we are not so sure of ourselves?

(3) What about our freedom to move freely at home and abroad? Is the day coming when we, too, will believe that gates and walls shall bar those who do not think as we do?

(4) Have we lost our right to freedom from arbitrary government regulations and control? Are we so entwined with bureaucracy and regulations that freedom is stifled?

(5) There are a host of other freedoms that we have placed in jeopardy by our indifference and our apathy. Where is our realization that life, liberty, and the pursuit of happiness are privileges with which go certain responsibilities, not only for ourselves but for our children and our children's children?

III. "O beautiful for patriot dream that sees beyond the years. . . ." These inspiring lines by Katharine Lee Bates see beyond the present, beyond our own time, and into the future. The men who formed our nation had a great dream in their hearts and a bright, burning hope for happier things to come.

(1) The spirit that made our country great was the belief in the rights that we possess. When we love America, we also will have the "patriot dream that sees beyond the years." We will see to it that now and for future generations we shall guarantee those rights for which men in the past were willing to cry: "Give me liberty or give me death!"

(2) Democracy, freedom, liberty, political and economic rights make up the

highway of hope for the government and the governed. It is for rich and poor; literate and illiterate; black, white, yellow, and red. The liberty in which Paul admonished the Galatians to stand fast does not just happen. By discipline and devotion, by precept and example, does it inspire hope now and in the years to come.

IV. Did liberty and freedom become established in our land by some quirk or happenstance? Or was the hand of God hovering over the pawn at the very beginning?

(1) The key men involved in the shaping of our nation's destiny took their fundamental belief in God with the utmost seriousness. Most of them had deep roots in a strong religious heritage and atmosphere.

(a) Perhaps Franklin spoke for most of them as, in his last year, he wrote: "I believe in one God, Creator of the Universe. That he governs it by his Providence. That he ought to be worshipped. That the most acceptable service we render him is doing good to his other children. That the soul of man is immortal."

(b) Washington expressed it as: "I am sure that there was never a people who had more reason to acknowledge a divine interposition in their affairs than those of the United States."

(2) As we look back in our history, does it not become apparent that God has been our Protector? From the dark days of the Revolution, when a handful of people won their freedom from a world empire, through the days of the Civil War, through two World Wars, in times of depression, civil strife, at moments when we have been driven to our knees because we had no place else to go—surely God's hand has been upon us.

(3) When as a nation we employ phrases such as "Under God" and "In God We Trust," we are recognizing God as the Supreme Sovereign of our land. There is no room for totalitarian ideals in our nation. For us it is the never-to-be-forgotten words of the psalmist as he spoke for all ages: "Blessed is the nation whose God is the Lord, and the people whom he has chosen as his." What takes place when we lose God?—Frank A. Kostyu.

Worship Aids

CALL TO WORSHIP. "He that dwelleth in the secret place of the most High shall abide under the shadow of the Almighty. I will say of the Lord, He is my refuge and my fortress: my God; in him will I trust." Ps. 91:1-2.

INVOCATION. Be gracious unto us, O Lord, and bless us. Stretch forth the right hand of thy protection to guard our country, that we, being devoted to thy service, may ever be defended by thy power.

OFFERTORY PRAYER. We thank thee, O God, for another anniversary of our nation's independence and pray that this rich gift may be an opportunity to serve one another in love.

OFFERTORY SENTENCE. "Offer the sacrifices of righteousness, and put your trust in the Lord." Ps. 4:5.

PRAYER. Almighty God, who hast given this land to be a heritage to all the inhabitants of it: make us gratefully conscious of our indebtedness to thee, our Maker and Defender, and to the pioneering builders of a free land. Assembled here under the challenge of a Declaration of Independence not yet fully realized, do thou deepen our appreciation of the worth of our common heritage. Give us the zeal fully to possess it and the wisdom and courage to safeguard it. Direct our efforts to achieve full freedom under an equal law for all our citizens, and make us one people in the desire and willing struggle for a nation indivisible under thy governance. Give to our nation wise and fearless citizens to defend our liberties and to preserve for us a land of order and peace, of unity and strength, and of faith and righteousness. Guide and encourage us through rightly purposed pursuits to earn thy favor and a worthy, responsible life for all.—Jesse Jai McNeil in *Minister's Service Book.*

Illustrations

WILL IT WORK? After the bitter debates and long arguments at the Constitutional Convention had been concluded, Dr. Benjamin Franklin was being carried from the convention hall in a portable chair. Along the way he was stopped by an anxious lady who inquired, "Dr. Franklin, is it finished?" His reply was, "Yes, madam, it is finished." Next she asked, "Will it work?" To this question Dr. Franklin replied, "That, madam, is up to you."—Frank M. Johnson, Jr.

SENATE PRAYER. O Lord, make us mindful of thee this day. Invest us with a sense of the eternal. Spare us from being little souls wrapped in the narrow confinement of our own selfish ways. But lift our eyes that we may behold the vision of that Kingdom which is yet to be, the Ruler of which is God, and the law of which is love. As we render high honor to the intrepid voyagers in the vast ranges of thy universe, make us explorers of the spirit and pioneers in a new order of brotherhood and peace. Equip the people of this land and their representatives here assembled with justice and righteousness, with wisdom and courage, with compassion and mercy, so as to be the servants of thy purposes upon this earth. Make us good enough, great enough, and strong enough for the age in which we live. Grant that goodness and mercy may so follow us all our days that we may abide with thee forever.—Edward L. R. Elson.

Sermon Suggestions

A NATION UNDER GOD. Text: Zech. 4:6. (1) Being a nation under God means we look for God's protection. (2) A nation under God realizes his justice. (3) A nation under God seeks his guidance.—Richard B. Douglass.

HONORING AMERICA. (1) We honor America because she has opened her heart and her doors to the distressed and the persecuted of the world. (2) We honor America because she has been the most generous nation in history. (3) We honor America because she has never hidden her problems and faults. (4) We honor America because she is honestly recognizing and is courageously trying to solve her social problems. (5) We honor America because she defends the right of her citizens to dissent. (6) We honor America because there is woven into the warp and woof of our nation faith in God.—Billy Graham.

EVENING SERVICE

Topic: Decisions That Shape Our Lives
TEXT: Luke 23:39.

When the crowd yelled, "Save thyself," our Lord said inwardly, "I will save myself—the higher, holier self, the self committed to doing the full will of God." This struggle was won on the Cross because it had been won on earlier moral battlefields.

I. That is the clue to our Lord's life, and so it must be the clue to all of our lives. It portrays a principle which has to be confronted by every man and woman and youth all along the way of life. No man can by his own acts achieve salvation. No man can save himself from his own sins. Salvation is the gracious gift of God. But in another sense—in his moral choices, in his daily decisions, in his judgments in a crisis—each one must choose which self is to be saved, the lower or the higher self.

II. That choice is no less great today than it was on a dark Friday; nor will it be two thousand years from now. The greatness of character, the quality of a human personality, is to be seen in the way this choice is made. Courage and character are developed by staying on the cross and going on in spite of fears. When hardship is encountered, when suffering is to be borne, when defeat overtakes one, when a cross looms on the distant horizon, there is always the tempting claim: "Save your skin. Take it easy. Don't get hurt. Save thyself." There is, however, another alternative: "To thine own self be true."

III. To find spiritual depth, man must look inward to discover three basic truths: Who he is, where he is, and where he is going. If an individual cannot do this he becomes an actor playing a role for exterior effect, reacting almost solely to the response of his superiors and his peers. He uses and responds to traditional values, not because he believes them, but because they are the proximate causation of exterior applause. Man must seek peace of mind and inner reserves of strength before he can commit himself to a higher cause or challenge.

IV. Each of us in our daily lives makes decisions that shape our lives, mold our characters. All choices are not earth-shaking, momentous milestones. Most come on little mouse feet. We can slide into a great collective cop-out that ill prepares us for the big dramatic crisis, the supreme test that will mark our lives, perhaps end them.

V. The heart of our Gospel is that you can never save yourself. You can only give yourself, and in giving, find life. Whenever a choice must be made as to which self is to be saved, let us make it by the wisdom and in the power of our faith. Nobility of character and inner worth come not by avoiding the small, onerous daily challenges that test and train us but by accepting them and thereby strengthening our higher self. —Senator William B. Saxbe.

SUNDAY: JULY EIGHTH

MORNING SERVICE

Topic: The World's Slow Stain
TEXT: Rom. 12:2.

Paul Elmer More, writing of Cardinal John Newman, claims that the cardinal's face revealed a "steady deterioration" as he reached old age. "The end is almost terrible," More says, "so plainly written on the old man's countenance are the marks of anxiety and strain and a kind of pathetic fear." Sad as it is to say, too many of us, with the coming of the years, readily succumb to the world's slow stain.

Youth is a precious gift; it is indeed "the glad season of life." All of us wish we could hold on to it much longer. But Time marches on inexorably. Yet we must never forget that even though we grow old physically, we can all be youthful in spirit, we can possess this certain frame of mind which to a great extent will insulate us from the world's slow stain.

Here are three suggestions.

I. Try to face each day with the enthusiasm and unstudied joyousness of youth. (1) Someone has said the young greet the dawn with a cheer. Young people do have a surprising enthusiasm for life; they have a certain radiant joyousness which seems to slip away from us the older we get.

(2) There are all types of enthusiasm. There is the raucous enthusiasm of the football stadium, the heroic enthusiasm of the explorer who makes his way across burning deserts or impenetrable forests, the inspiring enthusiasm of a great scientist or student as he diligently seeks after Truth, and the less spectacular enthusiasm which drives a talented man or woman in making her community a better place in which to live. Enthusiasm for life, of one sort or another, all of us can possess regardless

of what our age may be. A person does not lose his enthusiasm when he grows old; he grows old when he loses his enthusiasm.

II. An inquiring mind is another characteristic of a youthful spirit. (1) It is so easy to speak out sharply against our young folks. At times they are so flippant in their speech, so self-centered in their thinking, so selfish in their conduct, so indifferent to the higher things of life, and so defiant of the old and tested moral standards of life.

(2) Today we parents are perturbed by our young people. They seem so radical, so unconventional in their thinking. Many of us, naturally, are alarmed if not frantic, thinking that we have brought ingrates or rebels into the world. But much better would it be for us parents to remain calm and patient, even amused, for these young people are responding in a very normal manner. Their radicalism, their unconventional thinking are merely symptomatic of growing pains. They have begun to sense their intellectual strength and are eager to do independent thinking.

(3) Someone has very cleverly said that a woman is as old as she looks, and a man is as old as he feels. But I believe the truth of the matter is that a person is as old as he thinks. Whenever a person stops thinking, when he fails to be mentally alert, when he surrenders his inquiring mind, then old age for sure has got the better of him. Complacency with things as they are and a general hostility to change are characteristic of age. To be young in spirit one must seek daily to develop and discipline his mind.

III. A third characteristic of youth is its generous impulses and its devoted consecration to high ideals.

(1) The tragedy is that Christianity has not been able in this generation to capitalize on the idealism of its young people. There have, of course, been times such as in the first four centuries of its history, when Christianity swept at a phenomenal speed over the Graeco-Roman world; in the Middle Ages, at the time of the Crusades; and in the last generation or so when we have had a tremendous impetus in foreign missionary work under the slogan, "The World for Christ in Our Generation." Whenever the Church has captivated the hearts and minds of its young people, appealing to their idealism, demanding an uncompromising loyalty and devotion, it has made rapid progress.

(2) We so often are tempted to claim that our modern young people are degenerate in their thinking and conduct. But the truth of the matter is that they respond much more readily to an ideal than do older folk. A very prominent principal emphasized this fact when he said that he has never known the young people in his school to elect a rotter, a bad character, as the president of the student body. He also added these significant words: "I would trust the moral reactions of my students far more than I would the moral reactions of the forty-year-olds." Youth is idealistic.

IV. William Wordsworth in his famous poem, "Ode on Intimations of Immortality," tells of the "shades of the prison-house" which begin "to close upon the growing boy." All of us know what he means, for as we grow older we catch ourselves more and more compromising, if not forsaking, our ideals.

(1) The spirit of youth, its unbounded enthusiasm, its wonder, its trust, its radiance, and its faith, which we early in life deeply cherished, slowly seem to lose their pre-eminence, and we temporize, become expedient, mercenary, and mean. Inexorably we succumb to the contagion of the world's slow stain, and we slump into a deadly conformity with the world.

(2) Such an attitude is, of course, a betrayal of our faith, for Christianity implies action and vitality, growth and change. If we would be true to our heritage, we must, like St. Paul, be youthful in spirit, cultivating a joyous acceptance of the life which God has entrusted to our care, developing an inquiring mind, and cherishing high ideals

SUNDAY: JULY EIGHTH

which will be a leavening influence in the community.—John Schott.

Worship Aids

CALL TO WORSHIP. "How beautiful upon the mountains are the feet of him that bringeth good tidings, that publisheth peace; that publisheth salvation; that saith unto Zion, thy God reigneth!" Isa. 52:7.

INVOCATION. Eternal and ever-blessed God, come to us this day as we wait upon thee; and banish every evil thought, and restrain every wandering thought, that we, being pure in heart, may see thee.

OFFERTORY SENTENCE. "He that soweth bountifully shall reap also bountifully." II Cor. 9:6.

OFFERTORY PRAYER. O Lord, who hast given us the privilege of life, help us to magnify eternal values and to show forth by our lives and our tithes the Christ, whom to know aright is life eternal.

PRAYER. Gracious Father, whose will is our salvation and whose way is our peace: grant us patience and courage and faith that we may be more than conquerors through him who loved us and gave himself for us.

Keep us steady in the simple living of our days. With patience may we discipline our wills, cultivate our minds, and harness our powers. So may we be worthy instruments of thy purpose as we take up the common activities of every day.

Make us equal to life's crises. Let us not shrink from our responsibilities. Fortify us with valor to meet handicap, frustration, and conflict. May we conduct ourselves on life's field of honor as good soldiers of Jesus Christ.

Give us faith in life's greatness as we march into the future. Save us from impatience in the day of small things and from fear in times of peril. Make us strong to endure. Help us to march breast forward in hope and courage, faith and confidence. We make our dedication in the name of Jesus Christ, the Captain of our salvation.—Carl A. Glover.

Illustrations

CHANGE AND LOSS. A friend of mine, with an active, perceptive mind, said to me on her ninetieth birthday: "I feel as though I had lived for two hundred years, not ninety, so many and so rapid are the changes I have seen; and I don't like the age into which we are moving because, in losing many things we can do without, we are losing many we can't do without if our young people are to have a life that is worth living."—James Welch in *Foundations of Western Values*.

DISCOVERING. Most young people are not rebelling but discovering. The communication gap can be tightened by open minds between youth and adults.—Michael McGowan.

Sermon Suggestions

CHRISTIAN BRIDGES. Text: Rom. 12:10 (RSV). (1) Bridges of prayer and worship across which men may renew relationship to God. (2) Bridges of brotherly acceptance across which men of all races may see themselves as children of one Father and, therefore, see themselves as brothers. (3) Bridges of self-insight across which men may meet their true selves on the other side. (4) Bridges of hope for those caught in the whirlpools of despair and poverty. (5) Bridges of reconciliation across which men may walk to meet again brothers lost by bridges burned behind them.—Robert P. Bunch.

BASIC EDUCATION. The kind of education needed today is concerned with (1) the head and the heart, (2) mathematics and morals, (3) curriculum and character, and (4) grades and God.—Emerson S. Colaw.

EVENING SERVICE

Topic: The Treasure of Tribulation

I. If we are careful not to take it in superficial Pollyanna fashion, we may say that there seems to be a sense in which suffering is somehow intended—to improve character, to force us to grow in love, understanding, patience, and faith—much as pain in the physical body is intended to call our attention to something amiss and motivate us to correct it.

II. In suffering there often lies the power to help others. Tolstoy once asserted: it is by those who have suffered that the world has been advanced. The greatest of the Hebrew prophets reached a similar conclusion. The nation Israel was called not to be a great military power, bringing all nations under her control, but rather she was called to be a "suffering servant" and by her suffering to redeem the world. And among Christians it has been out of his suffering that the compassion of Jesus has spoken most convincingly the redeeming word to men and women across the centuries.

III. The hard reality is that suffering is a part of the life of every living creature. Death itself is as much a part of the life process as birth, and no man can avoid it.

(1) Either we will learn to accept suffering, to live with it and grow from it, or we will be beaten and embittered by it, for suffering in one form or another is an inescapable fact in the experience of us all.

(2) The religious problem of suffering is how we may, as Gerald Heard reminds us, so "take the initiative against the opponent, so answer the challenge, that suffering is transmuted into energy and creativeness."

IV. If we are to be honest, we must admit that there is much we do not know; with Paul we acknowledge that we "see through the drudgery of what seems like meaningless toil, or the handling of some personal problem, or whether it is undergoing the excruciating pain of some dread disease, it often seems that the suffering goes on and on long after any useful purpose has been served."

It is not escapism to answer with the firm conviction of religious faith that God wills goodness for his beloved children. His perspective is beyond our perspective, and it is often our experience that we do not at first comprehend what good things life has in store for us.—Ralph W. Odom.

SUNDAY: JULY FIFTEENTH

MORNING SERVICE

Topic: The Mile That Counts the Most

Text: Matt. 5:41.

Jesus lived in the little country of Palestine which had been conquered by Rome. Not only did Rome exact heavy taxes and hold those people under strict bondage, but they also never let them forget they were at all times subject to their orders.

(a) One of the most annoying laws was the one which allowed a soldier to compel any citizen to carry his pack for one mile. These were proud people, and you can imagine how they resented this. They would walk that mile cursing under their breaths. Since under the law just one mile was the limit a soldier could command a person at any one time, we can feel certain they would carefully count their steps and not go one step farther than the law demanded.

(b) Jesus said don't stop with just one mile. Go a second mile. The people must have thought him crazy, but he wasn't. He was giving them something to live by. The first mile was compulsory; the second was voluntary. The first mile one must go; the second mile one chooses to go. Jesus would have people know that living really begins after one has walked the mile of duty and then stepped out on the mile of privilege.

I. The Second Mile eliminates the drudgery of life. (1) Many people go through life doing only those things they are compelled to do. They find life to be hard, not much joy, and they are constantly tired. Other people go beyond the call of duty and freely give themselves on a voluntary basis. They find life to be a stimulating, thrilling adventure.

(2) Jesus divided life into two miles: the first mile is compulsion, the second is consecration. On the first mile a man is constantly demanding his "rights"; on the second mile he is constantly looking for his opportunities. The mile of duty is no fun; on the mile of consecration we find great joy.

II. The Second Mile is the mile on which we make our progress. The man who just thinks of his duty never really makes much success, but when a man thinks in terms of voluntary consecration, he gets enthusiastic. You never get enthusiasm over the things you are compelled to do, but you find enthusiasm in the things you want to do.

III. On the Second Mile we gain our largest rewards. The Second Mile rewards us in our relationships with other people.

(1) As you go along through life, somebody will do you wrong. There are four attitudes you may take: (a) "If he hurts me, I will hurt him worse." That is vindictive vengeance. (b) "If he hurts me, I will treat him the same." That is retribution, the old law of "an eye for an eye." (c) "If he hurts me, I will ignore him and have nothing more to do with him." That is indifferent disdain. (d) "If he hurts me, I will love and serve him." That is the Christian way, and that is the way that brings rewards.

(2) One day Jesus was nailed to a cross. He had been mistreated as no other man had been. His trials were not fair, and even as he was hanging there, he was scorned and ridiculed. He had the power to strike every one of them dead or to even utterly ignore them. But he did neither. Instead, he began to pray. What was his very first prayer? For the good of those who had done him wrong. He went the Second Mile, and on that mile multitudes have seen him as the Savior. He bore his cross of duty, but he went further, and in doing so he gained his greatest reward.—Charles L. Allen.

Worship Aids

CALL TO WORSHIP. "If a man love me, saith Jesus, he will keep my words: and my Father will love him, and we will come unto him, and make our abode wtih him." John 14:23.

INVOCATION. Almighty God, who hast given us minds to know thee, hearts to love thee, and voices to show forth thy praise, we would not know thee if thou hadst not already found us: so assist us again to know thee with pure minds, to love thee with warm hearts, and to praise thee with a clear voice, world without end.

OFFERTORY SENTENCE. "Every man shall give as he is able, according to the blessing of the Lord thy God which he hath given thee." Deut. 16:17.

OFFERTORY PRAYER. Dear Father, may we ever give thee a definite, consistent, and heartfelt service.

PRAYER. Our Father, thou who art from everlasting to everlasting the same, we turn to thee, the infinite, the good, the pure, the redemptive, the merciful. We lift our being to thee from our finiteness, our weakness, our follies and shortcomings. O God, we thank thee that thou hast given us the upward look, the desire somehow to overcome our failings and our disharmony, and the unhappiness and disquiet that beset us. Teach us the divine truth that peace and creativity, wisdom and love, meaning and fulfillment are in thee and thee alone. Thou hast made us restless until we rest in thee. So teach us to number our days that we may apply our hearts to thy wisdom, the only reality in life, and thus achieve the joys now of that fellowship with thee which is eternal.

In this solemn hour of worship, we would direct our minds from weakness to strength, from discord to harmony, from sin to holiness, from strife to love. We would gird ourselves with thy truth and face the many tasks of the coming week with confidence and trust, with wisdom and kindness, with a sense of gratitude for our high calling as children of thine. We thank thee that thou hast broken the shackles of sin and sorrow and planted within us the consuming desire to be fellow workers with thee. Keep our minds stayed upon thee, our Strength and Peace.

In the coming week, help us to mount up over those things that would unman us, fill us with fear, and cause us to lower the standards of Christ in thought or word or deed. Help us to run with patience and not be weary. Through Christ our Lord, whose mind we would have in us this week and always in order that his Kingdom may come in all of its fullness.—Alvin D. Johnson.

Illustrations

ON THE GOOD SAMARITAN. The splendid thing about the Good Samaritan was that he refused to imitate anybody. His action, far from giving effect to any fixed rule that might have been taught him by contemporary moralists, was a flat violation of the respectable morality of that time and place. We can imitate him, not by reproducing his act, but by being just as original, just as creative, just as indifferent toward fatuous morality as he was.—L. P. Jacks.

"YOUR" AND "MY." An American missionary in Africa was teaching some natives the Twenty-third Psalm. He had them repeat after him: "The Lord is my shepherd." Again and again they would say, "The Lord is your shepherd." Puzzled, the missionary asked them why they said "your" instead of "my." They explained, "You have homes, good food and clothes, but we don't." They had to wait for bodily needs to be supplied if they were to see the Lord as shepherd of the soul. Man's first approach to God may be through service of others.—Roud Shaw.

TREE OF BEING. We ask the leaf, "Are you complete in yourself?" And the leaf answers, "No, my life is in the branches." We ask the branch, and the branch answers, "No, my life is in the root." We ask the root, and it answers, "No, my life is in the trunk and the branches and the leaves. Keep the branches stripped of leaves, and I shall die." So it is with the great tree of being. Nothing is completely and merely individual.—Harry Emerson Fosdick.

Sermon Suggestions

WHO IS A CHRISTIAN? There are some minimums. (1) One is a deep-felt sense of need. (See Rom. 7:18-24.) (2) The recognition that something has been done for us. In spite of the fact that life is a miracle, something has been done that we could not do for ourselves. We have been lived for and have been died for. (3) Being a Christian involves the constant struggle to bring one's own life to its highest potential. (See 2 Cor. 5:17.) (4) A Christ-inspired social goal as inclusive as the love of God. Through a Christian light shines for every man, woman, and child.—Wesley P. Ford.

THE PAIN AND THE HOPE OF THE LONELY. Scripture: Ps. 142. (1) What is loneliness for you? You may be one of the lonely aged, the lonely poor, or the lonely youth. Loneliness is often experienced in a crowd. Loneliness is different from aloneness. Loneliness is different from solitude. Loneliness is the feeling of being cut off from others, of being different from others, of being alienated from others. (2) Is there hope for the lonely? The psalmist finds hope in turning from himself. He looks beyond himself as he opens up to God. The psalmist discovers people. Is it possible that you can turn toward that One who stood so utterly alone—"despised and rejected by men, a man of sorrows, and acquainted with grief"?—Wade P. Huie.

EVENING SERVICE

Topic: The Problem and Privilege of Faith

Every area of life is made up of two aspects, problem and privilege. (a) If a man tries to monopolize the privilege alone and forget the problem, he becomes a sentimentalist.

(b) If a man becomes so obsessed with problems, holds them so closely to his eye that he can see nothing else, he becomes dry, sophisticated, unhappy, uncreative, futile. And particularly in religion he ceases having strength and song and has only a debate.

I. Consider the central matter of religion—God. (1) Say that very word to some people today and their instinctive response is a puzzled awareness of difficulty. There have been generations when the thought of God brought back a singing answer: "Holy, Holy, Holy, Lord God of Hosts! Heaven and earth are full of thy glory." But today try the psychological test on many a casual Christian, saying, "God," and see what a stream of questions you start. Is there really a God? What is he like? How do you imagine him? How can you justify his ways with men?

(2) What a problem he is! Well, of course. He is a problem. Here we are with our little minds developing for a few millenniums upon this midget planet in an immeasurable cosmos. Do we expect that with our butterfly nets we can capture the sun at noon, that we expect with our wits to capture the blazing truth about the Power that made all things?

II. We do not need to solve all the problems about God before we can begin to be enriched by him.

(1) He is well worth discussion, and there are depths beyond depths there that the longest plummets of your debate will never reach, but for your soul's sake enjoy him, depend on him, live by him, be true to him.

(2) When you say "God" you mean spiritual life projected to the very center of the universe. But that spiritual life which you are projecting to the center of the universe is also here. Here is where you start with it. Wherever goodness shines or love and beauty sing, there is the near end of God. Love him here; be true to him; be enriched by him.

III. You have problems about Christ. Well, of course you do. (1) Such is the capacity of the human mind to be obsessed with problems, even when dealing with something singularly beautiful, that there are many people today who never get any nearer to Christ than that he is a problem.

(2) Do we really mean that in his teachings of the good life, that go before us yet like a pillar of cloud by day and of fire by night, we can see nothing but problems? In that luminous Personality that incarnated them and made those teachings beautiful, so that across the centuries men like George Matheson have said, "Again and again I have been tempted to give up the struggle, but always the figure of that Strange Man hanging on the Cross sends me back to my task again," do you see nothing but problems?—Harry Emerson Fosdick.

SUNDAY: JULY TWENTY-SECOND

MORNING SERVICE

Topic: The Secret of Permanence in a World of Change.
Text: Matt. 7:25.

A positive and perennial secret of permanence in a world of change is faith in God. What kind of God?

I. A creator God. (1) Consider the phenomenal universe. Scientists insist that if a ray of light traveling at the rate of 186,000 miles per second were to leave the outer observable periphery of the universe, it would require one billion years for it to cross over to the opposite boundary. We are advised that it would require the entire population of the world 10,000 years to count the atoms in a single drop of water. (See Ps. 8:3–4.)

(2) We are assured of being made in the image of God, "a little lower than the angels," and crowned with glory and honor. We marvel at the contributions of those who have anchored their faith in this universal, yet personal, God. Imagine Abraham going out into a streetless night, faith his sole light! We stand in awe and admiration before the transformed and magnificent Moses! Our tribulations seem woefully few when compared with the trials of Job! Our hardships are trivial when we recall the life of Paul, yet what a crusader was he!

II. An incarnate God. (1) No miracle of nature is comparable to the mysteries of Christ; no splendor of the skies as inspiring as the Son of God; no contribution of man equals God's unspeakable gift, Jesus the Christ, through whom God so uniquely invaded the world. He thus became available. (See John 3:16; II Cor. 5:19.)

(2) We need this Man. He is no ordinary soul. Jesus is God's supreme revelation. The prophets foretold his coming. (See Isa. 9:6.)

(3) Divine wonderment cradled his birth. Ethereal music announced his arrival. His was a marvelous ministry! It would seem that he came too soon, for he was crucified. But this did not defeat God nor did it discourage Christ. God took the most grotesque of man's offerings and transformed it into the secret of salvation.

III. A God who imparts. (1) The Church is God's idea. Through it God bestows his life-giving spirit. A man asked Quinton Hogg, "What did it cost to build the Polytechnic Institute of London?" He answered, "One man's life." Building the Church was likewise expensive. One Man's life was given that its foundation might be secure. Since the initial cornerstone laying, many lives have been offered to increase its witness, expand its service, and enhance its holiness.

(2) Paul declared the Church to be "the body of Christ." The Church does not mysteriously transfer one to fellowship in Christ, but one's faith in Christ admits one to membership in his mystical Body. The Church is the incarnation of the Gospel. It is both visible and invisible. The Church brings good tidings from afar. It makes mistakes because it is human; it will succeed because it is divine.

IV. An eternal God. No one would be content to be forever what he is. Man is by nature a bipolar creature. He is an amphibian. He lives in two realms: matter and spirit. It is to his glory that he can work below and live above. This world is not his permanent home. (See John 14:2–3.)—G. Curtis Jones.

Worship Aids

CALL TO WORSHIP. "Trust in [God] at all times; ye people, pour out your heart before him: God is a refuge for us." Ps. 62:8.

SUNDAY: JULY TWENTY-SECOND

INVOCATION. O God, whose word is quick and powerful, and sharper than any two-edged sword: grant us grace to receive thy truth in faith and love, that by it we may be taught and guided, upheld and comforted, and prepared unto every good word and work, to the glory of thy name.

OFFERTORY SENTENCE. "For ye know the grace of our Lord Jesus Christ, that though he was rich, yet for your sakes he became poor, that ye through his poverty might be rich." II Cor. 8:9.

OFFERTORY PRAYER. Dear Lord and Savior of us all, may we become obedient to thy will both in the dedication of our tithes and of our talents.

PRAYER. Gracious Father, thy children have come for prayer. In their hearts is the longing for communion. In their minds is the knowledge of the world. In their thoughts is the desire to reconcile their earthbound duties with their heavenly imaginings. They seek forgiveness for their many mistakes and willful misdoings: for their perversness in repeating what they know to be wrong, their obstinacy in continuing on a tortuous course of evil, for their selfishness in mistreating family and neighbors, for the prejudices that are so easily provoked and so strenuously held. We pray that thou wilt pity them, as Jesus on the Cross forgave his enemies.

They express their thankfulness for all of thy mercies by trying to walk in thy favor and live in thy righteousness. They rejoice in the insights which lead them into thy truth, in the love which surrounds them, in the light on their pathway, and in the fellowship and worship of the Church of Christ. We pray that thou wilt accept their giving of thanks, help them to live in thee and be inspired by thy spirit.—Herbert Beecher Hudnut.

Illustrations

CAPACITIES. In these days when nervous exhaustion is such a common experience, we should analyze our capacity to suffer without bitterness, to endure disappointment without loss of hope, to withstand strain without grumbling. Nothing shows more plainly what we are, and how we have been spiritually fed, than does a crisis.—Harold E. Kohn in *Thoughts Afield*.

DAY OF JESUS CHRIST. Our day may well be a day in which all of us, Christians and non-Christians alike, sin in evil thoughts and words and deeds as though we were not those who were justified and sanctified in Christ's life and death. It may well be a day on which the earth is covered, as once before the flood, by so much merited and unmerited suffering. It may well be a day when no moment passes in which death does not make what seems to be an irrevocable end of some human life. It may well be a day of the devil and demons, of yielding but still resisting darkness. This is true. But it is not decisive. The decisive thing is that it is also a day of Jesus Christ, a day of his presence, life, activity, and speech. It is concretely a day of his coming again in the full sense of the word, of his new coming in glory, here and now in this intervening time which is our place. —Karl Barth in *The Doctrine of Reconciliation*.

Sermon Suggestions

THE CHRISTIAN'S LIFE AND MIND. There are five important things which will help us understand better the close relationship between the intellectual life and the Christian life. (1) We must realize that man can serve God in all occupations. (2) We must acquire a mature understanding of Christ's message. (3) We must use our knowledge in service to our fellowman. (4) We must view all life as one integrated whole. (5) We must develop the inner principles which can guide us through the intricacies of life.—Willis D. Weatherford.

THE ROAD OF SHUT DOORS. Scripture: Acts 16:1–9. What prevented Paul and Timothy from doing what they had planned we shall never know. At any rate, the doors they hoped to enter were one by one shut in their faces and a door of which they had not dreamed was opened. So Chrsitianity crossed a narrow, shining sea—and entered Europe. (1) We, too, have often enough to travel the road of shut doors. Somewhere each one of us has a great store of things—quite wonderful and right things he meant to do or be—and they are still only dreams. (2) We have been forbidden—prevented—by forces beyond our control. But there has always been an open door beyond —and perhaps to a larger service and a better self. (3) How often we have found the road of shut doors to be at the end an open road to a fullness of life and service we might otherwise never have reached. But we must go to the end to know it.—Gaius Glenn Atkins.

EVENING SERVICE

Topic: A Christian View of Sex
SCRIPTURE: Gen. 1:26–28; I Cor. 6:9–20.
I. Our faith is based on the recognition of God as creator and sovereign ruler of the universe and all that is in it. "In the beginning God created . . . male and female created he them and God saw everything that he had made, and behold, it was very good." The Christian in all of his behavior patterns, including that of sex, is disciplined in the knowledge that God is with him and he is with God. This body is not a vehicle for pleasure, but an instrument for God's glory.

II. A Christian understanding of sex is built on an understanding of God's entire plan for unity for life.
(1) God's plan is for unity of the body and person. This means that the whole self is redeemed by Christ, not just that part of you that is going to heaven. The body as well as the soul of the Christian is involved in the process because the person is one.
(2) God's plan calls for a unity of the feeling and the fact. A genuine Christian union should be romantic in that it is deeply personal, but it also must have an element of the sacramental in that the outward sign is indicative of the inward reality. When sex is divorced from real love, it becomes mere lust.
III. The Christian control of sex is maintained when this unity of God and life is maintained.
(1) J. Wallace Hamilton uses an interesting analogy in comparing basic human instincts to a wild stallion that must be broken. In sex, as in other appetites, some use the theory of self-assertion by letting the wild horse run and by giving free rein to the natural instincts. Others go to the opposite extreme with self-negation. Instead of eliminating the rider and throwing the reins over the horse's head for him to run free they would eliminate the horse. The Christian way is neither self-assertion nor self-negation, but self-fulfillment. A wild horse can be trained and disciplined until rider and horse, the mind and the body, become one in using this strong, surging energy for good purpose.
(2) The temptations of sex in the twentieth century can be overwhelming. I quickly add that, with God's help, there is no temptation that you cannot handle if you establish and maintain the unity of God in life by throwing open the door of your heart to Christ and letting your body be the temple of the Holy Spirit.—John F. Anderson.

SUNDAY: JULY TWENTY-NINTH

MORNING SERVICE

Topic: Formula for Peace of Soul

A peaceful, untroubled mind, dedicated to human service, has always been the Christian ideal for living. Jesus, who lived an abundant life, left a rich legacy of peace to all his followers. (See John 14:27.) In practicing the poised spirit, symbolic of all New Testament teaching, one finds serenity for his confusion, security for his insecurity, and power for overcoming his frustrations.

I. Consider the first ingredient in this modern formula for attaining peace within oneself—humility. The art of being humble contributes both to poise and to health.

(1) The humble heart is teachable, genuine, honest. Moreover, the appreciative, humble man recognizes his indebtedness to all others. His chief concern is not outward appearances but inner righteousness. Seeking the quiet judgment of God, not the artificial praise of men, he is guided by what is true, and is not easily given to that which is merely expedient.

(2) Health and poise attend humility, revealing a peaceful kingdom which is not only above but also within. God delights to walk with the humble, whispering his secrets only to pure, searching minds. Always the humble is made "beautiful for salvation" because of what he is.

(3) The very gateway to good health and to social improvement is the same —humility. You may even apply your own interpretation, reading Moffatt's translation, "blessed are the humble," or Weymouth interpreting God's love for the "retiring, submissive," but the overtone of the New Testament is always this: "Happy are the humble!"

II. The second ingredient for peace of soul is tranquility. With Webster's help, tranquility is easily defined in such terms as "quiet," "calm," "undisturbed," but it is much more difficult to illustrate and still harder to practice.

(1) Who among us, following an unintended emotional outburst, has not wished he had remained both cool and collected? Impatience and irritability must be conquered if one is to have peace of mind.

(2) To possess a dependable confidence a person must always work at some part of it. Every day he eliminates under control some danger which otherwise could explode. He does it in little, easy ways which prepare him in advance of a crisis. He knows that, unlike Henry the Navigator's royal geographers, he cannot live his life in some cloistered fortress behind the hills. He, therefore, prepares himself to meet tranquilly the noises and disturbances about him.

(3) By what assurance do you possess this quiet, dependable, tranquil mind which puts you in the fortunate position of being the offended rather than the occasional offender? How can you, in the humdrum of everyday living with its split schedules, rushing traffic, etc., be so sure of yourself? The answer is simple. You have prepared yourself in advance to meet this, and any other emergency, before it arises. You pause and wait for the adjustment to eternal things. You are aware of the command: "Be still, and know that I am God." You say a prayer, gaze upon the wonder of a flower, or look at the stars as they twinkle in the overarching sky above. The peace you acquire in those moments alone with yourself and with God builds up reserve strength to meet and conquer personal conflicts which arise.

III. The third ingredient in the formula which brings us health, poise, and peace is equanimity. This element adds a completeness and a wholeness to life itself.

(1) And what is equanimity? It is equity, impartial judgment, evenness of mind. Other terms, too, might be added: calm temper, balance, composure. Poise has been described as the art of raising one's eyebrows instead of the roof. In actual practice, equanimity reaches out even further to overcome those subtler temptations, such as "wood swearing" (the kind of emotional disturbance indicated by door slamming), temper tantrums, or the "martyred air" (the emotional upset so commonly demonstrated through pouting and stony silence).

(2) The ability always to light right side up, to keep one's determined objective in spite of criticism, to fulfill one's obligation for being—that is the captivating satisfaction which brings peace of soul. The Apostle Paul evidences it, saying, "I know both how to be abased, and I know how to abound." This demonstration of equanimity made him the most significant figure in the early Church; for whatever his circumstances, he was always the same, pushing forward to fulfill his objective. No variation in temporal fortune, no fluctuation in outward things, made any real difference to Paul. And why should it—either to him or to you?—J. Richard Sneed.

Worship Aids

CALL TO WORSHIP. "O send out thy light and thy truth: let them lead me; let them bring me unto thy holy hill, and to the tabernacles." Ps. 43:3.

INVOCATION. Almighty God, who lookest upon the inward man, forbid us in thy presence the vain endeavor to hide from thee what we have thought and done and truly are. Give us candor to acknowledge freely to thee what must be forever hidden from the knowledge of others, and may no false shame keep us from confessing those sins which no proper shame kept us from committing.

OFFERTORY SENTENCE. "Upon the first day of the week let every one of you lay by him in store, as God hath prospered him." I Cor. 16:2.

OFFERTORY PRAYER. Our Father, help us to trust thee more fully and to accept our responsibility toward thy work and thy children who are our brethren in Christ.

PRAYER. Almighty God, Father of lights, in whose presence there is no night and in the light of whose countenance is perpetual day: we bless and praise thee as at the beginning of this our day of rest we are permitted to draw near unto thee. When we awake we are still with thee. Accept, we beseech thee, the worship of our hearts. Help us to realize thy nearness and thy holiness. Assist us by the power of thy Holy Spirit to free ourselves from the hindrances of our sinful nature. Forgive us our offences and cleanse our desires. Renew a right spirit within us. Remove our transgressions from us. Grant that we may acceptably worship thee this day; may we indeed know thy name and hear thy voice. Breathe in our ears thy message of peace. Give to us power to receive and understand. May the services of thy house be refreshment unto our souls and glory to thy holy name. Fill our hearts with love to thee. Satisfy us with thy mercy. Let thy Kingdom extend amongst us. May every member of thy Church be faithful to his vocation and ministry, that the earth may be filled with the glory of the Lord as the waters cover the sea.—*A Book of Family Worship.*

Illustrations

LAST THANKS. A little boy who was cared for in a Christian orphanage fell ill, and it became apparent that he could not live. The matron felt he should know that his time on earth was drawing short. How could she tell him? She decided to call in the chaplain and have him talk to the boy. The pastor sat down on the lad's bed and said to him, "Son, God made you. God loves you. God cares for you. And now God wants you to leave us and to live with him forever."

The little boy looked deeply into the eyes of the chaplain and was silent for a few moments. Then he said, very simply, "Will you thank him for me, please?"—Ernest R. Case.

DENIAL AND BELIEF. People may deny God with the top of their minds, but they believe him at the bottom of their hearts.—Robert J. McCracken.

CONTINUAL REMINDERS. Daily prayer and religious reading are necessary parts of the Christian life. We have to be continually reminded of what we believe. Neither this belief nor any other will automatically remain alive in the mind; it must be fed. As a matter of fact, if you examined a hundred people who had lost their faith in Christianity, I wonder how many of them would turn out to have been reasoned out of it by honest argument? Do not most people simply drift away?—C. S. Lewis in *Mere Christianity.*

Sermon Suggestions

IF YOU CAN'T TAKE CRITICISM. Scripture: Rom. 14:4, 10–13 (MOFFATT). (1) If you and I can't take criticism it may be because we need to grow up concerning ourselves and our relationships with others. (2) To grow up into a mature attitude toward ourselves and others means that we must evaluate the criticism and try to understand the critic. (3) Some criticism comes as a challenge to correct flaws and with Christian honesty may help us become more useful Christians. (4) When we find it difficult to take criticism we need the help which God's spirit is willing and eager to give. (a) We realize that we are all under the judgment of God. (b) The core of the cure is yielding one's total self to God. The secret is the surrendered self.—David A. MacLennan in *The Clergy Journal.*

THE LIFE OF PRAYER. The colonial Puritan preacher, Richard Baxter, gives us counsel on how we might pray alone: "We ought to find the fittest time and the fittest place and the fittest preparation of heart for prayer." (1) By the fittest time he meant that time when we are most awake, most alert, most in possession of our faculties. (2) By the fittest place Baxter meant that place where you can be alone and give that time to God. (3) By the fittest preparation of heart Baxter meant that personal inner experience that makes prayer a vital point of contact with God so that you are in reality in fellowship with him.—Carl H. Lundquist.

EVENING SERVICE

Topic: Worlds to Conquer

TEXT: Luke 2:49.

Alexander the Great, conqueror of the ancient world, died at thirty-three sighing for other worlds to conquer. Jesus at thirty-three, approaching his death on the Cross, said: "Be of good cheer, I have overcome the world." His followers do not need to sigh for other worlds to conquer, but in the spirit of the Christ to overcome the world. There are many worlds that must be conquered.

I. There is the world of starving millions, which must be conquered by production and distribution.

II. There is the world of class hatred, to be conquered by understanding and fair dealing.

III. There is the world of prejudice, to be overcome by education, justifiable racial pride, and opportunity.

IV. There is the world of bigoted religions, to be overcome by humility and tolerance.

V. There is the world of warring nations, to be conquered by goodwill and understanding.—Lester R. Templin.

SUNDAY: AUGUST FIFTH

MORNING SERVICE

Topic: Getting Off the Earth
Text: II Cor. 12:2.

We all need to get off the earth at times in order to see from a new perspective, to have a new sense of appreciation for this our earth as we view it from above, and come back with a new awareness of our possibilities as children of God and our responsibilities as heirs of God.

I. St. Paul had such an experience when he was lifted up, as he said, to the third heaven and was enabled to see things which were too magnificent to describe and to hear things that were too sacred to relate. It made him so proud that he was ashamed to boast about it, yet he was kept humble by the fact that he was given thorn in the flesh to make him know that he was human and that it was by grace that he lived.

II. We all need some moments of fresh insight, deepening of our understanding of who we are and where we stand, of finding some direction in life which can come as we feel ourselves free from the shackles of our earthiness and become part of a greater and more eternal universe.

(1) We can't command such an experience, of course, but we can prepare ourselves for its coming and we can look, with expectancy and great hope, for the open door of its coming and then avail ourselves of every opportunity to become a part of a world removed from the earth that will enable us to see ourselves in a new light.

(2) How many times have you said to yourself, "I've got to get away from it all!" And you know how you feel sometime—the pressure of the too-immediate, the monotony of things, the daily routine of what appears to be meaningless and trivial. Then you need to get away from it all, get off from the earth, and then come back to it afresh.

III. Religion at its best enables us to get off the earth by relating us to the God of the universe whose concerns are with eternal and universal values, as well as with men and their immediate problems.

(1) We place our trust in a great God—Creator of the heavens and the earth, the moon and the stars—all things are the works of his hands. But our faith is that God is not only great but good, as good as our Jesus Christ. "He knows the stars by name," but he also "heals the brokenhearted."

(2) No progress is made by simply standing. It is when you are willing to raise a foot into the air of dreams, of possibilities, of great hopes, of expectation, and then have faith that there will be "everlasting arms" to support you again when you come down from the lofty heights.

IV. The reason to get off the earth, of course, is to come back to it and begin over. One does not come back to it just as he left it. Something has happened to a man who really gets off the earth, something that makes him see life in a new way, with new eyes, from a changed perspective. A new sense of the value of, and appreciation for, life among the whole human race seems to radiate from our astronauts as they come back out of space. Lunar flight has cost in billions of dollars. One seems on safe ground to predict that a new spirit will come to us because of it. We have made a great step forward in science and technology, and it waits now for us to make a great stride forward in other areas of life—to make this a good world for all men to live in where peace may be established, the degrading aspects of poverty shall be eliminated, and where men shall walk together in a great exploration into God. We are all explorers at heart, and these explorers in the sky have shaken us from our boredom, our lack of faith in man and God, and will help us face forward and move into the unknown tomorrow with faith that God is there.—F. Harold Essert.

Worship Aids

CALL TO WORSHIP. "I will lift up mine eyes unto the hills, from whence cometh my help. My help cometh from the Lord, which made heaven and earth." Ps. 121:1–2.

INVOCATION. O God, whose name is great, whose goodness is inexhaustible, who art worshiped and served by all the hosts of heaven: touch our hearts, search out our consciences, and cast out of us every evil thought and base desire; all envy, wrath, and remembrance of injuries; and every motion of flesh and spirit that is contrary to thy holy will.

OFFERTORY SENTENCE. "Every man according as he purposeth in his heart, so let him give; not grudgingly, or of necessity: for God loveth a cheerful giver." II Cor. 9:7.

OFFERTORY PRAYER. Dear Father, help us to be ever concerned to find thy way for our lives, and may we never be satisfied to give thee our second best in return for thy great gift of love.

PRAYER. Eternal God, Father of our spirits, in the quiet of this hour we would commune with thee. Our souls are athirst for thee. Vainly have we tried to satisfy the deeper longing of our spirits with the things of time and sense. We come now seeking the living bread, and of the water of life that flows from the throne of God would we drink. Prepare our hearts for fellowship. Grant us expectant hearts that we may long for thee; pure hearts that we may see thee; penitent hearts that we may receive thee. May this service of worship be to us an open window through which eternal light and life will shine upon us and within us. In the spirit of him who has revealed that life, we pray.—Harold Cooke Phillips.

Illustrations

ALIENATION. Secular prophets have ripped the Band-Aids off humanity's hide and exposed the fatal wounds. It's obvious that we have lost our way—internationally, racially, morally, ecologically. Man is alienated from himself, from his fellowman, and from his world.—Leighton Ford.

RAW MATERIAL. Human nature is not a finished state which we can label good or bad, definitely one thing or the other. Human nature is the raw material of which character is the finished product. Life is what is given to us. Character is what we grow. Human nature is plastic clay—just homely, earthy stuff, but clay with all that it implies.—Hazen G. Werner.

Sermon Suggestions

YOUR GOD IS TOO SMALL. Scripture: I Kings 18:17–40. One of the greatest disclosures of Jehovah was the majestic experience with Elijah at Mount Carmel. (1) Elijah's God was adequate. (2) Elijah's God was available. (3) Elijah's God was authoritative.—Harold T. Bryson.

PRAY WITHOUT CEASING. Text: Luke 18:1. (1) The sheer necessity of prayer. "Men *ought* always to pray and not to faint" (v. 1). (2) The serious activity of prayer. "Men ought *always* to pray" (v. 1). (3) The simple reality of prayer. "Men ought always to *pray*" (v. 1).—Stephen F. Olford.

EVENING SERVICE

Topic: Christ's Hands and Ours
TEXT: Mark 9:27.
Jesus came to teach mankind a di-

vine ideal of life; and despite all the learning of the Greeks and all the religion of the Jews, neither Greek nor Jew had ever heard such an ideal of living as this one presented by Jesus.

I. According to Jesus, the good that you do is not important in itself; the important thing is the spirit in which you do it.

(1) Whenever he did something for others, he was giving his followers a good example. (a) When he washed the feet of his disciples, he gave them a lesson in humility.

(b) When he gave sight to the blind, he taught us that it is our obligation to remove the ignorance and the prejudices that make people blind to the beauty, the good ideals, and the wonderful truths of the Bible.

(c) When he made the lame walk, he taught us that it is our duty to help some brother or sister along the rough road of life.

(d) There is a golden lesson in all that Jesus did. And that golden lesson is that love is the basis and fulfillment of the law.

(2) In the text we see Jesus giving his hand to a man who was suffering from a terrible disease. From the world there was no word of comfort to that man, as there is still no word of comfort today to the man who has fallen in the midst of all the temptations that are rampant. The failure in life cannot expect much sympathy from the world. He is alone as far as the world is concerned, and he has earned it.

(3) If we look around us, we would soon see the less fortunate ones. The duty of Christians is to take them as by the hand and help to lift them up. Whoever they are! For they are our brothers and sisters, through Jesus Christ.

II. Now comes the hard bit—helping the disagreeable and cross characters!

(1) The man in our text suffered from an evil spirit. I'm sure that it was not easy to minister to such as he, and, as with lepers, people steered clear of them. But not Jesus; thus he gives yet another good example. It is easy enough to be kind to those who appreciate our kindnesses. But it was not only to the friends who smiled at him that Jesus showed his mercy. He prayed for the murderers who nailed him to the Cross; he healed the ear of the priest's servant who came to arrest him; he granted forgiveness to the thief who had scorned him at first from a neighboring cross.

(2) The old law demanded that kindness should be shown to friends, whilst enemies were to be repaid "an eye for an eye and a tooth for a tooth." Jesus came with the highest principle, based on love, saying that we should love all men, that we should love mankind. Jesus did this difficult thing, and we can do it too by following his example and having faith in him.

III. The last thing I want to point out was the "secret" by which Jesus fulfilled these deeds of kindness.

(1) "Why couldn't we do this?" his disciples asked him. "The only way," replied Jesus, "is through prayer and fasting." And that is the secret for doing good—keeping in touch with God and allowing his Spirit to mould itself into our natures and let it work through us.

(2) Jesus is still extending his arm in this world—to each one, not only the downtrodden and those who bear burdens hard to be borne, but also to those disagreeable ones and those who like to think they are self-sufficient.—A. Wynn Jones.

SUNDAY: AUGUST TWELFTH

MORNING SERVICE

Topic: **The Blessings of the Church**
TEXT: Matt. 16:18.

I. The Church in its worship brings an atmosphere of rest amid the world's restlessness.

(1) The Church does not belong to the changing order of things or to this age alone. Its methods may change and its ways of presenting truth may change, but the fundamental facts about God, about man, about sin, about salvation, about forgiveness, about divine power and the Kingdom of God, can never change so long as human life shall last on this planet.

(2) When we gather within its walls we are ushered into an atmosphere in which we can find God and know his peace, so that the burdens of life are lifted for a while.

(3) Every true church, whatever its denomination may be, where the Spirit of the Lord is, carries healing in its very atmosphere, as well as its message, for those who seek to escape for a while from the world's bustle and turmoil, a place where men and women, sometimes nearly beaten in the battle of life, can find new hope and courage to take up the threads of life again.

II. The Church is the trustee of the Divine Ideal. (1) The Church stands in the midst of the world today as the supreme trustee of God's way of life for man. It sets before mankind a standard in Christ.

(2) It stands in the midst of this changing and frightening world, bearing its distinctive witness to Christ's way of life for both individuals and nations, a way of life that can bring peace and brotherly love that could remove all our fears, a way of life which ever points man to the noblest ideals that can so easily fade in our contacts with the world.

III. The Church calls for our dedicated service. (1) Jesus says in our text, "I will build my church"; but although he is the Master-builder, he is not the only builder. Jesus never says, "I will build my church myself"; rather we are called to be "laborers together with God" in the work of building his Church. It is to be his work and our work together.

(2) It may well be that we cannot all work for Christ in the same way, but we can all work for him in some way. That is why the Apostle Paul included in his list of those who served the Church people whom he called "helps"; and that single word covers a tremendously wide range of service. Everybody, in some way or other, can be included in that descriptive word.

IV. These then are some of the blessings of the Church for each one of us. (1) Here in the Church we may find peace and strength amid the turmoil of life. Here we may gain clarity of vision when our ideals begin to fade. Here we can gather fresh inspiration for life and service.

(2) The Church has the message that the world desperately needs, and we have the assurance of Jesus, "I will build my church and the gates of hell shall not prevail against it." In this assurance let us face life courageously, for his stimulating grace will not fail.
—Wilfred J. T. Brown.

Worship Aids

CALL TO WORSHIP. "Ye shall know truth, and the truth shall make you free. God is a Spirit: and they that worship him must worship him in spirit and in truth." John 8:32; 4:24.

INVOCATION. Almighty God, whose chosen dwelling is the heart that longs for thy presence and humbly seeks thy face: deepen within us the sense of shame and sorrow for the wrongs we have done and for the good we have left undone. Strengthen every desire to amend our lives according to thy holy will. Give light to our wills and rest to our souls that we may do those things which are pleasing in thy sight.

OFFERTORY SENTENCE. "And whatsoever ye do in word and deed, do all in the name of the Lord Jesus, giving thanks to God and the Father by him." Col. 3:17.

OFFERTORY PRAYER. O God, in whose sight a contrite heart is more than whole burnt offerings: help us with these our gifts to dedicate ourselves, body, soul, and spirit, unto thee, which is our reasonable service.—John Baillie.

PRAYER. Eternal God, our heavenly Father, help us to believe this day that there is a power to lift us up which is far stronger than all the things that would hold us down. Make us to be sensitive to what is beautiful and responsive to that which is good, that day by day we may be quick to see and ready to encourage whatever brings a better understanding of life and a keener insight into human relationships.

Open the way for each of us, O God, to earn an honest living without anxiety. But let us never forget the needs of others; may we want only those benefits for ourselves which will also be a gain for our fellowmen. Make us patient and sympathetic with the shortcomings of others. Keep us sternly watchful only of our own deeds, judging ourselves in the light of the highest principles and ideals.

Keep us this day from the reach of any evil to the body, but more so, from any danger to clear thinking and moral living. Help us to believe that the ideals of religion are not a far-off dream but a power to command our loyalty and direct our lives. Bless each of us and those we love with the true joys of life —with freedom, integrity, happiness, and peace of mind.—Donald E. Riker.

Illustrations

INWARD PARTS. What the Church needs is the quality of saintliness, of goodness in the "inward parts." Had the Church this quality, it would experience revival, know spiritual power, conquer atheism and agnosticism, produce great leaders, move toward church union, and have "ebullient joy." —William E. Sangster.

CHURCH AT HOME. As for social, economic, and cultural revolution, a church that has survived Caesar's dictatorship, medieval feudalism, European monarchies, all manner of tribal governments, colonialism, laissez-faire capitalism, and managed economy wherever technology is king—a church that survived all that should be at home in our contemporary world of social turbulence.—John W. Meister.

THE LIVING DEAD. Jesus wanted us to have an abundant life in the here and now. The question which should occupy us most is not where we will be spending eternity but where we are spending it. Many people go through seventy or eighty years of life on earth without having lived at all. They act as if God did not exist. They never commit themselves to any great cause. They never take a stand on any moral issue. The fate of races and nations may hang in the balance, but they are silent, inactive, neutral. They never come face to face with the Cross of Jesus Christ, nor plunge into any heroic effort for the Kingdom of God. They are merely existing—dead while they yet live. They remind me of the old Pennsylvania Dutchman who, when asked how long ago his neighbor died, said judiciously, "If he had shust lived until next Tuesday he would be dead two weeks already."—Edwin T. Dahlberg.

Sermon Suggestions

GROWING THROUGH WORSHIP. Scripture: Isa. 6:1–8. There are three basic elements, reflected in Isaiah's experience, which have found their place in worship down through the ages. (1) Adoration or praise of God. (2) Contrition or confession, a sense of unworthiness, a recognition that we have failed to live before God as we should. (3) Consecration. Isaiah's vision of God, followed by confession and forgiveness, prepared him for personal converse with God and brought him into spiritual sympathy with his purpose.—Ernest Trice Thompson.

PUBLIC WORSHIP. Text: Ps. 111:1. (1) Public worship ought to give a unity of passion and purpose. (2) Worship is of value in the cultivation of the spiritual life of each individual. (3) Worship may reveal us to ourselves. (4) In worship we may find the inspiration of service in Christ's Kingdom. —Fred R. Chenault.

EVENING SERVICE

Topic: The Tyranny of Sin
TEXT: Rom. 3:23.
I. Sin involves us in separation from God. Sin means that we are estranged from the Father, lost in the far country, adrift from God. Sin is a cleavage between God and man; it is to forsake God and to be forsaken of God.

II. Sin involves us in unrequited love. Sin is spurning the love of God. (1) William Barclay puts it like this: "Since God is love, all sin is sin, not so much against law as it is against love. Sin is not so much a breaking of God's law as it is a breaking of God's heart."
(2) God's heart is broken because men have spurned his love and cast it aside with callous indifference. It is the tragedy of unrequited love. Sin, exclaims James Stewart, "is another nail hammered into love's cross, a clenched fist thrust up into the face of God. It is a blow struck at a loving heart."

III. Sin involves us in the remorse of conscience. Sin is the ghost that stalks through the house of conscience; sin is the specter that torments us in the lonely hours when there is none around but God. "A man may play the fool in the drifts of the desert," said Emerson, "but every grain of sand will seem to see." Remorse for sin is the searing accusation of conscience.— Frank Howie.

SUNDAY: AUGUST NINETEENTH

MORNING SERVICE

Topic: Living Victoriously
TEXT: Mark 11:22.
Three things are necessary for victorious living.
I. The first is stability, a sense of security, and assurance and confidence that our lives rest on firm foundations.
(1) The first thing we ask about a building is, "Are its foundations safe?" It is the first thing to ask about a man's life. A potent reason for the instability and insecurity which many people feel today lies in what we may call the absence of a sense of "peace" in their hearts. There is something shoddy about the foundations.
(2) Never before did men so need and crave this sense of security. Life has become so complicated; there are so many demands made upon life in our day. Our unanswered questions are so numerous; our problems, so portentous; our tasks, so increasingly heavy. Therefore, unless human existence can base itself on something sure and solid, it can never achieve that serenity, poise, and confidence necessary to victorious living.
(3) When one digs down deep and seeks to find rock-bottom, seeks to dis-

cover what Plato called some "safe and sure word of God" on which to rest the soul, it is to be found only in the conviction that behind all the mysterious manifestations of life, all its most tragic and inexplicable events, all the twist and tangle of circumstances is a loving if also an inscrutable purpose working in us and through us toward divine ends.

II. The second thing necessary to victorious living is the power of control, the strength of will necessary to use wisely and well the complicated apparatus of our modern world.

(1) The trouble with our modern world is that our material equipment and resources have outrun our power of moral control. The speed of life, its many opportunities for diversions and pleasures threaten the order, simplicity, and sanity of everyday living. What is needed is an inward power to effect control.

(2) No power of control is comparable to that of religion. Prudence, wisdom, sagacity—these are not enough.

(3) No worse thing can happen to a child today than to have him go forth without faith in God into this modern world with its bewildering appeals to the pleasure-loving instinct, with its plausible and seductive invitations to self-gratification and bodily indulgence. Only a consciousness of God within the human life can give control. Only a sense of God can give direction.

III. One more thing is necessary to victorious living: everlasting hope. (1) The Bible is to me the most wonderful book in the world because it does full justice to the power of evil in the world and yet never falters in its unconquerable hope and persuasion that in the end evil is headed for destruction and that truth and righteousness will be enthroned. The Bible ends its tragic story of human sin and defeat with the dramatic picture of Satan being cast into the lake of brimstone and fire and of the triumph and salvation of the people of God. I know of nothing but Bible religion that will put that hope into a man's life and keep it shining undimmed until the end.

(2) Jesus keeps saying: "Be of good cheer. . . . Do not be afraid. . . . Have faith in God." See what wonders that worked. It sent out into a world which was far worse than that in which we are living today a company of men and women filled with unconquerable courage, buoyant, and certain of victory.

(3) We find two types of people around us today. One is fearful, doubtful, discouraged, if not despairing. The other is full of hope and dauntless courage. Eternal hope comes only from faith in God. Optimism, courage, fearlessness—the very qualities indispensable to make victory in ourselves or in our world—spring only from faith in God.—Raymond Calkins.

Worship Aids

CALL TO WORSHIP. "They that wait upon the Lord shall renew their strength; they shall mount up with wings as eagles; they shall run, and not be weary; and they shall walk, and not faint." Isa. 40:31.

INVOCATION. O Lord our God, great, eternal, wonderful in glory, who keepest covenant and promise for those that love thee with their whole heart, who art the life of all, the help of those that flee to thee, the hope of those that cry unto thee: cleanse us from our sins and from every thought displeasing to thy goodness. Cleanse our souls and bodies, our hearts and consciences, that with pure heart and a clear mind, with perfect love and calm hope we may confidently and fearlessly pray to thee.

OFFERTORY SENTENCE. "Go, and sell that thou hast, and give to the poor, and thou shalt have treasure in heaven: and come and follow me." Matt. 19:21.

SUNDAY: AUGUST NINETEENTH

OFFERTORY PRAYER. Our heavenly Father, help us so to live and so to give that when others see us they will take knowledge of us that we have been with Jesus and that his spirit dwells in us.

PRAYER. Almighty God, make us aware of the powers with which thou hast invested us. Thou hast given us large tasks to perform and facilities with which to complete them. Though we quail before the responsibilities that are ours, we would not make a fetish of our hopelessness. Forbid that we should fail thee in the face of lavish materials or forget the example of men and women who in the achievement of great things have found courage that rose with danger and powers that increased as they spent them. When the fields are white unto the harvest and we stand idly by, bemoaning the world situation and forgetting that thou dost work through human agents, may we remember a Voice that has always spoken to Christians in trying situations: "My grace is sufficient for thee and my strength is made perfect in weakness." Out of such discovered strength may we dedicate ourselves to the building of thy holy Kingdom of love, justice, and peace.—Charles J. Lotz.

Illustrations

THAT WHICH IS WORTHWHILE. Often we allow ourselves to be upset by small things we should despise and forget. Perhaps some man we helped has proved ungrateful, some woman we believe to be a friend has spoken ill of us, some regard we thought we deserved has been denied us. We feel such disappointments so strongly that we can no longer work or sleep. But isn't that absurd? Here we are on this earth, with only a few more decades to live, and we lose many irreplaceable hours brooding over grievances that in a year's time will be forgotten by us and by everybody. No, let us devote our life to worthwhile actions and feelings, to great thoughts, real affections, and enduring undertakings. For life is too short to be little.—André Maurois in *Christian Herald*.

THE EDUCATED MAN. As specialized, professional training, higher education in the United States today is often magnificent. But the educated man, the man capable not of providing specialized answers but of asking the great and liberating questions, by which humanity makes its way through time, is not more frequently encountered than he was two hundred years ago. On the contrary, he is rarely discovered in public life at all.—Archibald MacLeish.

Sermon Suggestions

PRISONERS OF HOPE. Text: Zech. 9:12. (1) In bondage yet delivered. (2) Exiled and yet at home. (3) Confined yet consoled.—Charles A. McClain, Jr.

"AND HE SAID WITHIN HIMSELF." Texts: Mark 2:6; Luke 12:17, 16:3, 18:4. Every one of us does hold every day within himself secret conversations. This conversation is important beyond our reckoning. What we say within ourselves is fraught with blessing or peril, strength or weakness. "Man is so constituted that if he tells himself he is a fool, he will constrain himself to believe it. For man holds an internal intercourse with himself which ought to be well regulated, since even here 'evil communications corrupt good manners'" (Pascal). (1) Consider that how we meet trouble and disappointment is in large part determined by what we say within ourselves. (2) Consider that our inner resources for living with praise and courage are made larger or smaller by what we say within ourselves. (3) Consider that these words teach the bane or blessing of solitude. —H. Richard Rasmusson.

EVENING SERVICE

Topic: Why I Attend Church Regularly
I. I believe in God and feel the need to worship him.
II. I believe the Church is God's people, and I want to be a part of this company of Christians.
III. I feel the necessity of partaking of spiritual food if I am to be strong spiritually, even as I need physical food for a strong body.
IV. The Bible recommends church attendance. (See Heb. 10:25).
V. I wish to set a good example for my children and my friends.
VI. I realize that in staying away from church I am voting to close it.
VII. I need to start the week with an exposure to good music, thoughtful preaching, prayer, and Bible reading.
VIII. Nothing I can do is more important than my worship of God, and I must give him priority in my life.
IX. The Church needs me.
X. Jesus attended church regularly. (See Luke 4:16.)—Harold E. Buell in *Clergy Journal*.

SUNDAY: AUGUST TWENTY-SIXTH

MORNING SERVICE

Topic: They Were Called Christians (Festival of Christ the King)
TEXT: Acts 9:26.
I. It was seen in their attitude to themselves. The followers of Jesus Christ had accepted certain rigid personal standards. They were pledged to honesty and integrity in all their dealings. They were pledged to purity and their personal living and family relationships. They were set free from fear and anxiety. They had learned not to set great store by material gains. In all these ways they sought not to think of themselves more highly than they ought to think.
II. The distinctive quality of the Christians' living was seen in their attitude toward others. The beginning of Christian belief is in the God who became man, thus showing that human life matters to him. So from its earliest days Christianity has been marked by a profound respect for human personality. All the great humanitarian movements of the past nineteen hundred years have had their origins, directly or indirectly, in the Christian religion.
III. These first two characteristics of Christian living are rooted in a third. It was their attitude toward God that was the basic distinctive mark of the first Christians. For them he was not far distant but very near, their Companion in all that they did, and the Source of the strength by which they lived. It was this which enabled them to live daringly and to die courageously.
(1) There is little doubt that it is at this point that our own Christian witness so often fails. We make tremendous claims about our belief in the power of God to save and uphold us, but so rarely do we live as if we really believed that this is his world in which he is working still to fulfill his purpose of love.
(2) Yet unless we believe this in such a way that our living is revolutionized by our belief, there will never be seen in us anything which can be recognized as distinctive from a non-Christian way of living. It is the Christian's belief in a God who loves and cares and saves and changes men which is the heart of the Gospel.
IV. So often people are heard to say, and sometimes we are ourselves among them, that Christiantiy can only work in an ideal society, that it is only there that such attitudes to ourselves and to others and to God can be adopted. So we are told that we must compromise and adapt the Christian way of life to fit in with the imperfections of a sinful world.
(1) Yet it is quite clear that Jesus Christ expected his followers to live his

kind of life by faith in him in the world as it now is. He spoke of loving our enemies and of being persecuted in this way in an ideal society; there would be no enemies and no persecution! Quite clearly, if Christianity was meant for any world it was meant for this world, here and now.

(2) Most of us find ourselves today thrust out into a world where we must shoulder considerable responsibilities and where the eyes of all are upon us. By what name shall we be known? Shall we be recognized as great leaders or efficient administrators or enthusiastic organizers, but nothing more? Or shall we be called "Christians"? To merit this title is to live by a faith which enables us to think of ourselves and of others and of God himself after the example and in the strength of Jesus Christ.—Raymond J. Jones.

Worship Aids

CALL TO WORSHIP. "Delight thyself also in the Lord; and he shall give thee the desires of thine heart. Commit thy way unto the Lord; trust also in him; and he shall bring it to pass." Ps. 37:4–5.

INVOCATION. O spirit of the living God, who dwellest in thy Church and who art holiness, wisdom, and might: come thou now in this hour, fill the hearts of thy faithful people, and kindle within them the fire of thy love.

OFFERTORY SENTENCE. "This is the thing which the Lord commanded, saying, Take ye from among you an offering unto the Lord: whosoever is of a willing heart, let him bring it, an offering of the Lord." Exod. 35:4–5.

OFFERTORY PRAYER. We pray thee, O God, to give us sight to see the Christ, the insight to choose him, the steadfastness to follow him, and the stewardship of loyalty represented in these gifts offered in his name.

PRAYER. O Lord, our God, to whom be all glory and adoration, we come into thy presence that we might worship thee who art the King of kings and Lord of lords.

We thank thee and praise thy name for all thy manifold blessings that thou hast bestowed upon us. They are as many as the stars of the sky and the sands of the beach. We marvel that thou art mindful of us and that thou knowest our most insignificant thoughts and concerns. We thank thee for thy presence in our lives, for the undeserved right and privilege we know through thy love.

We confess that we have sinned in thy presence and have not walked in thy paths of righteousness. Forgive us, merciful Father, those sins we now confess, and grant that we shall not forsake thy guidance, which will lead us on to the light of the eternal truths.

We lift our soul torment and anguish up to thee and ask for thy divine comfort. We seek to know thee better, O Lord. Grant us a vision of thy grace and a dedication of life to thy service. —Warren W. Watts.

Illustrations

TIME FOR PRAYER. A practicing Christian who asks whether he has time for prayer is like a carpenter asking whether he has time to sharpen his tools. All one can say is that he had better take time. For to take time for prayer is to save time for work.—Douglas V. Steere in *Time to Spare*.

FAILURE? Kirtley Mather, the Harvard geologist at Smith College, stated and explained his religious conviction that there is a Divine Administration controlling this universe and guaranteeing its moral and spiritual values. During the question period he was asked, "How can you believe in a Divine Administration undergirding this universe and underwriting its values when Jesus of Nazareth was so cruelly defeated?" Professor Mather paused a moment and said: "In the light of what Jesus did when he was on the earth and in the light of what has been done in his name since, do you really think Jesus was defeated?"

THE CHRISTIAN IN THE WORLD. We mustn't go out into the world as if the world were our enemy and we had to conquer it. It is rather like the poor wounded man on the road to Jericho; it is hungry, and we want to give it something to eat; it is thirsty, and we want to give it something to drink; homeless, and we want to open the door and give it lodging and a home.—Vincent McNabb.

Sermon Suggestions

WITNESS TO THE LIGHT. A Christian has encountered "the true light that enlightens every man," and his principal business is to bear witness to that Light. (1) Because he has some place to go, he takes the ups and downs in stride. (2) Inspired by the view of his goal, he radiates hope and joy. (3) He is not dependent on immediate circumstances. (4) He offers himself in personal service, he cares, and he radiates hope. (5) Because he knows where he is going, some "seeing the sunlight on his face will drop their tools and follow him."—Wesley P. Ford.

JESUS AND HIS KINGDOM. (1) Jesus constantly brings the Kingdom forward as the inspiring hope which must be behind all of man's actions. (2) In the confidence that God will soon establish his Kingdom, men can put their trust in God. (3) The Kingdom is for Jesus the criterion of all values; for example, we must answer these questions in the light of Jesus' teachings: What things are worth possessing? What sort of conduct does God require? What type of character is honored? (4) The Kingdom of God is a reward on which men set their hearts. (5) Above all, the Kingdom is for Jesus the fulfillment of divine purpose.—Ernest F. Scott in *The Kingdom of God in the New Testament.*

EVENING SERVICE

Topic: Secrets of Pleasurable Living

I. *Take frequent excursions into the land of yesterday.* That is not a sign of age; it is a mark of wisdom. To be sure, we live in the present and we feel the lure of the future; but, for the good of our souls, we need the backward look. One sees a bit more clearly in an exercise of this kind how, step by step, God has guided and how, day by day, God has blessed. Out of a deep sense of gratitude to an overshadowing providence we move confidently ahead.

II. *Change the things that ought to be changed.* (1) All of us need to change the things that should be changed if we are looking for the most out of life. How many people would find a new joy in living if this secret were observed! There would be less human wreckage, fewer broken homes, less need for divorce courts, if people would only change the things that need to be changed.

(2) Christianity teaches that possibility. Christianity is a religion of power. That power is available for all who seek it. We have all seen that power work. The changes we all deeply desire in society as a whole have their beginnings with changed individuals.

III. *Get off the fence.* (1) Make up your mind! Get off the fence. There is little satisfaction in forever staying in the state of indecision. There is a sense of inner satisfaction when a decision is reached.

(2) The critical point in history where we find ourselves today is a clear challenge to convinced Christians to stand up and be counted. The Christian Church, which is our heritage, came down to us from our fathers who knew in whom they believed and who were of the stuff of which martyrs are made. We read of these convinced

Christians in Heb. 11:33-34. They were not on the fence. Their minds were made up.

IV. *Spend your life for something that will outlast it.* (1) Think of the rich heritage bequeathed to us: love, freedom, the Christian faith, all were here when we came. Builders of the future worked for us before we were born. Is it possible to look at life on a selfish basis in view of this?

(2) There are some things today demands. We must give attention to those things. But the range is longer than today. There are tomorrow and the day after. There is the future of which we in a signal sense are the architects. To be one who helps lay the foundations of a greater superstructure, to be one who, by faith, builds the City of God while the City of Man apparently is perishing, to strive to accomplish the thing that seems, at the moment, to be out of reach—in short, to live for something that outlasts our threescore years and ten—that makes living with ourselves a pleasure. The causes are limitless. They include, among other things, peace, sobriety, the creation of a society in which the pursuit of happiness is possible for all, and freedom.—George A. Fowler.

SUNDAY: SEPTEMBER SECOND

MORNING SERVICE

Topic: Our Right to Work (Labor Sunday)

Text: Eph. 4:28.

I. According to the Bible, man was created to perform useful work. In the opening chapters of the Bible, God reveals that he is the Creator who has created men in his image in order that they might perform worthwhile tasks. In the beginning God placed man in the Garden of Eden to dress it and keep it. (See Gen. 2:15.) As soon as man found himself in this world, he was confronted with responsible tasks with respect to his environment. Man was not allowed simply to accept the world as God's gift to him, but man himself had to be busy in it and with it. At the very beginning of human history work was mankind's obedient response to God's creation mandate. This creation mandate was re-emphasized when the Ten Commandments were given. In Exod. 20:9 we read, "Six days shalt thou labor and do all thy work."

II. The New Testament also indicates that men are created to work. The New Testament views work as necessary to insure that we have the right to receive the goods we enjoy. When the New Testament talks about the opposite of work, it does not talk about leisure, but it talks about stealing. In II Thess. 3:10 we read, "If any will not work, neither let him eat." The same idea is expressed in Eph. 4:28. This implies that we are obligated to produce something in exchange for the goods we enjoy. It is immoral to be a consumer without being a producer.

III. The Bible apparently wants us to understand that we must spend something of ourselves when we work. This is implied in the scriptural message concerning the importance of physical work. (See I Thess. 4:10-11.)

(1) This emphasis is found especially in the writings of the Apostle Paul, for he was well acquainted with physical labor. He was a tentmaker, and he spent a great deal of time with skilled craftsmen and laborers. He numbered slaves among his personal friends. Sometimes he encountered Christian people who, under the cloak of a false spirituality, left their ordinary work and spent all their time waiting for the end of the world. Paul contradicted this false form of Christianity whenever he found it.

(2) Jesus Christ knew well the joys and frustrations of the working man. He began his life in a carpenter's home and most likely became intimately acquainted with the trade. Later, earthly figures of speech, drawn from the building trade, marked his conversation and helped him speak directly to the hearts of the common people. Jesus Christ, the Son of the living God, came into the center of human life and with his presence sanctified the ordinary labor of all men.

(3) God who worketh all things after the counsel of his will has created men to work. A society in which many men are deprived of the right to work cannot expect to flourish.

IV. These scriptural facts concerning the nature of man are important elements in the problem of modern automation.

(1) The human element in production may not be eliminated. It would be disastrous for us if men would be reduced to the point at which their most productive performance would be the watching of machines.

(2) If automation continues without check, we can only expect that men will continue to become involved in certain useless forms of work. Most men will be too far removed from the opportunity to perform necessary and meaningful work. They will be consumers only, and men who are only consumers are not happy men who derive important satisfactions from their lives.

V. Only the biblical description of man and his destiny is sufficient to give direction in these swift-changing times. Certainly, all who find themselves in a position to regulate the introduction of automated equipment will perform great disservice to all of us, if they do not take the scriptural view of man into consideration as they make their decisions. Equipment that will do nothing more than displace men and deprive them of their work, most likely will not be beneficial for our society in the long run. The final decisions in each case will have to be made by men who are well qualified to make the many technical decisions involved. But the right of men to work must always be remembered when these decisions are made. If it is forgotten, automation's promised abundance may well provide modern man with universal disillusion.

VI. Some people are fascinated when they see a machine do the work of eighteen men. There is something fascinating about it. But it is more wonderful to see eighteen men working, performing a useful task, and acknowledging as they do, that they are working in the name of the Lord Jesus Christ. Such Christian laborers are the foundation of a society that cannot be shaken, for they enjoy in their lives the exercise of one of the most fundamental of all our rights, the right to work. If we are not careful, depriving men of the opportunity to work may be one of the most serious crimes of the twentieth century.—Joel Nederhood.

Worship Aids

CALL TO WORSHIP. "We are laborers together with God: ye are God's husbandry, ye are God's building. Let every man take heed how he buildeth. For other foundation can no man lay than that is laid, which is Jesus Christ." I Cor. 3:9–11.

INVOCATION. Lord, lift us out of private-mindedness and give us public souls to work for thy Kingdom by daily creating that atmosphere of a happy temper and generous heart which alone can bring the great peace.

OFFERTORY SENTENCE. "God is not unrighteous to forget your work and labor of love, which ye have showed toward his name, in that ye have ministered to the saints, and to minister." Heb. 6:10.

OFFERTORY PRAYER. O Lord Jesus Christ, who hast taught us that to whomsoever much is given, of him shall much be required: grant that we, whose lot is cast in this Christian heritage, may strive more earnestly, by our prayers and tithes, by sympathy and study, to hasten the coming of thy Kingdom among all peoples of the earth, that as we have entered into the labors of others, so others may enter into ours, to thy honor and glory.

PRAYER. O God, at whose word man goeth forth to his work and to his labor until the evening: be merciful to all whose duties are difficult or burdensome and comfort them concerning their toil. Shield from bodily accident and harm the workmen at their work. Protect the efforts of sober and honest industry, and suffer not the hire of the laborers to be kept back by fraud. Incline the heart of employers and of those whom they employ to mutual forbearance, fairness, and goodwill. Give the spirit of governance and of a sound mind to all in places of authority. Bless all those who labor in works of mercy or in schools of good learning. Care for all aged persons and all little children, the sick and the afflicted, and those who travel by land or by sea. Remember all who by reason of weakness are overtasked or because of poverty are forgotten. Let the sorrowful sighing of the prisoners come before thee; and according to the greatness of thy power, preserve thou those that are appointed to die. Give ear unto our prayer, O merciful and gracious Father, for the love of thy dear Son, our Savior Jesus Christ.—William Reed Huntington.

Illustration

THE BOSS AND THE LEADER

The boss drives his men; the leader coaches them.

The boss depends upon authority; the leader on goodwill.

The boss inspires fear; the leader inspires enthusiasm.

The boss says "I"; the leader says "We."

The boss assigns the tasks; the leader sets the pace.

The boss says "Get here on time"; the leader gets there ahead of time.

The boss fixes the blame for the breakdown; the leader fixes the breakdown.

The boss knows how it is done; the leader shows how it is done.

The boss makes work a drudgery; the leader makes work a game.

The boss says "Go"; the leader says "Let's go."

Sermon Suggestions

A CHRISTIAN LOOKS AT INDUSTRY. (1) The purpose of industry or business is not primarily the making of money, but the making of men. (2) The dominant motive in industry should be, not profit but service. (3) The method prevailing in industry should be, not unregulated competition, but growing cooperation. (4) The spirit of industry should be dominated not by the rule of gold but by the golden rule. (5) The conduct of industry should be, not a paternalistic autocracy but a developing democracy in growing cooperation for the mutual benefit of all.—Sherwood Eddy.

WHAT ARE YOUR GOALS? Text: Phil. 2:14–16. What are to be the Christian's goals? Paul says three things. (1) He says that the life that is to be lived by Christians in the midst of the world is to be one of submission to God. We are to do all things "without murmurings and disputings." (2) This life is one that is to be blameless before other people. "Blameless" and "harmless" are the words Paul uses. (3) Our lives are to be blameless in the sight of God also. We are to be without rebuke as his children.—James M. Boice.

EVENING SERVICE

Topic: Oaks of Righteousness
TEXT: Isa. 61:3 (RSV).
I. The oak tree has its rise in a very

small beginning. "Great oaks from little acorns grow." (1) Just as an oak tree grows from a little acorn so does great character grow from a great many decisions that may at the time seem very minor. The more I read the New Testament, the words of Jesus, the more I come to see that he always defined the Kingdom in terms of relatively minor things—giving a cup of cold water to a thirsty man, giving food to someone who is hungry, showing kindness to someone who was lonely, visiting someone who was sick or imprisoned.

(2) What I am saying is that men who can be called "oaks of righteousness" grow from small decisions about seemingly unimportant things, but together these decisions forge destiny.

II. If a man is to become an "oak of righteousness," he must feed his spirit upon the bread and the water of life and nourish his spirit upon the power of God. He must sink his roots down deeply into faith. The making of a man is dependent not only upon what he does for himself and what others do for him, but also chiefly upon the work of God within him, the strength that faith, and faith alone, provides.

III. If a tree is to grow strong and straight and tall, spreading its branches far and wide, then it must not be too much protected; it must be out where the winds of life can blow upon it. It must little by little learn to take the storms of life.

(1) So it is with people. People never grow strong and sturdy when and if they are sheltered, shielded, protected from all harm, danger, temptation, and difficulty.

(2) A child does not mature, a lad does not grow up, a girl is not really protected with the only protection that counts, unless little by little they are allowed to make their own decisions— first in very minor and trivial matters; later, in matters of a bit more importance. Finally, they are able to decide matters of great importance.

IV. Oak trees grow for a purpose. (1) I suppose that this purpose is usually multiple. That is, an oak can be used for shade; an oak reproduces itself; an oak is beautiful; an oak eventually may be used for lumber.

(2) So our lives, if we want to be called "oaks of righteousness," ought to fufill a purpose. We were put into the world for a purpose, God's purpose. We were put into the world to serve the needs of mankind, God's children. We were put here to stand fast and steadfast against evil, sin, and every pressure that would take away from other people their God-given heritage. —Ben M. Herbster.

SUNDAY: SEPTEMBER NINTH

MORNING SERVICE

Topic: The Church in a Time of Revolution

What ought New Testament believers like ourselves do in these troubled times?

I. I would urge that we clarify our thinking with respect to the role of the Church. (1) The Church's task is that of evangelism and witness and mission. The Church's task is that of worship and education and fellowship. The Church's task is to communicate and demonstrate the reconciling love of God in Jesus Christ, incarnate, crucified, and resurrected.

(2) So we must help the Church resist all pressures to abandon its own distinctive role, whether those pressures come from the right or from the left. The Church, we must affirm, is not an agency which serves either the Kremlin or the Pentagon. The Church is an

agency which pledges its undivided allegiance to the Kingdom of Heaven.

II. We must insist on the Church's freedom and responsibility to proclaim God's Word prophetically. What does this mean?

(1) The Church must tell the radicals on the left that revolution has always been a brutal, bloody, barbaric business; revolution has always been a monster that devours its own children; it has unfailingly inaugurated a reign of terror that has ended in the rise of a dictatorship like that of Joseph Stalin, a totalitarianism as bad or worse than the society it has violently smashed. The Church must preach in season and out of season that unless individuals are radically changed by the sin-forgiving grace of God, any radical change in institutions is impossible.

(2) No doubt all of us are in heartiest agreement with this Word of God to the left. But we must insist at the same time that in freedom and responsibility the Church proclaim the Word of God prophetically to conservatives on the right. So in the Name of the God of justice and mercy, we must have the Christian courage and humility to demand that the Church lay biblical truth on the line, no matter how it hurts anybody, including ourselves.

(3) In discharging its prophetic responsibility, the Church must be free to tell us, as the Bible does, that patriotism can sometimes be a smoke screen for greed and pride and arrogance. The Church must be free to tell us that self-righteousness can blind good people to frightful evils. The Church must be free to tell us that the American way of life is not to be treated idolatrously. Like every human system, it has its flaws and faults and failures. It is a system organized and operated by sinners for their own interests and not for the glory of God. As a human system, contrived and controlled by sinful creatures, it falls infinitely short of divine perfection. Therefore, it is no more than relatively superior to other ways of life, thus open to criticism and change.

(4) The Church must tell any of us who are politically as well as theologically conservative that God is concerned about the agonizing, agitating problems of society. To be sure, he is concerned most of all about the destiny of people in the world beyond this world. But he is likewise concerned about this world.

III. The Church must keep reminding us that God has his own program mapped out for changing the world by the personal intervention of Jesus Christ who will return to establish the Kingdom of Heaven on earth.

(1) Yet the Church must likewise keep reminding us that there is no biblical reason for concluding that massive evils cannot be significantly changed before our Lord comes back.

(2) The Church must keep reminding us as New Testament believers, whatever our political alignment, that we ought to be spiritual subversives, duplicating the redemptive radicalism of those first-century Christians who were condemned for turning the world upside down.

(3) Yes, the Church must keep reminding us that we are God's saboteurs working to bring about a revolution of faith and hope and love.—Vernon C. Grounds in *Eternity*.

Worship Aids

CALL TO WORSHIP. "I will bless the Lord at all times: his praise shall continually be in my mouth. O magnify the Lord with me, and let us exalt his name together." Ps. 34:1, 3.

INVOCATION. Our Father, we thank thee for thy Word and for the eternal truths which guide us day by day. We thank thee most of all for the living Word, Jesus Christ, and the sureness of his presence in the home, in the factory, in the field, in the mine, at the office, and on the road. Teach us how to turn unto thee so that thy thoughts may be our thoughts and thy ways our ways.—Carl J. C. Wolf.

OFFERTORY SENTENCE. "Every one of us shall give account of himself to God." Rom. 14:12.

OFFERTORY PRAYER. Our Father, forgive our indifference and neglect, and help us to hear thy call to partnership with thee in making a new heaven and new earth.

PRAYER. Our Father, again we give thanks in gratitude for life's unfolding opportunities and responsibilities; for the thrill that comes as we gain a new and fresh glimpse of the boundless fields, beyond us and at our feet, as we see them awaiting our discovery and our toil. We are grateful for the challenge to toil; for the fact that the One whom we have chosen as our guide and friend, our companion and Lord, knew through his own experience life's rigorous demands and rich rewards; that for him there were many blind alleys and lonely wanderings as well as occasional triumphs on life's sun-kissed mountaintops.

Grant, most holy and demanding God, that as we discern thee in the things nearby we shall learn to prize thee more; that we may seek beauty and happiness not afar but in the simple things of life spread out before us; and that seeking we may find.

Thou knowest our longings, our dreams, our hopes, our anxieties, our discouragements, our worries, and our concerns. Grant us, we pray thee, the strength, the insight, the understanding, which we so sorely need to meet them. And granting us this holy blessing thou wilt but the closer bind us to thee.

Hear our prayers, O God; hear and answer by quickening us to more resolute and courageous search.—Morton S. Enslin.

Illustrations

CULTIVATION. The man who supposes that he has no time to pray or to reflect, because the social tasks are numerous and urgent, will soon find that he has become unproductive, because he will have separated his life from its roots. It will not then be surprising if, in his promotion of what seems to him to be a good cause, he becomes bitter in his condemnation of others. Without the cultivation of the inner and the outer life, it is almost inevitable that a man deeply involved in social action should become self-righteous.—Elton Trueblood in *The New Man for Our Time*.

ASKING THE RIGHT QUESTIONS. We're giving wrong answers because we're not asking the right questions. Robert Frost probes the problem in "The Cabin in the Clearing." The mist and the smoke are talking together in the wintry gray dawn about a little cabin somewhere in the New England woods. The mist says to the smoke, "You see that cabin—do you think there's anybody in there?" The smoke replies, "Why of course there is. They're just asleep." Then the mist says, "Well, if there's anybody in there, do you think they know where they are?" The punch line comes in this earthy but mystical bit of poetry when the smoke answers, "Well, you know, I don't know if they know where they are or not, but I'll tell you this. Once they know *who* they are, they'll know *where* they are."—John F. Anderson.

Sermon Suggestions

THE FOUR AGES OF MAN. Text: Luke 2:52. (1) The calendar age of life. (2) The physical age of life. (3) The emotional age. (4) The philosophical age. A man's calendar age is beyond his power to alter. A man's physical age is often very much what he makes it. A man's emotional age can often be sadly underdeveloped. The wise man is the man who lives in the philosophical age in which he is growing all the time.—*The British Weekly*.

HOW TO BE GOOD—AND MAD. Text: Eph. 4:26. (1) Righteous anger is properly motivated; that is, it is inspired and animated by unselfish considerations. (2) Righteous Christian anger is properly focused and directed. That is to say, if it is really righteous and not sinful, it is directed not against persons, wrong though they be, but against wrong deeds, things, institutions, and situations. (3) Righteous Christian anger is properly implemented—that is, followed up by every possible kind of positive and constructive action to end the wrong that occasioned the anger.—Norman V. Hope.

EVENING SERVICE

Topic: The Parable of the Haunted House
SCRIPTURE: Matt. 12:38-50.

In this strange parable of the haunted house, Jesus used the medium of the popular mythology of the day to set forth lessons which are applicable in every age.

I. *The persistence of evil.* (1) Evil is not merely an absence of the good, but it is a force, a power at work in the world seeking to thwart God's will. The man in the parable kicked the demon out of his life (his house), swept it clean, and then sat back and rested. But the demon returned when he wasn't looking!

(2) Jesus doesn't tell us all that we'd like to know about evil, but he does tell us that it is a persistent thing, something against which we must always be on guard. Experience seems to bear out his words. Therefore, Jesus continually admonished his disciples to "watch and pray" that they "enter not into temptation" (Matt. 26:41).

II. *The peril of emptiness.* (1) A vacuum is always a dangerous situation. "Nature abhors a vacuum," and that holds true of our spiritual natures as well. An empty mind, heart, and life are like empty houses. They are invitations to evil.

(2) Negative goodness is not enough. Many times religious people tend to think of religion as a set of taboos, a set of "thou shalt not's" to which people must conform. Jesus' attack on the popular religion of his day was that it was primarily negative.

III. *Emptiness is impossible.* (1) If a life is not filled with positive good, it will soon become filled with positive evil. Neutrality is impossible. Life demands that we will have something at its center, something to which we can give ourselves with passionate intensity. If not God, then something else. Tillich was right when he said that man's basic problem is not *atheism* (no god) but *idolatry* (the wrong god).

(2) The problem of our world is that we have lost our center. As a Christian, I believe that Christ is intended to be that center. I believe that our choice today is the same as it has always been: CHRIST OR CHAOS. It is true of our personal lives. It is true of the world. Which will it be?—Donald B. Strobe.

SUNDAY: SEPTEMBER SIXTEENTH

MORNING SERVICE

Topic: Sound the Trumpet
TEXT: Lev. 25:9.

We must sound the trumpets and call upon people to repent and turn from their sinning and turn to the Lord.

I. The year of Jubilee was a year of redemption. The economically disinherited saw in its program a medium of redress, and the spiritually indifferent heard the trumpet calling to a new dedication of life.

(1) The church of Christ has the

Cross as the symbol of our redemption, and through the medium of a cross the Church must continually call people to repentance.

(2) The establishment of the Cross was possible because so many participated in it, and the justification of the Cross is established when all classes and conditions and races and nations are saved through it. To establish the Cross, the carpenters fashioned it, the metal workers forged the nails, the manual laborers dug the hole to receive it, the lawyers interpreted the law, the soldiers supplied the force, the priests gave it their blessing, and the stage was set.

(3) As men of all classes gathered around the Cross, so men of all conditions can find their redemption in the Cross.

II. The year of Jubilee was a year of restoration.

(1) Fundamentally speaking, the program of life is far more toward destruction than restoration. Our very food is only possible because the cardinal ingredients are sacrificed and destroyed. We manufacture shoes that they shall wear out. Clothes are supplied with one main purpose—that they shall be discarded. The very genius of business is to keep styles changing and patterns evolving to meet and create varying moods in life.

(2) With the ancient Jews, the idea of restoration had a personal or family connotation as well as a national significance. The Jewish people were people of the Covenant, hence heirs of the restoration of God to all he had promised them and all he had in store for them. Haggai, Zechariah, and Malachci are the great prophets of the Restoration. (See Mal. 4:2.)

(3) The ancient Jews missed the Sun of righteousness when he came to restore mankind to the spiritual inheritance that God had in store for them. We still miss him but he still calls, though few there be that find him. He will keep on calling that fallen man and woman may be restored to God.

(4) The purpose of the Jubilee was restoration, and one of the major purposes of Christianity is the restoration by God of those who have dispossessed themselves or been dispossessed of his salvation through Christ.

III. The year of Jubilee was a year of emancipation.

(1) The slaves were set free. No matter what wrong they had done, no matter how improvident they had been, no matter if they had sold themselves, body and soul, to any master, they were set free.

(2) That is the real and supreme message of Christ for our world today. He sets us free from the bondage of sin. He gives us a new start with pardon and power. He proclaims for us and through us the glorious fact that we have been separated from the things that enthralled us and the evils that ensnared us and the habits that have bound us, and with him we are free.—H. E. D. Ashford.

Worship Aids

CALL TO WORSHIP. "Having therefore, brethren, boldness to enter into the holiest by the blood of Jesus, by a new and living way, which he hath consecrated for us, let us draw near with a true heart in full assurance of faith." Heb. 10:19–20, 22.

INVOCATION. Almighty and everlasting God, in whom we live and move and have our being, who hast created us for thyself so that we can find rest only in thee: grant unto us purity of heart and strength of purpose, so that no selfish passion may hinder us from knowing thy will, and no weakness sway us from doing it; that in thy light we may see light clearly and in thy service find perfect freedom.

OFFERTORY SENTENCE. "Bring ye all the tithes into the storehouse, saith the Lord, [and I will] open the windows of heaven, and pour you out a blessing." Mal. 3:10.

OFFERTORY PRAYER. God of all good, who hath rewarded our labors, we acknowledge thankfully thy favor and do now dedicate a share of our material gains to the even more satisfying ministries of the spirit.

PRAYER. O thou eternal God, Father of love and mercy, in thy hands are the destinies of men and of nations. We pray that we may be blessed with a vital sense of thy sovereignty.

Show us anew that in our obedience of thy laws and in our living within thy will we are fulfilling the highest purposes of our lives. In these tragic times may we stand fast in the faith wherein thou hast made us free. Let the living of our days give testimony to the belief that thou art our refuge and strength, an ever-present help in time of trouble.

Amid a world of unrest and destruction we acknowledge our sin and bow before thee in humility. We have been a disappointment to thee for we have failed thee again and again. We confess our selfish aims, our pride, our self-dependence. We have been shown those whom the injustices of the world have bruised and beaten, and we have passed by on the other side. We have refused to heed the cries of our brothers who need thy love through us.

To thee alone do we look for direction when confusion encompasses us, for light when the way is dark. Interpret to us the mind of Christ, and grant us thy help in the task of applying his spirit in the world.

Grant unto us the love that we should have for one another. Teach us how to bear one another's burdens. May this house of prayer be a place where the lonely find companionship, the heavy-laden find rest for their souls, and those who sorrow are strengthened and upheld by the everlasting arms. —William Carman Trembath.

Illustrations

UNDER OBLIGATION. When I analyze my moral consciousness I cannot doubt that it sets up to be a consciousness of standards not of my own making, of ends not of my own choosing, of commandments not of my own issuing. The whole dignity of man, the whole much-boasted "value of human personality" resides in man's awareness of being thus under obligation to something greater than himself.—John Baillie.

BEYOND ONESELF. James Boswell once went to hear William Wilberforce speak in his crusade to make England stop the African slave traffic. Boswell said afterward: "I saw what seemed a mere shrimp mount upon the table; but as I listened, he grew and grew, until the shrimp became a whale." Wilberforce, the little hunchback, never had good health. Viewed as a physical specimen, Wilberforce might have been termed "but a walking shadow" of a man. He might have felt sorry for himself, but his bodily handicap made him sorry for others. Living in the shadow of pain, he gained a clarity of vision, a depth of insight, a breadth of sympathy, a force of persuasion which lifted the country he loved out of the cruelty which he hated.—Ralph W. Sockman.

Sermon Suggestions

HOW CHRIST HELPS US TO UNDERSTAND GOD. (1) Christ helps us understand God better by teaching us the truth about God as our heavenly Father whose love for us is unconditional, purposeful, and includes all mankind and to whom we respond in love for him. Christ sought to help us see our human life as God sees it. (2) Our Lord's deeds illustrated how Christ believed and accepted God as his loving Heavenly Father. (3) Christ helps us understand God by being God incarnate in a human being.—Robert W. Burns.

HOW CHRIST HELPS US TO UNDERSTAND OURSELVES. (1) Christ helps us understand ourselves by what he said, teaching us the truth about ourselves, what human nature really is, what manner of person each of us has been made by God. (2) Christ will help us understand ourselves more adequately if we will really look at his actions. What did he do? (a) His every movement was intended to be helpful. (b) Quietly going about his own higher business, he set the example of how to deal with rejection. (c) He helps us by his actions to understand our need for quiet and solitude. (3) Christ helps us understand ourselves by being the kind of person that he was, demonstrating forever the high potential of human nature. Every man has within him the possibility of greatness. Everyone has a Christ within his own life.—Robert W. Burns.

HOW CHRIST HELPS US TO UNDERSTAND OTHERS. (1) The dynamics of forgiveness are central to understanding other persons. All of us need forgiveness, and we cannot accept God's forgiveness of us when we have not forgiven one another. Christ helps us understand other persons by what he said about forgiveness. (2) He helps us understand other persons by what he did about forgiveness. How forgiving our Master was! We need to look at this part of his life and recognize what he did as a source for understanding our need to forgive other persons. Christ came into the world to make people happy, and men knew where he had been because of the trail of joy he left behind him. (3) Christ helps us understand others by being an illustration of what happens when a person gives and receives forgiving love, revealing at the same time the misery and destruction that result in failure to forgive.—Robert W. Burns.

EVENING SERVICE

Topic: Christian Baptism

I. Baptism is the Christian equivalent of and successor to Jewish circumcision. Just as Jews from the days of Moses have circumcised their male children and converts to mark them as members of the Jewish nation, so Christians have baptized their new members —both male and female—as a "sign" or "mark" that they belong to the new Israel.

II. Baptism is a rite instituted by our Lord. Not only did he present himself for baptism at the hands of John, but he also clearly commanded his followers to baptize as they went forth to make disciples of all nations. It follows that, if he commanded his disciples to baptize, he commanded would-be disciples to be baptized.

III. Baptism is a custom as old as the Christian enterprise. On the day of Pentecost Peter answered those who asked, "What must we do to be saved?" with, "Repent, and be baptized every one of you in the name of Jesus Christ." From then until now the overwhelming practice of the Church has been to initiate new members with baptism.

IV. Baptism is rich with symbolism. From time immemorial water has been the symbol of realities as varied as life and death and cleansing. A study of the place of water symbolism in the religions of mankind proves not only fascinating but also rewarding.

V. Baptism is an effective method of proclaiming the Gospel. What a true sermon does with words, baptism does with symbol and sign. It dramatizes in a way mere words never can that God was in Christ reconciling the world to himself, thereby instituting a new covenant between him and his people and bringing forth a new creation.—John W. Meister.

SUNDAY: SEPTEMBER TWENTY-THIRD

MORNING SERVICE

Topic: The Grace of God
TEXT: I Cor. 15:10.

Paul attributes all to the grace of God: his character, his achievements, and his position in the Church. He was a man of great intellectual ability, with a philosophical bent and a deep and penetrating insight, yet he resolutely attributed what he was and what he was able to accomplish to the grace of God.

The effects of grace so clearly discernible in the case of Paul are equally applicable to all men.

I. Grace humbles us and enables us to see ourselves as we are.

(1) Paul was brought to his knees on the Damascus Road. While pursuing his ruthless policy of persecuting the Christians he was floored by Christ and made to see himself as he really was: a boastful young man presuming to judge others without realizing that he himself was being judged; a self-righteous moralist arrogantly drawing his measuring line over others without realizing that he was being measured by the plumbline of God. The grace of God enables all of us to see ourselves as we are. We measure ourselves correctly only in the light of the Cross.

(2) Grace uplifts us and enables us to see things differently. If we are brought to our knees by the grace of God we are not left in the dust but lifted up, changed, and given a new outlook. Paul was raised from the dust of the Damascus Road and renewed. The bitter Pharisee became the inspired author of the Hymn of Love, the slave of the law became a free man.

(3) Grace preserves us and enables us to see the value of the fellowship of the Church. The small community of Christians accepted their former persecutor, nurtured him in the faith, and preserved him from the intrigues of his enemies. Paul never ceased to give thanks for the fellowship of the Church and counted it as one of the greatest blessings of his life.

(4) Grace enriches us to see the world in a new light. Paul never questioned the riches of grace. Christ for him was never on the circumference, as a mere addendum to his life, but at the center of his being and the main source of all his blessings. God in Christ had changed and enriched his life, and he believed that grace was the means of enrichment for all men. Much has come to humanity through the grace of God in Christ, and life would be greatly impoverished without it.

II. Among the blessings of grace is the gift of the Spirit, the Comforter, the Paraclete. A suggested translation of "Paraclete" is "the perspective-giver."

(1) Grace enables us to see things in their right perspective. This surely is the secret of living. We are worried by the insignificant things of life. Small, unimportant things affect us and make life a burden for us. The joy of living is ours when we are able to see all things in their right perspective.

(2) By the grace of God we are enabled to see our lives against a background of eternity, *sub specie aeternitatis*, which puts all the everyday happenings of our lives in the right perspective.

III. By the grace of God we are given a new hope. A hope not dependent on what we might desire, not self-manufactured. A hope that does not depend on what we see, for hope that is seen is not hope; that does not depend on what we might reasonably expect and is not governed by the law of cause and effect. Through grace we are given a new hope, centered in Christ and founded on his Resurrection, that this corruption will put on incorruption and that this mortal will put on immortality. The effect of this hope is to assure us that the world is ours, that life is ours, that the future is ours.—Glyn Richards.

Worship Aids

CALL TO WORSHIP. "Lift up your heads in the sanctuary, and bless the Lord. The Lord that made heaven and earth bless thee out of Zion." Ps. 134:2–3.

INVOCATION. Most holy and gracious God, who turnest the shadow of night into morning: satisfy us early with thy mercy that we may rejoice and be glad all the day. Lift the light of thy countenance upon us, calm every troubled thought, and guide our feet into the way of peace. Perfect thy strength in our weakness and help us to worship thee in the spirit of Jesus Christ our Lord.

OFFERTORY SENTENCE. "To do good and to communicate forget not: for with such sacrifices God is well pleased." Heb. 13:16.

OFFERTORY PRAYER. O Christ, may we walk constantly in thy way and work fervently for those causes which are dear to thee.

PRAYER. Our Father God, thou hast been patient with us: forgive our impatience with ourselves. Forgive us for the endless running away from the reality of today into dreams of tomorrow; for the senseless and ceaseless getting more and having less; for the impatience that drives us to be what we are not and leaves us bored with what we are.

Forgive our impatience with others. Forgive us for demanding our whims of them when they are wearied of work; for commanding them because another has commanded us; for throwing at them the past we have not had the grace to forget.

Forgive our impatience with thee. We are sinners, each of us, lonely and afraid to share it, hurt and ashamed to admit it, foolish and unwilling to confess it. Heal us, Father; our faith is sick, our hope is tired, our trust is thin and tattered. Create in us health, and grant us strength to bear the pain of patience.—Anderson D. Clark.

Illustrations

INDWELLING POWER. Grace is an indwelling power that re-creates from within and that is illimitable in its power to refashion broken human nature after the likeness of our Lord Jesus Christ.—Stephen Neill.

PAUL IN PRISON. Paul had fallen on calamity and whipped it into a blessing. He had turned a prison into a pulpit and a printing press for the Kingdom of God. He had taken a peck of trouble in his hands and made a bushel of stars out of it, for brave spirits to hang on in dark nights.—Paul Scherer.

WHAT IS GRACE? Grace is like getting two more days to complete an assignment even though you've goofed off for six weeks and missed the deadline.

Grace is like getting a warning from the traffic officer instead of a $50 fine and a suspended license.

Grace is getting another chance even though you haven't earned it or deserved it. (You may not even want it!)

Grace is God's unmerited favor, mercy, and love, by which we are justified freely.—Fritz Ridenour in *How to Be a Christian Without Being Religious*.

Sermon Suggestions

HOW JESUS TAUGHT. Text: Matt. 7:28–29. (1) Jesus Christ taught on his own initiative, responsibility, and authority, and not on the authority of anyone else. (2) Jesus Christ taught only what had come home to him with vital reality in his own personal experience, his own inner spiritual life. (3) The appeal Jesus made in his message was to the mind and heart, or in other words, to the experience of his listeners.—Norman V. Hope.

MAN'S JUDGMENT. Text: Matt. 7:1. We should remember four things about men's judgments. (1) Men must make judgments about other men's thoughts and conduct. Otherwise it would be impossible to enjoy an ordered society. The rightness or wrongness of the relations between men in civil and criminal affairs demands judgments. (2) All human judgments, those of believers and unbelievers alike, are subject to error, no matter how desirous men are to judge justly. In this sense their judgments are tentative and lack finality. Men see darkly, think erroneously, and often draw varying conclusions from the same set of facts. (3) Men need to be careful how they judge, because the basis on which they make their judgments will be the basis on which they themselves are ultimately judged by God. (4) There is a judgment that is final and without error. Paul speaks of this in his first letter to the church at Corinth. He says that neither the judgments of men about him nor his own judgment of himself is determinative. It is the judgment of God that counts, for God knows the secrets of men's hearts and brings to light the things that are hidden from men.—*Christianity Today.*

EVENING SERVICE

Topic: Vengeance in Christian Perspective

TEXT: Matt. 5:38–39.

Christians are called to a style of life that is totally free of vengeance. A wrong done to you does not give you license to inflict a wrong on someone else. The wisdom behind this counsel is visible from many angles.

I. Vengeance is harmful to the avenger as well as to the avengee. (1) Jesus absolutely negates hatred as inhuman, and vengeance always rises out of hatred. Vengeance produces in the human heart a disorganizing anxiety and displaces those positive and constructive dispositions where our well-being lies.

(2) For the man of vengeance, every sunset is bleached of color; every meal is rendered bland and tasteless; every dream is cankered; every relationship is soured. Vengeance stops prayer, represses joy, misdirects energy, robs the middle years of their productivity, and crowns old age with a thorny wreath of bitterness.

II. Vengeance is futile. Evil is not the true answer to evil. It never was and it never will be. Vengeance simply perpetuates the cycle of sin-against, hate; sin-against, hate; sin-against, hate. Better that we should meet the one who offends us with kindness, even on pragmatic grounds. (See Rom. 12:20–21.)

III. Vengeance reduces, when you think about it, to a denial of trust in God. (1) It's an easy matter to stamp our coins: "In God We Trust." But when we take matters into our own hands asd seek to execute judgment, we are in effect saying that we can't trust God to do this for us. "Shall not the Judge of all the earth do right?" (Gen. 18:25)—not only by the nations of the world, but also by those petty hurts that wound and crush the heart.

(2) "Shall not the Judge of all the earth do right?" Do you really believe in the law of God—that it generates its own conviction and exacts its own penalties? Does not the adulterer suffer because he is moving against the very structure of the universe? Does the man who steals really have it as easy as your eyes would make it out to be?

IV. Vengeance is wrong because something else is right. And that something else is forgiveness.

(1) Some people keep picking at their scar tissue so that the wounds will stay. Others massage their scars so that every trace may vanish.

(2) "Forgive us our debts as we for-

give our debtors." Not that there is a quid pro quo here, that God only forgives as we forgive. Rather, the assumption is that, unless we have learned how to forgive another, we haven't learned to receive forgiveness for ourselves. Francis Bacon said: "By taking revenge a man is but even with his enemy; but, by passing over it, he is supreme."—Ernest T. Campbell in *Pulpit Digest*.

SUNDAY: SEPTEMBER THIRTIETH

MORNING SERVICE

Topic: The Many and the Few
TEXT: Matt. 22:14.

All are invited: the offer of new life in Jesus Christ is extended to everyone without exception. The whole world is called into fellowship with the eternal God. Many are called, but few are chosen. Why?

I. Not all actually hear the invitation. (1) Four out of every ten people in the world, we are told, have never even heard of Jesus. And countless numbers of those who have heard something of Jesus have not really had it made clear to them who he is and what it is he offers.

(2) To us the gospel invitation has been made known, most of us have understood it, and many of us have responded to it. But we have failed to realize—or worse still, we may have realized but failed to act on the knowledge—that the invitation of Christ is given not only to us but also through us.

(a) It is through his Church, through each of its members, that he is calling, or trying to call, men and women into his eternal Kingdom. It is our task to see that it is made clear to all people, near and far, what the invitation of our Lord is, and that it is extended to all without exception.

(b) We have the greatest good news, the most urgent message in the world to pass on, and nothing must be allowed to keep us back from passing it on.

II. Not all who hear respond to the invitation. (1) There are many who hear the challenge and the invitation of the Christian gospel and give it little or no further thought. They are too preoccupied with other things.

(2) Others hear the Christian message and they think a little about it, but postpone any decision. For the time being they are too busy with other matters to give it fuller consideration.

(3) There are those who feel there is too much risk involved. They know that if they begin to follow Christ considerable sacrifices may be necessary, and they are unwilling to hazard all for him.

(4) In a completely different category are those who are most definitely interested, and indeed ready to respond to the call of Christ, but who feel that they are unfit or unworthy to do so.

III. Of those who do respond, not all are found to be fit to enter the Kingdom of God. (1) There is no written examination for entrance into God's Kingdom. We don't necessarily have to be A-1 either physically or intellectually to become followers of Jesus Christ. There may indeed be a very stern reality behind the notion of a Last Judgment, at which our fitness or otherwise to dwell within the eternal realm will be assessed. The examination, however, will be not of knowledge but of character. The standard of judgment will be whether or not we have shown compassion to others, and what use we have made of that which God has given us.

(2) We come to Christ just as we are. We approach the door, as it were, in our unredeemed, unrenewed, unchanged condition, but before we enter

the door we must be renewed and changed.

(3) If we wait until we can cleanse and renew ourselves, until we can make ourselves fit, before we approach God, we will never get into his Kingdom. On the other hand, if we try to "gate-crash" just as we are, without allowing Christ to transform us, to put on us the robe of his righteousness, admittance will be refused. For the robe of righteousness is a Christlike character.

(4) Not one of us is worthy of fellowship with God; not one of us, as we are, is fit for his Kingdom. Yet we need not despair, for he will make us fit, if we allow him. We cannot enter the Kingdom on our own terms. We must realize our unfitness, the defectiveness of our own unredeemed nature, and accept the new nature which God in Jesus Christ gives to us.—Douglas H. Cummins.

Worship Aids

CALL TO WORSHIP. "Lord, who shall abide in thy tabernacle? Who shall dwell in thy holy hill? He that walketh uprightly, and worketh righteousness, and speaketh the truth in his heart." Ps. 15:1-2.

INVOCATION. O Lord of light, in this hour of worship in thy house, make pure our hearts, and we shall see thee; reveal thyself to us, and we shall love thee. Strengthen our wills, and we shall choose the good from the evil, and day by day manifest in the world the glory and power of thy blessed Gospel, which thou hast made known to us through thy Son Jesus Christ.

OFFERTORY SENTENCE. "Every man hath his proper gift of God, one after this manner, and another after that." I Cor. 7:7.

OFFERTORY. Eternal God, give us a vision of thy glory that no sacrifice may seem too great, and strengthen us in every step we take from selfishness to generosity.

PRAYER. O thou who hast made us for thyself, our hearts are restless until they rest in thee. When we think of thee we forget our limitations and reach beyond ourselves to the realm of thy limitless power. In thy presence we find rest; in thy wisdom we find truth; in thy mercy we find forgiveness; in thy love we find an answer to the evil of the world.

O thou who dwellest in light unapproachable, may the shining of thy love drive the shadows from our lives, making them centers of health, cheerfulness, and courage. Break through the mists of doubt, dispelling the clouds that impede our progress and making clear the way that we should follow. Come nearer to us than we have ever known thee in our happiest moments of vision and teach us more of the wonder of thy laws.

Light the flame of faith upon the altar of our minds. Help us to praise thee with lives of radiant service. Because we have paused these moments and lifted our hearts to thee, may we be able to go forth into the world with love toward all men, with hope to impart to the discouraged, with support to offer in every good cause, and with faith in the ultimate triumph of right. —Robert M. Bartlett.

Illustrations

LINE OF HUNGER. Suppose, as you sat down to your dinner, the doorbell rang. You opened the door, and there before you, ragged and disease-ravaged, with pinched faces, stood the world's hungry in single file, each begging for a crust of bread. How far do you think the line would reach? Beginning at your door, the line would continue out of sight, over continent and ocean, around the world—25,000 miles—and return to the place it started; and it would do this, circling the globe not once, not five times, but 25, with no one in this line but hungry, suffering humanity.—A. Leonard Griffith in *Christian Herald*.

GODLESS WORLD. True, man can organize the world apart from God, but without God man can organize it in the end only to man's detriment. An isolated humanism is an inhuman humanism.—Pope Paul VI.

GROWING IN GRACE. In order to grow in grace, we must be much alone. It is not in society—even Christian society—that the soul grows most vigorously. In one single, quiet hour of prayer it will often make more progress than in days of company with others. It is in the desert that the dew falls freshest and the air is purest.—Horatius Bonar.

Sermon Suggestions

THE TASTE OF BETTER WINE. Text: John 2:10. Jesus offers a taste of better wine. (1) It comes to us in the form of his leadership as Master and Lord. (2) Jesus offers the taste of better wine when it comes to leadership. In Jesus there is no flaw of character or personality. He is the very best to follow and to whom to give your life in obedience and service. (3) Jesus offers us the taste of better wine when he offers us the true way of living the Christian life.—John R. Brokhoff.

TOO GOOD NOT TO BE TRUE. (1) There are memories that are too good to be dismissed. (2) There are hopes that are too good not to come true. (3) There are human encounters which are too good to ever end.—Clarence J. Forsberg.

EVENING SERVICE

Topic: The Church as the Body of Christ

TEXT: I Cor. 12:27.

I. "You are the Body of *Christ*": not just of congenial neighbors, not just of fellow Americans, not just of people drawn together by similar idealistic interests. Here in the Church, St. Paul is saying, is a society which we did not create, which the community did not create, which the government did not create. It owes its existence to Christ, not to any human design. It can never be true to its own nature, therefore, if it merely reflects the views of those who happen to be its members or its official board. It is really "the Church" only as it represents Christ. It fails to be "the Church" if it proclaims merely what people like to hear or easily adjusts its witness to the outlook of secular society.

II. "*You* are the Body of Christ": in Corinth the witness to Christ depends not on St. Paul, not on some leader, but on them. Yet who were they? A very ordinary lot, by no means remarkable for either saintliness or achievement. A large part of his Letter to the Christians in Corinth is taken up with their all-too-human shortcomings and failures. Yet he insists that it is they who represent the exalted Christ in a city that sorely needed a Christian testimony. The very name of Corinth was almost a byword for debased moral standards. Even today, when you visit Corinth, your guide points out where a great temple of Aphrodite stood, a visual symbol of sexual license glorified. In the midst of such conditions, it was through a little group of apparently inconsequential people that Corinth was to know what Christ meant for its life.

III. "You are the *Body* of Christ": his Body—not just a collection of individual units, each standing alone. The Church, that is to say, has an organic character, all the members being knit together in a common relation to Christ. It is the communion of the faithful who have fellowship with their Lord and with one another. The phrase "Body of Christ" doubtless sounds rather mystical, and so we tend to assume that it has reference to some invisible ideal rather than to a down-to-earth actuality

like a congregation on Main Street. But to St. Paul the "Body of Christ" meant the visible, concrete reality by which Christ continues to be manifest to the world and acts in human history. It is the human community in which the Risen and Living Christ dwells and through which his work is carried on. Just as my physical body serves my purposes as a person, so the Church as Christ's Body is to carry on his purposes in the world. There is a corporate Christian witness to be borne and a corporate function to be fulfilled.
—Samuel McCrea Cavert in *Pulpit Digest.*

SUNDAY: OCTOBER SEVENTH

MORNING SERVICE

Topic: Door of Fellowship (World Communion Sunday)
TEXT: Gal. 3:28.

For all divisions caused by ignorance, injustice, fear, and hatred, for every barrier which would deny and destroy our humanity, there is a healing bridge of fellowship, says Paul, in Jesus Christ.

I. This is a fellowship of dedication, of hearts united in loyalty to Christ and his Church. It is a loyalty which transcends all other loyalties. Hence, it is a fellowship which rises above all divisions of class and party, nationality and race, to unite us as God's children equal in his sight.

II. This is the fellowship of sinners, of people who have looked upon the excellence of Jesus Christ and thus know themselves to have fallen far short of their moral potential. Hence, it is a fellowship which rises above every human difference in position and attainment to unite people in the humility of mutual penitence and awareness of common need.

III. This is the fellowship of the redeemed, of sinners saved by the grace of God. It is a fellowship which surmounts every divisive pretense of pride to make us one in knowledge of dependence upon and gratitude to God, the Author of our salvation.

IV. This is the fellowship of understanding, of people sensitive to the needs and rights of others, who know and feel the hopes and hurts of others, who comprehend what they are trying to say in language without words. Hence, it is a fellowship which surmounts every barrier of loneliness and distrust, ignorance and injustice, to join us in a healing awareness of kinship.

V. This is the fellowship of concern, of those who, sensitive to the needs and rights of others, seek to serve their need in compassion. Hence, it is a fellowship which spans every barrier made of human want and weakness, disaster and despair, to unite us in practicing the intelligence of love.

VI. This is the fellowship of human unity and equality in Christ. It is a fellowship of dedication in loyalty that transcends every other loyalty; of sinners, alike in penitence and awareness of need; of the redeemed saved from their worst but by the grace of God; of those who understand and of those who truly care.

VII. This is the fellowship which feeds the hunger of every heart; the fellowship which can save twentieth-century mankind from itself.

VIII. In the name of and for the sake of this fellowship, we join in the commemoration of World Communion Sunday. With Christians of every race and nationality, on both sides of the "iron curtain" and of the "bamboo curtain," and in every part of the world, we pledge our lives anew to Christ and his Church. We join in affirming a loyalty to the King of kings which makes us one, above all differences. We bow in gratitude to accept a gift of Divine Love which makes us bound in honor to be the practitioners of love toward all men.—Everett W. Palmer.

Worship Aids

CALL TO WORSHIP. "The cup of blessing which we bless, is not the communion of the blood of Christ? The bread which we break, is not the communion of the body of Christ? For we being many are one bread, and one body: for we are all partakers of that one bread." I Cor. 10:16–17.

INVOCATION. Heavenly Father, we earnestly pray thee to bless this church and all who worship here. Bind us in a close fellowship of worship, work, and holy living. Give to each one of us some share in carrying out thy purposes for this place and for all mankind. Grant us love, faithfulness, and the spirit of cooperation and tolerance.

OFFERTORY SENTENCE. "We then that are strong ought to bear the infirmities of the weak, and not to please ourselves." Rom. 15:1.

OFFERTORY PRAYER. Accept, O Lord, these offerings thy people make unto thee, and grant that the cause to which they are devoted may prosper under thy guidance, to the glory of thy name.

PRAYER

Let us remember Jesus:
Who, though he was rich, yet for our sakes became poor and dwelt among us.
Who was content to be subject to his parents, the child of a poor man's home.
Who lived for thirty years the common life, earning his living with his own hands and declining no humble tasks.
Whom the common people heard gladly, for he understood their ways.
May this mind be in us that was in Christ Jesus.

Let us remember Jesus:
Who was mighty in deed, healing the sick and the disordered, using for others the powers he would not invoke for himself.
Who refused to force men's allegiance.
Who was Master and Lord to his disciples, yet was among them as their companion and as one who served.
Whose meat was to do the will of the Father who sent him.
May this mind be in us that was in Christ Jesus.

Let us remember Jesus:
Who believed in men to the last and never despaired of them.
Who through all disappointment never lost heart.
Who disregarded his own comfort and convenience and thought first of others' needs, and though he suffered long was always kind.
Who, when he was reviled, reviled not again, and when he suffered, threatened not.
Who humbled himself and carried obedience to the point of death, even death on the Cross, and endured faithful to the end.
May this mind be in us that was in Christ Jesus.

O Christ, our only Savior, so come to dwell in us that we may go forth with the light of thy hope in our eyes, and thy faith and love in our hearts.—Adapted from *A New Prayer Book*.

Illustrations

KINSHIP. A brief visit to a village in New Guinea during World War II underlined for me the depth of the kinship of humanity. Upon approaching the village, a lad came running toward us. He cried out, "My name Apo," and proudly escorted us into the village where we were met by friendly people.
The village leader recognized the cross on my lapel as identifying me with the Christian religion. He brought

out the New Testament in his language, and we read and compared the Word in his native tongue with the Word in my English Version.

He spoke with great affection for his missionary teacher who had been forced to leave because of the war. In some respects we had little in common, and yet how much!—John F. Cagle in *The Upper Room*.

BORN TO LOVE. The meaning of our life, according to the Gospel, is that we are made by love for love. This is not grasped all at once or realized in a single flash. It dawns on us through day-to-day experiences which may seem at first to have little to do with faith in God. As we acquire competence in caring and our craving for love from others is supplanted by ability to give love to them, a way is opened which leads toward God himself.—Roger Hazelton in *Knowing the Living God*.

PERFORMANCE. There is a spirit abroad in America, an esthetic spirit concerned with the quality of life that makes people want to participate in the art of human performance.—Anderson D. Clark in *Presbyterian Life*.

Sermon Suggestions

THE MEANINGS OF WORLD COMMUNION. (1) It means that we must dedicate ourselves to seeking a deeper understanding of the implications of the commission of Jesus to take his very life to all mankind. (2) It means that we must rededicate ourselves to providing adequately trained personnel and adequate resources to carry on, and bring to genuine fruition, the work which has been initiated by those who felt under divine compulsion to take Christ to all the world. (3) It means that we must recognize the seething situations throughout the world as personal challenges to those who take seriously their conviction that Christ is the answer to the real needs of every person.—Homer J. R. Elford.

WE BELONG TO THE SAME CHURCH. Christians share much in common, more probably than they are usually aware. (1) We have a common Bible. (2) We belong to the same church because we are heirs of a common life of prayer and devotion. (3) We belong to the same church in the sense that we have a common body of song, a common hymnal. (4) We belong to the same church in the sense that we share a common table.—Taylor E. Roth.

EVENING SERVICE

Topic: The Face of Our Brother

I. This is missions: to look upon the face of our brother and to know that he is a beggar just as we.

(1) He is our brother whether he is next door or thousands of miles away, whether he is our color of skin or not, whether he speaks our language or does not even know how to read.

(2) As we look upon his face we see that it reflects a revolutionary world whose foundations are shaking.

(3) We believe that it is God who is shaking the foundations. Then there wells up within us a compassion to shake the foundation even further, to disrupt his life with the good news of Christ.

II. What does it mean to be a missionary church?

(1) It means first to proclaim the good news in every place in the world.

(2) It means to disrupt the easy answers of life and proclaim that in Christ, who suffered for men, there is hope and purpose.

(3) It means to identify ourselves with our brother, to try to walk where he walks, to live where he lives, and to love him for what he is.

(4) Wherever there is revolution, wherever people are struggling to be a people, the Church of Christ must identify itself with them. As we draw closer to Christ we find ourselves drawn closer to the world in revolution.

III. To be a missionary church means to demonstrate our faith. By a repentant spirit the Church demonstrates to our brother the sincerity of our faith. By our giving and by our concern for the world we demonstrate the sincerity of our faith.

IV. Let us be excited about the shaking foundations. God is working. May he work through us who seek to come face to face with our brother. In our revolutionary world there is only one thing that does not change, and that is God himself. God will prevail though the mountains crumble. Our prayer is that we may be able to trust in him and be used by him.—Robert B. Wallace.

SUNDAY: OCTOBER FOURTEENTH

MORNING SERVICE

Topic: Who Are the Laymen? (Laymen's Sunday)

The word "lay" comes from a Greek word *laos;* it was used by early translators of the Bible to denote "the people of God." This idea is found, of course, in the Old Testament, in the people of Israel as God's "chosen people." When Christians in the New Testament Church tried to think about who they were, they took this same idea: they were God's people, the *laos*. Out of this fundamental meaning, three aspects arise:

I. The layman belongs to the people of God because in Christ he is becoming a "new man." He has been converted.

(1) Whatever our differing ideas may be as to the meaning of, and the way to, conversion, there is no mistaking the New Testament's insistence that only by being "born again" does an individual put off his old life and nature and enter into the new. And, however differing may be the interpretation and the administration of baptism among us, its essential meaning is that, through his baptism, the individual is confirmed in his new life, and has bestowed upon him the gift of the Spirit as the mark and the source of power for his new condition.

(2) If we take this point seriously as describing the beginning of a layman's life, we will have to do some hard thinking as to whether many of the people whose names appear on our church rolls rightly deserve the name of layman for themselves. Whatever else they may be, they do not seem to be this.

II. The layman belongs to the *laos*. (1) He is never a layman as a solitary individual. The new life he enters is a life shared with fellow Christians. While certain aspects of his life must be solitary—only I can answer for myself before God—his new manhood comes to him by his participation in the community to whom the new life is given.

(2) In this sense, it may be incorrect to speak of any single individual as a "Christian" or a "layman." It would be more precise to say: "He belongs to [with] the Christians"; "he is one of the laymen." The New Testament knows nothing of the "private Christian" so popular among us today.

III. He engages in ministry. (1) What he is, a new man, must show itself in what he does. Our question of those seeking membership in the churches should include, not only "Do you believe . . .," but also "What now are you going to do?"

(2) This is related to the Reformers' teaching about "the priesthood of all believers." They did not mean, as some people have supposed, that this teaching gave everybody the right to believe anything he wanted to believe, without interference by any authoritarian priesthood. What they did mean is that every person coming into the

Church of Christ has his particular service to undertake. Certain laymen were ordained for certain responsibilities within the life of the churches. But the ministry of the churches belong to all believers, in whatever condition they might find themselves.

IV. Laymen, then, are those persons who have entered into a new life in Christ, who share this life with one another, and who give themselves to the ministries Christ bestowed upon them. In fulfilling these ministries, laymen truly come into their own. They make the Church—which they are—faithful to its calling to be the servant of Christ among men in the world.—John L. Casteel.

Worship Aids

CALL TO WORSHIP. "Be strong and of a good courage, fear not: for the Lord thy God, he it is that doth go with thee; he will not fail thee, nor forsake thee." Deut. 31:6.

INVOCATION. O God of mercy, in this hour in thy house, have mercy upon us. O God of light, shine into our hearts. O thou Eternal Goodness, deliver us from evil. O God of power, be thou our refuge and our strength. O God of love, let love flow through us. O God of life, live within us, now and forevermore.

OFFERTORY SENTENCE. "And they came, every one whose heart stirred him up, and every one whom his spirit made willing, and they brought the Lord's offering to the work of the tabernacle of the congregation, and for all his service." Exod. 35:21.

OFFERTORY PRAYER. Help us to remember, O Lord, that a life is a more persuasive testimony than words, that deeds are more effective than arguments, and that these gifts are only a portion of the loyalty thou dost require of us.

A LAYMAN'S PRAYER. Our Father, with love and sincerity we bow and speak once more our thankfulness for the full measure of spiritual and physical care that comes from thee. Little as we have deserved them, thy blessings have gone with us every day, and no matter how faltering our steps, thy light has been our constant guide.

For thy Church, we thank thee, and for the opportunity to worship freely in it. For the faithful service of thy ministers, we give thanks. For the defenders of our nation and for its leaders, we ask thy guidance and protection, that Christian principles and right decisions may direct them.

For love and loved ones, for constructive work, and for thy attendance to our every need, we give thee praise. We ask of thee not easier lives but clearer vision to see the goals ahead; not lesser tasks but added strength to do thy work. Grant us the willingness, the enthusiasm, and the touch of thy spirit that will enable us, thy children, to gain new victories for thee.—Vic Jameson.

Illustrations

CHRIST'S LAYMEN. It is an interesting fact that all of the men who were originally chosen by Jesus to be his disciples came from the common walks of life. Four were fishermen. One was a tax collector. There was not a priest or member of the clergy in the group. None of the men had received any professional training of the kind available at that time. It is an open question whether all of the twelve could read or write. Only three among the group left any evidence of a written record behind them. All of them were, in every sense of the meaning of the word, laymen who somehow had a vital religious awakening and who then were part of that little group that upset the world at that time.—Richard Thomason.

LAITY AS SAINTS. St. Paul called all the laity of his day saints. He did not mean they were perfect. They were in most cases far from it. It was a tender, gentle, hopeful word. It meant that they had started on the way. I think the greatest miracle we know is the way a person suddenly rises beyond himself, gets attached to the eternal reservoir of God's grace and truth, and lets the streams of life pour through him. When that miracle takes place, we have a saint, and he is forthwith a transmitter.—Rufus M. Jones.

Sermon Suggestions

THAT SEARCHING LOOK. Text: I Sam. 16:7. What did God, with his all-searching, all-seeing eyes, see in David's heart? What qualities made it possible for God to say David was a man after his own heart? (1) God saw a man of deep faith. (2) God saw in David a man of great courage. (3) God saw in David a depending heart. (4) God saw in David's heart a deep capacity for sorrow and contrition for sin. (5) God saw in David a man capable of rising to the heights of worship and praise. (6) God saw in David a man sensitive to his works of creation. (7) God saw in David a man willing to share in a deep personal relationship with himself.—L. Nelson Bell in *Christianity Today.*

HOW CAN THE CHURCH LIVE ABUNDANTLY? Text: John 10:10 (RSV). Jesus might be interpreted as saying to the Church: "I came that you might have vitality and that you might overflow with it." (1) A church to live abundantly must be a united church. (2) A church to live abundantly must be a working church. (3) A church to live abundantly must be a giving church.—Rolla S. Kenaston.

WHAT IS A CHRISTIAN? (1) A mind through which Christ thinks. (2) A voice through which Christ speaks. (3) A hand through which Christ helps. (4) A life through which Christ lives.

EVENING SERVICE

Topic: The Capacity to Enjoy
TEXT: I Tim. 6:17.

We should be interested in our capacity to enjoy, for we only really live in those things we can do and do enjoy. Lacking that capacity, we are in danger of going to pieces, for we live by our satisfactions.

I. The paucity of our pleasures may not only be due to the failure of the self to develop within us, but also it may be due to our refusal to accept the authority and wisdom of the great positive ideas about God and life as found in the Gospel. If we truly live only in our capacity to enjoy, it is also true that our very capacity depends upon principles we believe and accept as true in the order of creation—yes, and trust!

(1) Does it come as a surprise that God has created life for our enjoyment? That is his intention, that is his motive, that is his purpose. Of course, we have to develop the capacity to enjoy—that is our part in the business of living, that is our responsibility as persons. The capacity to enjoy anything is never inborn; it is always developed. If we do not develop it, we cannot distinguish pleasure, for that is a personal evaluation we learn to make. We cannot possess what we fail to develop—a capacity to enjoy. Believe this purpose of God and work at it!

(2) Does it surprise you that God is a giving God? What does he give us? He "giveth us richly all things"— the good and the bad, the pleasant and the unpleasant, victory and defeat, birth and death, health and disease, truth and untruth, for without the one we could never distinguish the other. Without pain we could never know pleasure, without sorrow we could never know joy, without illness we could never know the value of health, without error we could never know the reality of truth.

(3) If you cannot accept life—and many of us obviously do not—perhaps the reason is that we have not accepted

the goodness of God in life. Therefore, we have not humility, which is another word for gratefulness; nor patience, which is another name for trust in a living God; nor even love for one another.

II. Christianity is an offer of power to find life and enjoy it. Jesus himself announced that he came from heaven to share our lives, that by his help we might have life and that abundantly.

(1) He was always begging people to "enter into life" by believing in the revelation of reality he came to give to worried, wearied, harassed people with all too few satisfactions.

(2) He asked them to surrender to his guidance and to develop their capacity to enjoy, to lay hold on eternal life—the abiding satisfactions with as much value in heaven as on earth.

(3) He called men to follow him. As they did so, he pointed out the hidden treasures, opened their minds and eyes and hearts to secret joys. As they followed, he led them out of illness, out of frustration and inhibitions, out of guilt and self-contempt, out of sin and all bondage, out of darkness and despair into light and gladness. They discovered an enormous capacity for enjoyment, which included even martyrdom. They were liberated from self-made chains and entered into their real inheritance through faith in Christ.

(4) It can be true for you, too, for Christ is not dead but a living presence in the Church, his visible Body. In the Church he calls you to him to believe his good news of available life and salvation. He charges you to come out of your self-centeredness into full possession of the joy of life through obedience to him.—Martin A. Klingberg.

SUNDAY: OCTOBER TWENTY-FIRST

MORNING SERVICE

Topic: Brotherly Love (World Order Sunday)
TEXT: Heb. 13:1.

I. *Love justifies the Christian claim.* Our claim that our religion is the truth will make the greatest impression among men when they see us living as men of love together and with love to all men everywhere. Therefore must we frequently recall the words of our Lord Jesus: "By this shall all men know that ye are my disciples, if ye have love one toward another."

II. *Love upholds in testing times.* Brotherly love will uphold us when we face the trial and testing of faith.

(1) We do know personally that in trials and sorrows the love and sympathy of an understanding friend can make us brave and hopeful. When we realize that we belong to another, who loves us in our testing, we are supported and upheld and enabled to hold on.

(2) We must hope that the same comfort comes to the Church overseas in circumstances so different from our own, when waves of love and honor go from our hearts to them, as they stand for Christ, and for us, against tyranny and Satan.

(3) We need the encouragement and strength that mutual trust and love can bring. We, too, must "wave our caps" and greet one another in the Lord as brethren, for we are all brethren for whom Christ died.

III. *Love sets a world standard.* (1) In the purpose of God part of the work and witness of the Church is for her to be a kind of living conscience in the midst of society. By her own life she is to stand as a measure or norm of human behavior, to which man should conform.

(2) In comparatively recent years, we know by the divine revelation to scientists, this world has become one neighborhood but not yet is it a brotherhood. We of this century have seen,

as it were, the arms of divine love gathered round this globe, pressing men together, closer and closer, so that they might come to see how much they need each other, whatever color or race, and that it is his purpose for brotherliness to rule instead of divisions and hatred.

(3) In this new situation, men need more than ever an example of brotherly love to follow. Is it not here that the witness of God's Church must come in? Should we not be showing what brotherly love can do between the followers of Christ across this world, and thereby giving all men a standard of life to follow?

IV. *Love the pledge of heaven.* (1) Our knowledge of that life which is to come is small. God has been pleased to veil our eyes from much which he is preparing for those who love him, and we dare not try to pry into that which is his own secret. But we do know that we shall go with Christ to a realm of love where all that is contrary to love will be banished forever, and the night of sin and sorrow will be over once and for all.

(2) Of this we are confident, and we are assured of it again and again on earth, when we taste something of the pure love as between brethren in the Lord. At once a shaft of revealing light seems to come of what is yet to be for us.—Walter A. Butcher.

Worship Aids

CALL TO WORSHIP. "Wait on the Lord: be of good courage, and he shall strengthen thine heart: wait, I say, on the Lord." Ps. 27:14.

INVOCATION. Our heavenly Father, we thy humble children invoke thy blessing upon us in this hour of worship. We adore thee, whose nature is compassion, whose presence is joy, whose Word is truth, whose spirit is goodness, whose holiness is beauty, whose will is peace, whose service is perfect freedom, and in knowledge of whom standeth our eternal life. Unto thee be all honor and all glory.

OFFERTORY SENTENCE. "Let the beauty of the Lord our God be upon us: and establish thou the work of our hands upon us; yea, the work of our hands establish thou it." Ps. 90:17.

OFFERTORY PRAYER. O God, help us so to practice by our gifts and our lives the divine principle of goodwill that in our homes, our communities, and among all the nations of the earth, men may enjoy the boon of peace.

PRAYER. O God of light and truth, in a strangely tangled time when confused cries echo through the world, we pray for the leadership of faith. Hear our prayer for the prophet vision and the light of the moral mind, lest we lose our way and wander in the dark. Thou mighty Seer, send us men endowed with the grace of insight, the gift of interpretation, and the accent of command. Speak to thy people, O Lord, for without vision they perish.

God of the prophets, give us men who share thy vision of eternal values and are not afraid of the loneliness of following the highest they know. Show us the shame of the second best, the bitterness of a joy bought at the cost of a mean timidity. O God, let thy living Word have saving power among us, rebuking our sin, working in us the miracle of love, and leading us out of the night into a new day of the Lord Jesus.—James Dalton Morrison.

Illustrations

ONE SURE ANCHOR. In the name of religion, men have wrangled over creeds and fought over theologies, each convinced that his own is the one true revelation. All through history, too, different peoples have held different official concepts of God and have ever waged war to support their beliefs. Yet, underlying all these varieties of creeds and religions one basic concept has always predominated. It is the view that there is a universal power greater than that of man's and that we must have faith in it as the one sure anchor that will support us throughout life.—Smiley Blanton.

ONLY A TOUCH. A man in a railway station saw a young blind veteran carrying a heavy suitcase step down from a train. The man offered to help with the luggage but was shrugged off. "But can't I help you?" "Yes," said the veteran, "I want to go to the information desk, but don't push me, pal. Don't possess me. All I want is the touch of your hand on my shoulder."—C. Harry Atkinson.

Sermon Suggestions

THE GOOD SAMARITAN. Jesus chose a Samaritan for his hero precisely because of what he was, what he did, and how he did it. (1) The Samaritan was a person who had found that happiness lies in living for others and not for himself. (2) The Samaritan not only saw the chance to help but also did something about it. (3) The Samaritan loved others and helped them because he first loved God and could see his fellowmen as his children.—Frank Rowley.

FIVE ATTITUDES. In the Good Samaritan the Lord has revealed the attitudes we have toward people. (1) The attitude of the thieves. They saw a victim to exploit. (2) The attitude of the priest and the Levite. To them the beaten man is a nuisance to avoid. (3) The attitude of the innkeeper. To the innkeeper, the man was only a customer to serve. (4) The attitude of the lawyer. To the lawyer, this man was a problem to discuss. (5) To the Samaritan the beaten man was a person to love and help.—Warren Wiersbe.

EVENING SERVICE

Topic: The Peril of Drifting

TEXT: Heb. 2:1 (NEB).

I. There is the lack of a goal, an objective in life. (1) People simply won't take the trouble to find out what life is all about. They have no sense of a destiny and nothing to live for beyond their own little personal aims and concerns.

(2) The true Christian has always been thought of as a pilgrim on his way to the Heavenly City. Here we have the chief safeguard against drifting—to have a goal for our life, a dominating purpose, which saves us from drifting aimlessly from one day to the next, liable to be carried away by sudden impulses and wayward desires.

II. Another great cause of drifting is indolence and slackness. (1) The Christian way is not for the indolent and spineless people whose one cry is "Let me alone and just let me follow the path of least resistance where there's no trouble and no effort required." It is for those who in the strength of God are prepared to "mount" to Eternal Life.

(2) Are we drifting or are we steering? Have we got the control of life in our own hands so that we can bring it into line with the will and purpose of God, or are we allowing external factors to carry us along, blindly and helplessly?

III. The last cause of drifting is lack of vigilance. (1) Many a man thinks he is the same as he was yesterday. But there is a difference, and every day it becomes more marked until he ends up by being just the opposite to what he was at first.

(2) But there is a difference. There is a downward drift which you don't realize, an almost imperceptible alteration, not obvious in successive days, but in years and decades enough to make the difference between heaven and hell. —Harold E. Berry.

SUNDAY: OCTOBER TWENTY-EIGHTH

MORNING SERVICE

Topic: **Our Unfinished Task (Reformation Sunday)**

I. If the Church is to lead our present world, it must reform from its petty small-mindedness.

(1) We of the Protestant churches have too long dissipated our strength in squabbles over the petty differences of denominationalism to the neglect of the great universal truths of the Gospel.

(2) The world doesn't care what the cultural or historical bases of our differences may be; they only want a spiritual faith that will redeem and unite it.

(3) It is encouraging to note the renewed emphasis on unity within the Church. If the Church is to be the redeeming force in our world, the reformation must continue until we can move with unity and not division in the task of building the Kingdom of God.

II. The Church needs to reform itself from the discrimination that it has been guilty of practicing.

(1) We have been quick to preach the brotherhood of man, but slow to practice it. Without exception, the major denominations of Protestantism have made bold and sweeping pronouncements against the evil of discrimination and enforced segregation within the Church and church-related institutions.

(2) Regrettably, it has not been the Church which has led in the practical application of brotherhood and equality for all peoples.

(3) The early Christian Church refused to allow its fellowship to exclude other races and nations. Peter broke the tradition and law of his day by entering the home of a Gentile. (See Acts 10:28.) Paul said there could be no racial distinction if one followed Christ. (See Gal. 3:28.)

III. A final consideration in the continuing reformation is the Church's need to awake from its apathy.

(1) Again and again in the life of the Church there have risen waves of apathy that have threatened to extinguish the fire of progress in the Church. Few things take less self-discipline than to drift into a state of indifference and complacency, nor is anything more contrary to the will of God. It has only been when the Church has overcome a state of apathy that progress for the Kingdom has been accomplished.

(2) Arnold Toynbee wrote that apathy can be overcome only by two things. One is an ideal that captures the imagination. The other is a definite and intelligent plan for putting that ideal into practice. The revival movements that have burned high and low throughout the life of the Church give evidence of this. In these revival periods there have always been great masses of people to respond to the ideal of Christian discipleship; but through lack of an intelligent plan for carrying that ideal into the framework of daily living, a large percentage of the so-called "converts" drift into a state of apathy.

(3) If "like a mighty army moves the Church of God" is to become a reality, then the reformation must continue until the Church has risen above the apathy that threatens to paralyze its progress. We have the ideal, but we must renew the plan of intelligent action. Only to the extent that an intelligent plan for Christian action is put into practice will the Church be able to reform from its apathy and work for the building of the Kingdom of God.—Donald E. Collins in *Pulpit Digest*.

Worship Aids

CALL TO WORSHIP. "O love the Lord, all ye his saints: for the Lord

SUNDAY: OCTOBER TWENTY-EIGHTH

preserveth the faithful. Be of good courage, and he shall strengthen your heart, all ye that hope in the Lord." Ps. 31:23-24.

INVOCATION. O thou who art the Light of the minds that know thee, the Life of the souls that love thee, and the Strength of the wills that serve thee, help us so to know thee that we may truly love thee and so to love thee that we may fully serve thee, whom to serve is perfect freedom.

OFFERTORY SENTENCE. "As every man hath received the gift, even so minister the same one to another, as good stewards of the manifold grace of God." I Pet. 4:10.

OFFERTORY PRAYER. O living Christ, help us to know the ecstasy of thine everlasting lordship that we may more perfectly become cheerful givers.

PRAYER. O holy Father, friendly to strangers and forgiving to straying sons: we bless thee for what thou art—God and Father of us all.

Continue, O God, to bear with us patiently as now in this holy place we put aside our human pride, unfasten our burdens, and kneel at thy feet. Prepare our hearts for thy mercy; make our minds sensitive to thy wisdom; convert our wills to thine.

In this presence we feel thy healing power. From the cross Christ's forgiveness comes into our spirits. We thank thee for Christ himself. We praise thee for thy saving love shown through him.

In the joy of our salvation we pray now for others. May all men come to kneel before thee, their Maker. Turn the mind of the world toward the God of men and nations. Confirm our leaders in the right as thou hast shown us the right in the Scriptures.

Beyond these prayers for others and beyond the cleansing mercy of this hour, we pray for thy companionship as we turn again to daily duties. Put a new faith in Christ within us. Make our feet obedient to thee.

May we take from this worship and from its spoken Word those thoughts which guide, that spirit which inspires, in order that we may be faithful servants of thine in the days to come.—Ralph Grieser.

Illustrations

THE STARTING POINT. The morally serious Christian asks in the midst of his concrete responsibilities and opportunities: "What ought I to do?" One answer he hears from theology is: "That is the wrong question. You cannot know what you ought to do, or can do, until you acknowledge what has been done for you and for the world. You must turn to him who is the source, power, and goal of personal life and history. Jesus Christ is the starting point; Jesus Christ the Incarnation of God, Jesus Christ the judgment of God, Jesus Christ the elect of God, Jesus Christ the victor over sin and death. Jesus Christ is the reality of moral life. He objectively rules. He is the King and Head of every man. He reveals God. What you ought to do is bear witness in your action to what has been done. Walk in the light. What you can do is express in your moral life the power of Christ who reigns within and without."—James M. Gustafson in *Christ and the Moral Life* (New York: Harper & Row, 1968).

ALTERNATIVE. Billy Graham told of a conversation with a leading theoretician of the new left. This radical leader said, "Within five years we shall have either revolution or dictatorship." "Can anything stop it?" Graham asked. "Only one thing can stop it, and that is a religious awakening."—*Christianity Today*.

Sermon Suggestions

WHAT HAVE YOU DONE TODAY THAT ONLY A CHRISTIAN WOULD DO? Text: Luke 11:28. (1) Did you put first the things of the Kingdom? (2) Did you seek to lift another's burdens? (3) Were you faithful in your God-given stewardship? (4) Did you seek to lead someone into the fellowship of Jesus Christ?—R. Frank Porter, Jr.

WHAT IN THE WORLD IS THE CHURCH FOR? Text: Rev. 2:7 (RSV). (1) Whether we approve or disapprove, the Church is here to be involved in our changing, confusing, and chaotic world. (2) The Church is here today to call us to a deeply committed fellowship. (3) The Church is here today to proclaim to the world a balanced, full-orbed gospel. (4) The Church is here to fulfill the evangelistic, missionary aim and passion.—Jerry Dooling.

EVENING SERVICE

Topic: Why the Church-Related College? (Youth Sunday)

I. Christianity, perhaps more than some other religions, must maintain reliable access to the past. It had a crucially historical origin and has had an important and continuous history ever since. Not to know the sense in which this is so is to lack an essential understanding of the religion which your church seeks to embody and in which, as member, you participate. For any church professing to be Christian, reliable access to the past is an essential life-line. In a certain sense, Christianity and its churches are at the mercy of responsible historical scholarship. A church-related college which leaves its customers unaware of this, and of the significance of this, is selling them short.

II. Christianity consists of a considerable body of doctrines or teachings. I do not know whether all of these are theological, but a great number of them are. To the extent that this is so, the theologian, like the historian, is essential to the life of Christianity and its churches, and therefore relevant to the life of the church-related college. My suggestion is not that a church-related college should be either a truncated theological seminary or a glorified Sunday School. But I suppose you can say that, as church-related, it is concerned to produce a liberally and relevantly educated laity.

(1) If you ask, "What does a college get, from being church-related?" one answer is: access to a class of persons who will benefit by the college's power to confer a liberal education in respect to the history, doctrines, and literature of Christianity. It may get more than this, and, as matters go, this is an advantage to the college.

(2) If you ask, "What does a church get from being college-related?" the answer is: a liberally and relevantly educated laity; and as matters go, this is an advantage to the Church.

III. With few exceptions, the church-related college is today the sole effective alternative to the state-related, tax-supported college. So long as church-related colleges are there, they stand as a small but important bulwark against a condition which I would regard as highly objectionable. If college education became a state-monopoly, comparable to legislation and taxation and armed services, so that receivers of such education were of necessity beholden to governments and to no one else, the results would be disastrous for education, for governments, for churches, and in the end for the nation as a whole. As matters stand today the church-related colleges provide a small but effective check on such a monopoly. Because they are so few and so small, it may be that their effectiveness lies in providing an untarnished symbol of alternativity.—Alburey Castell in *The Church-Related College Today: Anachronism or Opportunity.*

SUNDAY: NOVEMBER FOURTH

MORNING SERVICE

Topic: Accept the Challenge or Cease to Grow
Scripture: Heb. 5:12–6:2.

Life is a growing process. Where there is no growth, death sets in. But growth means effort, pain, and struggle. Every stage of growth is a challenge. Progress, or growth, takes place only when one is prepared to accept the challenge of life and all that that challenge entails.

I. It may take place when we are confronted with the truth of life. (1) The people in Jesus' time heard the truth of the Gospel, but only a handful of them had the courage to accept the challenge. These paid the price and received the fuller and more abundant life. We now know them as saints of God.

(2) Many people are similarly challenged today when they hear the truth of the Gospel preached. Those who accept the challenge experience the fuller life; those who fail to accept the challenge for fear of men postpone life. They have wronged themselves; they cease to grow!

II. Whenever we are confronted with human need, we are challenged. The story of the Good Samaritan reveals to us that when the priest and the Levite saw the poor, wounded man by the roadside, they were challenged to do something for that man. However, they simply excused themselves and passed by on the other side. They failed to accept the challenge. They saved themselves some trouble and financial loss, but they forfeited the larger and more useful life. We are surrounded by human needs which cry for relief. They are challenges to richer and more useful life. If we fail to accept, we cease to grow!

III. Whenever we are confronted with the crises of life, we are thereby challenged. In our intercourse with our fellowmen, we may be tempted to be dishonest. Here is a challenge! To accept the challenge may mean financial loss, but spiritual growth through the process.

IV. We may be tempted to be selfish. Perhaps no one will know that we have refused to accept the challenge to be unselfish. Our souls, however, have by that failure been deprived of the opportunity for growth, radiancy, and unselfishness.

V. We may be tempted to impurity of thought or life. If we accept the challenge to be pure, we may lose some friends or be laughed at by others, but our souls will surely be ennobled.

VI. We may be tempted to be unloving, malicious, and revengeful. It is not easy to overcome such human failings except by the help of the Holy Spirit and a firm determination to be loving under whatever circumstances. If we succeed, life instantly becomes sweet and beautiful, radiant with goodwill and love!

VII. Many people live under the false impression that the Christian life begins and ends with the only challenge being to accept Jesus as our Savior. That is just the beginning; we must be continually accepting challenges to the larger and fuller life, or else we cease to grow. The writer of the Epistle to the Hebrews had in mind those Christians who had stopped growing because they thought they could live on their past experiences. There are, at the present time, hosts of Christian laymen and ministers who have ceased to grow spiritually and are trying to live on their past experiences. The writer was impatient with Christians who had ceased to grow because they had not been accepting challenges to the larger and fuller life that is in Christ Jesus.—Chew Hock Hin.

Worship Aids

CALL TO WORSHIP. "Ho, every one that thirstest, come ye to the waters. Incline your ear, and come unto me: hear, and your soul shall live; and I will make an everlasting covenant with you, even the sure mercies of David." Isa. 55:1, 3.

INVOCATION. Eternal God our Father, who art from everlasting, thou hast made us and not we ourselves. Thou hast set us never far from thee, that we, thy children, may learn the ways of freedom and choose thee with all our hearts. Grant us now thy Holy Spirit, that confident in prayer, we may worship thee with gladness, and become as little children before thee.

OFFERTORY SENTENCE. "As we have therefore opportunity, let us do good unto all men, especially unto them who are of the household of faith." Gal. 6:10.

OFFERTORY PRAYER. Almighty God, whose loving hand hath given us all that we possess: grant us grace that we may honor thee with our substance, and remembering the account which we must one day give, may be faithful stewards of thy bounty.—*Book of Common Prayer.*

PRAYER. Father of Lights, in whom there is no shadow, Giver of every good and perfect gift, to thee cherubim and seraphim continually do cry, "Holy, Holy, Holy, Lord God of Sabaoth, heaven and earth are full of the majesty of thy glory." The glorious company of the apostles, the goodly fellowship of the prophets, and the noble army of martyrs praise thee. We would be worthy of the glorious company, worthy of the goodly fellowship, worthy of the noble army. Lift our hearts above the clamor and chaos of our time, above the darkness of our day, into the white light of thy presence.

Bring forth before our wondering eyes thy treasures both new and old: forgiveness for the contrite heart, joy for the stricken spirit, and the peace that passeth all understanding for the longing soul. Bury forever in the tomb of thy forgetfulness our restlessness, our fretfulness, our pettiness, and our waywardness, and enable us to view beyond the altar of sacrifice the mount of jubilation. Oft have we walked with Christ in Olivet, oft have we been his guests in the upper room, oft have we stood beneath his cross. Sanctify our thanksgiving as we remember his victory, and behold the King in his beauty, the Resurrection and the Life.—Walter A. Scholten.

Illustrations

GUIDANCE. When in doubt, do the most Christlike thing, and you will not go wrong. If any guidance seems to be at variance at any point with what you see in Christ, then doubt that guidance, for it cannot be of God, however implemented by reason or emotion.—E. Stanley Jones.

SPIRITUAL AND MATERIAL. The spiritually minded man does not differ from the materially minded man chiefly in thinking about different things, but in thinking about the same things differently.—William Temple.

Sermon Suggestions

ABIDING IN CHRIST. Text: John 15:5. How does one abide in Christ? (1) We must accept Christ as our Savior. We must "put on Christ" (Gal. 3:27). We abide in him by letting his Spirit abide in us. (2) We abide in Christ through his Word. (3) We abide in Christ by bearing fruit.—Jacqueline Westers.

OUR THIRST FOR GOD. Text: Ps. 63:1. (1) It is the most sacred thing about us. (2) It tells us of the purpose for which we were born. (3) It points to the end we are meant to find. (4)

It tells of the life we are intended to live. (5) It is only when we early seek God, when we remember him upon our beds and meditate upon him in the night watches, when our flesh longs for him, when our souls follow hard after him, that he meets us and we meet him.—Paul W. Hoon.

EVENING SERVICE

Topic: The Grace to Say No (World Temperance Day)

TEXT: Rom. 12:2 (PHILLIPS).

We are living in a permissive society, in a time when much that is evil goes unchallenged. It is not easy to go against current mores and to stand up and say no when one is convinced that something is contrary to the holy will of God. But exactly that is necessary. The Bible offers many examples of men who were able to say no at a crucial time in their lives.

I. Abraham said no to the natural desire to stay in his own home and with his own people when God had called him to go out, not knowing where he was going. He said no to the natural impulse to spare his son, Isaac. (See Heb. 11:17.)

II. Moses said no to the impulse to stay in the affluence and security of Pharaoh's household. (See Heb. 11:24–26.)

III. Joseph said no when tempted by a beautiful woman who offered her body and her companionship to a lonely young man. (See Gen. 39:9.)

IV. Daniel said no when confronted with a preferment that included turning from a Spartan way of life to eating food from the king's table. (See Dan. 1:8.)

V. Daniel's three companions said no to temptation to save their lives by bowing before the image Nebuchadnezzar had set up. (See Dan. 3:16–18.)

VI. Later Daniel again said no, confronted this time with the temptation to buy safety at the cost of compromise by obeying the king's decree against public worship. (See Dan. 6:10.)

VII. All of us face the seemingly overwhelming temptation to trim our sails in these days of permissive living. When temptation comes, it is so much easier to compromise a little to avoid criticism or even reprisals.

(1) The grace to say no must be exercised with the assurance that God has not left his children to grope in darkness. Rather, he has made plain a way of life that is alien to this world but just as real as the air we breathe and the food that sustains our bodies.

(2) The grace to say no is one that must be cultivated, not with a hard, unyielding stubbornness but with the joy of knowing that God is a personal God, that he is deeply concerned with every detail of our lives, and that he will surely open up the way he wants us to take.—L. Nelson Bell in *Christianity Today.*

SUNDAY: NOVEMBER ELEVENTH

MORNING SERVICE

Topic: We Need to Give (Stewardship Day)

TEXT: I Pet. 4:10.

Giving is good for the giver. To give without thought of getting a return meets a need in the giver. We generally think of giving as helping the receiver. The need is present in the person or the cause to which the gift is made. Giving benefits the receiver. Giving also meets a need in the giver. For his own good, he needs to give.

Why is giving necessary for the giver? Why do we need to give?

I. A person who always receives and never gives becomes like a stagnant pool without an outlet. His life becomes self-centered. He thinks only of what others can do for him, seldom of what he can do for them.

II. We need the thrill of helping someone or of having a part in furthering a cause that needs us. Life gets dull when we no longer have anything to give. The person who lives only for himself and spends money only on himself, soon gets tired of himself. He is missing one of the joys of living. Giving makes life worth living.

III. Giving is especially necessary for the Christian. He needs some way to express his gratitude. Gratitude is in the very foundation of Christian faith. The good news of the Gospel proclaims not what God demands of us but what he has done for us. He took the initiative of good will toward us. "While we were yet sinners, Christ died for us." This is cause for praise and gratitude.

IV. The emotion of gratitude needs to be more than a momentary feeling or an impetuous outburst. We need to do more than shout with joy: "Thanks be to God for his unspeakable gift." Paul wrote these words when he wanted to remind his readers of their need to give. Thanksgiving means giving with thanks. Gratitude for what we have received needs expression through giving.

V. All giving has two aspects. On the one hand, we would like to know whether our giving is meeting a genuine need. Good stewardship calls for careful selection in the causes for which one gives. On the other hand, the health, the spiritual health, of the giver is also involved. He needs to give for his own good.

VI. Wilfred T. Grenfell made a memorable statement concerning the good that giving does for the giver: "There is a flavor about the return for the money and time and strength that one spends, however indirectly, in accomplishing things for the benefit of others which no amount of money spent on self in any other way whatever can give. It is like the aroma of the early morning air in the country, not contributed by any one thing, such as the possession of a diamond ring or going around eighteen holes in bogey or driving in one's own Rolls Royce. It seems to make the whole of life over."—Rolland W. Schloerb.

Worship Aids

CALL TO WORSHIP. "Blessed is the man that trusteth in the Lord, and whose hope the Lord is." Jer. 17:7.

INVOCATION. Most humbly do we thank thee, O Lord, for thy mercies of every kind, and thy loving care over all thy creatures. We bless thee for the gift of life; for thy protection round about us; for thy guiding hand upon us and the many tokens of thy love; especially for the saving knowledge of thy dear Son, our Savior; and for friendship and duty; for good hopes and precious memories; for the joys that cheer us and for the trials that teach us to trust in thee. O heavenly Father, make us wise unto a right use of thy benefits, and so direct us that in word and deed we may show gratitude to thee.

OFFERTORY SENTENCE. "Thy prayers and thine alms are come up for a memorial before God." Acts 10:4.

OFFERTORY PRAYER. Our Father, we thank thee that thou art so generous to us. All that we have is a gift from thee. Help us to serve one another so that we may reflect thy spirit and goodness.

PRAYER. O Holy Father, have mercy upon us, and hasten the day when there shall be unity in the Church and friendship among the nations of thy world. May every barrier be broken down until brotherhood shall be fully manifested according to the mind of Jesus Christ our Lord, in factory, shop, store, field, mine, government, and wherever else men are. Grant that men shall hold money lightly and shall cease to defraud and oppress one another, and

SUNDAY: NOVEMBER ELEVENTH

that the stewardship of divine love be held so sacredly that we shall be restless and ill at ease because of the world's discontent and the coldness of unbrotherly attitudes. May thy Holy Spirit be less grieved as the days go by because of our impenitence, until the path of truth leads us into divine freedom.—*Prayers for the Christian Year.*

Illustrations

WORTH ADVERTISING. A little girl on her vacation in the country saw her first rainbow. As she looked at the colors against the sky, the little girl cried to her mother, "O, Mummy, what's it advertising?" The rainbow was advertising something that very much needs to be advertised, namely, those values in life which are of worth regardless of sale price.—Harold Cooke Phillips.

RESCUER. One simple, devoted Christian cried to God, "I don't want to be saved out of a damned world." I don't want to be saved and see others perish. I don't want to be one of the ninety-and-nine safe, comfortable ones. I want to be out on the hills with the Good Shepherd, seeking that poor, hunted miserable creature that is lost.—E. J. Webb.

Sermon Suggestions

GOD'S RICHEST MEN. (1) Those who are rich toward God are those who hold their lives faithfully as trusts under God. (2) God's richest men are those who invest their lives wisely. (3) God's richest men are those who give themselves generously.—Ralph W. Sockman.

PARTNERSHIP WITH GOD. There are three basic principles of partnership with God: (1) God owns all. "The earth is the Lord's and the fullness thereof." (2) Man owes all. "What hast thou that thou hast not received?" (3) Man occupies only. "Give account of thy stewardship." We only possess as a trust and are responsible and accountable to God.

EVENING SERVICE

Topic: **The Need and the Possession**
TEXT: I Cor. 6:19.

How careful one must be when it comes to acknowledging the great needs of one's life!

I. If we feel that we have been injured, mistreated, abused—then because of this treatment we will feel the need of revenge, that we must get even, that we must show certain individuals that they cannot overrun us with immunity. Thus feeling this need for hatred, revenge, jealousy, we come to be owned by these forces of life. They rule our judgment; they demand conduct of which we come to be ashamed. We discover that we are not acting as we formerly did; we are not our own, for we are possessed by these forces which we have come to feel we need badly.

II. Or we find the individual who feels the need of the pleasures of life, of the trivial things, which may not be bad in themselves but are simply trivial. We may feel the need of the wild excesses of life. We must have drink; we must find our thrill in gambling; we must waste ourselves in the wild excesses. Whatever it is that we have come to feel we need, whatever we have gone forth seeking to satisfy—lo! we discover that the very things we felt we needed have come to own us. We are possessed by the trivial, by the low and vulgar, by appetites for what will destroy body and soul. These things which we felt we needed now own us.

III. But there is the one who has felt the need in his life for the better things, the higher things, the spiritual things; and having felt that need, comes to discover that those very forces which he felt he needed have come to own him. This is beautifully expressed in one of the beatitudes of Jesus. (See Matt.

5:6.) The one who feels the great craving for goodness, for the right things of life, discovers that he is possessed by, owned by, those very things which he desired. Righteousness and goodness have come to own him, and through that ownership his soul finds its greatest peace and satisfaction.

IV. It is then we make the great discovery that the greatness of a man's life is not to be measured by the things which he possesses but by the forces which possess him. What needs me belongs to me, and what I need and seek comes to possess me. The recognition of these great truths is extremely necessary for successful, abundant living.—Guy O. Carpenter.

SUNDAY: NOVEMBER EIGHTEENTH

MORNING SERVICE

Topic: Thanksgiving This Time (Thanksgiving Sunday)

The gravest commentary on any institution is that it cannot be spoken of, thought about, or otherwise considered without those worn-out niceties and clichés which are absorbed by the mind without leaving a trace. As an institution in the American culture, Thanksgiving is reaching that point.

(a) To probe below the sugarcoated truisms we associate with this holiday and to attempt to redefine its relevancy to our time is to grope for something of the personal impact of the day's opportunities. It is a blind search because our sight has been filled with visions of abundance and comfort. We seek the personal impact which goes beyond the sentimentalities of family and home and much deeper than the traditionally overworked digestive tract.

(b) In our day, Thanksgiving implies and symbolizes plenty, the watchword of middle-class America. This is ironic because in seventeenth-century Massachusetts the thanks given by Colonists at Plymouth was for bare survival. The fact that a large number of their company perished during the first winter did not shatter their faith. They could still thank God.

(c) It is both fascinating and disturbing to note that throughout history when a nation or a person exemplified the spirit of thanksgiving, it was the result of a crisis experience through which faith had survived and been deepened. Whether in the ancient Hebrew holy days or the subsequent tribulations of history's afflicted peoples, the thanks-evoking factor was most strongly in evidence when a crisis had been passed and faith's survival marked a victory rather than when abundance and comfort prevailed.

(d) Protestations of sinfulness, two-minute prayers at the overladen table, and pictures of the Pilgrims notwithstanding, Thanksgiving is becoming a time of thanksgetting in the crassness of our age. We seem convinced that God is expressing appreciation for our goodness by blessing us with abundance.

I. Why this self-righteousness is becoming increasingly prevalent makes an interesting subject for speculation.

(1) Even with installment buying, it seems inconceivable to the mass of American humanity—living in abundance and comfort, isolated from the harshness of the world's struggles and revolutions—that their survival is in question.

(2) What is more, there appears to be no conception of having recently survived anything which should bring about the deeply personal giving of thanks we find manifested at critical points in our heritage.

(3) From our perspective of security, we fail to see anything to evoke a self-transcending sense of gratitude from the innermost chambers of our lives. But we are still a part of the thanksgiving heritage. So we offer our shal-

low and superficial expressions which reflect what may or may not be a conscious belief that we, the righteous ones, have been rewarded as we deserve by a grateful God.

II. It may be that we have survived a crisis, as far as life goes, unaware. Our faith may have been the victim. Our relationship to God may have atrophied and vanished.

(1) The crisis may have been galloping secularism; it may have been institutionalism or clericalism. It may have been, or still be, any of several other nebulous phantoms on which our attention is focused by theologians and sociologists. The price for survival, in a socially acceptable manner, may have been our faith in God.

(2) Society is becoming more and more willing to substitute religion for faith. The form and the institutions—religion—are beginning to satisfy the need of people to relate to that which is beyond them, without getting beyond the form by nurturing faith. The means of growth toward God is replacing the growth itself. It is as though we are content in having an organ without ever using it to create music.

(3) There is now a crisis which faith may not overcome and survive. Unless we recognize where we are in the development of man's growth toward God in the faith relationship and unless we nurture this faith so that it can survive the developing crisis, then our age will pass, leaving shells of creatures who once had a meaningful association with their God. Living, to be sure, but dead to the life.

III. Thanksgiving this time has to be a time for discovery and renewal.

(1) The discovery which must be made is the difference between "Let us say thanks" and "Let us give thanks." The renewal must begin with the confession that too often we have said "thanks" and let this end our response to God's love. In this discovery and renewal, Thanksgiving can take on redemptive significance. Even as we redeem this holy day, so also do we start again to be redemptively related to our God.

(2) "Thanks" is a rather vague concept. One doesn't give a basket of thanks or carry a satchel of it around. The easiest thing in the world, because this is true, is to assume that giving thanks means simply saying thanks. Saying thanks is not the same as giving thanks, any more than saying "I love you" is the same as testifying to love in acts of giving of oneself.

(3) It is in the engagement with God, in actively giving ourselves to him in gratitude, that the redemptive nature of thanksgiving develops. Consider for a moment what your thanksgiving will be this year. How much giving of yourself will there be? How much taking in will you do?—Richard N. Rinker.

Worship Aids

CALL TO WORSHIP. "O come, let us sing unto the Lord: let us make a joyful noise to the rock of our salvation. Let us come before his presence with thanksgiving, and make a joyful noise unto him with psalms." Ps. 95:1–2.

INVOCATION. O God, in glory exalted and in mercy ever blessed, we magnify thee, we praise thee, we give thanks unto thee for thy bountiful providence, for all the blessings of this present life, and all the hopes of a better life to come. Let the memory of thy goodness, we beseech thee, fill our hearts with joy and thankfulness.

OFFERTORY SENTENCE. "Offer unto God thanksgiving; and pay thy vows unto the most High." Ps. 50:14.

OFFERTORY. Almighty and everlasting God, who hast graciously given us the fruits of the earth in their season: we yield thee humble and hearty thanks for these thy bounties, beseeching thee to give us grace rightly to use them to thy glory and the relief of all in need.

PRAYER. O God, whose gift is faith

and hope through Jesus Christ, we bless thee also for the lovingkindness which has brought us comfort all along the way. Thine are these changing skies, this earth that ripens corn for bread and flowers for beauty, these walls that shelter us from cold and storm, these hopes that cheer. In every day's renewal of our life with thee, in countless gifts, unrecognized, which join to make our hearts content, in all the kindly affections of our human fellowship, we look to thee with grateful hearts. Enlarge our souls that those who love us may have more to love. Quicken our consciences that we may desire more of the beauty of thy holiness. Endow us with strength and wisdom that we may serve our generation before we fall asleep. And abide thou with us in purity and power forevermore.—Isaac O. Rankin.

Illustrations

THE PILGRIM'S THANKSGIVING. To the Pilgrim, a blessing was the security of firm soil underfoot after months of hardship at sea; the fragrance of newly cut grain as the first harvest was brought in; the sight of the first snowfall heralding a few months' reprieve from the peril of Indian raids; the joy of publicly praising God, unfettered by the dictates of old-world doctrine. To the Pilgrim, who deliberately chose suffering for the sake of freedom, there were no "small" blessings. The mere fact of survival was so precious a gift that Thanksgiving was more than a special day of gratitude; it was a continual state of mind.

THOSE WHO GIVE THANKS. A farmer was invited to dine with a city friend. Before partaking of the sumptuous meal, the farmer bowed his head and silently thanked God for the food.

His ungrateful host said: "You are old-fashioned, I see. I never pray before meals."

The farmer said: "I always give thanks to God before I eat the good things he has so graciously provided. There are some creatures on my farm, however, who never pray over their meals."

"Ah," said the host, "they are up to date and enlightened. Who are they?"

The farmer replied: "They are my pigs!"

Sermon Suggestions

WHY THANKSGIVING? (1) Let us be thankful for God, who provides all things temporal, and who "spared not his own Son" so that penitent sinners could gain a life fit for eternity. (2) Let us be thankful for life and health and shelter and food. (3) Let us be thankful for a land of liberty and for courageous young men still ready to put patriotism above self-interest. (4) Let us be thankful for a land in which persuasion and law still count for more than disorder and violence. (5) Let us, as Americans, be thankful for one another.—*Christianity Today.*

GIVE THANKS FOR THE UNSEEN. (1) How often do we thank God for the mind with its outlying islands: conscience, imagination, and memory? (2) How often do we thank God for the ties that unite family and friends? Don't these ties exist because of the presence in life of a spirit of love and understanding? (3) How often do we thank God for the promises, given by Christ, of a continuous life beyond the horizon of our mortal sight?— Ernest R. Case in *The War Cry.*

IN EVERYTHING GIVE THANKS. Text: Phil. 4:11–12 (PHILLIPS). How was Paul able to give thanks in all circumstances? (1) He was assured of his own personal salvation. (2) Paul was sure of God's continuous care. (3) Paul was enabled by grace. (4) Paul learned to look beyond the immediate.—Carl Herndon.

LESSONS FROM THE PILGRIMS. (1) The Pilgrims have left us an example of their deep, unwavering religious convictions. (2) The Pilgrims have left us an example of disciplined living. (3) They have left us the example of freedom under law. (4) The Pilgrims have left us their example of a people who had keen social concern. (5) The Pilgrims were evangelists who set us an example in sharing their spiritual and material blessings with others. (6) The Pilgrims were men of vision and hope.—Billy Graham in *Decision*.

THE GOODNESS OF GOD.   Text: Ps. 27:13. (1) In the goodness of God we possess life and live and move and have our being in God. (2) In the goodness of God life has one increasing purpose, and we are given the secret of entering into that purpose. (3) In the goodness of God life is destined to wear the crown of triumph if by faith in Christ we endure faithful to the end.—John W. McKelvey.

EVENING SERVICE

Topic: Charisma Is a Christian Word
TEXT: I Cor. 12:4–5.

Charisma, in the New Testament, derives from the Greek word *charis,* meaning "grace." (a) Grace is the little word that contains all we know of the Gospel. Our sense of God's presence—that is grace. His help when we are weak—that is grace. His forgiveness of our sins—that is grace. Grace is the love of God in action; grace is divine healing; grace is suffering transmuted into hope and joy; grace is everything that Christ means to those who know him.

(b) A charisma, then, is a gift of God that flows from his grace. It is an endowment of the Spirit and can take many different forms. "There are varieties of gifts (the word is *charismata*), but the same Spirit." The Church known in the earliest days as the community where ordinary men and women were transformed by the Spirit of God, and each one had his own special charisma. The Epistle to the Hebrews says, "God added his testimony by signs, by miracles, by manifold works of power, and by distributing the gifts [*charismata*] of the Holy Spirit at his own will" (2:4, NEB).

I. The Christian charisma is not the possession of a small elite. It is given to all who believe.

II. Charisma in the New Testament is the gift of the Spirit of Christ and is, therefore, exercised solely in the service of others.

III. Unlike this modern charisma which just seems to happen where the lightning strikes, Christian charisma is a gift to be sought and found and a gift that grows.—David H. C. Read in *Presbyterian Life*.

SUNDAY: NOVEMBER TWENTY-FIFTH

MORNING SERVICE

Topic: Has Suffering Any Meaning?
TEXTS: John 9:3; II Cor. 7:10.

I. Suffering has no necessary meaning in itself; it acquires meaning only as God is allowed to guide and direct it. That is to say, apart from God, suffering is just as apt to make its victims bitter as to make them better.

(1) If God is allowed to guide the suffering, it can make its bearers finer in character and more useful and profitable servants in the Kingdom of God.

(2) It can make its bearers more serious and less shallow, superficial, and frivolous. It can waken them to the fact that life is real and earnest and should be lived not flippantly nor thoughtlessly but greatly and worthily in view of the momentousness of its issues.

II. The pain that God is allowed to guide can make us more sensitive, more deeply aware of other people's needs, difficulties, and problems, and of how we can help in the overcoming of these problems.

III. The pain that God is allowed to guide can make us more serviceable to him through Jesus Christ; can, in fact, make us more fruitful agents of his cause and Kingdom.

(1) The clearest illustration of this in the New Testament is the case of Paul's thorn in the flesh, concerning which he speaks in II Cor. 12. Paul does not specifically state what this thorn was. All kinds of guesses have been made. Some have maintained that Paul was referring to the solicitations of the flesh. Others have contended that he was referring to a personal enemy, such as Alexander the coppersmith, who did him much harm. The more usual kind of interpretation, however, has suggested that Paul was speaking about some physical disease or handicap, such as malaria or opthalmia, so common in the East, and calculated to make life a misery.

(2) Whatever Paul's thorn was, clearly it interfered drastically with his work. It made him incapable of doing anything while it lasted and even made him appear loathsome in the eyes of strangers. He does not hesitate to speak of it as "a messenger of Satan to buffet me."

(3) Quite naturally, Paul besought the Lord thrice—and this means not simply three times, but repeatedly and continuously—that the thorn might depart. God, however, did not remove the thorn. Rather, he answered Paul's prayer by giving him grace to overcome the thorn. So Paul, having learned the lesson, having allowed God to guide his pain, says this: "Most gladly therefore will I rather glory in my infirmities, that the power of Christ may rest upon me" (II Cor. 12:9).—Norman Victor Hope.

Worship Aids

CALL TO WORSHIP. "We have thought of thy lovingkindness, O God, in the midst of thy temple. According to thy name, O God, so is thy praise unto the ends of the earth." Ps. 48:9–10.

INVOCATION. As we begin another day, most gracious Father, make us to know that we never drift out of thy love and care. Faces may change, conditions may alter, but thou art never so near to us as when we need thee most.

OFFERTORY SENTENCE. "He that hath a bountiful eye shall be blessed; for he giveth of his bread to the poor." Prov. 22:9.

OFFERTORY PRAYER. Our Father, who desirest the love and fellowship of all: enable us so to witness by our lives and by these our gifts that others may be drawn to thy Kingdom.

PRAYER. O Lord, our eternal God, we come to you in the quietness of this hour, just as we are. We make no claim of goodness in ourselves, but even so we come to worship. We come to praise. We come to give thanks. Accept us, Lord, as your children; we cannot ask for more. Help us to express our thanks in our hearts and lives rather than in words. We know that living what we believe to be right speaks with greater force than do the words we speak.

Bless us, Lord, as we wait before you. Each one of us needs your blessing and your forgiveness. We have done many things which we should not have done. Many of the things which we have done have not represented the best we could do. So, we pray, strengthen us in our resolve and determination to live a life more pleasing to you.

Comfort those who mourn; heal those who are sick, both in body and soul; bring peace to those who are troubled; stir up the lazy and indifferent, so that all might receive your blessing and your love.

Be near to those who are in authority in our land and in the nations of

SUNDAY: NOVEMBER TWENTY-FIFTH

the world. Give them guidance. May they always look to you for direction as they face the problems which are before them. Help them to deal with all people as brothers.

Grant, O Lord, that what is said and done here today be for your glory and for our good.—Fred J. Miller.

Illustrations

FAMILY LEGEND. Cousin Hannah was living through one of those winters when every known calamity descends on a family. She was a buoyant soul, but when her mother broke her hip, Hannah expressed her bitterness in a manner that has since become a family legend. She said, "I know the Lord won't send me more trouble than I have strength to bear, but I do wish he didn't have quite such a good opinion of me!"—*World Religious News.*

BALLAST. I regard the mixture of the sad and the joyous experiences of life after the analogy of a ship. There are parts of a ship so heavy that by themselves they would sink—the engine, the propeller, and other features. But built together in a ship, the craft floats. These parts of a ship which are heavier than water are necessary to make a ship sail. We cannot use a boat unless there is weight enough to give it draught. We even put ballast in a boat to make it serviceable. Likewise in life, without heavy experiences which sometimes threaten to sink us, burdens, sufferings we call crosses—without these our lives would lack the ballast to keep them going.—Ralph W. Sockman.

GREATEST MIRACLE. In Lourdes where people come to be healed by the miracle waters, a priest was once asked by a newspaper reporter the most impressive miracle he had ever seen at Lourdes. The reporter expected him to talk about the amazing recovery of someone who had come to Lourdes ill and walked away well. "Not at all," the old priest said. "If you want to know the greatest miracle that I have ever seen at Lourdes, it is the look of radiant resignation on the faces of those who turn away unhealed."—Charles A. McClain, Jr.

Sermon Suggestions

STRENGTH IN WEAKNESS. Text: II Cor. 12:10. Paul could speak about suffering for several reasons. (1) Because he had met Jesus Christ on the Damascus road. (2) Because he was overwhelmed by the love of God. (3) Because he had learned that almost from the beginning God worked in the pattern of bringing good out of evil, glory out of tribulation, strength out of weakness.—John Primus.

WHY PRAY? Again and again Jesus left a busy ministry among the multitudes to withdraw into a lonely place and pray. Why? (1) In prayer he found strength to fulfill his mission. (2) Our Lord evidently believed that his prayers had profound effects upon the lives of others. (3) Jesus prayed because he trusted in the Father's love, a love which seeks for fellowship, for communion.—William C. Brownson, Jr.

EVENING SERVICE

Topic: Show Us the Father
TEXT: John 14:9.

It was because the God whom Jesus knew, loved, and sought to reveal to men had such a high regard for man that Jesus did what he did and said what he said, and in the end could answer one of his disciple's requests, "Show us the Father," by saying, "He that hath seen me hath seen the Father." What did he do?

I. He put a supreme value on human life, making it crystal clear that people are of infinite importance to their Creator and, therefore, should enjoy respect and a dignified position in the eyes of all men.

II. He made it clear by his own relationship with God that it is not only possible, but the very desire of God, that men should have intimate fellowship with God. They should pray, believing that God hears prayer and that he is ready, willing, eager, and able to hear the prayers which ascend from humble, receptive hearts.

III. Jesus so gave himself to helping people live complete, fulfilled lives that he succeeded in getting it across to those from every walk of life that God wants to help them live life at its glorious best.

(1) In some instances this meant that they needed forgiveness; needed to be relieved of the past so that they could "arise, take up their beds and walk" out into an experience of life renewed.

(2) In other cases this meant finding a purpose which would really make life worth living, something over and above and beyond themselves.

(3) For all it meant such a complete devotion to the will of God, as they discovered it through careful thought and prayer, that they were overtaken with a sense of divine compulsion.

IV. Jesus, by living a life of absolute trust in God, revealed to us that God can be trusted. He is the undergirding, supporting Spirit which is ever present to give us healing for all our diseases of the body, mind, and spirit. He is the God of all comfort who never leaves us nor forsakes us, for underneath are his everlasting arms. He is the God of the living to whom our spirits return when the "fever of life is over and the weary world is hushed." He is the one who gives us peace at last, simply because we are his children and he is our Father.—Homer J. R. Elford.

SUNDAY: DECEMBER SECOND

MORNING SERVICE

Topic: The Dangerous Christ (Advent)

TEXT: Isa. 52:15, RSV.

We most often think of the Messiah as the Comforter who comes with healing in his wings, speaking peace to troubled hearts. But Isaiah writes: "So shall he startle many nations" (Isa. 52:15, RSV). Here the Messiah is seen as one who disturbs, startles, and confounds. For some he will be a Deliverer, for others a Disturber. Christ endangers the thought patterns and way of life of those who hear him.

I. Christ is a danger to closed and prejudiced minds. It has been said that there is no pain like the pain of a new idea. We all have our own little thought-world that we do not want disturbed.

(1) The closed mind of the first century passed Bethlehem by despite the Prophet Micah's word that the Messiah was to be born there.

(2) The closed mind of Nathaniel answered Philip's invitation to come and see Jesus with the question, "Can any good thing come out of Nazareth?" —and yet Jesus hallowed Nazareth by spending thirty years of his life there.

(3) The closed mind of the Jews who heard Jesus teach at the feast of tabernacles led them to ask, "How is it that this man has learning, when he has never studied?" Yet Jesus has been the inspiration for the founding of more schools and the writing of more books than anyone else. None of our prejudices are safe in the presence of Christ.

II. Christ is a danger to selfish interests. His stand on greed and exploitation is startling indeed. Listen to him: "Whoever would save his life will lose it; and whoever loses his life for my sake, he will save it." And again, "What does it profit a man, to gain the whole world and forfeit his life?"

(1) Was it not dangerous for the rich young ruler to come to Jesus with the question, "Teacher, what good deed must I do, to have eternal life?" For Jesus' reply was, "Go, sell what you possess and give to the poor . . . and come, follow me." The price was too great. The young man loved his possessions too much, and he went away sorrowful. But he went away.

(2) Was it not dangerous for the scribes and the Pharisees to expose themselves to Jesus' withering blasts about greed that hides beneath the cloak of religion? He said to them, "You devour widows' houses and for a pretense make long prayers; therefore you shall receive the greater damnation."

(3) Was it not dangerous for two of his disciples and their mother to request the chief seats in the coming Kingdom? Jesus let them know immediately that honors are not passed out in the Kingdom as politicians pass them out here. In reply to their request, Jesus asked, "Are you able to be baptized with my baptism?" And he gave us the guideline for our lives when he said, "Seek first his kingdom and his righteousness, and all these things shall be yours as well."

(4) Christ still stands as the greatest menace to greed and selfishness. We need desperately to learn that any evil promoted for selfish gain at the expense of human personality must face the condemnation of Christ. Slavery, the liquor traffic, prostitution, war, white supremacy—these stand in danger in the presence of Christ. For all of them, Christ spells ultimate doom.

III. Christ is dangerous to those who casually and formally profess religion.

(1) Whenever he comes in contact with them, he tears the cloak of pride and unreality from their shallow piety. To those who came to worship he said, "Beware of practicing your piety before men in order to be seen by them; for then you will have no reward from your Father who is in heaven."

(2) To be insincere in Christ's presence is always dangerous. It is perilous to attempt even a mild deception of God. "Whenever you stand praying, forgive, if you have anything against anyone; so that your Father who is in heaven may forgive you your trespasses."

(3) To boast of piety is always dangerous. The Pharisee who came to the temple to worship said, "God, I thank thee that I am not as other men." He did not receive the Lord.

(4) When we come into the Lord's presence we should always be searching our hearts to see what he sees. Too many of us have the outward form but inwardly are, as Jesus said to the Pharisees, "full of dead men's bones." Christ always sees us for what we really are. He detects our formality and our empty professions and declares that harlots and publicans will enter the Kingdom ahead of mere formal professors of religion.

IV. Christ is a danger to evildoers and those who defy God's moral order. This danger we recognize more readily than the others. We all can see that Christ imperils evil.

(1) Consider Herod. He was terrified when he heard of Jesus' birth. And his terror was well founded, for the Baby in the manger was a threat to everything Herod represented.

(2) None can defy God's moral order with impunity, because "whatever a man sows, that he will also reap." Not many of us openly defy God's moral order. We rather try to reconcile ourselves to an easygoing existence made up of too much evil and too little positive good. We excuse our sin: it is "just human nature" and we are not really responsible. Our mean disposition? Inherited from grandfather. And a really Christlike life is impossible these days, we tell ourselves.

(3) Yet all the while this dangerous Christ is making us uncomfortable in our complacency. He will not let us

rest. He is always saying to us: "I offer you more than an example; I offer you myself. Let me come in. Let me speak the healing word of forgiveness and peace. Let me release my power in your life. Let me be your Savior and Lord." And our answer to him will determine whether he is our danger or our deliverer, our ruin or our redemption.—M. Jackson White in *Christianity Today.*

Worship Aids

CALL TO WORSHIP. "O Zion, that bringeth good tidings, get thee up into the high mountain; O Jerusalem, that bringeth good tidings, lift up thy voice with strength; lift it up, be not afraid; say unto the cities of Judah, Behold your God!" Isa. 40:9.

INVOCATION. Out of our darkness we are come to thee for light; out of our sorrows we are come to thee for joy; out of our doubts we are come to thee for certainty; out of our anxieties we are come to thee for peace; out of our sinning we are come to thee for thy forgiving love. Open thou thine hand this day and satisfy our every need. This we ask for thy love's sake.—William Barclay.

OFFERTORY SENTENCE. "Of every man that giveth willingly with his heart ye shall take my offering [saith the Lord]." Exod. 25:2.

OFFERTORY PRAYER. Our Father, open our eyes, we pray, to the glorious opportunities of sharing with others our blessed experiences of fellowship with one another and with thee.

PRAYER. O God of hope, who hast awakened in all who have trusted thee through the centuries a great expectation, who dost more than fulfill the hopes of the men of old in the coming of Jesus, and hast made thy people look for even greater things: strengthen our confidence that every high and holy dream of men's hearts will be realized and that the anticipation of Jesus Christ for the whole world will certainly come to pass. Enable us to look at every woe and wrong and error and unhappiness under the sun as doomed to disappear and at every movement toward health and truth and justice and faith as sure to increase and succeed. And accounting no obstacle in men's prejudices or indifference or selfishness insuperable, may we resolutely set ourselves to prepare a highway for thee in our world's life. May the Lord Christ find us and our fellow countrymen a people made ready for him with national ambitions and business standards and household ways of which he can approve, with churches and places of recreation and schools in which he can feel himself at home.—Henry Sloan Coffin.

Illustrations

THE VOICE OF JESUS. Across this modern Babel, this chaos and distraction, the voice of Jesus rings like a bell. Into this fetid brawl he comes like a cool wind driven across the stars, saying do what you know to be right and ampler truth will dawn upon you as you walk. Carry your reason into sanctified energy. Fulfill your emotion in transfigured conduct. Let worship and neighborliness be the divine alternation of your life. Thus you gain the Kingdom as you help other gain it.—George A. Buttrick.

NO INVOLVEMENT. A cartoon showed a beggar sitting on a sidewalk and holding out his hat as an obviously sophisticated man and wife approached. The beggar, rather than using the typical "help me" approach, said, "Know the joy of helping someone without the slightest danger to yourself of getting involved."—William J. Krutza.

EXISTENTIAL REALITY. The coming of God's eternal Son into history and into the soul of man has revolutionary significance. It involves light and strength, understanding and experience, wisdom and power, meaning and grace, theology and action. The evangel is existential reality at its highest and best. It embraces the boundless love of Deity and the grand design for humanity which that love engendered.—John A. Mackay in *World Vision Magazine*.

Sermon Suggestions

THE DISTURBING CHRIST. Text: Luke 8:37. (1) Jesus disturbs by his sinless life. For in him, we see life as God intended every life to be. (2) Jesus disturbs (convicts) the sinner, for he is "not willing that any should perish, but that all should come to repentance" (II Pet. 3:9). (3) He disturbs the backslider, seeking to bring him again into right relationship with God. (4) Jesus disturbs his followers that they might make the most of their God-given ability. (5) Our Lord disturbs us by the needs about us. (6) Our Lord never disturbs merely for the sake of disturbing, but always he has a purpose. He disturbs us so that he might bring us into a right relationship with God. Thus he guides us into Christian maturity and directs us in right use of our God-given abilities. Christ causes disturbance in our lives to reveal his interest in us.—Carroll L. McNutt.

GOD'S CALL FOR SERVANTS. Text: Isa. 6:8. (1) The person who accepts God's call for servants must have a realization of the holiness of God as Creator of the universe. (2) He must have a realization of his own lost condition in the presence of his Maker. (3) He must have a realization of the need of lost humanity for a Savior. (4) He must have a realization of a personal faith in Christ as the only begotten Son of God. (5) He must have a realization of the complete forgiveness of his sins. (6) He must have a willingness to go and tell others about the Savior.—Dale Gates in *Devotion*.

EVENING SERVICE

Topic: Compelling Worship
TEXT: Ps. 90:9.

I. The first stage in worship is coming to God conscious of some need and seeking what he can give us. In one sense this is only a beginning; in another it is always a part of worship, though it should be purified and enriched in a continuing Christian experience.

II. The second stage in worship is when the mind moves on from what God can give to a realization of what God has done and is still doing. If the mark of the first stage is man's need, the mark of the second is thanksgiving for what God does.

III. The final stage in worship is reached when God becomes the center of our worship, desired not for what he can give, nor because of what he does, but for what he is, the only real Lover of men. "Exalt the Lord our God, and worship at his holy hill; for the Lord our God is holy." God is holy—the perfection of love. That is the climax of true worship; that is compelling worship. This surely recognizes that we owe God more for being what he is than for any benefit he bestows on us. To know this is to know God. To know this is to worship in the best and highest way open to us in this life and to have foretaste of what worship will be in the world to come.—James T. McNay.

SUNDAY: DECEMBER NINTH

MORNING SERVICE

Topic: Joy to the World (Advent)
SCRIPTURE: Luke 2:1-14.

When Jesus Christ was born at Bethlehem, God broke into time with the greatest announcement of joy contained in the whole Bible. Christianity was introduced to a world of darkness, sadness, and hopelessness with the message of great joy. At the heart of Christian experience is this pulsating, exuberant, irresponsible, contagious joy, which nothing on earth can match. It is:

I. *A liberating joy*. It was introduced with the words, "Fear not," or as the literal translation has it, "Let not fear hold you" or "Be gone fear." It is a liberating joy, and that becomes all the more evident when we understand something of the background of this glorious story of Christmas.

(1) *Political tyranny* (v. 1). The Emperor demanded that every man and woman should be registered for taxation. Now while taxation is a necessary measure for the economy of a country, history reveals that Caesar Augustus was a tyrant and had bludgeoned and bullied the entire land of Palestine into a false peace and security. No man or woman dare call his or her soul their own; no one dare raise a voice in protest. As a matter of fact, up until that moment it was the darkest hour in the world's history. So this beam of light from heaven, introducing the Savior, was a message of joy.

(2) *Social tension* (v. 8). Most authorities are agreed that these shepherds were not the sort who owned their own flocks. Rather, they were the miserable, ill-clad men who were employed by the religious leaders (then a decadent religion) for the rearing of sheep and goats for temple sacrifices in Jerusalem. So poor were they that they were the scum of the earth; they had nothing to call their own. They were constantly grumbling and complaining, and this appears to have been the condition of things all around. There was social tension, and people longed for liberty.

(3) *Spiritual tragedy* (v. 7). What a picture is captured for us in these words! Think, for a moment, of how Joseph must have felt. And what is even more pertinent, try to enter into the feelings and emotions of Mary the mother. So poor were they, so unknown, that they were found, not in a palace, nor an inn, nor even a traveler's enclosure, but in a stable amidst the beasts; and there she brought forth her Son, laying him in a manger. God manifest in the flesh—born in a stable! Why? Because there was no room for him. This symbolizes the spiritual tragedy of the hour.

(4) It was into the context of political tyranny, social tension, and spiritual tragedy that the shekinah glory of God burst forth with the message of joy. Here was a joy which was unaffected by circumstances because it was the joy of a transcendent God.

(5) This joy has persisted down through the centuries, even when blood has flowed like a river in the persecuted Church of Jesus Christ, when Christians have been reduced to poverty and brought down to distress.

II. *A limitless joy*. "I bring you good tidings of great joy, which shall be to all people" (v. 10). Here is a joy which knows no boundaries of capacity, color, class, or creed.

(1) *In terms of degree*. "Great joy" (v. 10). Whatever your capacity, God can fill it with joy. If your life is overwhelmed by sorrow, your capacity is enlarged for joy. If you are overtaken by persecution, your capacity is enhanced for joy. If your life is visited by blessing, your capacity is enriched for joy. However big your capacity be-

comes, God measures up to it by the joy which he gives.

(2) *In terms of design.* "To all people" (v. 10). I suppose if we were to keep to a strict exegesis, we should say that "all people" here means all the Jewish people. But that was only until the Cross. "All people" now includes every son of Adam's race. Because the mighty redemptive work of the Babe of Bethlehem who became the Christ of Calvary has been completed, this joy is now to "all people." Wherever the flag of the Church of Jesus Christ flutters in the breeze, the joy of Jesus Christ has been experienced.

III. *A living joy.* "I bring you good tidings of great joy. For unto you is born this day in the city of David a Savior, which is Christ the Lord" (vv. 10-11). Joy must have some Being in the universe who shall stand as its representation and end. Joy is not something abstract: it is essentially a moral quality. Joy, therefore, must be embodied in a Person, and that Person happens to be the Christ of Christmas. In fact, he is given his full name here in a very significant way: "a Savior . . . Christ the Lord" (v. 11), or "Jesus Christ the Lord." How is joy associated with his name?

(1) *As Savior, he established the joy.* Joy was not possible to the sons of men while there was no atonement for sin, but in the Epistle to the Romans we read: "We joy in God through our Lord Jesus Christ, by whom we have now received the atonement" (5:11). Man was banishsed from God because of sin, but Jesus Christ by his saving work came and dealt a mighty blow to the great enemy of joy. As the mighty, triumphant Savior, he burst through sin, death, and hell into resurrection life and made joy available to everyone who comes to him by faith.

(2) *As Christ, he expressed the joy.* The Evangelist tells us that in the life of the Lord Jesus there were occasions when he "rejoiced in spirit" (Luke 10:21). He was a "Man of sorrows and acquainted with grief," but even in all his sorrow there was never a moment in his life when the flame of joy was quenched.

(3) He manifested joy: (a) *At his birth.* "I bring you good tidings of great joy" was the message of the angel.

(b) *In his life.* (See John 15:11.)

(c) *In his death.* (See Heb. 12:2.)

(4) *As Lord, he extends the joy.* He extends joy to all who come to him. Hear what two of the New Testament writers have to say: (a) Peter: "Whom having not seen, ye love; in whom, though now ye see him not, yet believing, ye rejoice with joy unspeakable and full of glory" (I Pet. 1:8). (b) Paul: "Rejoice in the Lord always: and again I say, Rejoice" (Phil. 4:4). It really means: "Have your center, or spring, or well of joy, in the Lord; because he is the only One who ministers it."

IV. Do you know this radiancy, this joy? I am speaking of happiness. I know happiness is a Bible word, but it is always used in a very strict context. Happiness is something which depends on happenings, and when these go wrong happiness fails. Joy is something deep and abiding. It is liberating, limitless, and living, for it is centered in a Person, this Savior which is Christ the Lord. Have you any room for him in your life?—Stephen F. Olford in *The Calvary Pulpit.*

Worship Aids

CALL TO WORSHIP. "They that wait upon the Lord shall renew their strength; they shall mount up with wings as eagles; they shall run, and not be weary; and they shall walk, and not faint." Isa. 40:31.

INVOCATION. O God our Father, who dost dwell in the high and holy place, with him also that is of a humble and contrite heart: grant that, through this time of worship in thy presence, we may be made the more sure that our true home is with thee in the realm of spiritual things, and that thou art ever with us in the midst of our common walk and daily duties; that so the vision of the eternal may ever give meaning and beauty to this earthly and outward life.

OFFERTORY SENTENCE. "Give unto the Lord the glory due unto his name: bring an offering, and come before him: worship the Lord in the beauty of holiness." I Chron. 16:29.

OFFERTORY PRAYER. Our Father, enable all Christians to know that their lives may be lived with Christ in God and that their gifts are means by which thy love in Christ may reach into the lives of wayward and needy persons everywhere.

PRAYER. Almighty God, who art able to give the light which will make it possible for us to see in the darkness, the life which will cause us to rejoice amid the gloom of despair, the peace which brings quietness to our troubled spirits, we worship thee.

We confess in thy sight our ingratitude for thy continuing favor. Although thou hast richly blessed us, we persist in using these evidences of thy lovingkindnesses to satisfy our self-centered desires. We become so involved in a mad pursuit after those treasures which moth and rust can corrupt that we do not take time to meditate upon the mercy, thy loving care, and thy watchful providence.

We ask thee to be merciful to us because of the stubbornness of our wills and the hardness of our hearts. Deliver us, we pray, from that self-centeredness which drives us to dissipate the strength of our lives in a fruitless quest after transitory possessions; from that narrowness of vision which warps our sense of values; from that arrogance which tempts us to feel superior to those who are less privileged than ourselves; from that self-righteousness which offends the prodigal children.

Some of us have lost our sense of direction amid the confusion and the perplexity of these times. We seek the light of thy presence to illuminate the darkness of aimless living. Amid the desert trails of monotony of our daily tasks, grant us the insight to behold the burning bushes which remind us of thine everlasting presence.

We ask thee to calm those who are overcome with anxiety, that they may realize that their lives are always within the reach of thy loving care. Grant strength to those that are wearied in body and exhausted in spirit, that they may be able to run and not be weary. Kindle the faith of those who live without hope for the morrow.—Walter S. R. Powell.

Illustrations

GIFT OF LIGHT. Sometime when we are disheartened with ourselves and humanity in general, we should go into God's presence not with a neatly worded prayer, but into a dark room with an unlighted candle, to sit there long enough to feel the darkness, the blackout of hope in a world where no Christ has come, the hopelessness which the ancient world lived with daily, and then to light our candle and thank God for the gift of his light.—Allan Knight Chalmers.

IS THERE A FUTURE FOR MAN? The star over Bethlehem answers this question which troubles our time. We can trust the future, for the Star of Hope which arose over Bethlehem gives light to our troubled and darkened earth. Our hope is born anew at Christmas because Bethlehem's star, like Calvary's Cross, testifies to God's care for man. We can hope because God in Christ enters the fellowship of our experiences and proves himself able to help us in all our need. The Incarnation is the pledge of a future for man.—Willis Hubert Porter in *The Secret Place*.

ENCOUNTER. The Christmas event is the story of a dramatic encounter between pseudo-reality and reality, between a false estimate of the nature of life and a true demonstration of what life both is and has the power to become, between the cheerless rigidity of nonpersonal determinism and the buoyant—if perilous—freedom of the sons of God. The conflict lined up the most improbable antagonists: the mighty distances that separate the stars and the tiny strip of road that separates Bethlehem and Jerusalem, the voiceless silence of whirling galaxies and the song of angels with its theme of peace on earth, the awesome thunder of the heavens in convulsion and the poignant cry of fragile life in the form of a baby in a manger.—John E. Hines.

Sermon Suggestions

SEASON OF PREPARATION. (1) We prepare ourselves—our hearts, minds, and souls—to receive. (2) We prepare to be used of God. (3) We prepare for service.—Norman R. Lawson.

CHRISTMAS IS FOR CELEBRATION. (1) The celebration of hope. (2) The celebration of the home. (3) The celebration of benevolence.—*The Watchman-Examiner.*

EVENING SERVICE

Topic: God and His World
TEXT: John 3:16.
What do we mean by the world? It is the vast span of reality which owes its origin to God, its predicament to men, and whose destiny sways in the balances.
I. It is a *resourceful* world of staggering changes. It is a world in which man has learned to fly in space and to walk in outer space without cosmic dizziness, a world that halts the advent of human life by capsule and postpones the immanence of death by heart transplant, and which commutes astronauts to the moon and hangs stars in the sky. What a magnificently resourceful world this is!
II. It is also a *runaway* world wherein totalitarian tyrants trample human dignity and human rights, while denizens of democracy do the same thing in more subtle ways; a world in which war has not only gone global but has also taken to the heavens; a world in which man has split the atom and then splintered populous cities like Hiroshima in the mass cremation of humanity.
(1) The world's population balance is rapidly shifting to Asia and one-third of the globe's inhabitants are now in Communist China.
(2) It is a world which at the beginning of this century called 33 percent of its population Christian, but which at the close may claim less than 22 percent to be such; a world whose diminishing Christian remnant is starkly aware of the spiritual alienation of once friendly world powers like Russia.
(3) It is a world for which God has largely gone silent and in which long-repressed impulses of man's pagan nature are thrusting into view.
(4) It is a world nonetheless whose gods like science and sex and status and stocks have left life even emptier than it was. And from this world of their inheritance multitudes of young people seek an escape; they shrink from its invitation to a robot civilization that would feed their energies into mechanical computer buttons. Meanwhile an older generation, even in so-called welfare states, asks whether man can justify not destroying himself in a defiant act of final protest against such a world. It is indeed a runaway world—running away from the past, running away from itself, and running away from God.
III. It is still a *redeemable* world. Here is a marvel to dwarf all the wonders of modern science: this world is the object of God's love.
(1) The great Creator has not forsaken the rebellious creation, but with an amazing love, loves it still with a

love measurable only by the superhuman yardstick of the death of his holy Son.

(2) This world God loves—this wicked world that "lieth in the evil one" (I John 5:19). It is this world that God loves, that he considers salvageable.

(3) This world, despite its riot and rebellion, he made a rendezvous for redemption; through this world he seeks a new heaven and earth, the Kingdom of God in the midst of men, and in it he now proffers men of all nations and races a prospect of hope and happiness, of life and liberty, of peace and purity. To this world God's Gospel is addressed, to this resourceful but runaway, yet redeemable world.—Carl F. H. Henry.

SUNDAY: DECEMBER SIXTEENTH

MORNING SERVICE

Topic: The Christmas Word (Advent)
TEXT: John 1:14.

I. What do we mean by "the Word"? Protestant theology has sometimes been called the theology of the Word. By God's Word we mean his way of relating and revealing himself to men. God's Word is the channel through which he communicates himself and his will to his children. It is the means by which he discloses himself.

(1) We distinguish between four aspects of God's Word, and interestingly enough, the arrangement of our chancel gives all four individual emphasis. There is (a) the Word of God written, the Scripture (lectern); (b) the Word of God spoken, the sermon and the verbal interpretation (pulpit); (c) the Word of God enacted, the two Sacraments of Baptism and Holy Communion (table); and all three of these point to and are fulfilled in the (d) supreme Word, the Word of God incarnate, Jesus Christ (cross and window).

(2) One of the great doctrines at the heart of Christianity is the doctrine of the Incarnation. Incarnate means literally "in the flesh."

(a) Christians believe that in Jesus Christ, God became flesh. God took upon himself the form and burden of our humanity. He emptied himself and became a servant, a man for others who was like as we at all points, yet without sin. Christians do not always explain it in the same way, and they recognize that beyond their rational comprehension there lies considerable mystery. But nonetheless, the mainstream of Christian piety and thought has always included the belief that in Jesus Christ, the fullness of the Godhead dwelt bodily (Col. 1:19). God was in him reconciling the world unto himself. He was God's Son.

(b) In the fullness of time the Word was made flesh. Christians say that in Jesus Christ God's creativity and power have become manifest in a flesh-and-blood human being.

(3) In this astounding claim we find the real meaning of Christmas. Christians believe that Jesus was a real historical individual who confronted men with the eternal power and truth of God, not just in his message, but in his life and actions and person. Man was in Christ, man as God intended him to be at the Creation; and God was in Christ, reconciling his lost Creation unto himself. Both of these things must be said equally confidently if we are to do justice to the meaning of Christmas and properly understand what the Christian Church believes about the Christmas Word.

(4) The real issue is whether or not we believe that he is truly the One who embodies God's redemptive action, whether or not we believe that he is the absolutely unique and decisive figure in human history. The Church's claims about him are either true or

false. If they are true, we owe him worship and obedience; if they are false, our faith in Christ is blasphemy and our worship of him is idolatry.

II. The Christmas Word involves communication through speech as well as a person; it involves hearing as well as seeing. Words are used to convey the Word. What words would God speak to us at Christmas?

(1) "I am with you. My name is Emmanuel. I will not abandon you, foundlinglike, on the doorstep of an indifferent universe. I will not leave you comfortless. I, the great God Almighty, who formed the earth and created the heavens and spangled the night with the stars and hurled the sun out into space and breathed into a lump of clay the breath of life so that man became a living soul, I will love you with an everlasting love that tracks you across the margent of your world, pursuing you with patience and affection down the labyrinth of your years, never letting go of you, never giving up on you, bearing your burdens with you, always accompanying you to give you guidance and strength and comfort, just as a mother does with her sick child in the dead of night, or a father does with his prodigal son, believing in you, hoping for you, praying for you, standing with you—and this will be proof of it, this will be the sign that I give unto you, that in a Bethlehem manger you will find a Baby, born this day in the City of David, a Savior, Christ the Lord, whose name is Emmanuel, meaning that I am with you."

(2) "Trust, believe, know that I am with you, rest confident in my love which is surrounding you and accepting you even when you cannot accept yourself and sticking with you all the way. Do not be terror-struck."

(3) A third part of the message that God would speak to us through the Christmas Word is that peace will come on earth where and when men put positive goodwill to work, where and when they practice love, the kind of love that God is showing us in the gift of his own Son. The Christmas Word challenges us to express love in action. It says: bear each other's burdens with the kind of compassion and courage that God displayed in bearing our burdens when he took upon himself the form of a servant in Jesus Christ and became a man for others.

(4) The last Word of Christmas is a word of joy, of music in the heart. "Rejoice, be of good cheer, for Christ the Savior is born." (a) On the far side of despair, Christianity promises the beginning of a new human life. (b) On the far side of despair, Christianity points to a light that shines in the darkness and is not overcome by it. (c) On the far side of despair, Christianity introduces us to a Savior who loves us with an everlasting love and beckons us to lead a life of love and teaches us that love is the greatest thing in the world.—William H. Hudnut III.

Worship Aids

CALL TO WORSHIP. "Arise, shine; for thy light is come, and the glory of the Lord is risen upon thee. Lift up thine eyes round about and see." Isa. 60:1, 4.

INVOCATION. Almighty God, who in thy providence hath made all ages a preparation for the Kingdom of thy Son: we beseech thee to make ready our hearts for the brightness of thy glory and the fullness of thy blessing.

OFFERTORY SENTENCE. "Remember the words of the Lord Jesus, how he said, It is more blessed to give than to receive." Acts 20:35.

OFFERTORY PRAYER. Our Lord Jesus Christ, whose birthday has become a season of benevolence and giving, bless these our gifts which we offer in thankfulness for thyself, God's unspeakably precious gift.

PRAYER. O God, whose breath blows upon us as a refreshing breeze; whose faith in us revives us as cool, clear water does the parched tongue; whose hand rests upon us as gently, and yet as firmly, as does a mother's love; whose very power overcomes our weakness and becomes our strength, we pray for thy forgiveness.

Forgive us for being filled with our own self-importance, our own self-interest, our own self-sufficiency. Forgive us for having eyes and seeing not, for having ears and hearing not, for having tongues and speaking not, for having hands and serving not, for having minds and neglecting to use them. Forgive us for being content with that conversation that is but an echo of our own opinions; for hearing only that music that is none other than the blowing of our own horns; for shutting out the cacophonous sound that is the wail of the world; for being concerned only with those who fit into our limited circle; and for drawing into our selfish selves when we should be going out in love and service to mankind.

Now, our Father, we pray that thou wilt grant us the will and wisdom to use in thy service all the gifts and attributes with which thou hast endowed us. Help us to recognize that we serve thee best when we serve each other without thought of self. As we are forgiven for past follies and failures, may we be guided into fresh and fertile areas of Christian service.—Chester E. Hodgson.

Illustrations

BORN ANEW. Christmas is the most glorious tradition on the face of the earth, the greatest idea of profound simplicity ever uttered by the mind of man, the sweetest story ever told. But we must bring it to earth. What good to sing merely praises to a heavenly host? What good to look back two thousand years to watch a divine event of the incarnation of life, light, and love; of wisdom, truth, beauty, majesty, power, and might? What good unless Christ is born in us today?—*The P. E. O. Record.*

ANOTHER WORD FOR CHRISTMAS. One Christmas season General William Booth of the Salvation Army decided to send greetings to every unit scattered across six continents. But cable rates were so expensive, he knew he would be forced to confine his messages to a single word. What would best express the spirit and challenge of Yuletide? Finally, he made his choice. The messages read simply: "Others." That's Christmas in one word. The entire Salvation Army staff agreed.—Philip Jerome Cleveland.

THE ESCAPE OF CHRISTMAS. I'm quite glad that the storekeepers let people who never go to church listen to "Silent Night," even if the motive is to loosen up their pocketbooks for more purchases. This is the time of the year when Christmas escapes from the churches and surges through the streets. Perhaps the multitude will hear an echo of angel voices. Who knows what might happen over the loud speaker system of Gimbels?—*The Lutheran.*

EVERY MAN'S BETHLEHEM. Every man has his Bethlehem where possibilities and hopes are born, where history is invaded by novelty and the potency for action. At such times the tyranny of the past and the terror of the future give way before a new time of open possibility—the vibrant present.—Sam Keen in *To a Dancing God.*

Sermon Suggestions

CHRISTMAS IN THREE WORDS. Scripture: Luke 2:8–14. How can we explain the mighty influence of Christmas? I think there are three words which can help our thought. In a sense, these are the words by which a Christian lives. (1) Christmas is affirmation. (2) Christmas is assurance. We celebrate what God is doing as well as what he has done. (3) Christmas is anticipation. Christmas is celebration of anticipation in God.—Paul A. Duffey.

THE MEANING OF CHRISTMAS. (1) Christmas is a spirit, and the spirit of Christmas is peace. (2) Christmas is a gladness, and the gladness of Christmas is hope. (3) Christmas is a heart, and the heart of Christmas is love. (4) Christmas is an experience, and the experience of Christmas is giving. (5) Christmas is a celebration, and the celebration of Christmas is Christ confessed and adored.—Frank Johnson Pippin in *The Christmas Light and the Easter Hope*.

EVENING SERVICE

Topic: By the Leading of a Star
SCRIPTURE: Matt. 2:1–10.

I. These three were kings or Wise Men. God, in manifesting his Son to them, chose a vehicle with which they were already very familiar, which was almost a commonplace to them. A star which must have been seen by many besides the Wise Men might seem at first thought hardly dramatic or unusual enough to serve effectively as God's instrument in such an epoch-making purpose. But in spite of all that pious devotion has done to clothe the scene of the Nativity with wonder and awe is not its dominant note extraordinarily ordinary? God took on human flesh in totally undistinguished fashion: the birth of a child occurring in a stable which was the only place available.

II. The star is fixed; it is constant; it can be relied upon. (1) Man sought to trace out the path of the stars. Gradually they discovered an amazing order and pattern. They found movements could be precisely predicted years ahead. Through this knowledge, many found themselves led in awe into the presence of the Almighty. One such, a psalmist, sang long ago, "When I consider the heavens, the moon and the stars which thou hast ordained, what is man that thou art mindful of him?" Unless stars were fixed, they could not lead. A meteor or a comet is far more spectacular, but useless to set a course.

(2) People today often ask that religion be made relevant to life in the twentieth century. They would be wiser to ask the extent to which today's life is consistent with the way God put his world together. Are the principles of the Sermon on the Mount applicable today? Is not this putting the question the wrong way around? If our moral principles do not agree with those of the Sermon on the Mount, which is it that is out of step with the eternal and unchangeable truths of God?

III. God used the leading of a star, not the leading of the sun or the moon. (1) No matter how bright a star, its light to us is very pale compared to either. One could imagine that through the long hours of a moonless night the Wise Men in their journey across the desert might have yearned to see their path more clearly, to have the benefit of light which no mere star could give.

(2) It is natural for us to desire to be self-sufficient and to have clearly worked out plans as to where we want to go and how we are likely to get there. When this is vouchsafed to us, and sometimes it is, the experience is a pleasant and agreeable one. But at times for all of us the dim light of a leading star is all that is given us. Being human we may fret, complain, and get impatient. Yet as we look back on such periods in our life does not honesty compel us to admit that it was at just hard times as these rather than when everything seemed straight, clearcut, and evident, that God actually had most effectively manifested his Son to us?

IV. God chose a star because it is somewhat dim. (1) The Wise Men were free at any time to turn back from their arduous journey. God created man in his own image, free to obey or to disobey, to respond, to love, or to ignore that love.

(2) He sent his Son to dwell among us, and we have rejected him and in

the end nailed him to the Cross. Not even then would God give up on us. Not even then would he allow coercion to take the place of leading and waiting and hoping and suffering and still and always loving.—G. Gardner Monks.

SUNDAY: DECEMBER TWENTY-THIRD

MORNING SERVICE

Topic: This Dark World's Light (Christmas Sunday)

Text: John 1:5.

I. Mary bore Jesus in the night, but it was a deeper and darker night than that brought about by the setting of the sun in the west.

(1) It was the dark night of the soul of the Jewish people, penned in by pride and prejudice, fettered by folly, sickened by sin, disgraced by defeat, haunted by hopelessness, occupied and oppressed, anticipating only further abuse and agony as a nation.

(2) It was a time of twilight for Rome, though not many Romans realized it then. The power of the imperial purple was still intact, but the inner darkness of decay was already preparing to dissipate and destroy it. And with its destruction would topple the whole temple of Graeco-Roman culture. The dusk was beginning to descend on "the grandeur that was Rome."

(3) It was a dark time, indeed, for nations and empires and cultures, and it was a dark time, too, for individuals who felt the shackles of their sin chafe sorely.

(4) There is still much darkness and disorder in the world. War and the ever-present threat and fear of war are commonplace. Lost, blinded, fettered folk are forever seeking after strange saviors, grotesque gods, and weird witch doctors. Man has been clever enough to unmask and master powers in nature of almost unbelievable magnitude, but it remains to be demonstrated that he is wise enough to employ those powers for the world's well-being. And the ancient aching sickness in the soul of man survives—the deadly, soul-destroying power of his own folly and freely chosen sin.

(5) It is a dark world, indeed, yet into this darkness shines with unchanging brightness the same Light that began to shine beneath the lowest and least-inviting roof in all Bethlehem long, long ago.

II. It is very helpful and heartening to see in darkened days a light shining, and the men who saw the face and form of Jesus were blessed indeed.

(1) A light is good to look at, but a light does not exist merely to be seen. It exists to light up other things and to be reflected. We do well at Christmastime to remember that Jesus not only said: "I am the light of the world." He also said: "Ye are the light of the world."

(2) When we think of some Christian friends we realize that, though perhaps they had no spiritual light of themselves, their lives were beautiful because they continually reflected his. They threw back into this dark world a radiance that they received from him.

III. We ought to realize at Christmastime how many splendid enterprises there are in this dark world that take their radiance from him.

(1) If positive proof is needed to convince some that "the light is shining in the darkness," it will be found when they turn their attention to what the spiritual descendants of the first disciples are doing in Asia, in Africa, in South and Central America, and "in the uttermost parts of the earth." In the wake of the work of Christian missionaries of every communion, the blind are beginning to see, the deaf are starting to hear, the dead are being raised to life, slaves are being set free, and the poor are having the Gospel

preached to them. "The light is shining in the darkness."

(2) The tremendous tragedy of today's kind of Christianity is that so many professing Christians have failed to understand the meaning of a God who at Bethelhem came down-to-earth "to seek and to save that which is lost," and so few of them are really facing up to the far-reaching implications of the Incarnation. The Gospel of Christmas, therefore, presents an uncomfortable challenge to all who seek "ease in Zion."

(a) It tells of a God who plunged into the turmoil, the temptation, and the testing of life as it is. It declares that God has come very near to man—as near as a lowly home, as near as a woman's pain, as near as the cry of an ill-clad child, as near as a hunger pang and a heart-heavy sigh, as near as the tears of a sorry thief, as near as a cross of wood.

(b) It puts before us plain facts. It tells us a story of actual happenings. Bethlehem is a place on the map. Jesus was born, had a body, skin on his face, and breathed. Human eyes did see him —"lying in a manger," working with wood, pleading with people, praying to his Father, teaching, preaching, "doing good," supping with sinners and friends, sweating as it were great drops of blood in a garden, and hanging on a grim gibbet. There were people, just like us, who saw him after he had defeated death.

IV. The world is still dark and precariously poised between fellowship and hate, hope and cynicism, mercy and greed, although it is nearly two thousand years ago that the Son of God became the Son of Man to redeem the world through love.

(1) Yet Christmas still survives. "The light is shining in the darkness." The story of the Nativity is still being told in nearly every land; and men and women who are missionary-minded still harbor in their hearts the sure faith that, someday and somehow, the Christmas greeting of the angels will come true: "Peace on earth, goodwill among men." And through their faith, their efforts, their prayers, their service, their sacrifices, their daily lives, and their labors, the balance is gradually being tilted to the side on which the Wise Men of yesterday laid all they had along with their treasured gifts of "gold, frankincense, and myrrh."

(2) Isn't it rather wonderful that, when the world was most dark and times most bitter, God became human? He gave a gift to the world who was to become its Light. He gave the loveliest and liveliest gift this world can imagine. He sent his Son from the throne of the universe—down through patriarchs, priests, and prophets—to a barn in Bethlehem. He gave this dark world a Child of Light who was to rule, and yet was content in the service of men to be a slave.

When the meaning of Christmas becomes the motif of missionary enterprise, at home and abroad, its spirit becomes appealingly active where Christ is welcomed in faithful hearts, where his love is allowed to rule, where his light is allowed to illumine, where his will and his work are being done. The Christ of the crib, the carpenter's bench, the cross, and the empty tomb is still alive and "in another form" abroad in the world. "The light is shining in the darkness."—Johnstone G. Patrick.

Worship Aids

CALL TO WORSHIP. "Behold, I bring you good tidings of great joy, which shall be to all people. For unto you is born this day in the ctiy of David a Savior, which is Christ the Lord. Glory to God in the highest, and on earth peace, good will toward men." Luke 2:10-11, 14.

INVOCATION. O God who didst prepare of old the minds and hearts of men for the coming of thy Son, and whose spirit ever worketh to illumine our darkened lives with the light of his gospel: prepare now our minds and hearts, we beseech thee, that Christ may dwell within us, and ever reign in our thoughts and affections as the King of love and the Prince of peace.

OFFERTORY SENTENCE. "When they were come into the house, they saw the young child with Mary his mother, and fell down, and worshiped him. And they presented unto him gifts; gold, and frankincense, and myrrh." Matt. 2:11.

OFFERTORY PRAYER. O God, who didst give to us the gift of thy Son, stir us with such love toward thee that we may gladly share whatever thou hast entrusted to us for the relief of the world's sorrow and the coming of thy Kingdom.

PRAYER. O thou who in the worst of times proclaimed the best of hopes and sent the Christ child in the fullness of time: make receptive our hearts to receive this little One who changed the face of history. Make clean our lips and wash white our hearts. Let Scripture tell the story. Let music take us again through the paths of time. When we cannot grasp the fact, help our imaginations to lay hold of the story and make it live.

Help us to remember that many followers of this Bethelhem Babe will find it difficult to worship him. They are hungry through no fault of their own. While we worship in comfort and warmth, their bodies are cold. Maybe their hearts are bitter. Maybe they have lost the capacity to love. The world has been cruel. They have never felt our handclasp. God, are they bitter because of us? Do they hate their fellowmen because of us? Help us so to transform our love into deeds that they may know that this is thy world.

Incite us to act now. Let not this season of seasons pass without our giving ourselves to missions of mercy, errands of love, works of charity. Let not the day mock us. Help us to lay hold of the goodwill generated by this birth. Let it soften the wrath of those who misunderstand their fellowmen and those who hate their brothers. Help us to rejoice with exceeding great joy as we bring in thankfulness our gifts to the Christ, believing that, despite all the Herods, Christ's message shall yet be written on every lintel and sung at every hearth.—Fred E. Luchs.

Illustrations

A CHILD IS BORN. When God wants an important thing done in this world or a wrong righted, he goes about it in a very singular way. He doesn't release his thunderbolts or stir up his earthquakes. He simply has a tiny baby born, perhaps in a very humble home, perhaps of a very humble mother. And he puts the idea or purpose into the mother's heart. And she puts it in the baby's mind, and then—God waits. The great events of this world are not battles and elections and earthquakes and thunderbolts. The great events are babies, for each child comes with the message that God is not yet discouraged with man, but is still expecting goodwill to become incarnate in each human life.—Edward McDonald.

IF I HAD BEEN THERE. There are some of us who think to ourselves: "If I had only been there! How quick I would have been to help the Baby. I would have washed his linen. How happy I would have been to go with the shepherds to see the Lord lying in the manger." Yes, we would. We say that because we know how great Christ is, but if we had been there at that time, we would have done no better than the people of Bethlehem. Why don't we do it now?—Martin Luther.

HARVEST TIME. Christmas is the harvest time of love. Souls are drawn to other souls. All that we have read and thought and hoped comes to fruition at this time. Our spirits are astir. We feel within us a strong desire to serve. A strange, subtle force, a new

SUNDAY: DECEMBER TWENTY-THIRD

kindness, animates man and child. A new spirit is growing in us. No longer are we content to relieve pain, to sweeten sorrow, to give the crust of charity. We dare to give friendship, service, the equal loaf of bread, and love.—Helen Keller.

THEIR LOVELIEST CHRISTMAS. In a Western public school the sixth graders were told that in many other lands the religious expression of Christmas was much more important than gift giving. These lively youngsters were understandably surprised, and asked: "How then should we celebrate the holiday?"

Their teacher asked them all to find the answer in the Bible. One boy wrote this answer: "I was hungered, and ye gave me meat: I was thirsty, and ye gave me drink. As ye have done it unto the least of these my brethren ye have done it unto me."

That was a good beginning, the teacher told them, and suggested that they find the least of their brethren in their own town. They did, and collected their Christmas Fund in an empty jar.

On Christmas Day there was enough in the jar for Christmas dinners and gifts for two families. And the children themselves took their gifts to both families. On the way back one of the teachers saw a little girl tightly clutching the empty mayonnaise jar that had held the Christmas Fund.

"I'm going to put it under my tree at home," the little girl explained all aglow, "to remind me of the loveliest Christmas I've ever had."—Norman Vincent Peale.

STAR AND STABLE. The star here represents vision—that which reaches us from the other side, a moment of illumination that ignites the imagination and fires the will. The stable, on the other hand, suggests the harsh realities to which our visions often lead. We Christians have romanticized that stable. In truth it was a place of pungent, stubborn odors, dank, depressing, disappointing. But this is the way life comes to each of us—as a mix of star and stable. And we spend our years trying to reconcile and understand the two.—Ernest T. Campbell.

DECLARATION OF FAITH AT CHRISTMAS TIME

I believe in Jesus Christ, and in the beauty of the Gospel that began in Bethlehem.

I believe in him whose spirit glorified a little town;
Of whose coming only shepherds saw the sign;
And for whom the crowded inn could find no room.

I believe in him whom the kings of the earth ignored and the proud could never understand;
Whose paths were among the common people;
Whose welcome came from men of hungry hearts.

I believe in him who proclaimed the love of God to be invincible:
Whose cradle was a mother's arms;
Whose home in Nazareth had love for its only wealth;
Who looked at men and made them see what his love saw in them;
Who by his love brought sinners back to purity,
And lifted human weakness up to meet the strength of God.

I acknowledge the glory of all that is like Christ:
The steadfastness of friends,
The blessedness of homes,
The beauty of compassion,
The miracle of many hearts made kind at Christmas,
The courage of those who dare to resist all indifference, hate, and war.

I believe that only by love expressed shall the earth at length be purified.

—Thomas T. Oliver.

Poetry

KEEPERS OF CHRISTMAS

Tune your heart strings, O keepers of Christmas,
Draw the music of sheep bells and wind song at evening
With fingers soft-feathered.
Tune the voices of children's and angel's Hosannas,
Sing of home and the night that is silent and holy,
And of heart's love upgathered.

Sweep the strings softly, O keepers of Christmas,
Mute the harsh notes, recapture the carols
From the brow of the hill;
This night is measured by desires upswinging,
By a Star that eclipses the shadows, and by music
Echoing still.

—Leila Pier King. Reprinted by permission.

A TINY HAND

Christmas is love
tugging men back to God
with the powerful clasp of a tiny hand
reaching out from a bed of straw.

—Molly Brooks. Reprinted by permission.

BETHLEHEM'S STALL

The creatures there in Bethlehem's stall
Who looked upon the Christ-Child small—
I wonder if they knew at all

That someday his skilled hands would form
An easy yoke; a stable warm
To shelter them from wind and storm;

That o'er his head a dove's white wing
Would make the heavenly choirs to sing
That God was pleased his Son to bring;

That he would choose an ass's foal
To ride upon, in kingly role
To claim the Kingdom of the Soul.

The little Lamb of God was he
Who lay there sleeping silently,
The Shepherd of us all to be.

The creatures there within the stall
Looked down upon that Baby small—
I wonder if they knew at all!

—Jill Morgan in *Christianity Today*. Reprinted by permission.

YULETIDE

On hills we thought forgotten leans the light,
on hope's familiar steeples followed and lost:
this Star brings back all that has taken flight:
the loves, the childhood flames, the rivers crossed;
this Star reclaims, this light burns out our fear,
leaving us certain—All that has been is here,
and all that is will live, though grieved and torn,
because, each hour of faith, the Child is born.

—George Abbe in *Christian Century*. Reprinted by permission.

THE WORK OF CHRISTMAS

When the song of the angels is stilled,
When the star in the sky is gone,
When the kings and princes are home,
When the shepherds are back with their flock,
The work of Christmas begins:
To find the lost,
To heal the broken,
To feed the hungry,
To release the prisoner,
To rebuild the nations,

To bring peace among brothers,
To make music in the heart.

—Howard Thurman. Reprinted by permission.

MEDIEVAL MIRACLE STORY

Two midwives swept the barn and
  trimmed the manger
The night on which our blessed Lord was
  born,
And Mary's talk about the visiting angel
Flavored their conversation the next
  morn.
"There's only one true way to make a
  baby,"
The second midwife slyly said. "Now
  come
And tell me you agree, and don't say
  'maybe'!"
Before she knew it she was stricken
  dumb.

Years later at Bethesda's famous waters,
That healing pool received a stifling
  throng
Of transient dumb and blind and crippled squatters
Who came with hope to be made well
  and strong;
And one dumb creature growing old and
  older,
The midwife, elbowed yearly from her
  goal,
Was spied by Christ who reached and
  touched her shoulder—
The miracle she had doubted made her
  whole.

—Wilbert Snow. Reprinted by permission.

Sermon Suggestions

THE MEANING OF BETHLEHEM. (1) Bethlehem means love. (2) Bethlehem means God cares. (3) It means faithfulness, God's faithfulness, for Bethlehem is the fulfillment of the ancient prophecy. (4) Bethlehem means sharing. God has shared himself with us in his Son. (5) Bethlehem means that God is with us. (See Matt. 1:23.) "God was in Christ."—W. Morgan Patterson in *Western Recorder*.

THE TROUBLE IN BEING HEROD. (1) We should learn from Herod that we can fight against God. (2) We should learn from Herod that we can never win in our struggle against God. (3) There's a postscript to the Herod lesson: The longer we fight against God, the more we destroy of ourselves.—George Graham.

THE CLAIMS OF CHRISTMAS. Text: Luke 2:11. (1) A saving claim upon your life. "Unto you is born . . . a Savior." (2) A spiritual claim upon your life. "Unto you is born . . . a Savior, which is Christ." (3) A sovereign claim upon your life. "Unto you is born this day in the city of David a Savior, which is Christ the Lord."—Stephen F. Olford.

THE MYSTERY OF CHRISTMAS. Text: Phil. 2:5–7. At the center of the Christmas celebration there is a mystery so great that it goes far beyond our poor power to grasp the acts of a saving God. It is a threefold mystery. (1) The mystery of Jesus' person. (2) The mystery of the Savior's love. (3) The mystery of man's redemption.—Joel Nederhood.

WHAT CHRISTMAS REVEALS. Christmas shows us some things that we had not seen before or perhaps not quite so clearly. (1) The enormous gap between what we believe and what we do. (2) The vulgarity of which human beings are capable. (3) The emptiness of hundreds of human lives; how lonely, how twisted, how resentful some of them are. (4) Some of the good things that we do not always see. (5) That people do things you have no reason to expect them to do. (6) That God does things no one would expect him to do. —Theodore P. Ferris.

THE COURAGE OF CHRISTMAS. (1)

Courage of conviction. Mary believed what she could not see. She walked from the world's darkness toward God's glorious light. (2) Courage of character. Joseph was committed to do the will of God. He believed the word spoken by the angel. (3) Courage of nonconformity. Courage took the Wise Men from distant climes and sent them across the dusty desert to follow the way of God.—D. Thurlow Yaxley.

THE CASUALTIES OF CHRISTMAS. Text: Phil. 4:4 (NEB). (1) Peace is a continuing casualty of Christmas. Human conflicts distort heavenly music. Greed, power, and search for fame kill possibilities of peace. (2) Children are frequently casualties of Christmas. For a few mysterious days they are elevated to positions of prominence and showered with love. Afterward they are sometimes forgotten, allowed to shift for themselves. (3) The Church is a common casualty of Christmas; its people, weary of schedule, soon forget Bethlehem and question the relevance of worship on Christmas Eve or Christmas day! (4) Christ is often mutilated beyond recognition in the keen rivalry of the season. Christmas has become a season of our fashioning, not God's. —G. Curtis Jones in *The Clergy Journal.*

EVENING SERVICE

Topic: Celebrating the Word Made Flesh
TEXT: John 1:14.

Jesus is not man achieving deity but God accepting humanity, identifying with it, not wearing it as a make-believe but entering into a union with it that has permanent integrity. This has meanings and values urgently worth exploring by contemporary man.

I. The humanity of God in Jesus Christ points to the *primacy of the personal*—and that is something to celebrate at a time when much in our society works to depersonalize and dehumanize.

(1) The impersonal, though it be physically near, is always distant. It is the personal that gets inside of us. A psychologist, with his jargon in full gale, gives us his analysis of love. That is one thing. Two young people at a marriage altar say "I will." That is something else. "It is not abstractions but persons who most deeply influence us."

(2) The message is the medium— and that medium a Man! It's the primacy of the personal.

II. The humanity of God in Jesus Christ points to *the purity beyond the legal*—and that is something to celebrate when the phrase "law and order" is on everybody's lips, obscenely denounced by some, naïvely adored by others.

(1) Jesus was neither an anarchist nor a legalist. He paid taxes to Rome, which was a powerful autocracy. In word and by act, he kept saying, laws can restrain; they cannot redeem.

(2) On religious laws, the rules of the Establishment, Jesus came down with a heavy fist. He reverenced the Sabbath but refused to be bound by the man-made rules that encased it. He forgave and freed an adulterous woman who by law should have been executed. Resorting to physical force, he assailed a religiously sanctioned racket when he drove the money-changers from the temple.

(3) We need not better legalists but better men. (See Matt. 5:20, NEB.) And "better men," as he elsewhere told Nicodemus, means new men.

III. There is a third thought suggested by this power-packed phrase: *the identity with the marginal*—and that is something to celebrate in an hour when the lower classes of human society are restlessly, often bitterly, wondering who cares about their fate or fortune.

(1) Jesus was neither a class partisan nor a class antagonist. He is the Savior

of the lost, which all men are. But having said this, it remains to be seen and said that if men are unjustly rich, he judges them severely, and if they are unjustly poor, or deprived, or rejected, or demeaned, his sympathies are with them and their defense is his cause.

(2) Take the Magnificat of Mary in Luke 1. Each Christmas we say it. And each January we forget it! He scatters "the proud," puts down "the mighty from their thrones," exalts "those of low degree," fills "the hungry with good things," while "the rich" he sends "empty away."

(3) The main current of life and society sweeps along. But there are mean margins—the swirling, foul eddies near the banks—where multitudes are caught and held. And that is where the "Word made flesh" is found, saying: "These too are mine. These too have my love. These too I shall claim, that they may rise from lonely creaturehood to full-fledged sons in the heavenly Father's Kingdom."—Paul S. Rees in *World Vision*.

SUNDAY: DECEMBER THIRTIETH

MORNING SERVICE

Topic: Of Serpents and Doves
TEXT: Matt. 10:16.

The turbulence, division, anger, and humorlessness of the body politic are reflected in the Church, and therefore we meet in difficult times that in a special way require wisdom. We are not commanded by our Lord to be amiably naïve or courageously stupid; we are commanded to be wise as serpents. Our Faith proclaims that Divine Wisdom took human form and walked with us, so that, partaking of his life, we might leave our confusion, divisiveness, and shortsighted folly and become wise. Did he not promise to send the Holy Spirit, one of whose gifts is wisdom?

I. What is this wisdom? Wisdom, as we are using the word, is a practical virtue having to do with decisions. It is good judgment. It is a spacious view that takes into consideration all the facts and circumstances and does not squeeze out facts for the sake of a hard theory. It is a hard-headed virtue that counts the cost; for surely if a decision or policy has disastrous results, it is not wise. Wisdom is love choosing appropriately in the midst of real people and real circumstances and real debate. Let's admit that there is a lot of stupidity in us, for we belong to a sinful race of men. It is easy for man to lock into hard factions, but this is not wise! It is easy to squeeze the facts for the sake of my hard theory, but it is not wise! It is easy to crush the world into my party-line and not to listen, but it is not wise! "Be ye wise" to all the facts, all the circumstances.

II. Let's look at some wisdom as it comes to us from our faith and as it applies to our turbulent days.

(1) It is wisdom, as a great prayer says, to accept the things that cannot be changed. So a man said recently: "Pick up your cross and relax." Being uptight, resentful, humorless, raging against things in general is as much a sickness in us as it is in an alcoholic. It is not our fault that we live in turbulent times, but it is our responsibility to be tolerant, flexible, wise, and civilized.

(2) Another piece of wisdom is to see clearly the necessity for compromise. I don't mean compromising the Faith or principles. I mean a willingness to compromise on those issues on which people who hold the same faith and principles sincerely disagree. Compromise in this sense is not a weakness at

all. It is a necessity of social existence, based upon a decent humility and recognition that on many matters a difference of opinion is inevitable. He who insists on a victory can be a fool.

(3) It is wise for optimistic Americans to see in a turbulent age the delicacy and precariousness of the social order. Knowing the sinfulness of human nature, including our own, and the landslides of history, it is wise to keep our voices down, to avoid the heavy hand and the abrupt action. Diplomacy is a fine word. Be ye wise diplomats and walk with a godly fear.

(4) It is wise for us as Christian leaders and theologians to look beneath the obvious surface and see the real enemy. The real enemy who tempted Christ, who roams this world like a lion, who is the father of lies, is the power of evil itself, who is here and there and everywhere. This power does not want us to reason correctly; his methods always have been, and always will be, to confuse and to divide.

III. "And innocent as doves." This means that only a certain kind of person can be wise.

(1) If I am centered in myself, or a faction, or want above all the victory of my limited point of view, I cannot be wise. Only when a man sees that he is but part of the body, only when he knows his own sin as well as the sin of others, only when he sees his own limited creatureliness, only when he rises above self in a kind of childlike innocence to desire the common good, can he be wise.

(2) Love in action does not sin. It desires to serve whether it commends or criticizes. There is a wisdom of this world which is foolishness with God because it is self-centered, self-righteous, and factious. And there is a wisdom of the Holy Spirit which is gentle, temperate, and loves the common good.

(3) May the Holy Spirit come to us in our need! May he give us a wisdom and perspective, a judgment and an understanding, we do not naturally possess. By the Holy Spirit what a great life we can have, even in turbulent times. Let us look up and pray for a wisdom not our own that is promised to us.—Richard S. Emrich.

Worship Aids

CALL TO WORSHIP. "Great is the Lord, and greatly to be praised; and his greatness is unsearchable. One generation shall praise thy works to another, and shall declare thy mighty works." Ps. 145:3-4.

INVOCATION. Almighty God, accept our thanksgiving for this new year as evidence that thy love has not grown weary of men. Forgive the sinful pride that would destroy the universe itself if we did not find mercy before the Prince of ages. Strengthen our faith in the eternal purpose which finds completion in Christ Jesus. Grant that in this year of our Lord we may live and move and have our being in him, and so in thee, to whom be glory world without end.

OFFERTORY SENTENCE. "Thou crownest the year with thy goodness. . . . Samuel took a stone, and set it between Mizpeh and Shen, saying, Hitherto hath the Lord helped us." Ps. 65:11; I Sam. 7:12.

OFFERTORY PRAYER. Our Father, we bow in humble gratitude that as a new year dawns we may call on thee to guide, strengthen, bless, and forgive, and that through these gifts we may share thy love with all who call upon us and thee.

PRAYER. God of the Ages, once again we face a new year. Give us strength to forget our failures, our mistakes, and our fears, and to approach this year with faith and confidence. We thank thee for the gift of time, for years, for days, for hours, for moments. Grant that this year shall be for us a year of change, of growth, of discipline, of hard work. Give us greater wisdom and more patience and fill our hearts with love. Please, God, now and throughout the year, may we seek divine direction. Help us from our hearts to say, "Thy will be done."—*Link.*

Illustrations

PAST AND FUTURE. We must welcome the future, remembering that soon it will be the past, remembering that once it was all that was humanly possible.—George Santayana.

GOD'S GIFT. Time is a gift of God, the Lord of time. Our times are in his hand. The trouble is, we have forgotten how to accept time as a gift. No sooner do we receive a calendar than we make appointments and set deadlines. It is a subtle revelation of our pride that we make more appointments than we can keep, set more deadlines than we can meet. Thus the calendar becomes a source of pressure and anxiety, and time becomes a slave-driver's whip instead of a Father's gift.

Jesus' time was limited. He often spoke of that "hour" that would cut short his life. Yet he was almost never in a hurry. He was seldom unable to meet the need or celebrate the joy of a present moment because he had to prepare for a future engagement. With no schedule of meetings or list of appointments, he could hardly be a success in A.D. 1974. But then he was hardly a "success" in A.D. 30. He only managed to live the most authentically human life on record.—Albert Curry Winn.

Sermon Suggestions

FUTURE CERTAINTIES. Text: Rom. 8:38–39. The Christian has one sure center for his thoughts about the destiny of man. In the presence of Christ he sees the image of God restored and hears again the summons to the adventure of the Sons of God. (1) He is not afraid of the future, for Christ is the way. (2) He is not afraid of any discovery of science, for Christ is the truth. (3) He is not afraid of death, for Christ is the life. (4) Above all he is delivered from that one true fear of separation from God.—David H. C. Read.

ABRAHAM'S FAITH AND OURS. Several lessons of Abraham's life seem particularly relevant today. (1) If we are to be Abraham's spiritual children and heirs of the promise, we need to recognize that faith is true only when based on the objective word of God. (2) Abraham was a man of flesh and blood like ourselves and triumphed only after a tremendous struggle. (3) If we are inclined to be daunted by the prospect of the fight of faith (Heb. 13:13), we need to recall that Abraham was sustained, guided, and kept (I Pet. 1:5) by a faithful, merciful, loving, and sovereign God who first gave the word and then ensured its ultimate victory by overruling every weakness in the one to whom he had given it and every thwarting turn of events. (4) Just as Abraham was promised that God himself would be his "exceeding great reward," we should not lightly throw away our confidence (Heb. 10:35); for when Christ who is our life appears, then we also will appear with him in glory.—H. K. Stothard.

EVENING SERVICE

Topic: The Right Road for the New Year

TEXT: Prov. 3:6.

I. It means to receive his approbation in all that we do. (1) God never gives his approbation to those who do not sincerely seek it. It is true that God does send his rain upon the just and the unjust. Nevertheless, we must not forget that the moral and spiritual laws of God are irrevocable.

(2) No man's life can be enriched with divine benedictions whose will and purpose do not harmonize with the will of God. We cannot break the laws of

God. If we defy them, they will certainly break us.

II. It means to accept his leadership in all that he demands. (1) Jesus never compromised Truth. He demands of us the most in order that we may find the best. He reminds us that no man can serve two masters. He is eager to have Christian soldiers enlist in his services. He persuades but never compels.

(2) To accept Christ's leadership is to incarnate the Christ. God does not seek primarily to make us comfortable but to make us useful.

(3) Jesus did not say that if any man will come after him he must deny himself something, but, rather, he must get rid of himself by putting Christ in place of himself.

(a) To be a Christian is not simply to enunciate a creed but rather to express a character.

(b) It is not to comply with ritualism but rather to embody righteousness.

(c) It is not simply to manifest certain types of service but in love to become the servant of all.

III. When we acknowledge him in all our ways he empowers us, day by day, for a more abundant life and a more unselfish service.

(1) To have physical life only is merely to exist, but to have the spiritual plus the physical is to share the immortal. Where we live depends more upon what is on the inside of us than what is on the outside of us. We may dwell together in closest proximity and still our spirits may be as far apart as the poles. The world to us is no more than we are able to see, to appreciate, and to assimilate.

(2) The life abundant is something intangible and yet vital. It is a quality of life that radiates itself through the whole personality. We may own many things and yet possess nothing. A man may own very little of the material and yet possess all things. When Christ becomes the center of our lives, we can no longer live to ourselves but we must express his spirit in sharing what we have and what we are with others.—Fred R. Chenault.

SECTION XI. Focus on Key 73

KEY 73 is a flame to ignite our land with a holy zeal and concern for all men everywhere.

KEY 73 is a dove to bring God's peace to our anxious world.

KEY 73 is a key to unlock God's provisions for a spiritually hungry humanity.

In 1967, forty churchmen, seeking new possibilities for cooperative evangelism, met in a motel at the Virginia side of the Francis Scott Key Bridge which spans the Potomac River from Washington, D.C. Their discussions led to the launching in 1970 of KEY 73, which during this year will mobilize the resources and witness of more than 100 denominations and evangelistic agencies.

KEY 73 is an overarching Christian canopy in both the United States and Canada under which all denominations, congregations, and Christian groups may concentrate on evangelism during the year-long, continent-wide effort.

KEY 73 theme: Calling our continent to Christ.

KEY 73 text: "Jesus Christ is the same yesterday, and today, and forever." Heb. 13:8.

OBJECTIVES

KEY 73 objectives are the following: (1) To share with every person in North America more fully and more forcefully the claims and message of the Gospel of Jesus Christ.

(2) To employ every means and method of communicating the Gospel in order to create the conditions in which men may more rapidly respond to the leading of the Holy Spirit.

(3) To apply the message and meaning of Jesus Christ to the issues shaping man and his society in order that they may be resolved.

(4) To develop new resources for effective evangelism for consideration, adoption, adaptation, or rejection by the participating churches or Christian groups.

(5) To assist the efforts of Christian congregations and organizations in becoming more effective redemptive centers and more aggressive witnesses of God's redeeming power in the world.

ABBREVIATED CALENDAR

Phase I. Calling our continent to repentance and prayer

TEXT: "There is joy . . . over one sinner who repents." Luke 15:10.

Advent (1972). Period of repentance, prayer, and promotion.

Christmas to first full weekend in 1973. Two weeks of prayer preparation and noon prayer call.

January 6–7. Launch weekend including Sunday morning covenant celebrations.

Phase II. Calling our continent to the Word of God
TEXT: "For the word of God is living." Heb. 4:12.
Thanksgiving (1972) to Easter. Distribution of Luke and Acts and study guides to every home in the United States and Canada.
Advent (1972). Coordinated Bible study focusing on repentance and reflection in the Gospel of Luke.
January 7 to March 7. Coordinated Bible study focusing on the motivation and methodology of evangelism as found in Acts.

Phase III. Calling our continent to the Resurrection
TEXT: "He has risen, as he said." Matt. 28:6.
January 7 to March 7. Continent-wide religious census and survey carried out at the local level, focusing on training and highlighting opportunities for witness.
March 7 to Easter. Period of lay witnessing.

Phase IV. Calling our continent to new life
TEXT: If any one is in Christ, he is a new creation." II Cor. 5:17.
Easter to mid-summer. Teams of musicians, artists, among others, will tour parks, shopping centers, resort areas, and the like, to confront persons with the Christ and the new life available through him.

Phase V. Calling our continent to the proclamation
TEXT: "But we preach Christ." I Cor. 1:23.
June and July. Youth Outreach Weeks scheduled in a key city in every state and province.
August and September. State Fair Missions planned for a major fair or exposition in each state and province.
November 1-7. Area Impact Week held simultaneously in at least one strategic area in each state and province.

Phase VI. Calling our continent to commitment
TEXT: "If any man would come after me, let him deny himself and take up his cross and follow me." Matt. 16:24.
Advent. Reclaiming the Advent-Christmas season as a distinctly Christian festival, thereby illustrating the unity in Christ of Christians and their common commitment to his lordship.
December 30. A continent-wide covenant celebration in which congregations and individuals celebrate their own commitment, new commitments within their congregations, and challenge one another to a renewed commitment to Christ and his mission in 1974.

KEY 73 AND THE LOCAL CHURCH

The emphasis of KEY 73 is on the local church. Each church will determine the nature and extent of its participation. Local churches may become involved in the following ways:

(1) By appointing KEY 73 committees to set objectives and plan for participation.

(2) By evaluating evangelical potentials and the effectiveness of various programs.

(3) By relating local activities to some or all of the national KEY 73 emphases which will reach into thousands of local communities by way of mass media.

The local parish involvement may include the following:

(1) Midweek prayer and Bible study meetings and the initiating or implementating of small groups dedicated to the evangelistic witness of the Church; vacation Bible schools; church retreats.

(2) Training of laymen including youth for visitation and witness; distribution of New Testaments and Christian literature in schools, factories, etc.; telephone campaigns; audio and video taping of sermons for shut-ins and oth-

ers; writing of Bible expositions and inspirational materials for area newspapers and preparing of tapes for radio broadcasting.

(3) Sunday school evangelism; pastor's membership classes.

(4) Use of the various daily devotional materials and Sunday school and Christian publications.

(5) Programs for senior citizens, area college students, ethnic and minority groups; missionary conferences; drama and art festivals.

(6) Alerting church members to the high-visibility television and other programs of KEY 73.

(7) A cooperative ministry with area councils of church and other groups concentrating on the KEY 73 goals.

Central to the achievement of this year-long witness to Christ is the local pastor, his staff, and the church officials. Their knowledge, involvement, guidance, and enthusiasm will be contagious throughout the congregation. The pastor's Sunday role as leader in worship and interpreter of God's Word is crucial. In view of this, a special KEY 73 index identifies all worship and homiletic materials in this issue of *The Ministers Manual* with the various phases and emphases of KEY 73.

Executive director of KEY 73 is Dr. Theodore A. Raedeke. The office of KEY 73 is at 418 Olive Street, St. Louis, Missouri 63102.

SECTION XII. A Little Treasury of Illustrations

HEADLINES. A mother was helping a little girl with her bedtime prayer. Apparently the girl included a prayer for the safety of the astronauts. The mother said to her daughter, "Honey, wouldn't it be nice if tomorrow's headline read: 'God brings back astronauts!'" The little girl replied, "Mother, wouldn't it be nice if tomorrow's headline read: 'Astronauts bring back God!'"—James W. Lenhart.

BEAUTIFUL MORNING. Whenever the Nenney family was able to get all the members of the family together at the same time for a breakfast they took turns saying "grace." Finally it came to Dale's turn. Outside was gloomy and overcast, without a prospect of sunshine anywhere. Yet when he prayed, Dale said, "Thank you, dear God, for my family, for this good food, and thank you God for this beautiful morning! Amen." Dale's mother, thinking that perhaps he was getting a little bit perfunctory in his prayers, pointed out the window at the fog and gloom and said, "Dale, what on earth are you doing, thanking God for a beautiful morning on a day like this?" Dale thoughtfully replied, "Mother, never judge a day by its weather!"—Melvin E. Wheatley, Jr.

THAT'S MY JOB. Madeline, a little girl, had just finished her evening prayers: "Now I lay me down to sleep . . ." Her mother had taught her to close the prayer with these words: "And help me to be a good girl." That evening she omitted the last words. When her mother reminded her that she had not entirely finished the prayer, she said, "I don't have to tell the angels to help me to be a good girl; that's my job to make myself a good girl."

The mother explained: "But we need someone to help us to be good. What if you should forget?"

So Madeline prayed: "In case I forget, then help me to be good."—Myron C. Pogue.

IDENTITY. Some time ago I became engaged in conversation with one of our members and her not-quite-three daughter. Afterward, the mother turned to the child and said, "Do you know who that was?" The little girl replied, "Yes, that's our God!"—Brunson Wallace.

CONSIDERATION. My friend's little boy was having his evening prayer at his mother's knee. After his usual "Now I lay me" and requests for the family and his playmates, he sang a rather silly song.

Being a wise mother, she did not interrupt; but afterward, as she tucked him in his bed, she asked, "Alfred, why did you sing that silly little song when you were talking to God?"

His answer came quickly, "Well, Mother, I knew God heard so many sad things, I just thought he'd enjoy something funny."—Hilda P. Davis in *The Upper Room*.

WISE CHILD. The remark of a wise child we heard about continues to haunt us. Was it a threat? A simple statement of fact? A genuine psychological insight? In any case, the remark, made by a twelve-year-old boy to his female parent, was: "You'd better enjoy me now, Mom, because next year I'll be a teen-ager and it'll be too late."—*Presbyterian Life.*

THE BOY AND HIS WORLD. A boy had been given a beautiful globe of the world, and the little fellow became so interested in it the first evening that he insisted upon taking it into his room and placing it on a table right beside his bed.

Later in the evening the boy's parents got into a discussion of some far country, and the father said he would slip into the lad's room and bring out the globe so they could find the place in which they were interested.

Tiptoeing into the room, the father picked up the globe and was making his way toward the door when his son aroused and inquired sleepily: "Hey, Daddy, what are you doing with my world?"—Leo Bennett in *Sunshine Magazine.*

THREE BELIEFS. A young Jewish girl in the Warsaw ghetto managed to escape over the wall and hide in a cave. She died there shortly before the Allied Army broke out the ghetto. Before she died, she had scratched on the wall three things. First: "I believe in the sun, even though it is not shining." The second thing she wrote was: "I believe in love, even when feeling it not." The third thing she wrote was: "I believe in God, even when he is silent."—Gerald Kennedy.

A LITTLE GIRL'S LOVE. A Scottish college principal, John Cairns, told of a confirmed law-breaker who was often in the hands of the police. The one redeeming feature of his dissolute life was love for his little girl, who was the image of her dead mother. Once, having committed burglary, he was sentenced to a fairly long term in prison. During his imprisonment his little girl died. On the day he came out he learned of her death. The blow shattered him. He was broken. He could not bring himself even to visit the home from which she had been taken. Suicide seemed the only escape. So he resolved to throw himself off one of the bridges of the Scottish capital. At midnight he stood on the parapet. He found himself climbing it. For no reason he could explain, as he said later, there flashed into his mind the words of the creed: "I believe in God the Father Almighty." He repeated it. He knew nothing of God, but he did know something of fatherhood. "Why," he said, "if that is what God is, if God is like that then I can trust him with my lassie—and myself." Death receded, life began anew. Heartbreaking loneliness and despair gave way before the Presence of Jesus who brings the Father near.—David A. MacLennan.

NEXT OF KIN. A young rather innocent girl from a small country town went to seek work in a large city. She was given one of those massive forms to fill out: Name, address, family history, etc. When she came to the question, "In case of emergency, whom should we notify?" she called the personnel man over and said: "I don't understand." He said: "Well, you know, if some accident befell you on the job, or some emergency developed, whom would we call?" She said: "Why, the nearest human being, of course."—Ernest T. Campbell.

"AH-AH" WORLD. A friend of mine was watching his two little boys playing around the living room. The three-year-old was ever reaching for things such as pictures, the lamp and so forth. Each time as he reached, his mother would say, "Ah, ah, Billy, don't touch." Finally the little six-year-old brother said, "Billy, don't you know this is an 'Ah-ah' world?"—Ralph W. Sockman.

BREAD AND HARVEST. A small boy, feeling hungry as small boys do, watched his mother baking some bread, and he said to her, in anticipation of a delightful morsel, "How long does it take to bake a loaf?" She answered, "Six months!"—and told him of the miller and the farmer and the sower of the seed. She might have said, "Six million years!"—going back and back to those first creative acts of God whereby in his goodness he made the earth fruitful. The divine goodness is a large goodness, embracing the ages, and some sense of that is given to us in the harvest.

FIFTEEN CENTS. A little boy attended church school for the first time. When the class was over, he asked the teacher, "Is there a coke machine here?" "No," she replied. "Well, is there a candy machine?" "No," she said again. "Then why did my mother give me fifteen cents?"—Harold Leonard Bowman.

CURE. Charlie Brown and Lucy are arguing. Lucy says: "All right, I've had enough of your insults! Put 'em up! . . . We're going to have this out right here and now. Put 'em up!" Charlie Brown puts 'em up, and Lucy is bopped right in the nose. She runs off, telling the world what Charlie Brown has done. Then Charlie becomes remorseful about what a terrible thing he has done in hitting a girl. Overcome by guilt, he goes to see the psychiatrist, which is Lucy, of course. While he confesses, she reaches out and bops him good. Though on his back and seeing stars, Charlie Brown smiles to say: "I don't feel guilty any more. Psychiatry has cured me."—Tom A. Whiting.

FIRST DAY. Little Herman went to his first day of school, and when he came home, his mother asked, "What did you learn today?" Herman said, "I learned to write." "Oh," she said, "to think my little Herman on his first day of school learned to write. What did you write?" "How should I know?" replied Herman. "I haven't learned to read yet."—Charles A. McClain, Jr.

TROUBLED CONSCIENCE. An old fellow had a conscience that troubled him. At last he went to a farmer and said, "Master, I'm sorry. I stole a rope from you a while back." His master forgave him and the countryman went away. But he still had no peace of mind. For he had not told the farmer that there was a cow at the end of the rope when he stole it.—Peter Howard.

PARTISAN DEITY. One day when Jackie was about four his father was giving him a terrific row for not eating his supper properly. It was quite near Christmas time, and his father reminded Jackie that he was a big boy now, that he must let Santa Claus see how well he could eat his supper, and, if he did not eat his supper, Santa Claus might not bring him very much. Jackie listened to his father's lecture quite unconcerned. And then at the end of it he said: "That's all right. God's on my side."—William Barclay.

HOW NOT TO GET LOST. A class of nine-year-old boys and girls were going the forty miles or so to New York to visit a museum. One mother was rather worried about this complicated trip into such a bewildering city. She knew what a job it was to keep up with two children, and how were the teacher and her assistant going to handle forty? The teacher and class seemed unconcerned. When they returned, the mother asked her son what happened. He said nothing. "But didn't you have any trouble getting around New York?" "Nope." "Well, what did the teacher tell you?" "Nothing." "Well, didn't she say anything?" And the youngster answered, "All she said was, 'Don't any of you let go the rope.'"—Emerson S. Colaw.

CHIPPING AWAY. A sculptor had just finished an enormous statue of an elephant. He invited a group of friends to his studio to view it.

"Did you use a model?" asked one.

"No," said the sculptor.

"Amazing. How did you get such a perfect likeness?"

"I just kept chipping away at the pieces that didn't look like an elephant," replied the sculptor.—Orval D. Peterson in *World Call*.

GOD'S LOVE. Little Mary rushed into the house deeply disturbed and sobbingly said to her mother, "Mommy, God doesn't love me anymore." "Why, Mary, dear," said the surprised mother, "should you say such a thing?" "Well, I just tried him on a daisy and it came out, 'He loves me not.' "

ROBIN'S ALIBI. Young Robin was more clever than anyone at making up alibis. When he brought home his grades at the end of the first report period, his father observed, "I see you failed in math." "That's true, Dad," Robin explained brightly, "but my grade was the highest of all those who failed."—Seth Harmon.

EXPLANATION. "Mother, Bobby just broke your kitchen window." "How did it happen?" "I threw a rock at him, and he ducked."

GOD'S LIGHT. The light had just been put out, and the child was a bit afraid of the dark. But she saw the bright moonlight outside her window, and she asked, "Is the moon God's light?"

"Yes," replied her mother. "The moon and the stars are God's lights."

"Will God turn out his light and go to sleep, too?"

"No, God's lights are always burning."

"Well, Mama," said the child, "while God is awake I am not afraid."

DOING WHAT HE PLEASES. Little Roger had just been scolded for not doing something that he had been told to do. In disgust he asked his father, "How old will I have to be before I can do whatever I please?" "I really don't know, son," replied the amused father. "Nobody has ever lived that long yet."—Seth Harmon.

PERFECT SOLUTION. At his vacation home, Skibo Castle, in his native Scotland, Andrew Carnegie had a beautiful rose garden in which red, white, and yellow blossoms waved in colorful profusion.

One day Mr. Carnegie's gardener came rushing to him. "The village folk are picking your flowers," he exclaimed excitedly. "Shall I order them away?"

"No, never do that," replied Carnegie.

"Then what shall I do?" asked the gardener.

"Why," said the famous philanthropist with a smile, "plant more roses."—Jack Kytle.

ULTIMATUM. Overheard from the next room, where our friend's small son was being pestered by a visiting cousin: "If you won't go away and leave me alone, I'll find somebody who will!"—*Presbyterian Life*.

POINT OF VIEW. I recently took a photograph of two little girls. When I picked up the prints, I took each child a copy. At the first home, the child said happily, "Oh, what a nice picture you took of me." In the second home, the little girl said with great glee, "Oh, Mother, come look. Isn't this the prettiest picture you ever saw of Janet?"—Mary Louise Kitsen.

TAULER'S KINGDOM. Johannes Tauler, when asked by a man on the road to Strassburg how he fared, replied: "I am full of praise to God. When the sun shines, I thank God. When the heavens pour down their rain, I rejoice in God. I am a king!" "A king?" said the man. "Where is your kingdom?" "My kingdom," replied Tauler joyously, "is in my heart."—Edwin T. Dahlberg.

FINDING GOD ANEW. A soldier, who had spent three months in the hospital in great pain and often at death's door, finally pulled through and recovered completely. That fall, at his church's Thanksgiving Day service, he heard the minister speak of a lad who, having served in World War II without a scar, had said, "I thank God for the bullets that didn't hit me." The soldier, pausing at the door after the worship, remarked to the minister, "You know, some of us are thankful, too, for the bullets that did hit us." And the clergyman, who had ministered to him during his long illness, understood what he meant. The soldier had found God anew in "the stress and strain of life," and it had meant everything to him. He had felt the Father's "chastening rod" and, yielding to it, had found spiritual blessings far more valuable than the richest material gifts man can know.—Russell F. Auman.

GOD'S VESSEL. My father, John Roach Straton, had a reputation as a defender of the faith. A young man had come to him and said, "I want to preach." My father in questioning him discovered that he had not finished high school, much less college or seminary. So his advice was to complete all three. The fellow replied, "But I believe that God will fill my mouth." Father responded, "Yes, God will fill your mouth if you fill your head first."—Hillyer H. Straton.

WRITTEN FROM EXILE. I am a child of this age, a child of unfaith and scepticism and probably (indeed, I know it) shall remain so till the end of my life—and yet God gives me sometimes moments of perfect peace. In such moments I love, and believe that I am loved. In such moments I have formulated my creed, wherein all is clear and holy to me. This creed is extremely simple. Here it is: I believe that there is nothing lovelier, deeper, more sympathetic, more rational, more manly, and more perfect than the Savior; and I say to myself with jealous love that not only is there no one else like him, but that there could be no one.—Fëdor Dostoevski.

THE THINGS WE FEAR. Fear does not prevent the approach of that which is feared. It only exhausts beforehand the strength one needs to meet the thing feared. Most things we fear to meet are not in reality so terrible as they appear to be when looked at from afar. When they meet us they can be borne.—Carl Hilty.

SOUL FREEDOM. Back in 1936 an American woman came home from Italy where she had lived for thirteen years. She had seen the growth of Fascism. She had seen Mussolini's rise to power, his march on Rome, his efforts to reconstruct Italy. She had sympathized with the movement at first, for she believed Italy needed a strong hand. Then came the disillusionment, and as she stepped off the gangplank of the ship in New York it was with a feeling of great release. She knew she was getting away from something sinister—the whispers, the suspicion; "Be careful what you say," "Be careful what you write," "Be careful whom you telephone." She had seen lovable, lighthearted people frightened into silence, suspicious of each other, spying on each other. "Then suddenly I knew," she said, "what America is, and that I wanted to hear somebody talk back. And I wanted to hear somebody laugh —spontaneously laugh out loud in the freedom of the soul."—J. Wallace Hamilton.

PASTORAL ADMISSION. One of the most cultured spirits of modern Methodism, a man whose style is as strong as his thoughts are lofty, has given this judgment as he looked back upon the years of his ministry: "I have not failed to study; I have not failed to visit; I have not failed to write and meditate; but I have failed to pray. Now why have I not prayed? Sometimes because

I did not like it; at other times because I hardly dared; and yet at other times because I had something else to do."—John Henry Jowett.

SHARING LOVE.   Love is not a scarce commodity which has to be hoarded. Many of us act as if it were! Actually, like joy and the other good things of life, love grows as it is shared. The more love we give to others, the more we have to give. We have all seen and experienced this in small ways. Parents don't run out of love when the third or fourth child arrives. Love for a new friend does not diminish love for the old. Love is like a muscle. It grows stronger with exercise.—Cynthia Clark Wedel.

BIBLE WITHIN THE BIBLE.   The world of the Bible is a great world. I have wandered through it all, but I have never made it all my own. But some friendly hills and valleys in it are mine by right of experience. Some chapters have comforted me; some have made me homesick; some have braced me like a bugle call; and some always enlarge me within by a sense of unutterable fellowship with a great, quiet Power that pervades all things and fills me. Such passages make up for each of us his Bible within the Bible, and the extent and variety of these claims he has staked out in it measure how much of the great Book has really entered into the substance of his life.—Walter Rauschenbusch.

PROOF POSITIVE.   Adelina Patti, the great singer, instructed her home post office to forward her mail to a post office in a small French village. There she planned to pick it up.

"Any mail for Adelina Patti?" she inquired of the postmaster to whom she was a stranger.

"Yes," replied the postmaster, "but have you anything with which to identify yourself?"

She presented a visiting card which the postmaster said was insufficient evidence.

"What can I do?" she mused. Then a brilliant idea came to her. She began to sing! In a few moments the post office was filled with people listening in wonderment to the rapturous voice. As she concluded her song she asked the postmaster, "Are you satisfied now that I am Adelina Patti?"

"Abundantly satisfied!" said he apologetically. "Only Adelina Patti could sing as you have sung," he said as he gave her a large bundle of mail.—*The War Cry.*

FOUNDATION.   Judy, with rapt concentration, was industriously piling blocks on the large family Bible. She carefully placed each block as the structure towered higher and higher. Frequently she sat back and surveyed her progress. Then lining them up straighter, she continued to build.

Becoming aware of me, she looked up, her face radiant, and said: "Look, Mommy. I'm building my house. Isn't it beautiful? The big Bible makes a won'erful foun'ation, like Daddy says we have." Then she explained: "The blocks stand straighter and taller on the Bible. The rug is too wavery."—Elsie Jefferies Thomas in *The Secret Place.*

LOST FAITH.   A little girl had been attending a Sunday School session where each student had made a little plaque with the words "Have Faith in God" as the motto. She boarded the bus that would take her to her home, and as the bus was starting to move, she realized that she did not have her little motto with her. She jumped from her seat, and dashing up the aisle to the driver, shouted: "Stop the bus. I've lost my 'Faith in God.'"—C. Reuben Anderson.

CHRIST IN AFRICA.   Eric Severeid in his book *Not So Wild a Dream* has a penetrating observation on the power of the spirit of Christ in Africa. He states that you can draw a line by the condition of the people where the missionaries have brought in culture, new ideas, schools, medicine, and the spirit of Christ. On one side of the line there is hopelessness, superstition, ignorance, and unconcern for the misery of life. On the other side life has been lifted, not by twentieth-century industry but through sacrifice of individuals in the timeless spirit of Christ.—Frank A. Court.

CRISIS MAN. Jim Elliot was a classmate in college. He was a young wrestler, good looking, and tough of body. He was also a deeply spiritual young man. Jim Elliot, every morning, arose at five or five-thirty and read his Bible and took notes in his diary. One day, in his praying about the people overseas, he thought to himself: "Why shouldn't I go? There is one minister for every 500 people in the United States, and one for every 500,000 overseas. Why shouldn't I go?" And he went. He went to the Auca Indians in Ecuador, and he was murdered. You may remember the story. After his death, they found, scattered along the shore, a river-soaked diary. In that diary, Jim Elliot says this: "Make me a crisis man, O Lord; not just a signpost on the highway of life, but a fork in the road so that men who meet me will come to know Jesus Christ." Today God numbers among the Auca Indians of Ecuador many believers in Jesus Christ because one young man was willing to follow him all the way, even unto death.—Ernest J. Lewis.

BROOKS AND RIVERS. In his novel, The Gauntlet, James Howell Street wrote about a bewildered young minister. When the story opens the hero is in college and is very much at sea both theologically and spiritually. He had been driven into the ministry by an inner compulsion which he could neither explain nor ignore. Now facing the ministry ahead of him he is seeking for some great river of truth, but has become disheartened in his search. About this Mr. Street made a very wise statement: "In seeking a great river he hadn't learned the importance of brooks; that the easiest way to find a river is to follow the nearest brook."—Emerson S. Colaw.

THE REAL THING. An American airman was shot down and landed in the Pacific Ocean near a South Sea Island to which he made his way. He crept into the bushes to hide. And no wonder. Within living memory he would have been captured by savages, boiled, and eaten. But not now. He was found and cared for, his injuries treated, and he himself nursed back to health.

He wrote home to his parents. In his letter he said he had never been much of a Christian and had regarded many churchgoing folk as hypocrites. "But now," he said, "I have seen the real thing." In that island, once cannibalistic, where dark orgies were indulged in and sorcery practiced, where dirt and disease abounded, where men and women had lived like animals, there had been a transformation.

The airman had an interview with the Chief during which he was told that there had not been a murder during his lifetime. There was no jail. There was no poverty, no drunkenness, no divorce, no venereal disease, no brothels, and practically no disease. There was one doctor, "but," said the Chief, "he spends most of his time fishing." Orphans were promptly absorbed into other homes. Honesty was taken for granted.—Leslie D. Weatherhead.

MORE THAN A PICCOLO. Jack and Alice had recently been married. They seemed admirably suited to each other and they were. In almost every way they got along superbly. The one thing on which they disagreed was their interpretation of the Christian Faith. Alice had made a decision for Christ and had joined the church; but Jack remained outside, attending services only now and then.

One night they went to the local symphony. It was an exciting night, for the great South American composer-conductor, Villa-Lobos, was the guest conductor. They were delighted with the intricate melodies, the unusual rhythms, the rich beauty of the composer's music as he interpreted it through the medium of the orchestra. Alice noticed that Jack kept watching the piccolo player.

That night, when they came home, Jack said, "Alice, I've learned that you can't play a symphony on a piccolo."

"What do you mean?" asked Alice.

"I mean just that," said Jack. "How would it have sounded if they had tried to play on one little piccolo all the rich music Villa-Lobos wrote?"

Alice looked at him inquiringly and said, "I still . . . Well, that's true, but I don't quite get what you are driving at."

"Don't you see, Alice? You've been telling me for a long time that my Christian faith would be richer if I became a part of the church. I have been trying to play all of God's symphony on my little piccolo. Next Sunday I'm coming back, and I'm going to speak to the minister about joining the church. I want to play my part in God's orchestra."

Jack had discovered that the church is God's fellowship in human history. It has its origin in the heart of God, its center in Jesus Christ, its life in the Holy Spirit. It is made up of those who have found God through Christ, who believe in him through his Spirit, and are bound to him and to one another by love.—John E. Skoglund in *Come and See.*

FRUITFUL LABOR. An old minister in Scotland was nearing the end of a long ministry in an obscure parish. He felt dreadfully disappointed about the results of his work because he could point to no seemingly clearcut conversions. He was telling his disappointment to a very distinguished minister whose work had appeared so fruitful. The famous preacher listened till the old man had finished. Then he said, "Do you remember a young woman who used to worship in your church some twenty years ago?" When he had described her, the old minister said, "Yes, I remember her. She came for quite a while, but she never joined the church." "Well," replied the great man, "that young woman had a younger brother who was rapidly becoming a drunkard. She would come home from church and talk to him about your sermons until he finally changed his habits. That young man was myself."—Ralph W. Sockman.

SHOCKED PARENTS. Most parents would be apprehensive, certainly puzzled, and perhaps shocked, if they learned that the church school planned to make active Christian disciples out of their children. Christian character is a fine thing, but Christian discipleship is likely to mean taking religion too seriously and carrying it too far.—James D. Smart in *The Teaching Ministry of the Church.*

DUAL MEMORIES. There is a Greek legend about a woman who came down to the River Styx to be ferried across to the region of departed spirits. Charon, the ferryman, reminded her that it was her privilege to drink of the waters of Lethe and thus forget the life she was leaving. This seemed to be a wonderful idea, and she said, "I will forget how I have suffered." "And," added Charon, "remember, too, that you will forget how you have rejoiced." She said, "I will forget my failures." The old ferryman added, "And also your victories." She continued, "I will forget how I have been hated." "And also how you have been loved," added Charon. So, when she considered the whole matter, she decided not to drink the Lethe potion, but retain her memory even of the bad that she might never forget the good.—Gerald Kennedy.

WALKING TOGETHER. A very happy

little girl came home from Sunday School, eager to tell what she had learned that day. "Mother, we learned all about Enoch." Then she quoted these words: "And Enoch walked with God, and he was not; for God took him." After that she explained it all in her fluent childish way: "It means that Enoch was a good man. God came to his house one day and asked him to go walking. Enoch went, and God showed him many wonderful things. Day after day they went walking together. Then one day Enoch got very tired during their walk. God saw it, and said, 'You have walked with me a long time and you are tired, aren't you? You need not go 'way back home today. You come to my house and rest!' So God took him."—Howard D. Jane in *The Secret Place.*

PRAYER. Merciful God, deliver us from being so uptight with the few who wear long hair and beads that we never give a thought to the multitudes who go hungry. Deliver us from being so worried that children might hear four-letter words that we are unconcerned that they hear every day violent words of obscenity: murder, riot, casualties. Help us, gracious Lord, to keep our priorities straight. Amen.—Robert L. Carlson in California State Senate.

RELIANCE. I believe that God both can and will bring good out of evil. I believe God will give us all the power we need to resist in all time of distress. But he never gives it in advance, lest we should rely upon ourselves and not on him alone.—Dietrich Bonhoeffer.

BIG JOB. Many years ago a young man went out to China as a Christian missionary on an annual salary of about $2,500. He was so outstanding that there was competition for his services. A commercial concern wanted him, so they offered him $5,000 salary, but he declined. They raised it to $7,000. When he declined again, they raised it to $10,000, but he refused this, also.

They couldn't understand, so they asked why he refused. He said that he preferred to stay with the job he had. They asked if it was a questtion of the salary not being big enough. He answered, "Oh, the salary is big enough, but the job isn't."—Clarence W. Kemper.

INDEX OF CONTRIBUTORS

Abbe, George 246
Ainslie, Peter 7
Albaugh, Dorothy P. 42
Allen, Charles L. 171
Allen, E. L. 108
Alsobrook, W. Aubrey 35
Anderson, C. Reuben 18, 24, 119, 261
Anderson, Harrison Ray 62
Anderson, John F. 176, 196
Anderson, Leroy Dean 107
Angell, James W. 28
Appelman, Hyman J. 55
Arkansas Baptist 8
Ashford H. E. D. 198
Athanasius, St. 96
Atkins, Gaius Glenn 162, 176
Atkinson, C. Harry 215
Atkinson, Lowell M. 36, 81, 131
Atkinson, Walter P. 114
Augustine, St. 7
Auman, Russell F. 260

Baillie, John 199
Barclay, William 76, 232, 258
Barker, Frank 150
Barrail, Herbert M. 132
Barratt, Stanley 80
Barrie, James M. 9
Barth, Karl 175
Bartlett, Gene E. 34
Bartlett, Robert M. 155, 205
Batchelder, Max L. 70, 74
Bell, L. Nelson 212, 221
Bennett, Leo 257
Berkhof, Hendrikus 7
Bernhardt, Clara 40
Berry, Harold E. 215
Beverage, John H. 64
Bigler, Vernon 146
Bingham, W. B. 14
Blackwood, Andrew W. 35, 132, 153
Blackwood, Andrew W., Jr. 33
Blair, Edith 60
Blanton, Smiley 215
Blazer, Robert 6
Bodo, John R. 160
Boice, James M. 193
Bonar, Horatius 206
Bonhoeffer, Dietrich 264
Book of Family Worship, A 178
Book of Common Prayer 220
Book of Common Worship 113
Booth, William 28
Bosley, Harold A. 22, 141
Bowman, Harold Leonard 94, 358
Boyd, Don R. 20, 110

Brasier, Inez 30
Braunstein, Richard 9
Breeze, G. E. 75
Brengle, S. L. 128
Bridgman, Amy S. 62
British Weekly, The 196
Brokhoff, John R. 13, 130, 159, 206
Brooks, Molly 246
Brooks, Raymond C. 88
Brown, H. C., Jr. 58
Brown, Wilfred J. T. 183
Brownson, William C., Jr. 229
Bryson, Harold T. 181
Buber, Martin 8
Buck, Charles H., Jr. 24
Buck, Pearl S. 62
Buell, Harold E. 188
Bulwer-Lytton, Edward 9
Bunch, Robert P. 169
Burket, Gail Brook 52
Burkholder, Esther York 50
Burns,. Robert W. 85, 134, 199, 200
Burtchaell, James T. 35
Bush, Vannever 149
Butcher, Walter A. 214
Buttrick, George A. 232

Cagle, John F. 209
Calhoun, W. E. 152
Calkins, Raymond 186
Calvert, Tom 118
Campbell, Ernest T. 9, 145, 204, 245, 257
Campbell, K. J. 19
Carlson, C. Emanuel 9
Carlson, Robert L. 264
Carpenter, Guy O. 224
Case, Ernest R. 179, 226
Casteel, John L'. 211
Castell, Alburey 218
Cavert, Samuel McCrea 207
Chafin, Kenneth 18, 159
Chalmers, Allan Knight 236
Chamberlain, William E. 15
Chartier, Myron R. 104
Chase, Mary Ellen 9
Chenault, Fred R. 185, 252
Chilvers, Gordon 128
Christianity Today 27, 149, 203, 217, 226
Churchill, Winston 8
Clark, Anderson D. 202, 209
Clarke, James W. 17, 105
Clem, Paul L. 20
Cleveland, Philip Jerome 240
Clinebell, Howard J., Jr. 45
Coffin, Henry Sloane 232
Colaw, Emerson S. 152, 169, 258, 262

INDEX OF CONTRIBUTORS

Collins, Donald E. 216
Conn, Charles W. 50
Coogan, Frederick Donald 6
Cooper, Don R. 149
Copenhaver, Charles L. 111
Corson, Fred P. 98
Court, Frank A. 17, 146, 147, 162, 262
Crosby, Ralph Mitchell 31
Crowe, W. Burton 154
Cummins, Douglas H. 205
Currie, Stuart D. 60

Dahl, Edward C. 138
Dahlberg, Edwin T. 184, 259
Dampier, Ross H. 41, 85
Dando, Norman E. 96
Davis, Hilda P. 256
Day, Albert E. 17
Decision 8, 88
Deckert, Robert E. 28
Deschner, John W. 62
DeVore, J. E. 143
Dewberry, Willis E. 15
Dooling, Jerry 218
Dosch, Walter L. 20, 92, 94
Dostoevski, Fëdor 9, 260
Douglass, Earl L. 7, 42, 107
Douglass, Richard B. 166
Duffey, Paul A. 241
du Maurier, Daphne 6

Eakin, Thomas 84
Earnshaw, George L., Jr. 17, 54, 139
Eberling, Gerhard 9
Eddy, Sherwood 193
Edgar, Robert A. 44
Edgeworth, Maria 9
Eisenhower, Dwight D. 8, 104
Eldersveld, Peter 16, 32
Elford, Homer J. R. 114, 209, 230
Elizabeth II 61
Elson, Edward L. R. 166
Emrich, Richard S. 250
Enslin, Morton S. 196
Essert, F. Harold 181
Eternity 8
Evans, Bergen 54
Evans, Bruce 12
Evans, W. Lionel 56

Fairbairn, A. B. 8
Family Devotions 64
Ferré, Nels F. S. 7, 8
Ferris, Frank Halliday 36, 142
Ferris, Theodore P. 114, 131, 247
Findley, Cecil R. 103
Fischbach, Julius 79
Fisher, William 23, 55
Fletcher, Grace 53
Foote, Gaston 7
Ford, Leighton 7, 60, 181
Ford, Wesley P. 139, 172, 190
Forister, Raynette 30
Forsberg, Clarence J. 135, 143, 206
Forward 73
Fosdick, Harry Emerson 125, 172, 173
Fowler, George A. 191
Frank, Robert W. 21

Fredericks, Mildred 80
Frick, Ivan E. 136
Fridy, Wallace 92
Frost, Robert 7
Fry, C. George 56
Fryhling, Paul P. 12, 91, 152

Gardner, John W. 51
Gates, Dale S. 233
Georges, Thomas W., Jr. 9
Gernert, I. W. 110
Gerrard, Eleanor 42
Gettelman, Frances 30
Gezork, Herbert 7
Gibbs, J. M. 38
Gide, André 9
Gladstone, H. H. 144
Glascow, Arnold H. 9
Glass, Bill 7
Glover, Carl A. 124, 169
Good, Andrew J., Jr. 38
Gough, Wilbert Donald 39
Graham, Billy 27, 40, 51, 166, 227
Graham, George 247
Gregg, John H. 98
Grieser, Ralph 217
Griffith, A. Leonard 158, 206
Griggs, Edward Howard 9
Grounds, Vernon C. 195
Grubb, Luther 122
Guptill, Nathaniel M. 32
Gustafson, James M. 217
Gustafson, Roy W. 19

Hall, George Hunter 16
Hall, Marvin E. 53
Hall, Mary Lee 42
Halle, Louis J. 6
Hamill, Robert H. 120
Hamilton, J. Wallace 117, 260
Hargroves, V. Carney 72
Harmon, Seth 259
Harnish, J. Lester 50
Harris, Doris 76
Harris, Mary Imogene 63
Havner, Vance 9
Hay, Lewis S. 13
Haynes, Marjorie 65
Hazelton, Roger 209
Henrichsen, Margaret 66
Henry, Carl F. H. 298
Henry, Lorne J. 77
Herbster, Ben M. 110, 194
Herndon, Carl 226
Hesburgh, Theodore 6
Hevey, Jerome J. 18
Higgins, Paul Lambourne 38
Hill, A. Stanley 99
Hilty, Carl 260
Hin, Chew Hock 219
Hines, John E. 237
Hobbs, Herschel H. 10
Hodges, Graham R. 73
Hodgson, Chester E. 91, 240
Hodgson, Leonard 7
Hoffman, Fred W. 139
Holland, Robert Cleveland 110
Hoon, Paul W. 221

INDEX OF CONTRIBUTORS

Hope, Norman Victor   197, 203, 228
Horne, Chevis   19
Howard, Peter   258
Howie, Frank   185
Hubbard, David A.   140
Hudgins, W. Douglas   98
Hudnut, Herbert Beecher   127, 175
Hudnut, William H. III   239
Huffman, John A., Jr.   134
Hughes, Albert Ashbden   97
Huie, Wade P.   173
Hunter, John   26
Huntington, William Reed   193
Huxhold, Harry N.   132

Jacks, L. P.   172
Jacobs, Charles F.   161
James, William   8
Jameson, Vic   211
Jane, Howard D.   264
Jaspers, Karl   8
Jenkins, David H.   45
Jewish Digest, The   41
Johnson, Alvin D.   145, 172
Johnson, Frank   7
Johnson, Frank M., Jr.   166
Johnson, Gordon G.   109
Johnson, L. Ted   57
Jones, A. Wynn   182
Jones, E. Stanley   59, 100, 139, 220
Jones, G. Curtis   174, 248
Jones, Ilion T.   103
Jones, J. D.   29
Jones, Medford   46, 155
Jones, Raymond J.   119, 189
Jones, Rufus M.   212
Jowett, John Henry   134, 261
Joynt, Carey B.   94

Keen, Sam   240
Keller, Helen   245
Kemper, Clarence W.   264
Kenaston, Rolla S.   212
Kennedy, Gerald   257, 263
Kenseth, Arnold   35
Kernan, William C.   104
Kestle, James Allen   23
Kierkegaard, Sören   9
Killinger, John   7
King, Bernard N.   19
King, James W.   58
King, Joseph F.   116
King, Leila Pier   246
King, Levon G.   95
Kitsen, Mary Louise   259
Klingberg, Martin A.   213
Knight, Richard S.   22
Kofahl, Duane A.   98
Kohler, Charles W.   9
Kohn, Harold E.   71, 81, 175
Kostyu, Frank A.   165
Krueger, O. E.   73
Krutza, William J.   232
Kytle, Jack   259

Lamb, Charles   7
Laue, Richard   156
Lawson, Norman R.   237

Lazarus, Henry   8
Lee, Charles V.   77
Lee, Robert G.   6, 80
Lehmenn, Titus   48
Leitner, Della Adams   61
Lenhart, James W.   256
Lennen, Elinor   71
Lewis, C. S.   179
Lewis, Ernest J.   262
Likins, William H.   18, 143
Lindsell, Harold   41
Link   8, 251
Long, Kermit   8
Longfellow, Henry Wadsworth   40
Lotz, Charles J.   187
Luchs, Fred E.   244
Lundquist, Carl H.   179
Luther, Martin   7, 8, 244
Lutheran, The   59, 240

McCabe, Joseph E.   148
McCarthy, David   143
McClain, Charles A., Jr.   13, 124, 187, 229, 258
McComb, J. Roy   125
McCracken, Robert J.   135, 179
McDavid, Joel D.   30
McDonald, Edward   244
McGowan, Michael   169
MacGregor, W. M.   128
Mackay, John A.   11, 233
McKee, Glenn L.   151
McKelvey, John W.   227
MacLeish, Archibald   187
MacLennan, David A.   35, 179, 257
Macleod, Donald   124
McMillion, Claude A.   52
McNabb, Vincent   190
McNay, James T.   233
McNeil, Jesse Jai   166
McNutt, Carroll L.   233
MacQueen, Angus J.   85
Mabie, Hamilton Wright   9
Magnuson, Ray F.   7
Mann, Louis L.   8
Marney, Carlyle   122
Marshall, Peter   8
Martin, H. V.   86
Martin, Iris Weber   68
Martin, Ralph P.   121
Maurois, André   187
Meckel, Aaron N.   113
Meister, John W.   184, 200
Melanchthon, Philip   9
Merck, John   125
Methodist Christian Advocate, The   12, 23, 27, 129
Metts, James N., Jr.   128
Micklem, Nathaniel   29, 162
Miller, Alexander   6
Miller, Arthur   8
Miller, Fred J.   229
Miller, Keith   95
Miller, Kenneth D.   138
Miller, Samuel H.   113
Mills, Bruce E.   31
Monks, G. Gardner   242
Mook, Jane Day   67

INDEX OF CONTRIBUTORS

Morgan, Jill 246
Morrice, Charles S. 93
Morrice, William C. 114
Morris, Fred 82
Morrison, James Dalton 214

Nash, Ogden 53
Nederhood, Joel 192, 247
Neill, Stephen 202
New Prayer Book, A 208
Niemoeller, Martin 29
Niles, Daniel T. 29, 39

Odom, Ralph W. 170
Oldham, J. H. 9
Oldsen, Armin C. 122
Olewiler, Robert W. 110
Olford, Stephen F. 25, 107, 116, 181, 235, 247
Oliver, Thomas T. 245
Orchard, William E. 7
Organ, Arthur 115

Palmer, Everett W. 21, 208
Palmer, Harrison 31
Parker, Clyde N. 70
Parker, George Gerald 21, 24
Pascal, Blaise 7
Pastor's Round Table 78
Paton, Alan 104
Patrick, Johnstone G. 243
Patterson, W. Morgan 247
Paul VI, Pope 206
Peak, J. Francis F. 25
Peale, Norman Vincent 8, 245
Pearson, Linnea 52
Pearson, Roy M. 8
Pennington, Chester A. 18
P. E. O. Record, The 240
Percy, Charles H. 88
Perkins, James Croswell 162
Peterson, Orval D. 259
Phillips, Harold Cooke 181, 223
Pippin, Frank Johnson 241
Platt, Charles A. 33
Pogue, Myron C. 256
Poling, Daniel 7
Porter, R. Frank, Jr. 218
Porter, Willis Hubert 236
Powell, Walter S. R. 236
Primus, John 18, 101, 229
Prayers for the Christian Year 36, 233
Presbyterian Life 257, 259
Proust, Marcel 7
Pulpit Digest 17
Pulitzer, Ralph 7
Purviance, A. E. 68

Qualben, Lara Peterson

Ramsay, John G. 43
Rankin, Isaac O. 226
Rasmusson, H. Richard 187
Rauschenbusch, Walter 261
Read, David H. C. 60, 227, 251
Reader's Digest 9
Redding, David A. 9

Reeder, D. H. 163
Rees, Paul S. 9, 249
Religion in American Life 53
Richards, Glyn 202
Richter, Jean Paul 8
Ridenour, Fritz 202
Rightmyer, Nelson Waite 158
Riker, Donald E. 184
Rinker, Richard N. 225
Roth, Taylor E. 209
Rowlett, Herman E. 122
Rowley, Frank 215
Rubin, Maude 51
Rupert, Hoover 22, 50, 135

Salazar, Lloyd J. 95
Salmon, Wilfred 89
Sanderson, John 7
Sangster, William E. 184
Santayana, George 251
Saxbe, William B. 167
Scharfe, Howard C. 157
Scherer, Paul 202
Schiller, Johann 7
Schloerb, Rolland W. 222
Schmiechen, Samuel J. 88
Scholten, Walter A. 220
Schott, John 70, 169
Schultz, Harold A. 30
Schweitzer, Albert 162
Scott, Ernest F. 190
Scroggie, W. Graham 7
Seamands, J. T. 62
Shaw, Roud 172
Shelby, Robert F., Jr. 24
Sheppard, Dick 50
Shillinglaw, Joseph 123
Skeath, William C. 9
Skinner, Tom 101
Skoglund, John E. 263
Sleeth, Ronald E. 84
Smart, James D. 263
Smith, Cliff 49
Smith, George B. 27
Smith, Logan Pearsall 53
Sneed, J. Richard 178
Snow, Wilbert 247
Snowden, Rita F. 69
Sockman, Ralph W. 41, 74, 127, 199, 223, 229, 257, 263
Sparks, Duron 145
Stafford, John Paul 8
Steere, Douglas V. 189
Steimle, Edmund A. 14
Stephens, John Underwood 151
Sternberg, William H. 81
Stone, Sam 68
Stothard, H. K. 251
Stott, John R. W. 8
Strait, C. Neil 6, 116
Straton, Hillyer H. 260
Strobe, Donald B. 14, 54, 197
Studer, Gerald C. 48
Sublette, Roy T. 38
Sunshine Magazine 67

Task Force 61
Taylor, Gardner C. 100

INDEX OF CONTRIBUTORS

Temple, William   159, 220
Templin, Lester R.   179
Ten Boom, Corrie   7
Thielicke, Helmut   85, 158
Thomas, Elsie Jeffries   261
Thomas, G. Ernest   98
Thomas, Winburn T.   34
Thomas a Kempis   8, 9
Thomason, Richard   211
Thompson, Ernest Trice   21, 88, 117, 185
Thompson, Rhodes   12
Thurber, James   9
Thurman, Howard   247
Tillich, Paul   7, 92, 100
Tillman, Sadie Wilson   61
Tittle, Ernest Fremont   107
Today   149
Torrey, Reuben A.   107
Townsend, John H.   39, 152, 155
Trembath, William Carman   199
Trueblood, Elton   9, 196
Tupper, Charles B.   100

Ullmark, Marion   74
Unamuno y Jugo, Miguel de   6
Underhill, Evelyn   8
United Presbyterian Church   57
Universalist Leader, The   139

Van Alen, Russell   119
Van Halsema, Dick L.   156
Vernier, Phillippe   85

Wade, John W.   82
Wagner, Charles   8
Walker, Harold Blake   127
Wallace, Brunson   256
Wallace, John T.   125
Wallace, Robert B.   210
War Cry, The   9, 56, 261
Ward, William Arthur   50, 95
Ward, W. Ralph   51
Watchman-Examiner, The   37, 237

Watermulder, David B.   119
Watson, Kenneth   31
Watts, Warren W.   189
Weatherford, Willis D.   176
Weatherhead, Leslie D.   28, 262
Webb, E. J.   59, 223
Webb, Ernest   63
Wedel, Cynthia Clark   261
Weinlick, John R.   156
Weir, John   7
Welch, James   169
Werner, Hazen G.   181
Wesson, Steve   104
Westers, Jacqueline   220
Wheatley, Melvin E., Jr.   23, 41, 79, 256
White, M. Jackson   232
White, William Allen   8
White, Willie   8
Whitfield, James O.   69
Whiting, Tom A.   258
Whitman, A. E.   40
Whittier, John Greenleaf   6
Whyte, Lloyd N.   74
Wiebe, Bernie   79, 163
Wiersbe, Warren   49, 52, 215
Wiggins, Harry H.   119
Wilcox, Jackson   34, 58
Wilkins, Minnie B.   61
Williams, Roberta Dillon   72
Williams, Thomas A.   40
Willkie, J. C.   8
Wilson, Grover   78
Wingard, Robert W.   27
Winn, Albert Curry   251
Wodehous, Helen   122
Wolf, Carl J. C.   196
Woodrum, Lon   7
World Religious News   229
Wright, Don   146
Wyand, Fred B.   131

Yaxley, D. Thurlow   248

SERMON TITLE INDEX

(Children's stories and sermons are identified with a "C"; sermon suggestions with an "S")

Abiding in Christ (S) 220
Abraham's Faith and Ours (S) 251
Accept the Challenge or Cease to Grow 219
Aftermath of Christmas 10
Alone But Never Lonely (S) 128
"And He Said within Himself" (S) 187
Apostles' Creed, The 46
Ascension Affirmations 17

Backing Our Faith with Our Brains (S) 92
Baptism of Jesus, The (C) 68
Bases for Thankfulness (S) 149
Basic Education (S) 169
Beautiful Hands (C) 70
Beauty of the People of God, The 18
Being Good Is Not Enough 19
Belief Is Not Enough 20
Benjamin Franklin's Philosophy (C) 79
Best Gift, The (C) 82
Beyond Courage 126
Biblical Basis for Evangelism 108
Billy and Pedro (C) 65
Birds and Men (C) 72
Blessings of the Church, The 183
Blood We Share, The (S) 100
Brotherhood in Christ 47
Brotherly Love 213
B's That Don't Sting 16
But There Is Judgment 92
By the Leading of a Star 241

Calvary: The Divine Paradox 26
Calvary Today 15
Can the Gospel Save the World? 24
Capacity to Enjoy, The 212
Caring Enough (S) 104
Casualties of Christmas, The (S) 248
Caught between Shock and Assurance (S) 135
Celebrating the Word Made Flesh 248
Characteristics of Great Preaching (S) 110
Charisma Is a Christian Word 227
Christ Calls All Christians 47
Christian Baptism 200
Christian Bridges (S) 169
Christian Challenge (S) 116
Christian Communicator, The 57
Christian Life in a Time of Change 119
Christian Looks at Industry, A (S) 193
Christian Sensitivity (S) 104
Christian's Life and Mind, The (S) 175
Christian's Social Obligations, The 21

Christian View of Sex, A 176
Christmas in Three Words (S) 240
Christmas Is for Celebration (S) 237
Christmas Word, The 238
Christ's Appeal to Youth 18
Christ's Hands and Ours 181
Christ: The Only Hope (S) 98
Church and Civil Rights, The 102
Church as the Body of Christ, The 206
Church Growth (S) 156
Church in a Time of Revolution, The 194
Church in Social Relations, The 20
Church of the Open Door, The 13
Citizens of Eternity 117
Claims of Christmas, The (S) 247
Closing the Door (C) 69
Communion Meditation 34
Compelling Worship 233
Confession of a Witch Doctor (C) 78
Consider the Rainbows 160
Courage of Christmas, The (S) 247
Crucial Hour, The 123
Cure of the Church Division, The (S) 159

Dangerous Christ, The 230
Death Hath No Dominion (S) 88
Decisions That Shape Our Lives 166
Denying Yourself (S) 95
Dimensions of the Gospel, The 12
Disturbing Christ, The (S) 233
Divine Guidance 85
Door of Fellowship 207

Easter Event, The 27
Easter Is Today (S) 132
Easter: Our Commencement Day 132
Enemy Within, The (S) 95
Evangelism in the Early Church 56
Everyone Needs a Savior (C) 68
Exclusiveness 21

Face into the Storm (C) 81
Face of Our Brother, The 209
Faith and Freedom under God 93
Faith and Health 17
Faith in an Age of Science 18
Fears of Love, The 12
Five Attitudes (S) 215
Footprints (C) 63
Forever 19
Formula for a Full Life 23
Formula for Peace of Soul 177
For Whom the Bells Toll (C) 81

SERMON TITLE INDEX

Four Ages of Man, The (S) 196
Four Things Jesus Could Not Do 26
Frame of Reference 27
Future Belongs to God, The 25
Future Certainties (S) 251

Garden Clock (C) 73
Getting Off the Earth 180
Give Thanks for the Unseen (S) 226
Glory of Going a Little Farther, The 15
Glory of His Coming, The 24
God and His World 237
God of All, The 99
God's Call for Servants (S) 233
God's Foresight (C) 70
God's Formula (S) 122
God Speaks to the Generation Gap 13
God's Richest Men (S) 223
God's Workmanship 105
Goodness of God, The (S) 227
Good Samaritan, The (S) 215
Good Shepherd, The 19
Gospel Affirmations 18
Gospel Drama, The 83
Grace of God, The 201
Grace to Say No, The 221
Great Day in the Morning 34
Great Motivator, The (S) 146
Great Woman, A (S) 143
Growing through Worship (S) 184

Hands of Labor (C) 75
Has Suffering Any Meaning? 227
Hearing God Speak (C) 76
Heart of Our Message, The 133
Helping a Brother (C) 78
Hill of Three Crosses 15
Holding an Elephant (C) 74
Holy Spirit's Coming, The (S) 155
Honoring America (S) 166
Hope for Life Situations 48
Hound That Couldn't Make Up His Mind, The (C) 79
How Can the Church Live Abundantly? (S) 212
How Christ Helps Us to Understand God (S) 199
How Christ Helps Us to Understand Others (S) 200
How Christ Helps Us to Understand Ourselves (S) 199
How Jesus Taught (S) 202
How to Be Good—and Mad (S) 197
How to Destroy Prejudice (S) 104
How to Finish What We Start (S) 85
Humanity One in Christ (S) 100

"I Am the Way" 96
I Believe in the Church 153
If You Can't Take Criticism (S) 179
In Everything Give Thanks (S) 226
Isle of Nightingales, The (C) 71

Jesus and His Heavenly Father 159
Jesus and His Kingdom (S) 190
Jesus' Conditions of Stewardship 23
Jesus' "Go" Movement (S) 98
Jesus Looks Great in Black 101

John's Certainties 24
Joy in Worship 114
Joy to the World 234

Kindness of God's Creatures (C) 73
King's Lesson, The (C) 75
Knowing the Will of God (C) 71

Ladder for Youth, A (S) 139
Leaves of Healing (C) 68
Legend of the Glowworm, The (C) 81
Lessons from Airline Pilots (C) 74
Lessons from the Pilgrims (S) 226
Life of Faith and Doubt, The 135
Life of Prayer, The (S) 179
Lift Your Anchors and Sail (S) 152
Living by Faith (S) 149
Living Victoriously 185
Look to the Cross 27
Lord, the Giver of Life, The 157

Making Common Cause for Christ 86
Making of Christian Homes, The 136
Making Your Marriage Secure (S) 139
Man at the Center of History, The (C) 82
Man's Greatest Discovery 12
Man's Judgment (S) 203
Man Who Missed Easter, The 16
Man Who Sang Like a Lark, The (C) 67
Many and the Few, The 204
Marks of an Effective Ministry 18
Meaning of Bethlehem, The (S) 247
Meaning of Christmas, The (S) 241
Meaning of the Crucifixion, The (S) 125
Meanings Defined by the Cross 128
Meanings of World Communion, The (S) 209
Message of Evangelism, The 55
Message to Scouts (C) 64
Mile That Counts the Most, The 170
Mission and Evangelism 56
Missions Education in Your Church 57
Mistakes (S) 108
Modern St. Valentine, A (C) 65
More than Meets the Eye (S) 110
Mystery of Christmas, The (S) 247

Nation's Needs, The 18
Nation under God, A (S) 166
Need and the Possession, The 223
Neighbors (C) 77
New Testament Life (S) 119
New-Time Religion, A 111
Nineveh Road, The 57
Not Ashamed of the Gospel 111
No Night There 37

Oaks of Righteousness 193
Of Serpents and Doves 249
On Accepting Yourself (S) 92
On Being Holy 113
On Being Part of a Family 156
Oneness in the Body 10
On Trial 27
Our Right to Work 191
Our Thirst for God (S) 220
Our Unfinished Task 216

SERMON TITLE INDEX

Pain and the Hope of the Lonely, The (S) 172
Parable of the Haunted House, The 197
Partnership with God (S) 223
Passing the Test (C) 75
Passion of Evangelism, The 55
Pathways to God through the World Around Us 146
Patient God, The (S) 85
Peril of Drifting, The 215
Prayer: The Source of Wisdom 144
Pray without Ceasing (S) 181
Prisoners of Hope (S) 187
Problem and Privilege of Faith, The 173
Proclamation of the Easter Angel, The (S) 132
Proof of God's Love 14
Public Worship (S) 185

Questions Facing Youth 22
Questions Jesus Asked 46

Radical Trust 38
Raising Children for God's Kingdom 139
Reaping Requires Sowing 149
Revitalizing Pentecost 18
Revival and Evangelism 55
Rich toward God 117
Right Ingredients, The (C) 63
Right Road for the New Year, The 251
Road of Shut Doors, The (S) 176

Sacramental Dinner Table, The 33
Sacrament of Life, The 34
Sacrifice Move, A (C) 71
Salvation through Christ 98
Season of Preparation (S) 237
Secret of Permanence in a World of Change, The 174
Secrets of Pleasurable Living 190
Selfish and Selfless Persons (C) 63
Shall We Know Each Other in Heaven? 38
Sharing the Gospel 58
Show Us the Father 229
Sin of Doing Nothing, The (S) 162
Six Tests of Love 17
Some Marks of the Christian (S) 122
Sound the Trumpet 197
Sources of Hope and Confidence (S) 119
Splendor of Eternal Life, The 38
Star and the Seal, The (C) 80
Star of Bethlehem, The 24
Strangler Tree, The (C) 67
Strength in Weakness (S) 229
Suggestions from Church History (S) 155
Supreme Incentive, The 122

Table that Circles the Globe, The 33
Target Lincoln Rejected, The (C) 66
Taste of Better Wine, The (S) 206
Teaching Them (S) 139
Tears for a Time of Joy 129
Ten Commandments for Husbands and Wives 16
Thanksgiving Every Day 23
Thanksgiving This Time 224
Thank You (C) 80
That Searching Look (S) 212

That They May Be One (S) 156
They Were Called Christians 188
Thieves of the Cross (S) 114
This Dark World's Light 242
This I Believe 23
Together with God (S) 107
To Heal the Split 104
Too Good Not to Be True (S) 206
Touch of Greatness, The (C) 76
Touch that Blesses, The 146
Toward a More Effective Church 88
Treasure of Tribulation, The 170
Tree to Climb, A 150
Trouble in Being Herod, The (S) 247
True Religion 21
Two Greedy Men (C) 74
Tyrannies that Thwart Discipleship 17
Tyranny of Sin, The 185

Unanswered Prayer 108
Understanding the Bible (S) 88
Unseen Presence, The 163
Unworthy Question, An 95
Upward and Forward (S) 152

Value of Contentment, The 21
Various Aspects of the Cross of Christ 48
Vengeance in Christian Perspective 203
Victory over Death 37
View from the Summit, The (S) 135
Virtues of a Good Home, The 140

Walking through the Valley 38
Watch that Temper! (C) 69
Way of His Passion, The 48
Way to Salvation, The 56
We Belong to the Same Church (S) 209
We Need to Give 221
We, Too, Face Goliath 20
What Are Your Goals? (S) 193
What Christmas Reveals (S) 247
What Do You Mean You Are Not a Minister? 22
What God Said (C) 68
What Have You Done Today that Only a Christian Would Do? (S) 217
What if We Follow Christ? 14
What in the World Is the Church For? (S) 218
What Is a Christian? (S) 212
What Is Christianity All About? 120
What Is Your Name? (C) 64
What It Means to Be a Christian 11
What Jesus Borrowed (S) 116
What Rubs Off (C) 69
What's in Me for It? (C) 78
What the Angel Might Have Said (S) 131
What the Liberty Bell Says (C) 72
What the Resurrection Meant 27
What the World Needs Now (S) 143
What We Do Thoughtlessly (C) 73
When Is Enough Enough? (S) 128
When Jesus Spoke 14
When the Tide Turns (C) 69
Where Freedom Ends and License Begins (S) 95
Where Jesus Places Life's Emphasis (S) 162

Who Am I? 89
Who Are the Laymen? 210
Who Is a Christian? (S) 172
Why Are We Here? 33
Why a Social Creed for the Churches? 22
Why I Attend Church Regularly 188
Why Missionaries Are Missionaries 58
Why Pray? (S) 145, 229
Why Thanksgiving? (S) 226
Why the Church-Related College? 218
Why We Say Grace (C) 67
Why Worship? (S) 159
Wishing Is Not Enough (C) 80

With Jesus at a Wedding Feast 152
Witness to the Light (S) 190
Word from the Sentenced, A (S) 125
Word to Change Lives, A 143
World's Slow Stain, The 167
Worlds to Conquer 179
Worthy Heritage and Spiritual Fortitude 163

Yoked to Christ 125
You Do Matter (S) 114
Your God Is Too Small (S) 181

INDEX OF SPECIAL DAYS AND OCCASIONS

Advent   24, 81, 230, 234, 238, 241, 242
Ascension Sunday   17, 152

Boy Scout Sunday   64
Brotherhood Week   13, 47, 65, 66, 77, 78, 99, 102, 207, 209, 213

Children's Sunday   49–54, 136, 139, 140, 156
Christ the King, Festival of   82, 188
Christian College Day   135, 218
Christmas   10, 24, 81, 82, 234, 238, 241, 242, 248
Communion   33–36, 76, 207
Commencement   13, 49–54, 63, 82, 89, 135, 146, 156, 160, 163, 179, 185, 190, 209, 212, 219

Easter   16, 27, 69, 129, 132, 133

Family Week   13, 16, 33, 136, 139, 140, 156
Father's Day   71, 136, 139, 140, 156, 159
Funeral services   37–42, 227

Good Friday   15, 26, 27, 48, 123, 128

Independence Sunday   18, 72, 93, 163

Labor Sunday   75, 105, 191
Laymen's Sunday   22, 210
Lent   14, 15, 26–32, 48, 67, 68, 111, 115, 117, 120

Lincoln's Birthday   66

Missionary Day   55–62, 63, 77, 178
Mother's Day   136, 139, 140, 156

Nature Sunday   67, 72, 73, 146, 160
New Year's Sunday   10, 25, 82, 85, 197, 251
Palm Sunday   15, 68, 126
Passion Sunday   15, 26, 27, 48, 68, 122, 123, 128
Pentecost   18, 68, 111, 153, 157, 183, 200
Prayer, Week of   11, 108, 144

Race Relations Sunday   13, 47, 65, 99, 101, 102
Reformation Sunday   88, 153, 183, 194, 216
Rural Life Sunday   73, 146, 149

Stewardship Sunday   17, 23, 74, 80, 117, 221
Thanksgiving Sunday   23, 65, 80, 224
Trinity Sunday   157

Valentine's Day   12, 16, 17, 65, 143, 213

World Communion Sunday   11, 21, 33, 34, 99, 206, 207
World Order Sunday   20, 21, 22, 194, 213
World Temperance Day   221

Youth Week   13, 18, 22, 49–54, 218

INDEX OF KEY 73 EMPHASES

Phase I. Calling our continent to repentance and prayer   12, 83, 108, 144, 163, 185, 197, 200, 215

Phase II. Calling our continent to the Word of God   55, 56, 108, 188, 197, 204, 210, 230, 237

Phase III. Calling our continent to the Resurrection   16, 22, 27, 129, 132, 133, 157

Phase IV. Calling our continent to new life   17, 18, 85, 96, 111, 119, 125, 143, 150, 201, 234, 251

Phase V. Calling our continent to the proclamation   12, 13, 18, 24, 47, 57, 58, 111, 179, 194, 206, 209

Phase VI. Calling our continent to commitment   11, 14, 20, 23, 33, 93, 120, 216, 219

POETRY INDEX

(Names of poets are listed in the Index of Contributors)

A newborn infant's hands   30
A wild duck in its flight may briefly pause   41
Be with them as they try to grope their way   52
BETHLEHEM'S STALL   246

Christmas is love   246

FACING DEATH   42
FOREIGNERS   60

Grant me time   53

HEALING   61
HIS HANDS   30
HOMING INSTINCT, THE   41

I thought that foreign children   60
I, TOO, AROSE   31
I walk beside a wall   42
If I should die and leave you here awhile   42

KEEPERS OF CHRISTMAS   246

LENT'S JOURNEY   30

MAUNDY THURSDAY   30
MEDIEVAL MIRACLE STORY   247

No mortal mind can comprehend the vastness   61

Not London, not New York, not Singapore   62

On hills we thought forgotten leans the light   246
On such a night as this   30
Over the Red Sea going   42

PENITENCE   30
PRAYER FOR YOUTH   52

She poured the spikenard on his feet   30
STEPS   30

The creatures there in Bethlehem's stall   246
The steps to immortality   30
THEY REACH FOR SKY   51
This is a pilgrimage we make   30
TINY HAND, A   246
Tune your heart strings, O keepers of Christmas   246
TURN AGAIN TO LIFE   42
Two midwives swept the barn and trimmed the manger   247

WHEN DEATH DIVIDES   42
When Jesus rose on Easter morn   31
When the song of the angels is stilled   246
WORK OF CHRISTMAS, THE   246

YOUTH'S PRAYER, A   53
YULETIDE   246

SCRIPTURAL INDEX

Genesis 1:26–28...176
  1:27...92
  2:7...89
  3:14–24...22
  18:23–25...92
Leviticus 25:9...197
Numbers 2:34...156
  24:17...24
Deuteronomy 29:29...25
I Samuel 12:38–50...197
  16:7...212
  17:45...20
  28:15...108
I Kings 18:17–40...181
II Kings 4:8–37...143
II Chronicles 6:18...163
  29:3...13
Psalms 23...19
  27:13...227
  61...119
  63:1...220
  90:9...233
  103:3...17
  107:23–24...152
  111:1...185
  122:1...114
  139...38
  142...172
Proverbs 3:6...251
  14:34...18
Ecclesiastes 3:11...117
Isaiah 6:1–8...184
  6:8...233
  9:6...24
  52:15...230
  61:3...193
Micah 6:6–8...13
Habakkuk 3:2...55
Zechariah 4:6...166
  9:12...187

Matthew 2:1–10...241
  3:11...24
  4:1–11...17
  5:38–39...203
  5:41...170
  6:10...21
  6:19–21...117
  6:20...119
  7:1...203
  7:7–12...140
  7:25...174
  7:28–29...202
  8:20...116
  9:35–38...55
  10:16...249
  11:2–6...24
  11:28–30...125
  12:38–50...197
  13:3...149
  14:1–12...24
  16:15–17...12
  16:18...183
  19:27...95
  22:14...204
  22:37...92
  22:37–40...19
  26:39...15
  28:1–10...38
  28:6...131
  28:16–20...98
  28:20...139
Mark 2:6...187
  8:27–38...14
  8:34...23
  9:27...181
  11:22...185
  16:2...132
  16:14–18...58
Luke 2:1–14...234
  2:8–14...240
  2:11...247
  2:17...10
  2:49...179
  2:52...196
  8:37...233
  9:51...126
  9:62...85
  10:1...55
  10:25–37...21, 162
  11:28...217
  12:13–21...117
  12:17...187
  14:12–14...33
  14:27...114
  14:28...139
  15:11–32...83, 133
  16:3...187
  18:1...181
  18:4...187
  19:1–10...150
  22:53...123
  23:39...166
  23:39–46...15
  24:1–12...131
  24:32...135
John 1:5...242
  1:14...238, 248
  2:10...206
  2:11...152

3:16...12, 237
  6:1–14...146
  9:3...227
  10:10...212
  14:6...96
  14:9...18, 229
  14:13...88
  15:5...220
  16:32...128
  17...146
  17:11...156
  18:12–19:16...27
  20...159
  20:11–18...129
  20:24, 26...16
Acts 1:8–9...152
  1:9–11...17
  2:1–13, 41–42...18
  9:26...188
  10:34...20
  16:1–9...176
  16:6–8...85
  17:16–23...21
  17:26...100
Romans 1:16...111
  3:23...185
  3:29...99
  7:7–25...95
  7:24–25...98
  8:38–39...251
  12:2...167, 221
  12:3...114, 135
  12:10...169
  14:4...179
  14:10–13...179
  15:5...85
I Corinthians 2:9–12...38
  3:9...107
  6:9–20...176
  6:19...223
  12:4–5...227
  12:13...21
  12:27...206
  13...16, 143
  13:2...17
  14:15...145
  15:10...201
  15:51–58...38
  15:55–58...37
II Corinthians 4:18...110
  5:11–20...57
  5:14...122
  5:19...26
  5:20—6:10...143
  6:14—7:1...13
  7:10...227

SCRIPTURAL INDEX

12:2...180
12:10...229
Galatians 3:28...207
5:1...93, 163
5:13...95
6:2...104
6:9...149
6:17...122
Ephesians 2:10...105
3...33
4:1–7, 11–24...18
4:26...197
4:28...191

4:32...16
5:1...136
5:25...153
6:1–2...139
Philippians 2:5–7...247
2:14–16...193
4:4...248
4:11...21
4:11–12...226
Colossians 1:3–5...120
1:17...104
3:11...100
I Thessalonians 5:16–18...23

I Timothy 6:17...212
Hebrews 2:1...215
5:12—6:2...219
11:1–10...149
13:1...213
James 1:5...144
I Peter 2:7...22
4:10...221
I John 3:2...89
4:10...14
4:18...12
Revelation 2:7...218
21:22–25...37

TOPICAL INDEX

Abraham 251
Advent 24
affirmation 18
alienation 181
alone 128
America 149, 163, 166, 224, 260
anchor 152, 214
angel 131
anger 197
animal 73
apathy 94, 216
apology 73
Apostles' Creed 46
appeal of Christ 18
Ascension 17, 152
aspiration 160
assurance 135
astronaut 92, 256
attitude 188, 215

Baden-Powell 64
ballast 229
baptism 68, 200
baseball 70
Baxter, Richard 179
beauty 18, 70
beginning 39
belief 20, 23, 28, 115, 257
bell 81
Berggrav, Elvind 110
Bethlehem 236, 240, 246, 247
Bible 61, 88, 110, 157, 261
Bill of Rights 51
bird 72, 81
birth 244
Body of Christ 206
Bok, Edward 71
books 69
borrowing 116
boss 193
Boy Scouts 64
bread 34, 258
bridge 169
brook 262
brotherhood 13, 47, 78, 102, 104, 209, 213
Browning, Robert 39
burial of Christ 88

Calvary 15, 26
capacity 175
caring 104
celebration 237
certainty 237

challenge 116
change 50, 119, 169, 174, 190
charisma 227
chess 71
chickadee 81
children 53, 139, 156, 244
choice 166
Christian 11, 59, 64, 122, 188, 190, 212
Christian life 19, 86, 119, 175
Christianity 18, 120
Christmas 10, 81, 236, 237, 238, 239, 240, 241, 242, 243, 244, 245, 246, 247, 248, 249
church 13, 18, 20, 49, 52, 76, 88, 102, 153, 155, 156, 157, 183, 184, 194, 206, 209, 212, 216, 218
church attendance 68, 188, 263
church unity 11
citizenship 102, 117
civil rights 102
climbing 40, 150
clock 73
closed mind 230
code 59
college 135, 218
comfort 40
commencement 132
committal 41
communicator 57
Communion 33, 34, 35, 76, 207, 209
concentration camp 28
confession 29, 77
conquer 179
conscience 258
contentment 21
control 106
conversion 39, 58
criticism 179
cross 15, 26, 27, 28, 29, 48, 99, 114, 128, 208
crossroads 62
crucifixion 15, 125
cure 258
cynicism 95

danger, Christ as 230
darkness 40, 242, 243
day 175

death 37, 38, 39, 40, 41, 42, 88, 129
decision 85, 166
Declaration of Independence 72, 164
dedication 116, 151
delinquency 50
denunciation 53
Descartes, René 117
discipleship 17
discovery 12, 169, 225
disturber, Christ as 233
division 159
Domitian 75
door 13, 69, 176, 207
doubt 135, 146
dove 249
drifting 215

earth 148, 180
Easter 16, 27, 31, 69, 129, 131, 132, 133, 135
eating 33
education 152, 169, 187
Eisenhower, Dwight D. 40
elephant 74
Elliot, Jim 262
emancipation 198
emphasis 162
emptiness 197
end 39
endurance 160
enemy 95
enjoyment 212
Enoch 264
enthusiasm 167
equanimity 177
Eternal City 37
eternal life 37, 38, 133
evangelism 55, 56, 58, 59, 60, 61, 62, 108
evil 197
exclusiveness 21
expectation 51
eye 70, 85, 110

faith 17, 18, 92, 93, 115, 116, 120, 135, 146, 149, 156, 173, 251, 261
family 16, 41, 136, 140, 142, 156
farther 15
father 71, 85
father, God as 159, 199, 229, 230
fear 12, 260

278

TOPICAL INDEX

feeling 12
fellowship 19, 62, 207
finish 85
flowers 73, 259
following Christ 14
footprint 63
foreigner 60
foresight 70
forever 19
forgiveness 200
formula 122
fortitude 163
foundation 261
Francis of Assisi 67
Franklin, Benjamin 79, 165, 166
freedom 93, 95, 133, 164, 165, 260
friends 52, 69
funeral 39, 155
future 25, 34, 84, 126, 236, 251

garden 162, 259
generation gap 13, 49
Gethsemane 124
gift 79, 81, 82, 133, 140, 236, 251
giving 221, 222
Glenn, John H. 92
glowworm 81
goal 193
gold 69
Goliath 20
good 19, 263
goodness 227
Good Samaritan 162, 172, 219
Good Shepherd 19, 215
Gospel 12, 18, 24, 58, 110, 111
grace 67, 92, 201, 202, 206
gratitude 222
greatness 76
greed 74
Grenfell, Wilfred T. 222
growth 53, 78, 139, 219
guidance 85, 220

habit 74
hand 30, 70, 75, 181, 246
handicap 199
hate 63
healing 61, 68, 104
health 17
heart 259
heaven 38, 40, 41, 42
helpfulness 78
heritage 163
Herod 247
history 28, 82, 155, 157
holiness 13
Holy Spirit 155, 157
home 52, 136, 137, 138, 140, 141, 142
hope 35, 48, 98, 121, 132, 172, 186, 187, 201
human nature 181

humility 177
hunger 205
husband 16, 137

idealism 53, 168
image of God 90
importance 51, 71
individual 137, 172
industry 193
influence 40, 61
instruction 114
intercession 145
invitation 59, 204
involvement 232

Jerusalem 29, 126, 127
journey 30, 98
joy 114, 129, 234
judgment 28, 92, 203
justification 133

kindness 73, 182
Kingdom of God 190, 204
kingfisher 70

labor 75
lark 67
Laubach, Frank 62
law of God 21
layman 22, 210, 211
leadership 88, 193
Lent 30
lesson 103
liberty 72, 164, 165
Liberty Bell 72
library 69
license 95
life 23, 34, 39, 42, 79, 219
light 40, 60, 190, 236, 242, 259
Lincoln, Abraham 66
listening 93, 95
loneliness 128, 172
Lord's Table 33, 34, 35
lost 258
love 12, 17, 35, 120, 143, 149, 213, 214, 259, 261
love of Christ 123
love of God 14

man 54, 89, 196
marriage 139, 152
Martin of Tours 74
Mary Magdalene 129
Maundy Thursday 30
memory 263
Michelangelo 116
Mickman, Philip 69
Miller, Keith 54
mind 92, 175
ministry 18, 22, 210, 260, 263
miracle 229
missionary 45, 57, 58, 60, 61, 62, 63, 77, 172, 209, 262, 264
missions 55, 56, 57, 58, 59, 60, 61, 62, 209

missions education 57
mistake 108
money 80
More, Paul Elmer 167
mother 41
motive 61

name 64
Napoleon, Louis 41
nation 18, 166
nature 146, 148
need 40, 223
neighbor 77
Newman, John 167
night 37
nightingale 71
Nineveh 57
"now" generation 49, 52

obedience 96, 97, 140
old age 167

pain 227, 228
Palm Sunday 68, 126
Paraclete 201
paradox 27
parent 53, 54, 139, 140, 263
partnership 223
Passion 48, 123
past 218, 251
patience 85
Patti, Adelina 261
Paul 201, 202, 228
peace of soul 177
penitence 30
Pentecost 18, 68
permanence 174
permissiveness 221
person 18
philosophy 119
Pilgrim Fathers 224, 226, 227
pilot 74
pleasure 190
Poling, Daniel 59
possession 223
power 147
praise 67, 114
prayer 67, 71, 114, 118, 144, 145, 146, 150, 179, 181, 189, 229, 256, 260
prayer unanswered 108
preaching 110, 132
prejudice 104
Prodigal Son 83
promise 160
purpose 194

question 22, 28, 29, 46, 51, 92, 95, 196

race 65, 99, 100, 101, 102
rainbow 160
reaping 149
reconciliation 18
redemption 15, 159, 197, 237

TOPICAL INDEX

Red Sea 42
reform 216
regeneration 105, 106
religion 111
remembrance 34, 35
reminder 179
renewal 35
repentance 15
resolution 53
restoration 198
Resurrection 27, 29, 30, 31, 39, 130, 132
reverence 161, 162
revival 55
revolution 194
righteousness 193
road 176, 251
rose 162

sacrament 33
sacrifice 48, 71, 87, 162
Salanter, Israel 41
salvation 56, 59, 98
Savior 98, 235
science 18, 148
seal 80
second mile 170, 171
secularism 225
security 185
self 89
self-acceptance 92
self-denial 95
self-identity 101
selfishness 63, 230, 231
sensitivity 104
sepulchre 131
serpent 249
servant 233
servant, Christ as 128
service 150, 183
serving 70
sex 176
sharing 58
shepherd 172
silver 69
sin 67, 83, 162, 185
single-hearted 85
slavery 159
social creed 22

social obligation 21
social relations 20
song 67
sorrow 38
sound 76
sowing 149
split 104
stable 245
star 24, 80, 236, 241, 245
start 85
steps 30
stewardship 23, 117, 221, 222
stone 48
storm 81
strength 229
suffering 48, 170, 227, 228, 229
summit 135
surrender 87, 121
swimming 69
sympathy 39, 40, 153

task 216
teacher 139, 202
teaching 62
teamwork 18
tears 129
teen-ager 50, 51, 257
temper 69
temptation 221
test 17, 75
testament 41
thanksgiving 23, 80, 149, 178, 224, 225, 226
thieves 114
thinking 117
thirst 220
Thomas 16
tide 69
time 251
togetherness 107
tool 72
touch 146, 215
tranquility 177
transformation 153
treasure 117
tree 67, 139, 150, 172, 193
trial of Christ 27

tribulation 170
trouble 229
trust 38
tyranny 17, 234

understanding 199, 200, 207

Valentine, St. 65
value 141
vengeance 203
Vibert, Jehan Georges 61
virtue 83, 135
vision 151

warrior 62
Washington, George 165
way, Christ as 96, 100, 122
weakness 229
weather 256
wedding 152
Whyte, Alexander 145
Wilberforce, William 199
will of God 71
window 155
wine 34
wisdom 144, 249, 250
wish 74, 80
witch doctor 77
witness 47
Word, Christ as 238, 248
words of Christ 14
work 149, 191, 192
workmanship of God 105
world 24, 33, 110, 146, 155, 179, 190, 237, 238, 242, 243, 257
worship 35, 113, 114, 119, 132, 150, 159, 161, 184, 185, 233

year, new 251
yesterday 190
yoke 125
youth 13, 18, 22, 49, 50, 51, 52, 53, 54, 139, 167

Zacchaeus 150

72 73 10 9 8 7 6 5 4 3 2 1